This Land, This Nation
Conservation, Rural America, and the New Deal

This book combines political with environmental history to present conservation policy as a critical arm of New Deal reform, one that embodied the promises and limits of midcentury American liberalism. It interprets the natural resource programs of the 1930s and 1940s as a set of federal strategies aimed at rehabilitating the economies of agricultural areas. The New Dealers believed that the country as a whole would remain mired in depression as long as its farmers remained poorer than its urban residents, and these politicians and policymakers set out to rebuild rural life and raise rural incomes with measures tied directly to conservation objectives – land retirement, soil restoration, flood control, and affordable electricity for homes and industries. In building new constituencies for the environmental initiatives, resource administrators and their liberal allies established the political justification for an enlarged federal government and created the institutions that shaped the contemporary rural landscape.

Sarah T. Phillips is an assistant professor of history at Columbia University.

This Land, This Nation

Conservation, Rural America, and the New Deal

SARAH T. PHILLIPS

CAMBRIDGE
UNIVERSITY PRESS

CAMBRIDGE UNIVERSITY PRESS
Cambridge, New York, Melbourne, Madrid, Cape Town,
Singapore, São Paulo, Delhi, Tokyo, Mexico City

Cambridge University Press
32 Avenue of the Americas, New York, NY 10013-2473, USA

www.cambridge.org
Information on this title: www.cambridge.org/9780521617963

First published 2007
Reprinted 2011

A catalog record for this publication is available from the British Library.

Library of Congress Cataloging in Publication Data
Phillips, Sarah T., 1974–
This land, this nation : conservation, rural America, and the New Deal /
Sarah T. Phillips.
    p. cm.
Includes bibliographical references and index.
ISBN-13: 978-0-521-85270-8 (hardback)
ISBN-13: 978-0-521-61796-3 (pbk.)
1. Conservation of natural resources – United States – History – 20th century.
2. United States – Politics and government – 1933–1945. 3. New Deal, 1933–1939.
I. Title.
S930.P54   2007
333.760973´09043 – dc22   2006020584

ISBN 978-0-521-85270-8 Hardback
ISBN 978-0-521-61796-3 Paperback

Contents

Plates follow page 148.

Abbreviations Used in the Footnotes

CUOH	Columbia University Oral History, New York, NY
FDRC	Edgar B. Nixon, ed., *Franklin D. Roosevelt and Conservation* (1972)
GPO	United States Government Printing Office, Washington, DC
GPSP	Giant Power Survey Papers, Morris Cooke Papers, Franklin D. Roosevelt Library, Hyde Park, NY
HBP	Miscellaneous Papers of Hugh H. Bennett, National Archives, Washington, DC
HHL	Herbert Hoover Library, West Branch, IA
HP	Lyndon B. Johnson House Papers, Lyndon B. Johnson Library, Austin, TX
HPCP	Herbert Hoover Commerce Papers, Herbert Hoover Library, West Branch, IA
HSTL	Harry S. Truman Library, Independence, MO
LBJL	Lyndon B. Johnson Library, Austin, TX
LCRA	Lower Colorado River Authority Papers, Lyndon B. Johnson Library, Austin, TX
LVF	Loeb Library Vertical File, Harvard University, Cambridge, MA
MF-LBJ	Microfilm "Documents Concerning Lyndon Johnson from the Papers of Franklin Roosevelt," Lyndon B. Johnson Library, Austin, TX
MOH	Memphis State University Oral History, University of Memphis Special Collections, Memphis, TN
NA RG	National Archives Record Group

NFRS   Morris Cooke Papers, General Correspondence, Numerical
            File, Red Series, Franklin D. Roosevelt Library, Hyde Park,
            NY
PPA   *The Public Papers and Addresses of Franklin D. Roosevelt*
REN   *Rural Electrification News*
SA-HB   "Speeches and Articles by the Late Dr. Henry Garland
            Bennett," Henry Bennett Papers, Harry S. Truman Library,
            Independence, MO
SG   *Survey Graphic*
TVAH   *Hearings Before the Joint Committee on the Investigation
            of the Tennessee Valley Authority*, 75th Cong., 3rd sess.,
            1938
WP   M. L. Wilson Papers, Montana State University Archives,
            Bozeman, MT

Preface

Although I didn't realize it at the time, this study began in the summer of 1995. I was a rising college senior, an aspiring musician, and I had taken a summer job outside my South Georgia hometown harvesting canola to make some quick cash for a trip to Europe. I worked with a local farmer, a genial and soft-spoken man. He was not a farm owner but a farm manager who found freelance jobs here and there. I opened and closed the sacks of seed while he drove the combine. It was not sweaty work: we sat in the comfort of an air-conditioned cab and darted into the June heat only as long as it took to pluck some wayward stalk out of the machine or to gulp down our lunch.

From our conversations I caught my first glimpse of a contemporary agrarian worldview. This was a man who believed that a society depended on its farmers. They produced the food and fiber that yielded national affluence and national security. Farmers embodied the American work ethic, and they represented the operating definition of economic freedom. Unlike welfare recipients, who in his view "had decided not to work," farms deserved government protection and federal assistance. Had I spent more time in college studying history, I would have immediately recognized the Jeffersonian strains, not to mention the inconsistent definition of government "welfare"; as it was, I could only ponder the puzzle of a farmer who lived in town, worked intermittently for large, subsidized landowners, and yet saw himself as a piece of the country's moral and economic foundation. Furthermore, this man loved the outdoors – he hunted or fished every chance he got and purposely sought out unspoiled swimming holes. Yet he deemed the vast environmental ills of modern agriculture to be necessary costs in preserving the nation's food supply and the farmer's standard of living.

This experience played not a small part in my decision to study American history at the graduate level, and it helped launch an academic interest in the relationships among political ideology, agricultural and environmental policy, and American government. In this study I've chosen to examine a crucial episode in the formation of that coevolution, an episode I hope will contribute not just to my own desire to understand the updated agrarianism I witnessed that summer but also to scholars' understanding of the New Deal era more broadly.

I have incurred many debts. First thanks go to my graduate adviser, Bruce Schulman, for his encouragement and friendship over the years and for his unfailing ability to inspire and instruct. I didn't intend to retrace so many of the steps he covered in *From Cotton Belt to Sunbelt*, but I did so anyway and he never reminded me of it. I cannot imagine having completed this project without Bruce's editorial guidance and paternal presence. James McCann introduced me to the field of environmental history and has served as a most generous colleague ever since. Louis Ferleger has continuously supplied invaluable mentoring assistance, often providing direction through dangerous periods of low morale. I am also grateful to Deborah Fitzgerald and Jess Gilbert for their warm welcome to agricultural history, and to Neil Maher, Paul Sutter, and Brian Black for inviting me to join the New Dealers' club within environmental history. Others who deserve mention for providing inspiration at a crucial moment in the past or for sustaining it in the present are Richard Andrews, Ellen Baker, Regina Blaszczyk, Kyri Claflin, Peter Coclanis, Lisa Colletta, Elysa Engelman, Evan Haefeli, David Hamilton, Douglas Helms, Heather Hoag, Stacy Holden, Neil Jumonville, Amy Kittelstrom, Jill Lepore, Nicole Marwell, Paul Milazzo, Sara Pritchard, Martin Reuss, and Mary Summers.

Grants from the Boston University Humanities Foundation, the Franklin and Eleanor Roosevelt Institute, the Harry S. Truman Library Institute, the Hoover Presidential Library Association, and the Lyndon B. Johnson Foundation funded archival research. The Miller Center of Public Affairs at the University of Virginia provided support for one glorious fellowship year, and I thank Brian Balogh and Ed Russell for their help during that time and in the years following. I'm especially grateful to Columbia colleagues Elizabeth Blackmar, Casey Blake, Alan Brinkley, Eric Foner, Ira Katznelson, and Alice Kessler-Harris for reading parts of the manuscript and for strengthening all of it. Three anonymous reviewers for the Press provided crucial advice and contributed much to the final product. Because of Janis Bolster the writing is clear and the text presentable. For the remaining faults I offer the usual mea culpa.

Finally, I would like to express my deepest appreciation for my family: Marilee and Jerry Phillips, Susan and Michael Meriwether, Nicholas and Amanda Meriwether, Charles and Cindy Corsentino, Inez Corsentino, and my love, Tony Corsentino. In the end, I've written this book for my mother, who never forgoes the opportunity to rant against injustice or to ask why Americans have forgotten the Constitution's injunction to promote the general welfare.

Introduction

Great Depression & environmental tragedies

It is impossible to imagine the Great Depression in the United States without envisioning the era's environmental tragedies. Seared onto the national memory by novelists, filmmakers, and government photographers, portraits of uprooted and impoverished people mingle with images of scarred land, abandoned farms, and swollen rivers. Dust clouds darken the Great Plains and move threateningly toward the nation's capital. A lone, broken windmill looms over parched cattle and crumbling fields. Migrants, fleeing dirt and drought, trek along Route 66 to California's unwelcoming fruit orchards. A black sharecropper stands helpless beside the deepening gully that has stolen his farm's precious topsoil. Clutching their few belongings, refugees race the rising water and watch from a nearby hill as the river claims their homes.

These images of environmental disaster are matched by equally familiar stories of state-sponsored environmental renewal. The president dedicates a new national park with a stirring address. Young men receive jobs battling soil erosion, replanting damaged forests, and constructing campgrounds. The federal government builds new farms for some and manages migrant camps for others. High dams rise along the Tennessee and the Colorado. "Your power is turning our darkness to dawn," sings Woody Guthrie, "so roll on, Columbia, roll on." Despite the indisputable importance of these episodes, however, historians have never made them central to their interpretations of the New Deal, nor to their analyses of American political development. Such stories provide a colorful sideshow, and they often serve as evidence for the government's increased inclination to intervene, for good or for ill, in economic or environmental affairs;

but resource conservation never stands alone as an essential component of American liberal ideology.

This Land, This Nation combines political with environmental history to present conservation policy as an arm of New Deal economic reform, one that embodied the promises and limits of New Deal liberalism. During the Depression of the 1930s many Americans felt betrayed by the sudden economic collapse, and they decided that a more interventionist federal government might provide some degree of protection from the unregulated free market. Though this ideological turn had been well under way for decades, the New Deal sealed the shift and ushered in the modern liberal state. Franklin Roosevelt transformed the political party system by assembling a "New Deal coalition" composed of groups that supported an active government, such as farmers, urban workers, African Americans, and capital-intensive businesses. For the first time, Americans received direct aid in the form of welfare benefits and work relief, farm subsidies, and retirement pensions. Less successfully, the Roosevelt administration also attempted to introduce more far-reaching institutional and regulatory reforms.

At the center of the New Deal's attempts at recovery and reform were the conservation programs of the 1930s and 1940s. These programs introduced a set of federal strategies aimed at rehabilitating the economies of agricultural areas. Industrial America had not yet vanquished its agrarian past. In 1933, farmers still constituted nearly one-third of the nation's workforce, but rural incomes lagged far behind urban incomes. Farm prices had swung wildly during the 1920s, plunging to levels below those required to maintain operations – never mind to turn a profit, to pay taxes, or to repay a loan. Unlike large industrial concerns, most individual farmers produced for volatile commodity markets they could neither control nor predict. What could correct the crippling disparity between the country and the city? What could make farming more secure?

For many of the politicians and policymakers who launched the New Deal, rural parity required that natural resources be distributed more equitably and used more sustainably, a vision that required a repertoire of tools far broader than the commodity price supports usually assumed to represent the entire farm program. These New Dealers argued that rural poverty was caused by poor resource use and unfair resource distribution, and they set out to rebuild rural life and to raise rural incomes with measures tied directly to conservation objectives – land retirement, soil and forest restoration, flood control, and cheap hydropower for farms and new industries.

Believing that farmers' low living standards helped trigger the Depression, the New Dealers assumed that when farmers achieved an "American standard of living," they would be able to purchase manufactured goods and maintain employment for industrial workers. Industrial recovery, in other words, was initially assumed to depend on the revival of *agricultural* purchasing power. Economic formulations of national underconsumption began with the farmer and radiated outward to include the factory laborer and urban worker. Consequently, once this question of national responsibility for improved rural living standards gained a foothold, it required consideration of the renewable natural resources upon which farming depended – soil and water primarily, though forested land could be included as well. Such resources were not just renewable but improvable, and theoretically capable of supporting a permanent farm culture. Behind much of what we can call New Deal conservation lay the assumption that the sustainable and equitable use of these rural resources would help agricultural America "catch up," thereby bringing the country into economic balance with the city and preventing future depressions.

Conservation policy was never the only answer offered for the farm crisis, of course, nor was it intended to work independently of the other farm recovery programs. Still, the inclusion of rural resource issues within a growing state apparatus signaled an important shift. For the first time, national administrators linked conservation with agricultural programs, and considered environmental planning vital to the nation's economic renewal and long-term vitality. In building both rural and urban support for the conservation initiatives, a new policy community of natural resource administrators and their political allies established the justification for an expanded federal reach and an enlarged federal government. Alongside the federal government's regulatory initiatives, its recognition of organized labor, and its commitment to social insurance, the natural resource agencies functioned as engines of government growth and as instruments of voter realignment.

This process was critical to the Democratic Party's transformation during the 1930s – to its success in fusing farmers and industrial workers into a new coalition in support of active, redistributive government. And even though many farmers returned to the Republican fold once good times returned, the New Deal initiatives created a set of permanent institutional structures, administrative mechanisms, and liberal assumptions about the necessity for government-sponsored farm support and rural industrialization that have escaped serious partisan debate. While the predominant approach to rural development would shift by the 1940s, and while the new Democratic coalition would lose its Depression-era strength, the majority of Americans never lost faith that federal resource policy could and should equalize rural and urban incomes. The principle that national welfare required rural welfare underlay both New Deal and postwar liberalism, and also inspired American efforts to build an international framework for assisted modernization in the developing world. In short, the new patterns of environmental regulation introduced during the 1930s and 1940s formed the lasting model for federal resource management and decisively shaped the evolution of the modern American state.

One reason for the absence of environmental policy from interpretations of the New Deal era is that historians still tend to view each conservation project as a discrete episode. As a result, the attention paid to these individual events detaches them from each other and masks consideration of the larger national and political context for the conservation initiatives. The assumption that resource policy was peripheral rather than central to the New Deal's political importance has also reinforced the historiographical tendency to define state development solely in terms of government-business relations and the provision of social welfare. For the most part, state influence is measured by inspecting the extent of the federal government's regulatory reach, its relationship with organized labor, and its commitment to social insurance. By focusing on the weak American state, and by asking why it differed from its stronger European counterparts, historians have indeed compiled a convincing story of intellectual and political constraints. But in doing so they have overlooked natural resource policy as a decisive force in shaping the contours of American government.[1]

---

[1] For a small sample of this vast literature, see Edwin Amenta, *Bold Relief: Institutional Politics and the Origins of Modern American Social Policy* (1998); Alan Brinkley, *The End of Reform: New Deal Liberalism in Recession and War* (1995); Lizabeth Cohen, *Making a New Deal: Industrial Workers in Chicago* (1990); Alan Dawley, *Struggles for Justice: Moral Responsibility and the Liberal State* (1991); Marc Allen Eisner, *From Warfare State to Welfare State: World War I, Compensatory State-Building, and the Limits of the Modern Order* (2000); Louis Galambos, *The Rise of the Corporate Commonwealth: United States Business and Public Policy in the Twentieth Century* (1988); Neil Gilbert, *Transformation of the Welfare State: Tax Expenditures and Social Policy in the United States* (1997); Colin Gordon, *New Deals: Business, Labor, and Politics in America, 1920–1935* (1994); Linda Gordon, *Pitied but Not Entitled: Single Mothers and the History of Welfare, 1890–1935* (1995); Jacob S. Hacker, *The Divided Welfare State: The Battle over Public and Private Social Benefits in the United States* (2002); Ellis Hawley, *The New Deal and the Problem of Monopoly: A Study in Economic Ambivalence* (1966); Alice Kessler-Harris, *In Pursuit*

This absence is all the more puzzling considering the widespread influence of a pathbreaking monograph on federal resource policy and Progressive-era state building published over forty years ago. Samuel P. Hays's *Conservation and the Gospel of Efficiency* offered an unprecedented and persuasive fusion of environmental and political history. Taking as his bête noire the idea that Progressivism could be best explained as a struggle between the people and concentrated business power, Hays argued that the conservationists were motivated not by the desire to rein in the power of the trusts, but by their loyalty to the ideals of the emerging scientific professions. Battling big business, after all, cannot have been the primary aim of planners and administrators who often collaborated with large cattle and lumber companies and who incurred the wrath of small proprietors. Instead, a new spirit of efficiency required expert personnel and administrative methods that bypassed the "irrational" and "unscientific" practices of pressure-group politics and congressional logrolling. Housed within a more protected executive setting, a new professional class of foresters, hydrologists, and geologists attempted to protect the supply of the nation's natural resources while harvesting those resources for sustained economic growth. Of course, some critics have pointed out that the gospel of efficiency cannot by itself explain the intellectual and political

of Equity: Women, Men, and the Quest for Economic Citizenship in 20th-Century America (2001); David Plotke, *Building a Democratic Political Order: Reshaping American Liberalism in the 1930s and 1940s* (1996); Jill S. Quadagno, *The Transformation of Old Age Security: Class and Politics in the American Welfare State* (1988); Bruce J. Schulman, *From Cotton Belt to Sunbelt: Federal Policy, Economic Development, and the Transformation of the South, 1938–1980* (1991); Theda Skocpol, *Protecting Soldiers and Mothers: The Political Origins of Social Policy in the United States* (1992); Stephen Skowronek, *Building a New American State: The Expansion of National Administrative Capacities, 1977–1920* (1982); Margaret Weir, Ann Shola Orloff, and Theda Skocpol, eds., *The Politics of Social Policy in the United States* (1988). To be fair, certain works have examined the importance of agriculture and natural resource policy to American political and organizational development; in addition to works cited in subsequent notes see Louis Ferleger and William Lazonick, "The Managerial Revolution and the Developmental State: The Case of U.S. Agriculture," *Business and Economic History* (1993); Kenneth Finegold and Theda Skocpol, *State and Party in America's New Deal* (1995); Richard S. Kirkendall, *Social Scientists and Farm Politics in the Age of Roosevelt* (1966); and Elizabeth Sanders, *Roots of Reform: Farmers, Workers, and the American State, 1877–1917* (1999). Daniel Carpenter's *The Forging of Bureaucratic Autonomy: Reputations, Networks, and Policy Innovation in Executive Agencies, 1862–1928* (2001), includes an examination of natural resource administration; also see Donald J. Pisani, "The Many Faces of Conservation," in Morton Keller and R. Shep Melnick, eds., *Taking Stock: American Government in the Twentieth Century* (1999). Taking a global perspective, James Scott views resource conservation policy as essential to twentieth-century state power: *Seeing Like a State: How Certain Schemes to Improve the Human Condition Have Failed* (1998).

complexity of Progressive environmental thought, and others have noted that Hays failed to look at how national policy actually affected the landscapes under consideration. Yet any serious student of American political history must be familiar with Hays's analysis, for he brilliantly demonstrated that resource policy was inextricably bound with changing conceptions of federal responsibility.[2]

Conservation and the Gospel of Efficiency, however, proved in some ways too influential. Instead of serving as a model for those wishing to revisit the character of New Deal liberalism, Hays's interpretation worked instead to convince both political and environmental historians that the major intellectual framework for resource conservation had been constructed in the early twentieth century. Because the grand projects of the 1930s appeared to represent the fulfillment of Progressive-era dreams, they were assumed to have sprung from the exigencies of the Depression and from the coffers of a more sympathetic federal government, not from new ideas or new reform movements. Recent work on the environmental ideas of the 1920s has begun to challenge such assumptions, but the dominant picture has not yet been overturned.[3] It is still assumed that continuity of purpose and rationale, not alterations in the intellectual or political climate, explains the pattern and timing of the first half century of federal conservation policy.

Hays is not to be faulted for the subsequent assumption of continuity, because his work helped initiate a much-needed reorientation of American political history. For many years, most observers had assumed that political change in the United States was fueled by the persistent struggle between liberals and conservatives, and that in this struggle liberals occasionally gained the upper hand and initiated periods of progressive reform. Since the 1970s, however, historians have argued that the guiding

---

[2] Samuel P. Hays, *Conservation and the Gospel of Efficiency* (1959). Recent challenges to Hays's interpretation include Brian Balogh, "Scientific Forestry and the Roots of the Modern American State," *Environmental History* 7 (2002); and Donald J. Pisani, *Water and American Government: The Reclamation Bureau, National Water Policy, and the West, 1902–1935* (2002).

[3] See Kendrick A. Clements, *Hoover, Conservation, and Consumerism: Engineering the Good Life* (2000); Paul S. Sutter, *Driven Wild: How the Fight Against Automobiles Launched the Modern Wilderness Movement* (2002); and Neil Maher, *Nature's New Deal: Franklin Roosevelt's Civilian Conservation Corps and the Roots of the American Environmental Movement* (forthcoming). On the missing historiography of the interwar years, see Paul S. Sutter, "Terra Incognita: The Neglected History of Interwar Environmental Thought and Politics," *Reviews in American History* 29 (2001). A new anthology also promises to fill the gap: Henry L. Henderson and David B. Woolner, eds., *FDR and the Environment* (2005).

political force of the twentieth century has been not waves of reform but rather the growth of large-scale, national institutions such as the modern business corporation, the professional organizations, and the administrative state. Like Hays's conservationists, the organization builders prized efficiency rather than equity, and they favored bureaucracy over democracy. In other words, too single-minded a focus on the rhetoric of reform and reaction had obscured other, more continuous influences: technological change, the gradual mobilization of scientific and social scientific expertise, the cozy cooperation between business and government, even – as a persuasive new book argues – consumer and labor mobilization for a low-price, high-wage economy. The previous attention to reform movements and traditional reform periodization now appears antiquated, more a testament to the liberal assumptions of past historians than an accurate reflection of political reality.[4]

Environmental historians have also accepted a picture of continuity. For the most part, their work has cast American environmental sentiment as a duel between two competing worldviews: conservation and preservation. "Conservation" is often used interchangeably with "environmental protection," but the two ideas have different meanings for environmental history. Conservationists, such as those who staffed the U.S. Forest Service under Theodore Roosevelt and those who built Hetch Hetchy Dam in Yosemite National Park, believed that natural resources should be managed professionally and scientifically for the public good. Represented most prominently by Gifford Pinchot, Roosevelt's chief forester, conservationists thought natural resources should be used, developed, even commodified, just not wasted. The preservationist outlook, usually traced to John Muir in the late nineteenth century, encompassed a wider appreciation for the intrinsic value of natural and scenic places (or at least an appreciation for how mankind might benefit from the uncultivated landscape). Public manifestations of preservationist thinking included the establishment of national parks, the movement for wilderness

---

[4] On the organizational synthesis, see Louis Galambos, "The Emerging Organizational Synthesis in Modern American History," *Business History Review* 44 (1970); Galambos, "Technology, Political Economy, and Professionalization: Central Themes of the Organizational Synthesis," *Business History Review* 5 (1983); and Brian Balogh, "Reorganizing the Organizational Synthesis: Federal-Professional Relations in Modern America," *Studies in American Political Development* 5 (1991). The "persuasive new book" that fits somewhat into the trend is Meg Jacobs, *Pocketbook Politics: Economic Citizenship in Twentieth-Century America* (2005). Jacobs emphasizes a more continuous force – the high cost of living – but also elegantly captures the way modern state building required debates about the equitable distribution of profit, not simply its efficient management.

areas, and the ecological attitudes of the modern environmental movement. Because most environmental historians have cast their lot with
John Muir rather than with Gifford Pinchot, they view the history of
twentieth-century resource policy as a battle between development and
preservation, and see both Progressive and New Deal conservation as
dominated by the similar impulse to use and to exploit the nation's natural
resources.[5]

In short, political and environmental historians have failed to join
together to reexamine the New Deal and its lasting effects on American
institutions and public policy. While a few political historians have continued to emphasize reform movements, many others have placed reform on
the back burner and examined the developments that appeared more influential: big business, expert management, public-private collaboration, and
technological change. While recognizing that New Deal liberalism constituted a significant departure from the past, they have downplayed its
differences from the "conservative" 1920s and portrayed the New Deal
as the interplay of more continuous forces. Environmental historians have
also understood that the Depression prompted a greater number of conservation initiatives, but they too have assumed these projects represented the
final outcome of unchanging desires to control and develop the country's
rivers and its land. More continuous forces have appeared at work here as

---

[5] The most influential work on conservation in the 1930s analyzes New Deal policy as a
missed opportunity to restrain capitalist exploitation: Donald Worster, *Dust Bowl: The
Southern Plains in the 1930s* (1979). For an overview of the environmental literature,
see Richard White, "American Environmental History: The Development of a New Historical Field," *Pacific Historical Review* 54 (1985). On conservation versus preservation,
see Roderick Nash, *Wilderness and the American Mind* (1967); and Stephen Fox, *The
American Conservation Movement: John Muir and His Legacy* (1981). This is not to
say that environmental historians are unaware of the limitations of the conservation/
preservation distinction. Clayton Koppes has replaced this dualism with a tripartite model,
arguing that three shifting emphases can explain twentieth-century environmental policy –
efficiency, equity, and esthetics. I enthusiastically concur that this additional category
("equity") should be included in order to analyze the distribution of benefits among
social and economic classes. See Koppes, "Environmental Policy and American Liberalism: The Department of the Interior, 1933–1953," *Environmental Review* 7 (1983),
and "Efficiency/Equity/Esthetics: Towards a Reinterpretation of American Conservation,"
Environmental Review 11 (1987). Char Miller's work on Gifford Pinchot also offers a
more nuanced interpretation of conservation ideology: *Gifford Pinchot and the Making
of Modern Environmentalism* (2001). Neil Maher and Paul Sutter have begun the much-
needed task of reexamining the New Deal era; see Maher, *Nature's New Deal*; Maher,
"'Crazy Quilt Farming on Round Land': The Great Depression, the Soil Conservation
Service, and the Politics of Landscape Change on the Great Plains During the New Deal,"
Western Historical Quarterly 31 (2000); and Sutter, *Driven Wild*.

well: capitalist expansion, technological development, and government-booster collusion.

While we have learned much from these new scholarly directions, the assumptions about continuity, efficiency, and exploitation have acted as a powerful barrier to historical inquiry. For the most part, scholars have failed to imagine the possibility of meaningful reform, or to look again at the New Deal as a struggle over the equitable division of economic resources. We have also become blind to the possibility that resource conservation could have meant anything but capitalist exploitation. Despite all the familiar images of environmental tragedy and government action, despite all the pictures of human desperation and state-sponsored renewal, we have missed an essential concern of New Deal environmental policy. It was poverty – in particular, rural poverty.

Poverty!

New Deal conservation was new because it linked natural with human resources, and took as its foremost concern the environmental imbalances of inhabited rural areas. The policy intellectuals who designed and implemented the programs believed that the free market had failed: unabated individualism had yielded an overinvestment in agriculture but an underinvestment in agriculturalists. Farmers continued to till eroded and exhausted land, leaving the nation pockmarked with chronic rural poverty. The New Conservationists concluded that land and water resources should therefore be protected and developed not just for efficiency's sake but to raise the living standards of the people living nearby. And the federal government, they insisted, had an obligation and a mandate to expand the economic and political opportunities of rural people by means of conservation policy.

New Conservationist beliefs

The favored methods for rural rehabilitation changed during the course of the New Deal and World War II. Tension had always existed between those who believed that farmers had to "get big or get out" and those who claimed that more could be done to help farmers remain on the land. The onset of the Depression tipped the balance in favor of the latter – those whom this study terms the agrarians. Between 1933 and the early 1940s, federal programs aimed to sustain the rural way of life and to help people remain on the land. The lack of alternative employment opportunities during the Depression provided the immediate context for this agrarian strategy, but the industrial slump simply provided a window of opportunity, not the underlying rationale. More important was the New Dealers' belief that all farmers, rich and poor, might find security of tenure and income when a region's natural resources were used properly and distributed fairly. This ideology inspired substantial achievements; it also helped the Democratic Party to build a new rural constituency. With government assistance, farmers received inexpensive electricity and altered destructive land use practices. They also asked to be included in resettlement communities and to take part in tenant-purchase and farm security programs.

Ultimately, however, the balance of power shifted toward those who believed that there were just too many farmers. Planners and policymakers began to wonder whether the very poorest rural people would be able to compete, economically and politically, with those farmers best able to stay on the land and to expand their operations with government assistance. Several groups – both liberal and conservative, and both from within and from outside the administration – also began to argue that only industrial jobs yielded sufficient incomes, and that small and marginal farmers might be best served by policies that encouraged out-migration, industrialization, and urbanization. Almost by accident, World War II provided exactly this opportunity. As a coalition of wealthier farmers and conservative congressmen from the South and West extinguished New Deal efforts to assist tenants, sharecroppers, and migrant workers, liberal conservation policy helped to bring about an alternate solution to the problem of the rural poor. Large, multipurpose dam projects powered war factories, drew migrants from the farms, and served as catalysts of regional and industrial growth.

To be sure, use of the word "solution" denies the complex and often disastrous results of government policy. Federal policymakers did not "solve" the problem of rural poverty: country migrants suffered unjustly when they entered an urban-industrial order rife with racial discrimination and segregation. Nor did policymakers ever seriously challenge the most egregious instances of agricultural class stratification. At best, federal aid in places like Mississippi or California served as a Band-Aid during hard times; at worst, it reinforced an exploitative and racist system of wage labor. The rural poor, as historian Anthony Badger has noted, "suffered from the failure of national farm policymakers to understand that agricultural relations on southern plantations and on western factory farms were not the same as relations on the family farms of the Midwest."[6] The lack of understanding, however, can explain only so much. Liberals also suffered from a lack of capacity, for the economics of race and region often precluded political solutions. "The problems facing the various sectors of the American farm economy were institutionalized," as the late Theodore Saloutos has remarked, "and overcoming them in a democratic

---

[6] Anthony J. Badger, *The New Deal: The Depression Years, 1933–1940* (1989), 184.

society required a unanimity of purpose among a majority that was difficult to obtain."[7]

Nor did federal policy bring about the sustainable social and environmental landscape that so many New Dealers desired. And here the fault
lies not simply with regional ignorance or with the outside forces arrayed
against reform – it must also be traced to the ideological conflicts at the
heart of the new rural conservation. At bottom, the program rested on two
paradoxes. First, these liberals hoped to preserve the family farm by modernizing it. They valued both efficiency and equity, yet failed to see that
the desire to raise rural incomes to urban-industrial standards could justify the political abandonment of the small farm. Related to this paradox
was a second: conservation was promoted as a tool for expanded production. It should therefore come as no surprise that farmers welcomed
environmental adjustments when they served this purpose and cast them
aside when they did not.

But "solution" is not used here as a way of avoiding such facts. Rather,
it is used to describe the influential and pervasive industrial paradigm
that emerged from the crucible of war, from the tensions within liberal
thought, and from the increasing power of newly secure farmers and their
conservative allies to preserve the dominance of large-farm interests. This
industrial paradigm held that farmers could capture a fair piece of the
nation's economic pie only after they were helped to expand their operations, and after public investments in regional and rural industrialization
encouraged farm out-migration. Despite the shortcomings of this final
outcome, however, liberal policymakers did achieve a certain measure of
social and environmental justice. Within a limited political and ideological
framework they negotiated a variety of internal and external constraints
to provide postwar America with what they hoped was a self-sustaining
industrial order.

While the New Conservation constituted a significant departure from the
past, these ideas did not spring forth, fully formed, during the 1930s.
Indeed, the intellectual background for the New Deal's rural resource
philosophy emerged from the Progressive conservation movement and
from its equally influential contemporary, the Country Life movement.
The conservation movement had its origins in the second half of the

---

[7] Theodore Saloutos, *The American Farmer and the New Deal* (1982), xv. The absence of
liberal capacity during the New Deal era is elegantly developed in Ira Katznelson, *When
Affirmative Action Was White: An Untold History of Racial Inequality in Twentieth-
Century America* (2005).

nineteenth century, when urgent concerns about the nation's disappearing natural resources first arose. Most antebellum Americans had regarded the country's forests, minerals, and soil as inexhaustible; the government merely needed to get this bounty into the hands of private citizens as quickly as possible. But as the country began to industrialize rapidly in the decades following the Civil War, scientists, journalists, and politicians warned that the nation faced a future resource shortage. These reformers criticized the ethos of laissez-faire capitalism, arguing that the federal government should supervise a system of public forests and more systematically manage the country's public domain and its waterways. Dire predictions of a resource famine also joined post-frontier fears about the declining availability of arable land and strengthened the bargaining power of those who wanted to develop the water supplies of the arid West.[8]

Gifford Pinchot, Theodore Roosevelt's chief forester, acted as the conservation movement's primary intellect and foremost publicist. To assuage the fears of those who thought conservation meant locking away resources from use, Pinchot declared that "the first principle of conservation is development, the use of the natural resources existing on this continent for the benefit of the people who live here now." To this first principle, he added two more: prevention of waste, and development for the many rather than for the few. The inevitable outgrowth of conservation, Pinchot claimed, would be "national efficiency"; the science of sustained yield would underpin the economic prosperity of current as well as future generations.[9]

[8] The classic work on Progressive conservation remains Hays, *Conservation and the Gospel of Efficiency*. Also see Char Miller, ed., *American Forests: Nature, Culture, and Politics* (1997); Donald J. Pisani, "Forests and Conservation, 1865–1890," *Journal of American History* 72 (1985); Pisani, *To Reclaim a Divided West: Water, Law, and Public Policy, 1848–1902* (1992); Pisani, *Water and American Government*; Elmo R. Richardson, *The Politics of Conservation: Crusades and Controversies, 1897–1913* (1962); William G. Robbins, *Lumberjacks and Legislators: Political Economy of the U.S. Lumber Industry, 1890–1941* (1982); William D. Rowley, *U.S. Forest Service Grazing and Rangelands: A History* (1985); Donald Worster, *Rivers of Empire: Water, Aridity, and the Growth of the American West* (1985); and William K. Wyant, *Westward in Eden: The Public Lands and the Conservation Movement* (1982). Contemporary sources include *Proceedings of a Conference of Governors on the Conservation of Natural Resources* (GPO, 1909); Gifford Pinchot, *The Fight for Conservation* (1910); Pinchot, *Breaking New Ground* (1947); Charles Van Hise, *The Conservation of Resources in the United States* (1921); and Richard T. Ely, *The Foundations of National Prosperity: Studies in the Conservation of Permanent National Resources* (1918).
[9] Pinchot, *Fight for Conservation*, 43–50.

Too narrow a focus on the conservation movement, however, can conceal equally formative thinking about rural resources during the Progressive era. The Country Life movement also set forward an analysis of agricultural life that influenced New Deal conservation policy. This alliance of academics, social thinkers, and government officials called attention to the disparities between the city and the country and worked to bring efficiency and organization to farming. With regard to resource use, these rural advocates argued that the country suffered from eroded land and depleted soils because American farmers still clung to primitive methods of cultivation. As one reformer put it, "The farmer, now the chief waster, must become the chief conservator." The Country Life reformers also believed that individual farmers faced tremendous disadvantages vis-à-vis more organized business interests, and that as a result of this poor bargaining position rural communities were often unable to control the disposition of nearby forests and streams. Indeed, the Country Life and the conservation movements shared similar rhetorical tropes: sustained development without waste or resource monopolization. If Pinchot defined conservation as "the greatest good to the greatest number for the longest time," Liberty Hyde Bailey, chairman of Roosevelt's Country Life Commission, similarly sought "a permanent agriculture that will maintain itself century by century … without despoliation or loss, or without a damaging monopoly."[10]

For Country Life commentators, a "permanent agriculture" meant a settled system that nurtured and protected its natural and human communities. Farming should be "self-sustaining" and "self-perpetuating,"

---

[10] Sir Horace Plunkett, "Conservation and Rural Life," *Outlook* (29 January 1910), 260; Pinchot, *Fight for Conservation*, 48; Liberty H. Bailey, *The Holy Earth* (1915; reprint, 1943), 20–1. Plunkett, a close adviser to Roosevelt and rural life propagandist, described the two movements as twin policies and credited Gifford Pinchot with first bringing this relationship to his attention. See Plunkett, "Conservation and Rural Life," "The Neglected Farmer," *Outlook* (5 February 1910), and *The Rural Life Problem of the United States* (1911). Bailey also viewed the two movements as complementary; see *The Country Life Movement in the United States* (1911) and *Outlook to Nature* (1905). Secondary literature on the Country Life movement includes William Bowers, *The Country Life Movement in America, 1900–1920* (1974); David B. Danbom, *The Resisted Revolution: Urban America and the Industrialization of Agriculture* (1979); Danbom, "Romantic Agrarianism in Twentieth-Century America," *Agricultural History* 65 (1991); Donald J. Tweton, "The Attitudes and Policies of the Theodore Roosevelt Administration Toward American Agriculture" (Ph.D. diss., University of Oklahoma, 1964); and Scott J. Peters and Paul A. Morgan, "The Country Life Commission: Reconsidering a Milestone in American Agricultural History," *Agricultural History* 78 (2004).

thereby leaving the land "better and richer" for each succeeding generation. Rural advocates did not assume everyone born on a farm should remain there, but they did believe that closer-knit, more prosperous neighborhoods would follow from intensive (as opposed to extensive or "pioneering") farming practices. Consequently, they chastised Americans for not moving beyond the pioneering stage of settlement. "We excavate the best of the coal and cast away the remainder," Bailey lamented, sounding very much the conservation crusader. "We box the pines for turpentine and abandon the growths of limitless years to fire and devastation; choke the streams with refuse and dross; rob the land of its available stores, denuding the surface, exposing great areas to erosion ... We are not to look for our permanent civilization to rest on any species of robber-economy." [11]

Both the conservation and the Country Life movements emphasized natural resources – soil, forests, and rivers – as critical to improving the conditions of farm life, and castigated "established business systems" for depriving the "permanent agricultural inhabitants" of the benefits from nearby rivers and forests. Rural stability, they argued, required that farmers acquire primary claims to the surrounding resources; forests and streams should be managed and conserved so as to benefit an area's most immediate inhabitants. However, both sets of reformers blamed individual farmers, not institutions or economic systems, for eroded and exhausted soils. Recommendations to bring about improved rural conditions occasionally included suggestions for business regulation or the communal purchase of waterpower sites and forested land. But when it came to soil management on private land, conservationists and rural advocates most emphatically endorsed voluntary farmer education efforts, especially the experiment and demonstration programs of the U.S. Department of Agriculture (USDA). In the end, they had decided that more education, not direct government intervention, would help farmers improve their conservation practices. [12]

The Country Life reformers' emphasis on education reveals how the conservation and rural life movements diverged despite their ideological similarities. While Country Life advocates and conservationists agreed

---

[11] Bailey, *Holy Earth*, 14, 19.

[12] *Report of the Commission on Country Life* (GPO, 1909; reprint, 1911), 64–6, 68–74, 83–91; Bailey, *Country Life Movement*, 48–50; Plunkett, *Rural Life Problem*, 136; Pinchot, *Fight for Conservation*, 31–9; "Address by E. A. Burnett," *Proceedings of a Conference of Governors*, 184–6; "Resolutions of the Third National Conservation Congress," *Proceedings of the Third National Conservation Congress* (1912).

that the individual misuse of private agricultural land posed a significant problem, neither set of reformers attempted to craft new regulations for farm resources or to place their concern for inhabited rural regions at the forefront of conservationist action. Liberty Bailey, for one, lamented this state of affairs. The conservation movement, he ruefully concluded, had barely touched "the plain problem of handling the soil by all the millions who, by skill or blundering or theft, produce crops and animals out of the earth." Instead, Bailey thought that Gifford Pinchot and his cohorts had garnered support for their resource policies by vilifying "entrenched property interests" such as lumber companies and utilities rather than individual farmers. Bailey's analysis was correct. Although, contrary to his assertion, the conservationists often forged alliances with the very propertied interests they denounced in order to promote scientific management across entire industries, they still embraced a more active federal role in the ownership and management of natural resources, and they sought to use the full power of the managerial state to promote the efficient use of the public domain and the nation's rivers. Rural reformers, on the other hand, consistently sought to use the less coercive influence of state-sponsored education and demonstration work to change the organizational strategies and cultivation practices of individual farmers.[13]

As a result, each movement cast a separate shadow across the 1920s. Conservationists secured federal supervision over navigable rivers and hydropower sites within the public domain, and they worked within the established agencies to expand programs in forestry, river development, and waterways improvement. Farmers, aided by the land-grant colleges, government experiment stations, and a new Extension Service, increasingly modernized their operations and organized cooperatives to assert their collective interest. But growing slowly beneath the surface was discontent with the nation's failure to link conservation goals with rural planning. In fact, the 1920s witnessed an extension of thinking about rural resources and farm poverty that broadened the conservation agenda and set the stage for the New Deal.

This book begins in the 1920s by tracing the emergence of a set of conservationist concerns closely linked with analyses of rural welfare. The

[13] Bailey, *Country Life Movement*, 180, 183, 200; Plunkett, "The Neglected Farmer," 298–9. Also see William H. Harbaugh, "The Limits of Voluntarism: Farmers, County Agents, and the Conservation Movement," in John M. Cooper and Charles E. Neu, eds., *The Wilson Era: Essays in Honor of Arthur S. Link* (1991).

first chapter shows how rural electrification advocates such as Morris Cooke and George Norris, and land planning specialists such as Lewis C. Gray and M. L. Wilson, recast the problem of farm parity as one of proper resource use and fair resource allocation. Troubled by the social and economic disparities between the country and the city, this policy community believed that regional planning for land and water resources would alleviate farm distress and restore the viability of rural living.[14] The New Conservationists attempted to shape federal programs, but the decade's prevailing political ideology prevented the New Conservation from becoming national policy during Herbert Hoover's presidency. However, the new rural conservationists were able to capture the ear of Franklin D. Roosevelt, the governor of New York and the Democratic candidate for president in 1932. The chapter concludes with an examination of Roosevelt's conservationist background and considers the role of agrarian thinking in the formulation of his economic worldview and his successful political strategy.

Chapter 2 follows this policy community into Roosevelt's administration, and traces the national influence of the new rural conservation within the New Deal programs designed to rehabilitate and reconstruct rural areas. The Depression provided Roosevelt and the Democratic Party with an opportunity to bring the New Conservationists into the federal government. Given wide administrative discretion, these rural advocates attempted to craft conservation policies to help farmers remain on the land. Arguing that national welfare required farm welfare, the New Conservationists and their bureaucratic allies – Rexford Tugwell, Henry Wallace, Hugh H. Bennett, and Tennessee Valley Authority (TVA) Chairmen A. E. Morgan, H. A. Morgan, and David Lilienthal – established the political justification for an expanded federal role and laid the groundwork for new federal responsibilities. The chapter analyzes TVA as the source of both programmatic and legal precedents, and takes the story beyond TVA to examine the rural resource programs designed for the rest of the country – land retirement, rural rehabilitation, soil conservation, rural electrification, and farm security.

The third chapter shifts the focus from Washington, D.C., to Central Texas to investigate New Deal conservation from the bottom up.

[14] The idea of a "policy community" comes from John W. Kingdon, *Agendas, Alternatives, and Public Policies* (1984); and Julian Zelizer, *Taxing America: Wilbur D. Mills, Congress, and the State, 1945–1975* (1998).

Analyzing the early political career of Lyndon Johnson, it illustrates the relationship between environmental policy and the New Deal Democratic coalition. Johnson served as a liaison between the farmers of his congressional district and the federal government, channeling money for agricultural conservation, flood control, hydroelectric development, and rural electrification from Washington to the Texas Hill Country. Johnson's experience demonstrates how the New Deal succeeded in building a new constituency for rural assistance. His career also straddled the agrarian and industrial New Deals. The young politician understood that long-term trends did not augur well for small and marginal farmers, and he seized the opportunity provided by World War II to test a new approach. Rather than formulating more programs to keep the very poorest farmers tied to the land, Johnson worked to build an industrial infrastructure based upon cheap hydropower from the region's newly completed set of hydroelectric dams. By the end of World War II, the congressman foresaw a future with fewer farmers but with more factories, more wage workers, and more city dwellers.

Chapter 4 returns to national administration to examine this shift in rural development strategy during the late 1930s and World War II. In contrast to the rural policy of the New Deal, the federal conservation programs during and after the war encouraged farm out-migration, urbanization, and industrialization. The hope that animated much of the New Deal's rural rehabilitation philosophy – the idea that every farmer might find security on the land when a region's natural resources were used properly and distributed fairly – faltered when confronted by the insurmountable difficulty of reconciling the needs of the poorest and smallest producers with the interests of their wealthier and more commercially oriented counterparts. Those who were able to remain on the land and to expand their operations with federal help now resisted government attempts to support small and marginal ("inefficient") producers.

The New Deal, in other words, was unable to sustain a constituency composed of the poorest farmers. This does not mean, however, that New Deal liberalism died completely or that popular support for federal action faded. Liberals now argued that the landless could find employment in a newly decentralized industrial sector powered by large hydroelectric installations and sustained by military contracts. In fact, the industrial transition revealed the New Conservation's resilience: both Democratic and Republican politicians supported water engineering schemes, commodity price supports, soil conservation districts, and rural economic diversification. However, the principle of state-sponsored rural resource development did not survive the war unaltered. Never again would Americans seriously debate the merits, environmental or social, of maintaining a stable farm population.

An epilogue considers the international influence of U.S. conservation policy during and immediately following World War II. Many Americans felt sure they had indeed found the tools for conquering the problem of rural poverty. In fact, it was this uncritical confidence that provided a path from the domestic to the international stage, where the New Deal experience played a formative role in the country's postwar foreign assistance programs. The resource administrators who shaped the bilateral and multilateral programs believed that the federal government had successfully integrated poor, rural regions into the national economy and that U.S. foreign policy could do the same for other areas of the globe. The postwar export of the American conservation models underscored their domestic political importance as acknowledged agents of state-sponsored rural rehabilitation and of regional economic development. In facilitating the adoption of the American conservation models overseas, especially the industrial paradigm, the New Conservationists helped to usher in the modern era of globalization.

The international story also suggests how attention to resource policy might revise the conventional understanding of the "weak" American state. The United States exported neither its patchwork system of social policy nor its imperfect approach to business regulation. Developing countries sent their most promising students to study America's experimental farms and its hydraulics laboratories, not its understaffed welfare departments. Other historians have recently suggested that the existence of a large public domain, coupled with the nation's "population imbalance," decisively shaped the character of American government. They have persuasively argued that conquering the West and marshaling its resources for settlement and economic expansion furnished the United States with a distinctive engine of state development.[15] While drawing from these insights, this study instead suggests that American resource policy might have become influential overseas not because of its managerial roots in

---

[15] See Richard White, *"It's Your Misfortune and None of My Own": A New History of the American West* (1991); Karen R. Merrill, "In Search of the 'Federal Presence' in the American West," *Western Historical Quarterly* 30 (1999); Gerald D. Nash, *The Federal Landscape: An Economic History of the Twentieth-century West* (1999); and Pisani, *Water and American Government.*

a vast, empty continent, but because it appeared to offer a road-tested solution for rural modernization.

The book is not meant to be an exhaustive treatment of agricultural or conservation policy, nor will it examine the actions of individual farmers or the perception of policy as it was felt on the ground. Rather, I intend to offer a thematic interpretation of New Deal conservation: how it differed from what came before, why that newness was significant, and what this period of resource management meant for the country's institutions and its landscapes. To illuminate this national story I have chosen to downplay regional differences, and I willingly accept the risks that follow from this decision along with the rewards. This is not to say regional differences play no part at all. As the country's poorest and most rural region, the South shows up as the first example of the New Conservation's potential and functions as the representative site of its social limitations. The Great Plains and the Great Basin states, with their farm settlements undeterred by the region's aridity and recurrent drought, will serve as the primary setting for analyzing the New Deal's environmental limitations. Finally, California and the Pacific Slope states appear near the story's end to illustrate the ultimate direction of conservation policy nationwide. The New Deal never asked residents of the Far West to lower their expectations, as had been attempted elsewhere in the country, but rather whetted their appetites for "expanding horizons" by means of massive hydroelectric and irrigation facilities serving both industrial farms and industrial factories.[16]

The question of what obligation Americans have to their rural citizens and to their farm landscapes still presses upon us. It is neither nostalgic nor backward-looking to understand that farmers not only produce the nation's food and fiber but also occupy the front line of any effort to preserve the nation's land and water, not to mention its rural community life. How many farmers are needed on the land to accomplish these tasks? The market cannot answer this question for us. I was drawn to the topic of New Deal conservation because the Depression opened a wide national debate on rural sustainability, a debate Americans have largely failed to recapture despite the admirable and growing efforts of many contemporary reformers. My intention with this study is not to bemoan the passing of that moment, however, or to predict how we might retrieve it in

[16] I borrow this interpretation from Richard Lowitt, *The New Deal and the West* (1984), 64, 220.

the future, but to demonstrate that the questions that occupied the New
Dealers – questions that still resonate about the place of natural resources
in economic planning, and about the proper relationship between the city
and the country – were inseparable from revolutionary shifts in American
politics and public policy.

The New Conservation

On a June afternoon in 1931, Franklin D. Roosevelt addressed his fellow governors assembled in Indiana for their annual conference. The severe economic situation, he said, called for positive leadership, tangible experiments, and government guidance. Yet Roosevelt confined his remarks that day to one particular aspect of the nation's troubles – the "dislocation of a proper balance between urban and rural life." Describing how hundreds of farmers clung to exhausted lands and eked out an existence far below the "American standard of living," he outlined measures New York State had initiated to classify lands, relieve tax burdens, purchase and reforest submarginal farmland, and bring cheaper electricity to the agricultural areas. He looked forward to a time when farmers cultivating land too worn to yield a profit would find alternate employment in factories close to rural communities. Planning for "a permanent agriculture," Roosevelt explained, was the state's ultimate purpose.[1]

Roosevelt's calls for "a proper balance" and "a permanent agriculture" encapsulated a new style of conservationist thinking, one largely developed in the decade before the New Deal. Conservationists in the Progressive era had essentially confined their efforts to waterways, forests, and recreational lands, and they advocated public ownership (mostly in the sparsely settled West) as the primary remedy for individual and corporate misuse. While the Progressives failed to win provisions for national, multiple-purpose river basin planning after World War I, the movement continued to influence natural resource policy during the 1920s. A new

[1] Franklin Roosevelt, "Acres Fit and Unfit: State Planning of Land Use for Industry and Agriculture," 1931, *PPA*, 485–95.

Federal Power Commission exercised supervision over hydropower sites within the public domain and over navigable waterways, and resource agencies within the Agriculture, Interior, and War Departments gradually expanded programs in reclamation, forestry, and river engineering.[2] But the 1920s also witnessed a critical extension of conservationist thought. A loosely connected coterie of engineers, politicians, intellectuals, and government officials voiced dissatisfaction with the nation's failure to meet the social and environmental needs of inhabited rural regions and privately held agricultural land. They believed that regional planning for land and water resources would alleviate farm poverty, modernize farm areas, and restore the viability of rural living. These concerns, labeled the "New Conservation" by one observer in 1925, broadened the resource policy agenda and set the stage for the New Deal.[3]

Two independent groups constructed the intellectual components of the New Conservation. The first of these policy communities was a collection of eastern planners and politicians who desired a more balanced regional life. They believed the modern business and financial system exploited the human and natural resources of rural areas, exhausted the nation's soils and forests, and pulled impoverished people to overcrowded city centers. Rural stability, these advocates argued, depended on a "permanent," rather than an extractive, relationship with nature. They maintained that governments must take active steps to halt the waste, stem the exodus, and promote a settled and prosperous farm culture. Bringing electricity to the countryside, decentralizing industry, and classifying land according to its proper use could improve farmers' living standards and protect their surroundings. For rural electrification promoters Gifford Pinchot and Morris Cooke, this vision justified their belief that utilities should serve farms with nondiscriminatory rates. Other rural reformers, such as Lewis Mumford, maintained that comprehensive regional planning would remedy the ills of urban congestion by stabilizing the farm population.

A group of government officials in the U.S. Department of Agriculture formed the second policy tributary. Land economists such as L. C. Gray and M. L. Wilson believed that the agricultural depression of the 1920s reflected structural and environmental imbalances within farming. Other

[2] For a long time the only treatment of conservation in the 1920s was Donald Swain, *Federal Conservation Policy, 1921–1933* (1963). Much-needed recent additions are Kendrick A. Clements, *Hoover, Conservation, and Consumerism: Engineering the Good Life* (2000); and Paul S. Sutter, *Driven Wild: How the Fight Against Automobiles Launched the Modern Wilderness Movement* (2002).

[3] Lewis Mumford, "Regions – To Live In," *SG* (May 1925), 152.

farm advocates argued that merely equalizing the farmer's terms of trade (making the tariff "effective" for agriculture) would correct disparities in income and living standards. But these planners insisted the underlying problems stemmed not from the absence of a protective tariff or from the inability of farmers to organize collectively, but from the failure of agricultural systems to adapt to proper land use.

Though these groups only occasionally acted in concert, by the late 1920s and early 1930s their ideas coalesced into an influential body of work. Both the rural electrification advocates and the land use planners *linking* linked social with environmental goals. They believed that proper resource use and fair resource distribution could relieve rural poverty and raise rural incomes, and they called upon the government to execute this vision. In this effort they enlisted as occasional allies Senator George Norris of Nebraska, a persistent advocate of public power and rural assistance, and Hugh H. Bennett, an equally relentless foe of soil erosion who campaigned against land degradation from his position in the Department of Agriculture. Because the same prescriptions for rural underdevelopment – cheap electricity, industrial decentralization, land planning, and land retirement – emanated from so many different quarters, these proposals received wide circulation and entered the political marketplace.

Presidential politics proved to be the critical arena. By the late 1920s, Herbert Hoover had earned his stripes as a sincere, if not fanatical, conservationist and farm advocate. He negotiated the first interstate water allocation compact in 1922, spearheaded efforts to conserve oil and timber, championed outdoor recreation initiatives, and supported federal outlays for flood control. He also believed that the federal government should assist the farmer by improving waterways, sponsoring and disseminating scientific research, and coordinating the work of agricultural marketing cooperatives. Initially, most of the New Conservation advocates approved of Hoover's activities. These men moved in similar professional and social circles, they voted Republican, and they shared Hoover's faith in enlightened management and associational methods.[4] But they gradually grew disenchanted with the president's rigidity on the electric power and farm issues. While he steadfastly promoted interstate utilities coordination and

---

[4] Ellis W. Hawley has presented the most influential interpretations of American associationalism. See "Herbert Hoover, the Commerce Secretariat, and the Vision of an 'Associative State,' 1921–1928," *Journal of American History* 61 (1974), *The Great War and the Search for a Modern Order: A History of the American People and Their Institutions, 1917–1933* (1979), and Hawley, ed., *Herbert Hoover as Secretary of Commerce: Studies in New Era Thought and Practice* (1981).

multipurpose river development, Hoover remained firm in his opposition to government transmission of power or regulation of utilities to achieve areawide coverage. This put the president on a collision course with those who desired more active government involvement in securing the fair distribution of electric current. Hoover also appeared insensitive to the rural distress of the early Depression. He supported continued farm research and marketing assistance but held the line against interest-group solutions (raising prices directly) or rural rehabilitation schemes. He did know of marginal and exhausted lands, and even believed that the federal government should begin to take them out of production, but he did not believe the state had the authority or the funds to sponsor comprehensive adjustments in environmental and economic relations.

By insisting that the government never provide electrical service to the end consumer, and by asserting that farmer self-organization alone would correct economic disparities, Hoover underestimated the strength of the New Conservation. The president's failure to adopt its tenets, particularly in the face of economic collapse, provided a political opportunity for any rival willing to promise immediate assistance for rural Americans. Into this opening marched Franklin Roosevelt, who believed that restoring the viability of rural living meant directly addressing the relationship between rural resources and social conditions. This strategy was honed during his years as governor of New York, when he sponsored a series of initiatives to classify soils, to purchase and reforest marginal lands, and to bring hydroelectric power to the state's agricultural areas. Dismayed by high levels of farm desertion and by overgrown metropolitan centers, Roosevelt hoped that improved agricultural practices and urban amenities would extend the American standard of living to rural areas. "The ultimate goal," he explained, "is that the farmer and his family shall be put on the same level of earning capacity as his fellow American who lives in the city."[5]

These ideas shaped Roosevelt's presidential campaign strategy, in which he appealed to America's "forgotten man" and promised direct assistance to those at the very bottom of the economic ladder. Most remembered for his efforts as governor to provide relief for unemployed industrial workers and the urban poor, Roosevelt nonetheless adopted an analysis of the Depression that traced it to the absence of farm purchasing power. For the 1932 campaign, Roosevelt hitched his wagon to the domestic allotment plan, to government generation and distribution

[5] "Annual Message to the Legislature," 1929, *PPA*, 82.

of electric power, and to a new philosophy of government-assisted rural development. Conservationists, farm advocates, and land use planners now put their efforts behind a new presidential candidate and a new political party.

GIANT POWER, RURAL ELECTRIFICATION, AND REGIONAL THOUGHT

Gifford Pinchot, former chief forester and principal spokesman for the "old" conservation, fired one of the first shots of the New Conservation. After he assumed the governorship of Pennsylvania in 1923, Pinchot convinced the legislature to approve a "Giant Power Survey" of the state's water and fuel resources. The national demand for electricity in homes, businesses, and factories had risen dramatically during the first two decades of the century. The governor saw tremendous potential in the introduction of powerful production systems and long-distance transmission lines. In addition to delivering abundant supplies of electricity, such technologies could ease load difficulties by enabling the "interconnection" of local, regional, and interstate power resources. "We have been slow to recognize that distance is a rapidly disappearing factor in public utility development," Pinchot declared. But these technological improvements also facilitated vast business combinations. In 1924, the seven largest holding companies controlled almost half of all the generating capacity in the country; by 1929, just three accounted for the same proportion. Pinchot fretted over the increasing concentration in the power industry, yet wanted Pennsylvania's consumers to reap the rewards of large generating plants and electrical interconnection. "From the power field," the governor predicted, "we can expect the most substantial aid in raising the standard of living, in eliminating the physical drudgery of life, and in winning the age-long struggle against poverty." He conceived the Giant Power Survey as part of a larger attempt to strengthen state supervision over the power industry and to provide the nation (and the federal government) with an innovative regulatory model.[6]

---

[6] Pinchot, "Giant Power," *SG* (March 1924), 561. Holding-company statistics are included in the Federal Power Commission's National Power Survey of 1935, *Principal Electrical Utility Systems in the United States* (Power Series No. 2), 10. Treatments of Giant Power include Jean Christie, "Giant Power: A Progressive Proposal of the Nineteen-Twenties," *Pennsylvania Magazine of History and Biography* 96 (1972); and Leonard DeGraaf, "Corporate Liberalism and Electric Power System Planning in the 1920s," *Business History Review* 64 (1990). Also see Philip J. Funigiello, *Toward a National Power Policy: The*

To direct the Giant Power Board Pinchot appointed Morris Cooke, an engineer who had led an effort to reduce electric rates in Philadelphia. Cooke believed that the utilities discriminated against small and domestic users and that they failed to extend electric service to areas where demand existed. Because Pennsylvania's bituminous coal deposits, not its streams or rivers, comprised the state's primary source of energy, Cooke and his associates developed an ambitious proposal to achieve statewide electrical coverage by locating large generating stations at the mines and by building a distribution system of high-voltage, long-distance transmission lines. The planners claimed that such an integrated system of production and distribution would eliminate waste, reduce freight costs, and lower prices. Not only would this integrated, interconnected system assure low power charges, those rates would become standardized and less discriminatory. "Already the leaders in the industry are beginning to face the fact that it will be difficult to maintain differences in rates *for similar service and use in one interconnected system,*" Cooke wrote to Pinchot. "The arguments for such differences become weaker and weaker day by day."[7]

Cooke and Pinchot soon combined this mission for reduced rates with a crusade to electrify the countryside. By the end of the 1920s, as historian David Nye has shown, American farmers faced two kinds of economic disadvantages in the power market: 90 percent could not get distribution lines strung to their homes, and the lucky 10 percent who did often paid double the urban rate. The private utilities and electric companies had decided that most farmers simply did not have the income to put them in the "customer class"; it was far more profitable to serve more densely populated areas and to increase appliance sales among urban consumers. However, a crucial ideological transition began during the 1920s that would bear fruit only in the following decade: rural electrification would become a "social program ... discussed less in terms of profit and loss than in terms of rights and minimal standards."[8] Morris Cooke, a central agent in this reformulation, castigated the industry's slow and inconsistent efforts to bring electricity to the farm, and in the mid-1920s he

---

New Deal and the Electric Utility Industry, 1933–1941 (1973); D. Clayton Brown, *Electricity for Rural America: The Fight for the REA* (1980); Jean Christie, *Morris Llewellyn Cooke, Progressive Engineer* (1983); and Thomas P. Hughes, *Networks of Power: Electrification in Western Society, 1880–1930* (1983).

[7] *Report of the Giant Power Board to the Governor of Pennsylvania* (1926); Cooke to Pinchot, 25 October 1923, 3 March 1924 (italics in original), NFRS, Box 36.

[8] David E. Nye, *Electrifying America: Social Meanings of a New Technology* (1990), 287, 297, 304.

persuaded Pinchot that the Giant Power Survey should be expanded to include investigations of rural electrification. To this end Cooke diligently gathered information on Pennsylvania's agricultural population, on rural demand, and on the potential costs of rural service.[9]

Cooke and Pinchot saw far more than satisfied farm customers; they envisioned electrification as the basis for a new rural society. Pinchot claimed that the first economic revolution, based on steam power, had bypassed the farms and concentrated factories and workers in the cities. As a result, country life declined and small communities decayed. "Neither the farmer's productive power nor his comforts and conveniences increased in proportion with those of other workers and investors," the governor declared. But electricity could be delivered many hundred miles away from where it was produced, thereby reversing the "social tendencies" of the age of steam. Pinchot and Cooke believed the government must take an active part in providing electric service to rural areas, for this revolutionary source of power would decentralize industry, restore country life, and "put the farmer on an equality with the townsman." They well understood that this vision constituted a significant extension of conservationist thought. Many farmers, Cooke remembered, supported Theodore Roosevelt's efforts to protect streams, waterfalls, and mines from corporate monopolization because they were simply "good citizens." "Now," he wrote, "the term conservation takes on an entirely new meaning, for it spells cheap power for the farm."[10]

What is more, the Giant Power designers intended these proposals to jumpstart the regulatory powers of the federal government. Neither Cooke nor Pinchot favored government ownership of the utility industry – they wanted to sidestep that question altogether – but they desired a strong federal commitment to reduce rates. While the Giant Power Board understood that Pennsylvania's electrical future hinged on coal, it forecast

---

[9] Cooke, "The Long Look Ahead," *SG* (March 1924); Cooke, "The Early Days of the Rural Electrification Idea," *American Political Science Review* 42 (1948); Cooke to Pinchot, 12 December 1923, 18 December 1923, NFRS, Box 36; Cooke to Myrick, 26 December 1923, Cooke to Willits, 17 December 1923, 11 November 1924, Willits to Cooke, 28 January 1924, GPSP, Box 191; Blasingame to Cooke, 16 September 1924, 20 November 1924, GPSP, Box 192.

[10] Pinchot, "Interconnection and Service to the Farm," 21 May 1924, address before the National Electric Light Association, GPSP, Box 200; "Electric Farm Rival of City," *North American*, 9 December 1924; Cooke, "The Farmer's Interest in Conservation," n.d. (ca. 1923–25), GPSP, Box 200. Also see Cooke to Pinchot, 12 December 1923, NFRS, Box 36; and "Pinchot Urges Electric Power as Aid to Farms," *North American*, 23 January 1924.

that the nation's electrical future would depend on hydropower. "Water power will last forever," wrote Philip Wells, Pinchot's attorney general. "Its use will greatly prolong the life of our mineral deposits... And the great bulk of it remains within Federal jurisdiction." Therefore the Pennsylvania reformers based their state program on a piece of national legislation, the Water Power Act of 1920. This act established the authority of the federal government to set the conditions of hydroelectric power development on navigable streams and for sites within the public domain. Furthermore, the legislation gave "preference" to states and municipalities with proposals to construct and operate hydroelectric projects. But the Federal Power Commission, the three-person board charged with approving power licenses, rarely met and did little but prevent the duplication of leases. Wells, Pinchot, and Cooke expected that the vigorous implementation of the Water Power Act on the state level (and applied to coal deposits) could inaugurate a new decentralized society, with particular benefits for rural people. This Pennsylvania experiment, they hoped, would inspire national action. "The Great State," Cooke affirmed, "is going to grow up out of a revivified agriculture and a re-inspiration in small town life and the utilization of these in placing the government of our individual states on a plane of effective social purpose... It is fortunately a law of growth that we don't need more than one conspicuous example in order to move the mass."[11]

Pennsylvania reformers unrelentingly emphasized their vision of low rates and rural electrification in order to contrast Giant Power with "Super Power," a competing energy plan put forward by Secretary of Commerce Herbert Hoover during the same period. Like Giant Power, Hoover's proposals aimed to meet the growing demand for reliable electric service in the Northeast and along the Mid-Atlantic seaboard. The commerce secretary envisioned a regional system of interconnected electric lines that enabled the transmission of power in the same way standardized equipment allowed the interchange of railroad cars. Interconnection, Hoover maintained, would allow isolated generating plants to abandon their individual power reserves and rely upon a central reserve. His goals – centralized production, waste reduction, and cheap power – were not unlike those of Pinchot, but the Giant Power proponents denounced Super Power as an attempt to grant the utilities all the monopolistic advantages of

---

[11] Pinchot, "Giant Power," 562; *Report of the Giant Power Board*, 6–7; Cooke, "The Farmer's Interest in Conservation"; Wells, "Our Federal Power Policy," *SG* (March 1924), 570; Pinchot to Smith, 9 March 1923, GPSP, Box 206; Cooke to Pinchot, 10 March 1924, NFRS, Box 36.

combination without requiring them to distribute those benefits to society. "Widespread interconnections do not necessarily give access to the cheapest power or spell low rates to the consumer," argued Cooke. The Pennsylvania reformers asserted that the country must follow the Giant Power example to lower rates and thwart a dangerous electric monopoly. "Giant Power," wrote Pinchot to each member of Congress, "proposes to break down and put an end to the present unfair discrimination in rates ... Giant-power means regulation by the people, Super-power means control of the people by the monopoly."[12]

Hoover vehemently denied these charges, claiming that industrial stability and interstate coordination would indeed reduce costs and consumer prices. "Interconnection," he claimed, "does not imply capital consolidation or the building up of great trusts. It implies the sale and resale of power from one utility to another." As an example of the type of interstate agreement he favored Hoover touted the Colorado Compact of 1922, which apportioned the water of the Colorado River among six western states and cleared the way for the river basin's multiple-purpose development. He hoped that the northeastern states would follow the same voluntary strategy to ensure the "fluid" transmission of electric power. Furthermore, Hoover maintained that the states possessed sufficient authority to regulate the distribution of power generated outside their borders (a claim reformers disputed). The secretary of commerce recognized the difficulties posed by rural electrification, but claimed those difficulties did not justify any new regulatory initiatives because industrial cooperation would soon correct the situation. "The agricultural problem," as he wrote to Morris Cooke, "is one of first getting our primary system onto right lines."[13]

---

[12] "A League for Superpower," *Literary Digest*, 13 November 1920; William Hard, "Giant Negotiations for Giant Power: An Interview with Herbert Hoover," *SG* (March 1924); "Summary of Statement of Secretary Hoover to the Super Power Conference," 13 October 1923, "Address by Herbert Hoover to Convention of National Electric Light Association," 21 May 1924, HPCP, Box 162; Cooke to Pinchot, 25 October 1923, NFRS, Box 36; Pinchot, "Interconnection and Service to the Farm"; "Governor Urges Right Citizenship, Warns of Electric Monopoly," *Philadelphia Inquirer*, 5 July 1925; "Pinchot Asks Help of Congressmen" *New York Times*, 20 July 1925. Also see DeGraaf, "Corporate Liberalism," for an excellent comparison of Giant Power and Super Power.

[13] Hard, "Giant Negotiations," 578; Hoover, "Interconnection Is Now Road of Electrical March," *Philadelphia Chamber of Commerce News Bulletin*, June 1925, 11; Hoover, "Why the Public Interest Requires Local Rather Than Federal Regulation of Electric Public Utilities," 14 October 1925, HPCP, Box 591; Hoover to Cooke, 2 April 1924, GPSP, Box 207. On the Colorado River Compact, see Norris Hundley, Jr., *Water and the West: The Colorado River and the Politics of Water in the American West* (1975); and Daniel Tyler, "The Silver Fox of the Rockies: Delphus Emory Carpenter and the Colorado River Compact," *New Mexico Historical Review* 73 (1998).

The advocates of Giant Power drew inspiration not from the Colorado Compact, which yielded few benefits during the 1920s, but from the Hydro-Electric Commission of Ontario, Canada. Set up by the provincial legislature in 1907, the "Hydro" distributed electrical power at cost from plants at the Niagara and St. Lawrence Rivers to communities in southern Ontario. It constructed and administered the production and transmission systems, while the municipalities retained ownership of the operation. The Hydro delivered power not only to cities and towns but also to smaller villages and farming communities. Canadian and American reformers believed Ontario's magic combination of low rates and rural electrification had inaugurated an economic revolution in the province. "One of the impressive points about the Hydro is the fact that all the small towns have access to power on relatively equal terms," Pinchot wrote in a special Giant Power issue of *Survey Graphic* in 1924. "Here industrial development is widely diffused and even small towns are on the same footing as larger centers." Journalist Martha Bensley Bruère agreed. She asserted that cheap electricity had diversified the economies of Ontario towns, raised incomes, and relieved farm women from drudgery. The Canadian experiment, she wrote, had "checked the human tide toward the great cities, and created a land with no visible signs of poverty."[14]

This heightened emphasis on rural living standards defined the New Conservation. To be sure, these reformers still sought in good Progressive fashion to eliminate waste by designing more efficient production and transmission methods. But this goal served a larger purpose. Equity, they insisted, should be the outcome of the streamlined system; benefits should be distributed in accordance with social needs. Power – electric power, manufacturing power, economic power – need no longer be confined to the city center.

A group of community designers, architects, and social scientists embraced and expanded the Giant Power idea, placing it within a "regionalist" framework of metropolitan and rural planning. Bound by a shared distaste for large cities (and for urban planning that only increased congestion), reformist thinkers such as Lewis Mumford, Benton MacKaye, Stuart Chase, and Clarence Stein formed the Regional Planning Association

---

[14] Cooke, "Ontario Hydro-Electric," *New Republic*, 21 June 1922; Adam Beck, "Ontario's Experience," *SG* (March 1924); Pinchot, "Giant Power," 562; Martha B. Bruère, "Following the Hydro," *SG* (March 1924), 594. Also see Robert W. Bruère, "Pandora's Box," in the same issue of *SG*. Cooke corresponded throughout the 1920s with Adam Beck, chairman of Ontario Hydro, and F. A. Gaby, its chief engineer – see NFRS, Box 35.

of America (RPAA) in 1923. Along with Gifford Pinchot and Morris Cooke, the regionalists deplored the social and cultural effects of industrial centralization and hoped that a new generation of "human engineers" might harness the power of modern technology, especially hydropower, to check the growth of large cities and to bring about a stable and prosperous village life. "Regional planning sees that the depopulated countryside and the congested city are intimately related," declared Mumford in 1925. "Regional planning [means] the reinvigoration and rehabilitation of whole regions so that the products of culture and civilization, instead of being confined to a prosperous minority in the congested centers, shall be available to everyone at every point in a region."[15]

The British garden city greatly influenced the early direction of the RPAA. The garden city design offered an alternative to urban slums and urban crowding by creating completely new rural-urban communities. Reformers hoped such communities would decentralize population and industry, provide inhabitants with low rents and health benefits, and impart all the virtues of a country setting – meadows, woods, fresh air, even part-time farming. These ideas drifted across the Atlantic and inspired RPAA members to launch similar, if not identical, models of garden cities in New York and New Jersey. Gradually, however, a few American regionalists distanced themselves from the garden city idea because it appeared too closely akin to the "back-to-the-land" movement, a movement they thought failed to address the problems of existing rural communities or the institutional inequality between the hinterlands and the metropole.[16]

Largely inspired by Benton MacKaye, a professional forester who proposed a rehabilitation scheme for Appalachia, the regionalists developed a more pointed environmental and social critique of urban concentration. The depletion and exploitation of soils, forests, and rivers, they argued, resulted from a parasitic relationship between rural regions and the metropolis. "To see the interdependence of the city and the country,"

---

[15] Mumford, "Regions – To Live In," 152. Mumford published this article in a special regional planning issue of the *Survey Graphic* (May 1925), which also contained articles by MacKaye, Stein, Chase, and others. On the RPAA see Roy Lubove, *Community Planning in the 1920s: The Contribution of the Regional Planning Association of America* (1963); Carl Sussman, ed., *Planning the Fourth Migration: The Neglected Vision of the Regional Planning Association of America* (1976); and Edward K. Spann, *Designing Modern America: The Regional Planning Association of America* (1996).

[16] Paul K. Conkin, *Tomorrow a New World: The New Deal Community Program* (1959), 61–70; Lubove, *Community Planning*, 1–2, 86–7; Mumford, "The Regional Community," *SG* (May 1925), 129.

wrote Mumford in 1924, "[is to see] that the growth and concentration of one is associated with the depletion and impoverishment of the
other...Instead of regarding the countryside as so much grist [for] the
metropolitan mill, we must plan to preserve and develop all our natural resources." Choice waterpower sites, for example, should be retained
for the benefit of the people living closest to them, rather than leased to
remote firms committed only to serving distant city dwellers. Farmland
should be occupied, cared for, replenished rather than abandoned. The
local stewardship of water, woods, and land would correct the imbalance
between man and nature; community-controlled resources would correct
the imbalance between city and country.[17]

Mumford's analysis of recent history provided the foundation for this
conservationist critique of the urban-industrial landscape. He believed the
first conservation movement was a necessary response to the pioneering
mindset, but it was largely a "negative" one, developing programs to halt
the most heinous examples of resource exploitation but doing little to set
out programs for social and regional development. The task ahead for
a new conservation movement was to give the whole continent a stable,
balanced, settled, cultivated life. "Regional planning is the New Conservation – the conservation of human values hand in hand with natural
resources...permanent agriculture instead of land-skinning, permanent
forestry instead of timber mining, permanent human communities." With
these words the RPAA positioned itself at the vanguard of conservationist thought. Regional planning, Mumford made clear, entailed neither the
impractical promotion of rural self-sufficiency nor an exodus of urbanites
in search of Arcadia. Rather, it looked to the creation of economic and
environmental balance.[18]

[17] Mumford, *Sticks and Stones: A Study of American Architecture and Civilization* (1924; reprint, 1955), 96–9; Stuart Chase, *The Tragedy of Waste* (1925), 257; Mumford, "The Fourth Migration," *SG* (May 1925): 130–3. For MacKaye's proposals see "An Appalachian Trail: A Project in Regional Planning," *Journal of the American Institute of Architects* (October 1921), and "The New Exploration: Charting the Industrial Wilderness," *SG* (May 1925). For analyses of MacKaye's influence see Mumford, introduction to *The New Exploration: A Philosophy of Regional Planning* (1962); John L. Thomas, "Lewis Mumford, Benton MacKaye, and the Regional Vision," in Thomas P. Hughes and Agatha C. Hughes, eds., *Lewis Mumford, Public Intellectual* (1990); Spann, *Designing Modern America*; and Paul Sutter, "'A Retreat from Profit': Colonization, the Appalachian Trail, and the Social Roots of Benton MacKaye's Wilderness Advocacy," *Environmental History* 4 (1999).
[18] Mumford, "The Fourth Migration," 130, 131; Mumford, "Regions – To Live In," 152; Mumford, "The Theory and Practice of Regionalism," *Sociological Review* 20 (1928), 25.

The regionalists looked approvingly upon state-level initiatives to integrate natural resource development with rural uplift. They admired Pinchot's efforts in Pennsylvania and helped Governor Alfred Smith of New York formulate a set of similar proposals, ones that would influence his successor, Franklin Roosevelt. The regionalists also lauded Senator George Norris of Nebraska. An ardent conservationist who had sided with Pinchot during the battles of the Progressive era, Norris believed in the multiple-purpose development of the nation's natural resources for the benefit of ordinary people, not for the profits of private firms or monopolistic trusts. He saw great promise in a Giant Power network of long-distance electric transmission lines. This vast system, Norris envisioned, would halt the growth of large cities and distribute electricity to small towns and rural areas. Though he did not share Pinchot and Cooke's optimism about the possibilities of regulation (Norris supported the government ownership of all resource development projects), he agreed that cheap power would strengthen farm communities and bring manufacturing to the country. No longer, he claimed, would the nation's farmers be forced to take jobs in urban centers, thereby inflicting permanent damage on the country by weakening its agrarian base.[19]

Norris also drew inspiration from Ontario Hydro and publicized Canada's experiment as part of his strategy to defeat a series of Republican-led efforts to dispose of the Muscle Shoals properties in northern Alabama. During World War I, the federal government had constructed two nitrate plants and a hydroelectric dam along the Tennessee River to manufacture explosives during the conflict and fertilizer afterward. In the early 1920s, the Harding and Coolidge administrations favored measures to sell or to lease these properties to private interests such as Henry Ford or the American Cyanamid Company. The bills fell into the hands of Norris, who chaired the Senate Committee on Agriculture and Forestry. Norris claimed that these businesses coveted the completed hydroelectric facilities, and that they deviously disguised their primary interest in power by promising to deliver cheap fertilizer to southern farmers. He also believed that the federal government should retain Muscle Shoals as the starting point in a more ambitious scheme to develop the entire Tennessee River basin. A trip to Ontario in 1925 confirmed

[19] *Congressional Record*, 68th Cong., 2nd sess., 8 December 1924, 122; "Senator Norris' Reference to Super Power, 23 September 1924," HPCP, Box 590; George W. Norris, *Fighting Liberal* (1945); Richard Lowitt, *George W. Norris: The Persistence of a Progressive, 1913–1933* (1971).

Norris's view that a large public power system could be operated effectively and efficiently: in Canada, the consumption of electricity increased as power prices decreased. So Norris fought a two-front war; on one side he battled legislation that would have placed Muscle Shoals in private hands, while on the other side he fought to establish a large public power project, to be realized eventually in the creation of the Tennessee Valley Authority. In the latter crusade Norris won support from the Giant Power reformers, who certainly believed that any measures to lease hydroelectric sites such as Muscle Shoals must require guarantees of low rates and rural electrification.[20]

On both fronts Norris frequently sparred with the secretary of commerce. While Hoover remained on friendly terms with Pinchot and Cooke, he had no patience for Norris and his philosophy of government ownership. Yet Hoover was no proponent of laissez-faire. He wanted to see Muscle Shoals put to work for southern agriculture, southern manufacturing, and national defense. And in general he favored the public development of rivers and waterways, arguing that lower shipping costs would help farmers and that the federal government could save millions of dollars in interest charges by financing large works such as hydroelectric dams. But Hoover's commitment ended there. He insisted that the government could never go into the power business; it could not compete with its citizens by distributing and marketing electricity to the end consumer. Essentially, Hoover concluded, a government that competed with its citizens by going into the power business violated the American commitment to economic freedom.[21]

Little came of Norris's Muscle Shoals proposal, or Pinchot's Giant Power scheme, or even Hoover's Super Power initiative during the 1920s. Coolidge, followed by Hoover, vetoed each public ownership bill that

[20] Richard Lowitt, "Ontario Hydro: A 1925 Tempest in an American Teapot," *Canadian Historical Review* 44 (1968); Lowitt, *George W. Norris*, 197–216, 244–71; Wells to Cooke, 28 February 1923, GPSP, Box 207; Pinchot to Cooke, 10 April 1924, NFRS, Box 36; Cooke, "In Re Muscle Shoals, Before the Senate Committee on Agriculture," 28 April 1924, NFRS, Box 36. On Muscle Shoals see Norman Wengert, "Antecedents of TVA: The Legislative History of Muscle Shoals," *Agricultural History* 26 (1952); Judson King, *The Conservation Fight: From Theodore Roosevelt to the Tennessee Valley Authority* (1959); and Preston J. Hubbard, *Origins of the TVA: The Muscle Shoals Controversy, 1920–1932* (1961).

[21] Hoover, "Muscle Shoals," 6 November 1925, Hoover to McGugin, 18 November 1925, HPCP, Box 422; Hoover, "A National Policy in Development of Water Resources," 21 August 1926, HPCP, Box 688; Hard, "Giant Negotiations," 579; Hoover, *American Individualism* (1922), 4, 60.

Norris wrote and the Congress passed; the Pennsylvania legislature rejected the Giant Power program not once but twice; and utilities executives persistently disappointed Hoover by their reluctance to cooperate in securing electrical interconnection for the Northeast. Of course the lack of immediate political success disappointed many Giant Power advocates. "Where are the engineers and statesmen," pleaded economist Stuart Chase, "to [bring about] ordered cities, impounded waters, tended forests, the sweep of great transmission lines, clean rivers, workshops planned with the dignity of cathedrals, and the end of grime and despair?"[22]

Despite the appearance of initial failure, these reformers had crafted an influential new agenda. By claiming that the country's natural resources should be protected and developed for farms and farm areas, they persuasively put forward an innovative set of social and environmental considerations. It is difficult for modern Americans, who now live in a time when electric service is deemed a right and an entitlement, to appreciate how the power issue could have inspired such passions. These conservationists understood the promise of this new technology, but also witnessed its uneven distribution and its unnecessarily high cost. Of course, the new rural conservation represented only a limited ecological advance: instead of working to reduce resource use, it clearly contained the potential to encourage an intensification of that use, however sustainable or permanent its spokesmen hoped that intensification could become. "Balance" was imagined primarily as economic balance, as the equitable distribution of goods between urban and rural areas; ecological balance was a secondary consideration. One cannot promise ever-higher living standards without making environmental compromises.

Still, to highlight the New Conservation's environmental shortcomings is to miss its political significance as a defining moment in the ongoing debate over the role of the federal government in managing a modern industrial economy. Industrialism and modernity were taken as givens; how best, then, to distribute the fruits? Here was the argument that inexpensive electric power and industrial decentralization – developments requiring state intervention – would alleviate rural poverty and raise rural living standards. Furthermore, this argument was certainly not confined to reformers from urban backgrounds, as the discussion of rural electrification has so far implied. During the same period a group of country-born farm advocates and agricultural economists reached similar conclusions,

---

[22] Stuart Chase, "The Tragedy of Waste," *New Republic* 44 (September 1925), 40.

though they approached the problem from a different perspective: the agricultural market.

THE FARM CRISIS AND THE LAND UTILIZATION MOVEMENT

Bitter complaints from rural citizens and their political advocates punctured the celebrated prosperity of the 1920s. While more and more industrial workers and city dwellers experienced rising wages and a dazzling array of consumer choices, most farmers received an unwelcome taste of the Depression to come. Emboldened by high prices and government encouragement, they had expanded agricultural production during World War I, often pushing into marginal or arid lands where success was far from certain. Insurance companies and rural banks fueled this expansion, providing loans on dubious real estate and boosting land values in a speculative frenzy. In just three years, from 1916 to 1919, the nation's farm income almost doubled. But it dropped just as precipitously after 1920, when overseas demand for American agricultural products plummeted. Besieged by this postwar contraction, farmers found themselves caught between the low prices they received for farm products and the high prices they paid for nonfarm items. Though most commodity prices gradually rose again after 1923, the farm situation did not improve. Wheat and other commodity markets suffered from overproduction throughout the decade. Commercial farmers increased their vulnerability to economic shocks by borrowing heavily to purchase land and machinery. In addition, tenants and sharecroppers remained stranded on exhausted, marginal lands.[23]

In response to the farm crisis of the 1920s some farmers' groups attempted to organize agricultural producers into marketing cooperatives. Many farm supporters saw private action as the way that the highly individualistic farm sector could secure the advantages of efficient business organization and assert its collective interests alongside industry and labor. Most cooperative marketing initiatives proved unsuccessful; such voluntary schemes had difficulty controlling the farmers who failed to reduce acreage or store their products. In 1921, George Peek of the Moline Plow Company proposed that the federal government could resolve this "outsider dilemma" by raising farm prices directly. National legislation,

[23] Theodore Saloutos and John Hicks, *Agricultural Discontent in the Middle West, 1900–1939* (1951); James Shideler, *Farm Crisis* (1957); Donald Worster, *Dust Bowl: The Southern Plains in the 1930s* (1979); David E. Hamilton, *From New Day to New Deal: American Farm Policy from Hoover to Roosevelt, 1928–1933* (1991); Deborah Fitzgerald, *Every Farm a Factory: The Industrial Ideal in American Agriculture* (2003).

he and his supporters argued, could restore the terms of trade to those of 1909 to 1914, a period when farmers felt satisfied with the exchange value between the prices of farm commodities and industrial goods.

The plan found concrete expression in the McNary-Haugen bills, which emerged as the focal point of congressional farm relief legislation during the 1920s. The McNary-Haugen legislation proposed to raise domestic prices by selling surplus stocks abroad. This two-price system, its proponents believed, did not entail special protection for agriculture; it would simply extend the benefits of the tariff (already enjoyed by American businesses) to farmers. A newly formed agricultural lobby in Washington composed of the American Farm Bureau Federation (AFBF), other farm organizations, and several key members of Congress strongly favored the McNary-Haugen bills, but the legislation faced decisive opposition from the Coolidge and Hoover administrations.[24]

Other reformers criticized this government-sponsored export dumping. From a new institutional base within the Bureau of Agricultural Economics (BAE), an influential group of farm experts crafted a radically different set of solutions to the farm crisis. These analysts insisted that any effort to reorganize American agriculture should begin with internal adjustments on individual farms and within the agricultural economy. Building upon the example of the USDA's Extension Service, the BAE economists believed that concerted research and education efforts could help farmers maximize income, conserve natural resources, and plan cooperatively. To this end the BAE published farm statistics, developed price-forecasting models, and sponsored research in farm management, land tenure, and land use. The BAE supported the McNary-Haugen bills, but only as an emergency measure, not as a substitute for agricultural planning. And more than most McNary-Haugenites or the AFBF, which represented commercial farmers, the farm economists worried about inequalities within agriculture, and claimed that the application of social-science expertise could alleviate chronic rural poverty.[25]

Research and recommendations on natural resources constituted an essential part of this alternative approach to the farm crisis. Land

---

[24] Hamilton, *New Day to New Deal*, 13–21; Gilbert Fite, *American Farmers: The New Minority* (1981), 38–48.

[25] Hamilton, *New Day to New Deal*; Jess Gilbert and Ellen Baker, "Wisconsin Economists and New Deal Agricultural Policy: The Legacy of Progressive Professors," *Wisconsin Magazine of History* 80 (1997). Also see Richard Lowitt, ed., *Journal of a Tamed Bureaucrat: Nils A. Olsen and the BAE, 1922–1935* (1980); and Henry C. Taylor and Anne D. Taylor, *The Story of Agricultural Economics in the United States, 1840–1932* (1952).

economists in particular argued that improper land use created instability in the agricultural economy and that comprehensive land use adjustments would bring stability to rural areas. The field of land economics, along with agricultural economics in general, had emerged from the institutionalist school of political economy at the University of Wisconsin. Richard Ely, who first formulated the field's goals and research methods, had joined with a handful of other economists in the late nineteenth century in rejecting individualistic, neoclassical principles. Institutionalists such as Ely and his colleague John R. Commons asserted that economic outcomes sprang from a complex matrix of social conditions and organizational constraints, and they sought a "middle way" between classic liberalism and radical socialism. The institutionalists endorsed the first conservation movement as a positive example of this middle way. In 1922, the field of land economics found an institutional base in Washington within the BAE's Division of Land Economics. Under the direction of Ely's student Lewis C. Gray, this division sponsored research and provided the leadership for the emerging land utilization movement, a movement that soon became an influential component of the new rural conservation.[26]

Perhaps influenced by his history teacher Frederick Jackson Turner, L. C. Gray interpreted World War I as the final closing of the frontier. Imprudent agricultural expansion onto poorer and drier lands had created a postwar legacy of abused resources and a marked rise in farm tenancy. "It seemed clear," Gray remembered, "that the continued increase of population would necessitate the occupancy of poorer and poorer lands and the operation of diminishing returns." Such an unfortunate scenario led Gray and his BAE colleagues to conclude that the era of unrestricted land settlement should be brought to a swift close. Land scarcity combined with population pressure required a cautious new approach to natural resources and agricultural development. The country could no longer trust individual initiative or private enterprise to provide for future needs. Careful consideration of whether land ought to be used for crops, pastures, or forests – even towns, roads, or utilities – must therefore precede any new settlement and guide farm management decisions. This approach,

---

[26] L. C. Gray, "The Evolution of the Land Program," 22 March 1939, LVF; Gray, "The Field of Land Utilization," *Journal of Land and Public Utility Economics* 1 (1925); Gilbert and Baker, "Wisconsin Economists"; Richard T. Ely, *The Foundations of National Prosperity: Studies in the Conservation of Permanent Natural Resources* (1918), 16; Leonard A. Salter, Jr., *A Critical Review of Research in Land Economics* (1948); Margaret R. Purcell, "A Quarter Century of Land Economics in the Department of Agriculture, 1919–44," October 1945, manuscript in possession of author.

Gray maintained, had the potential to stabilize agricultural prices, preserve natural resources, and repair the fabric of rural society.[27]

The cutover timberland of the Lakes states provided the land economists with an initial focus. During the final decades of the nineteenth century, lumber companies had removed the white pines and hardwoods from northern Wisconsin and Michigan. State governments, land colonization companies, and other boosters expected that the cutover counties could become profitable farms, and between 1900 and 1920 settlers flooded into the region. However, the new farmers did not produce very much for the market – their farms were small, they improved few acres, and they owned comparatively little livestock. The farm experts sharply criticized the process by which poor lands had been sold to hopeful farmers without any accompanying guidance and institutional support. State governments, they concluded, should restrict settlement to lands best suited for agriculture and should purchase the remaining portions of the cutover for reforestation and recreational use.[28]

The process of land classification in the Lakes states began in Michigan with the 1922 Land Economic Survey, sponsored by Michigan State University and the state departments of agriculture and conservation. The survey assembled a statewide inventory of data on soils, vegetative cover, tenure conditions, tax burdens, and trade areas, and it operated under the assumption that cutover lands would eventually be earmarked for one of three uses: farming (cropping or pastures), forests, or recreation. Wisconsin emulated Michigan's example but proceeded past the inventory stage with legislation aimed at actual land adjustments. In 1927, a Forest Crop Law granted subsidies to individuals and counties for reforestation, and two years later the legislature passed a zoning law authorizing county boards to determine the areas to be used for farming, forestry, and

---

[27] Gray, "Evolution of the Land Program," 5; Gray, "Field of Land Utilization"; Gray, "The Utilization of Our Lands for Crops, Pasture and Forests," *Agricultural Yearbook 1923* (GPO, 1924); Purcell, "Quarter Century of Land Economics"; Richard S. Kirkendall, "L. C. Gray and the Supply of Agricultural Land," *Agricultural History* 37 (1963); Albert Z. Guttenberg, "The Land Utilization Movement of the 1920s," *Agricultural History* 50 (1976); Tim Lehman, *Public Values, Private Lands: Farmland Preservation Policy, 1933–1985* (1995), 9–17; Melissa G. Wiedenfeld, "The Development of a New Deal Land Policy: Fergus County, Montana, 1900–1945" (Ph.D. diss., Louisiana State University, 1997), 138–67.

[28] Gray, "Field of Land Utilization"; P. S. Lovejoy, "Theory and Practice in Land Classification," *Journal of Land and Public Utility Economics* 1 (1925); Salter, *A Critical Review*, 20–2, 83–129; Robert J. Gough, "Richard T. Ely and the Development of the Wisconsin Cutover," *Wisconsin Magazine of History* 75 (1991); J. D. Black and L. C. Gray, *Land Settlement and Colonization in the Great Lakes States* (GPO, 1925).

recreation. Several planners touted the legislation – the first of its kind in any state – as a model for a national land program.[29]

The concept of economic marginality guided both the Michigan and the Wisconsin surveys. Land economists believed that there existed certain classes of land upon which no farmer, however bright or hardworking, could achieve a decent standard of living. "Marginal" and "submarginal" farms simply did not yield returns commensurate with the amount of labor and capital invested. The land might be too rocky, for example, or the soil too thin or unsuitable in some other way. Of course, this economic definition often blended with a sociocultural construction of marginality that justified critical judgments of character. Perhaps "marginal" farmers had no one but themselves to blame if they lacked the intelligence to avoid or to vacate unprofitable areas. "For the most part, there is little that can be done for these men," admitted Richard Ely. "Like other business men, farmers who have accepted the risk of operating the submarginal land must take their losses."[30] Such constructions of marginality left little room in the moral imagination for farmers who might have willingly chosen a lifestyle apart from profit maximization.

This question whether marginality arose from poor land, from ignorant farmers, or from an inflated definition of the "American standard of living" points to critical and unresolved tensions within the new rural conservation. As Deborah Fitzgerald has shown, a newly professionalized class of farm engineers and farm economists (many trained alongside the personnel of the land utilization movement) analyzed the farm crisis of the 1920s as the result of backward and preindustrial modes of farming. Viewing the agricultural depression as an opportunity to spread the "industrial ideal," they worked with banks and insurance companies to introduce more businesslike methods of accounting and more factory-like systems of production. These professionals sincerely wanted to help farmers; indeed, many had come from farm backgrounds themselves. Nonetheless, they denigrated traditional rural rhythms – rhythms that we now understand as having kept the exploitation of the soil in check – and harbored deep doubts about the capacity of rural people to become mechanized and efficient producers. Ultimately, Fitzgerald writes, "they

[29] Lovejoy, "Theory and Practice"; Vernon Carstensen, *Farms or Forests: Evolution of a State Land Policy for Northern Wisconsin, 1850–1932* (1958), 90–116; George S. Wehrwein, "A Social and Economic Program for Submarginal Agricultural Areas," *Journal of Farm Economics* 13 (1931).

[30] Richard Ely, "Worthless Land: What Can We Do for the Men on It," *Country Gentleman*, 25 October 1924, quoted in Gough, "Richard T. Ely," 28.

had as their goal, whether tacitly or explicitly, to bring agriculture kicking and screaming into the modern world."[31]

Modernity and efficiency: these goals are perhaps compatible with rural-urban equity, but not always with *intra*rural equity, nor, for that matter, with environmental permanence. Was the intent to help each and every farmer achieve a tolerable, though bounded, standard of living, or to assist and sustain those farmers who embraced industrial practices and deployed the latest labor-saving and profit-maximizing technology? In the end, the industrial ideal would triumph, but not inevitably. During the 1920s and the 1930s the new rural conservation attempted to reconcile efficiency, equity, and sustainability. Though many agricultural analysts believed that eventually the least intelligent and the least adaptable farmers would have to find new employment, they could be just as optimistic about possibilities for widespread rural rehabilitation. The planners and policymakers examined in this study jumped to the understandable conclusion that poverty was not voluntary, and they were not yet ready to surrender the agrarian ideal to the industrial ideal. In fact, they fused efficiency, equity, and sustainability in a manner that only in retrospect proved paradoxical: they hoped to preserve the family farm by modernizing it. To jump ahead of the story, the prospects for equitable rural modernization appeared even more propitious during the Depression decade, when no one predicted the quick return of prosperity or a revived, let alone expanded, industrial sector.

During the 1920s, many reformers hoped something could be done for those farmers who found themselves located on poor land or in environmentally risky areas without guidance, information, or assistance. One such risky region was the northern plains, where aridity – not tree stumps or stony soil – determined whether land was suitable for farming. Along with the northern Lakes states, Montana experienced a wave of new agricultural settlement in the first decades of the twentieth century. Enticed by larger homesteads, boosters, and high levels of rainfall, migrants streamed onto the short-grass frontier and plowed up the virgin sod to plant acres and acres of wheat. Fortunes fell rapidly after World War I, when prices dropped and drought set in. An epidemic of tax delinquency, foreclosures, bankruptcy, and farm abandonment swept the state. Many farmers lost their land to banks and insurance companies only to become tenants on property they had once owned; wags replaced the slogan "Montana or Bust" with "Montana *and* Bust." As John Wesley Powell had predicted,

---

[31] Fitzgerald, *Every Farm a Factory*, 77.

small parcels of 320 acres might work well in the humid East but did not provide a secure foothold in the arid West. "We had to design a new pattern of occupation for Montana," remembered M. L. Wilson, a Wisconsin-trained land economist and the state's director of agricultural extension. "We had to find out how we could work out an adjustment here, and farm so as to stay."[32]

Wilson – a perfect example of how the goals of efficiency, equity, and sustainability could coexist in unresolved tension – had moved to Montana in 1908, hoping to strike it rich himself. He and his business partner used crop data from the USDA's Bureau of Statistics to calculate that a single cash crop, flax, would yield the highest profits. They invested heavily in land and machinery, and borrowed money to cover the first year's operating costs. The venture failed; dry weather and hot winds crippled the crop, and the bank repossessed their new tractor. From this experience Wilson concluded that even educated farmers and highly capitalized operations might fail in the region's volatile environment. To succeed, farmers must have guidance and information based on thorough research. In 1911, Wilson went to work for the state's land-grant college, where he supervised its dry-land demonstration farms and experimental plots and soon accepted a job as Montana's first county agricultural agent. From his research and extension experience, Wilson concluded that cash cropping alone was likely to fail and that farmers should shift large portions of their operations to raising livestock. More pastures and less plowing, he believed, would sustain Montana's rural communities.[33]

The widespread distress of the 1920s only strengthened Wilson's resolve to spread the word. He worked with the BAE, the experiment stations, and the Extension Service on studies of plains farming and rural poverty. Researchers and county agents toured existing farms and operated others for demonstration. They convinced many banks, which owned most of the foreclosed or abandoned land, to sell only to those farmers who agreed to follow the directions of the area's supervisors. The experts encouraged the consolidation of small tracts of land, arguing that

---

[32] Mary W. M. Hargreaves, *Dry Farming in the Northern Great Plains, 1900–1925* (1957); Fitzgerald, *Every Farm a Factory*; Wiedenfeld, "Development of a New Deal Land Policy," 107–37; Milburn L. Wilson oral history, CUOH; Russell Lord, *The Wallaces of Iowa* (1947).

[33] "M. L. Wilson: Thirty Years of Social Engineering," USDA Division of Extension Information, 16 February 1944, WP 00003, 10:36; Harry C. McDean, "M. L. Wilson and the Origins of Federal Farm Policy in the Great Plains, 1909–1914," *Montana: The Magazine of Western History* 34 (1984).

only large, mechanized farms would guarantee sufficient incomes. The researchers also introduced techniques to reduce soil loss and encouraged farmers to diversify by raising stock and growing forage crops on small, irrigated sections.

The focal point of Wilson's efforts was the Fairway Farms project, a corporation of seven farms that Wilson established with his former economics instructor and BAE boss. Wilson and his partner wanted to demonstrate that tenants could become farm owners when provided with sufficient credit and expert guidance. Only by "adjusting the relations of farmers to the land," Wilson explained, could Montana's agricultural economy be rescued and its farms operated by the people who owned them. The Fairway experiment suffered large financial losses, but it demonstrated that enormous farms, with maximum machine power and very little human labor, could compete in the depressed world market. Wilson remained ambivalent about Fairway's implications, however, and continued to hope that the "old-time family farm" might not be swept away.[34]

The poor social, economic, and environmental conditions of the cutover regions and the northern plains during the 1920s appeared to confirm L. C. Gray's contention that the best lands in the country had already been taken and that settlements in marginal areas faced serious obstacles. This cautious approach to farm development also underlay Gray's opposition to the western reclamation program. In this effort to restrict agricultural expansion he ran headlong into the ambitions of Elwood Mead, the Bureau of Reclamation's new director, who planned to enlarge its program. Deeply influenced by his experience in Australia, where he helped design a state-sponsored irrigation and land settlement program, Mead returned to the United States convinced that the federal government could relieve poverty and enhance economic opportunity by coordinating the nation's industrial, commercial, and agricultural life. Mead did not view every vocation equally; he clung to the Jeffersonian belief that even a modern, industrial nation like the United States depended on the well-being of its farmers. Mead argued that ill-conceived land policy (including the practices of the Reclamation Bureau itself) threatened this agricultural foundation. Rural communities suffered from speculation,

---

[34] M. L. Wilson, "The Fairway Farms Project," *Journal of Land and Public Utility Economics* 2 (1926), 156; Harry C. McDean, "Social Scientists and Farm Poverty on the North American Plains, 1933–1940," *Great Plains Quarterly* 3 (1983); McDean, "Federal Farm Policy and the Dust Bowl: The Half-Right Solution," *North Dakota History* 47 (1980); Fitzgerald, *Every Farm a Factory*; Wilson oral history, CUOH; Lord, *Wallaces of Iowa*, 300.

tenancy, wasted soils, and the departure of farm youth in search of better opportunities. The reclamation program, Mead maintained, could create entirely new communities based on the most up-to-date scientific, social, and economic research.[35]

Throughout the 1920s the BAE waged an unsuccessful war to rein in the reclamation program. Why bring more farms into production, the economists asked, if instability and competition already plagued agricultural markets? Mead, a committed agrarian, countered that rural depopulation and the ceaseless drift of farm youth to urban centers weakened the nation. The federal government, he asserted, should stem this tide with concerted efforts to revamp rural life. The reclamation program's current difficulties – settler repayment problems, poor crop yields, little community "spirit" in the projects – could be corrected by proper land classification, sufficient credit, and technical advice. In addition, Mead sought to establish new planned settlements in the South, a "backward" farming region plagued by poverty and tenancy but "favored with good soil and climate and near the great consuming centers."[36] Therefore, despite the conflicting worldviews – Mead desired to create new farms while Gray wanted to restrict that expansion – this feud actually strengthened the land utilization movement. The two men shared a similar confidence in the ability of competent planners to correct the agricultural mistakes of the past, thereby opening the door to the coexistence of and occasional cooperation between the land retirement initiatives and the expanded reclamation programs of the early New Deal.

Developments in the field of soil science also strengthened the land utilization movement. Land classification and land planning decisions ultimately depended on whether a particular soil would sustain a particular agricultural activity, and from Hugh H. Bennett, a researcher at the USDA's Bureau of Soils, the land economists began to hear terrible news about the failure of agricultural practices to adapt to soil type and soil conditions. During the first part of his career surveying and mapping the soils of the South, Bennett became increasingly alarmed by the high

---

[35] Gray, "Field of Land Utilization"; Paul K. Conkin, "The Vision of Elwood Mead," *Agricultural History* 33 (1960). The best work on the reclamation program in the early twentieth century is Donald J. Pisani, *Water and American Government: The Reclamation Bureau, National Water Policy, and the West, 1902–1935* (2002).

[36] Brian Q. Cannon, "'We Are Now Entering a New Era': Federal Reclamation and the Fact Finding Commission of 1923–1924," *Pacific Historical Review* 66 (1997); Pisani, *Water and American Government*, 136–53; Elwood Mead, Preface to *Southern Reclamation: Planned Colonies of Farm Owners* (GPO, 1929).

rates of erosion he found. While gully erosion practically announced itself to observers because the land was so scarred, sheet erosion – the washing away of thin layers of topsoil – threatened more farms by its very invisibility. Based on his observations of sheet erosion, Bennett concluded that decreased agricultural production and low incomes in some areas might be explained by this gradual, imperceptible loss.[37]

Armed with this new analysis, Bennett launched a national campaign to publicize his work. With W. R. Chapline he coauthored *Soil Erosion: A National Menace* for the USDA in 1928, and he also wrote articles for popular magazines to reach a wider audience. Central to Bennett's message was the idea that proper land use practices could halt soil erosion. He demanded that "every loyal citizen of the Nation lessen this tremendous evil" by building terraces and dams, planting grasses and trees on the unstable soils and sloping areas, and reducing the number of livestock on overgrazed regions. Bennett also believed the federal government should assist the individual farmer. He wanted to establish eighteen new research and demonstration centers in regions particularly vulnerable to soil erosion, and he convinced several experiment station directors to assist him in this endeavor. Armed with examples of land degradation and alarming figures on lost farm income, Bennett testified before a Senate subcommittee and asked the Congress for money to begin work. Representative James Buchanan of Texas responded favorably, and he introduced legislation to begin the soil program. The final appropriation, approved by Congress in 1929, authorized erosion surveys, investigations of soil and water loss, and new conservation methods for erosion control. By 1931, eight experiment stations were in operation and ten more were in the works. These would become the basis for Hugh Bennett's vastly expanded responsibilities under the New Deal.[38]

During the 1920s, land economists and soil scientists concluded that improper land use resulted in unprofitable agricultural operations, tax

[37] Gray, "Evolution of the Land Program"; David Weeks, "Scope and Methods of Research in Land Utilization," *Journal of Farm Economics* 11 (1929), 597–8; Hugh H. Bennett, *The Soils and Agriculture of the Southern States* (1921); Douglas Helms, ed., *Readings in the History of the Soil Conservation Service* (GPO, SCS Economics and Social Sciences Division, Historical Notes No. 1, 1992).

[38] Helms, *Readings in the History of the Soil Conservation Service*, 4; Hugh H. Bennett, "Soil Erosion Takes $200,000,000 Yearly from U.S. Farmers," *USDA Yearbook of Agriculture* (GPO, 1927), 593; "Soil Conservation: Report of H. H. Bennett to Chief of Bureau," HBP, NA RG 114, Entry 21, Box 2; Hugh H. Bennett, "Soil-Erosion Problem Under Investigation in National Control Program," *USDA Yearbook of Agriculture* (GPO, 1932). Also see Swain, *Federal Conservation Policy*.

delinquency, and farm abandonment. Their analysis, which linked the
"farm problem" to the availability and use of natural resources, constituted an important contribution to the new rural conservation. Like the
Giant Power advocates, these farm experts extended conservationist principles to inhabited rural areas. Land, they argued, should be protected and
used correctly not just for its own or for efficiency's sake, but to raise the
living standards of the people living on it.

Clearly, the new rural conservation bore little resemblance to modern environmentalism, which takes as its concern entire ecosystems – not
simply their income-producing components. While improved agricultural
stewardship can certainly retard environmental deterioration, the conservationists of the 1920s developed their ideas with income benefits in mind
and for those resources that promised the greatest short-term returns. It
can be argued whether or not the new rural conservation constituted any
significant advance in environmental thought, but what is certain is that it
helped force open a series of volatile political questions about the obligation of the state and the nation to its rural areas. Indeed, both the electric
power and the farm advocates found a partially receptive ear in Herbert
Hoover's White House. In the end, however, Hoover's increasingly rigid
political philosophy gradually alienated the New Conservationists from
his administration and helped set the stage for the presidential election of
1932 and the political realignment of the New Deal.

HERBERT HOOVER AND RURAL CONSERVATION POLICY, 1928–1932

Herbert Hoover entered the White House in 1929 with plans for a "new
day" in American public life. He envisioned a country in which men
and women walked in "ordered freedom in the independent conduct of
their occupations," where they enjoyed "the advantages of wealth, not
concentrated in the hands of the few but spread through the lives of
all," and where freedom from "poverty and fear" allowed opportunity
for greater service to the community, the country, and the world. The
president offered this picture as the justification for his particular associational vision. He claimed that the increasing complexity of modern
life required the federal government to gather information and assemble
informed suggestions for the nation's improvement. However, Hoover
insisted that these tools be used primarily to assist the voluntary activities
of the people and their local or state governments. Too large or too intru-
sive a national state, he feared, would threaten liberty by regimenting

and dominating the country's economic life. Therefore the federal government might relieve poverty, guide prosperity, and preserve freedom by coordinating (and occasionally financing) the organization of those interested in collective self-help. This vision of state-sponsored voluntarism, as Kendrick Clements has elegantly argued, guided the president's approach to conservation.[39] It also steered his response to hydroelectric power development and to the farm crisis.

Hoover drew from his experience with the Mississippi flood of 1927 to illustrate his political philosophy and to set forward a national program of river development. Never had the lower Mississippi experienced such a deluge: during two weeks in April the river broke through levees in Missouri and Mississippi, killed over 250 people, and covered parts of seven states. President Coolidge appointed Hoover to direct the relief and reconstruction efforts, and the commerce secretary did this to great national acclaim by coordinating the resources of the federal government with those of private agencies such as the Red Cross and the U.S. Chamber of Commerce. Hoover helped publicize the U.S. Army Corps of Engineers' plans to improve flood control measures along the Mississippi, and he endorsed congressional actions to authorize large new federal outlays for this purpose. Hoover also saw an opportunity in the Mississippi tragedy to move beyond a single river and to advance a more aggressive agenda for the nation's waterways. "I am convinced," he wrote in 1928, "that the flood serves to bring home to the American people the increasing dangers which lurk in our great streams if not adequately controlled." Hoover believed that the improvement and administration of waterways had once been simple: navigation had been the single concern and the task had fallen to one agency, the Corps of Engineers. But the modern economy and a growing population meant that flood control, irrigation, and electrical power development would become as important as navigation, and Hoover asserted that the federal government must take the lead in coordinating the work of public and private interests in those pursuits.[40]

Hoover argued for comprehensive, multiple-purpose development of the nation's water resources. Each drainage system – the Mississippi, the

---

[39] Ray L. Wilbur and Arthur M. Hyde, *The Hoover Policies* (1937), 2, 3, 42, 46–7; Clements, *Hoover, Conservation, and Consumerism*.

[40] Bruce Lohof, "Herbert Hoover, Spokesman of Humane Efficiency: The Mississippi Flood of 1927," *American Quarterly* 22 (1970); Clements, *Hoover, Conservation, and Consumerism*, 111–27; Wilbur and Hyde, *Hoover Policies*, 264–5; Hoover, "The Improvement of Our Mid-West Waterways," *Annals of the American Academy of Political and Social Science* 135 (1928), 15, 22; Hoover, "A National Policy."

St. Lawrence and Great Lakes, the Colorado, the Columbia, the Tennessee – should be studied with a view to understanding its potential for transportation, flood control, irrigation, and electric power. He also understood that the country faced "a problem of determining the limits of private and public development." He explained that the federal government had long financed navigational improvements because of its responsibility for interstate commerce, and it also contributed to flood control works on a cost-sharing basis with local and state governments. In addition, the federal government loaned capital for irrigation and reclamation projects with the understanding that the cost would be recovered. But Hoover admitted the problems became "more complex" when electric power was involved, and he stood by his opinion that the government should never go into the business of generating and distributing electricity. If a site was developed for power only, then it should be leased to a private party. When power was a "by-product" of government works constructed for navigation, flood control, or reclamation, the federal government should lease the power rights to recover the cost of the investment.[41]

This position explained Hoover's divergent approaches to the two most significant waterpower proposals of the 1920s: Boulder Dam and Muscle Shoals. The Boulder Project represented the culmination of Hoover's earlier work as chair of the Colorado River Commission, which had negotiated the interstate Colorado River Compact in 1922. Despite continued conflict over the compact's water allocation provisions, especially between California and Arizona, Congress passed the Boulder Canyon Bill in 1928. This legislation authorized the federal government to build a high dam on the lower river to protect the Imperial Valley from floods, to provide irrigation water and an "All-American canal" for the Southwest, and to furnish municipalities with hydroelectric power and a domestic water supply. Before the government could begin construction, it needed to secure contracts for the sale of power in order to pay for the project. Public power advocates wanted the federal government to operate the power facilities so as to expose the exorbitant rates of the power trust, but Hoover and his interior secretary, Ray L. Wilbur, held the line against such notions. They made it clear that the federal government would purchase the dam, tunnels, powerhouse, and penstocks, but that the cost of the generating machinery would be repaid by the lessees. In addition, the lessees would build and operate their own transmission lines. "This will

---

[41] Hoover, "A National Policy," 6, 19; Wilbur and Hyde, *Hoover Policies*, 254–86.

place the technical problems of generation and transmission of power in the hands of the purchasers," Wilbur explained. It also protected the boundaries Hoover had drawn between public investment in multipurpose water projects and private enterprise: the federal government would not enter the electric power business. In keeping with the belief that the federal government could strengthen local initiatives, Hoover and Wilbur did nothing to restrict smaller nonprofit groups from distributing current; in fact, the administration agreed to lease the lion's share of the power – over 90 percent – to public entities such as the Metropolitan Water District of Southern California, the city of Los Angeles, and other municipalities.[42]

Still, many public power advocates felt betrayed by this government "giveaway." The Boulder Dam power contracts, though they favored public entities, did not provide a way for regulators to force down private utility rates, nor did they establish any provisions to ensure that rural consumers received electricity. Power progressives such as George Norris were equally outraged that the administration agreed to lease 9 percent of the power to the Southern California Edison Company. Even this small amount of power, they felt, violated the preference clause embodied in reclamation law and the Federal Water Power Act. Norris, of course, favored the public ownership and operation of water projects, and he continued to sponsor Muscle Shoals legislation that would place the property in the hands of the national government. Coolidge pocket vetoed one such bill in 1928, but Norris hoped Hoover would approve a similar measure passed by Congress in 1930. Hoover favored development of the Tennessee River basin for flood control, navigation, power, and the production of fertilizer. But Norris's bill would have allowed the government to build transmission lines and to sell power to nonprofit public groups, especially farm organizations. Hoover believed the properties should be put into the hands of private interests, and censured Norris's bill in his veto message of 1931. "The power problem is not to be solved by the Federal Government going into the power business," the president declared.

---

[42] Slattery to Cooke, 20 October 1927, Cooke Papers, NFRS, Box 49; Norris Hundley, Jr., "The West Against Itself: The Colorado River – An Institutional History," in Gary D. Weatherford and F. Lee Brown, eds., *New Courses for the Colorado River* (1986); Linda J. Lear, "Boulder Dam: A Crossroads in Natural Resource Policy," *Journal of the West* (1985); Jay L. Brigham, "Public Power and Progressivism in the 1920s" (Ph.D. diss., University of California, Riverside, 1992), 126–8; Department of the Interior, Press Releases, 21 October 1929, 28 December 1929, and 30 December 1931, in Hoover Cabinet Papers, Interior, Reclamation, HHL.

"I hesitate to contemplate the future of our institutions, of our Government, and of our country if the preoccupation of its officials is to be no longer the promotion of justice and equal opportunity."[43]

At issue was the definition of equal opportunity. For Norris, the idea meant that each citizen should have equal access to property he owned – the nation's natural resources. For Hoover, equal opportunity meant that the government should not hinder its citizens by setting up competing businesses. Instead, the president continued to recommend that the Muscle Shoals properties be leased or sold to "competent and experienced industrialists" who would produce and distribute fertilizer and power on a "cost plus, public service" (i.e., regulated) basis. This would allow the government to recover the cost of federal investments in flood control and navigation, just as the power leases and irrigators' reclamation payments would pay for the Boulder Project. In stark contrast to the Boulder Project legislation, Norris's Muscle Shoals proposals included no provisions for repayment and committed the federal government to produce and distribute electricity without the aid of private capital. Essentially, Hoover feared that by going into the power business, the government would enfeeble the nation's economic system by eliminating the incentives for individual effort and local self-government. And he wholeheartedly disapproved any scheme that might drain the federal treasury.[44]

Hoover's most politically damaging scrap over the issue of cheap hydropower occurred with Franklin Roosevelt, the governor of New York. Throughout the 1920s Hoover had recommended the expansion of the "Great Lakes System" of inland waterways, arguing that a ship channel connecting the Lakes with the Atlantic would reduce transportation costs for midwestern farmers and manufacturers. Such plans, however, depended on successful negotiations with Canada over the joint development of the St. Lawrence River. Into this diplomatic conflict entered Roosevelt, who insisted that New York's Power Authority take part in the discussions. Continuing a policy initiated by his predecessor, Alfred Smith, Roosevelt had successfully reserved the state's waterpower

---

[43] Lowitt, *George W. Norris*, 454–67; Norris, *Fighting Liberal*; Judson King, "Power Records of Hoover and Roosevelt" (National Popular Government League, Bulletin No. 157, September 1932); veto message quoted in Thomas K. McCraw, *TVA and the Power Fight, 1933–1939* (1971), 24.

[44] "A Comparative Report on the Boulder Canyon and Muscle Shoals Projects," December 1930, "Principles Adopted by the Muscle Shoals Commission on October 29, 1931," McMullen to Newton, 20 December 1930, 16 September 1931, Hoover Papers, President's Subject File, "Muscle Shoals" HHL; King, "Power Records."

sites – including that portion of the St. Lawrence within the state's boundaries – from unregulated private development. Like Norris, Roosevelt was impressed by the low rates and service record of the Ontario Hydro-Electric Commission. In 1931, he established the New York Power Authority to conduct studies on the transmission and distribution of low-cost current on the New York side of Niagara Falls, and he persuaded Morris Cooke of Pennsylvania's Giant Power Survey to join the authority. Roosevelt staked much of his political and economic strategy on the development of New York's power sources, and called especially for rural electrification as part of a statewide plan to revivify farm areas.[45]

Roosevelt argued that New York's participation in the international negotiations was necessary to begin the project and to determine his state's share of the construction costs. "I am deeply interested in the immediate construction of the deep waterway as well as in the development of abundant and cheap power," Roosevelt wrote Hoover. "May I respectfully point out that such action would hasten greatly the initiation of . . . cheap electricity from the State-owned and controlled resource, to be developed for the primary interest of homes, farms, and industries." In sharp contrast, Hoover insisted that the domestic distribution of power – the "by-product" of navigation works – was a secondary matter, and he rebuffed New York's request to participate.[46]

What may have been the president's legally justified attempt to restrict international negotiations to the federal government appeared as a veto of cheap hydropower. By continuing to classify electric current as the "by-product" of other developments, Hoover sidestepped the question that gripped Roosevelt, Norris, Cooke, and many other rural advocates – whether any government, state or federal, had the authority to require that inexpensive electricity be distributed on an areawide basis and at equal cost to scattered farm customers. Hoover insisted that solving the rural problem did not require government production and transmission of electricity or a vastly expanded regulatory system. Cheaper electricity, he convinced himself, would materialize as a result of prudent investments in waterways infrastructure and after private interests (not upstart state

[45] Herbert Hoover, "Statement Before House Committee on Rivers and Harbors," 30 January 1926, and "The Waterways Outlet from the Middle West," 9 March 1926, HPCP, Box 687; "St Lawrence O.K., Smith Checkmate," *New York Evening Post*, 3 January 1927; Wilbur and Hyde, *Hoover Policies*, 270–5; PPA, 159–206. Also see Daniel R. Fusfeld, *The Economic Thought of Franklin D. Roosevelt and the Origins of the New Deal* (1956).

[46] Roosevelt to Hoover, 9 July 1932, Hoover to Roosevelt, 10 July 1932, PPA, 204–5.

governors) made arrangements to distribute current with the public's interest in mind.

A similar worldview guided Hoover's approach to the farm crisis. Along with the economists from the USDA's Bureau of Agricultural Economics, Hoover believed that farming suffered from internal weaknesses and that its rescue depended not on export-dumping schemes, but on a program of government-assisted self-organization. Though Hoover's solution – the 1929 Agricultural Marketing Act – drew little enthusiasm from farm organizations or farm-state congressmen, it represented the first time any administration committed itself to a comprehensive farm policy. The legislation created a Federal Farm Board, an agricultural "action" agency whose members quickly decided upon a two-part plan: to modernize the farm marketing system by sponsoring centralized commodity associations, and to develop a cooperative and voluntary system of production control. These goals reflected the president's analysis of agriculture's ills; farming, he thought, lacked the kind of managers who had successfully organized the efficient systems of production and distribution in American industry. Hoover hoped that the Farm Board's efforts to build cooperative marketing and production control systems would create opportunities to fill this managerial void.[47]

As David Hamilton has demonstrated, both the attempt to create centralized marketing structures and the attempt to institute a program of voluntary acreage reduction were unsuccessful. The board assumed that national commodity cooperatives could stabilize prices by holding products off the market, but as prices declined sharply after 1929 it became clear that the cooperatives could not remain solvent without large infusions of government credit. There was little hope that the cooperatives could become independent; it seemed that only continuous state assistance would allow them to act as market stabilizers. Additionally, the board itself began buying up certain quantities of wheat and cotton as its members increasingly framed the farm problem as one of overproduction. As a corollary to these stabilization operations, the board tried to cajole farmers into reducing their acreage, but its efforts fell flat. In the end, the board was simply unable to resolve the tension between individual and collective interests – farmers could hope to reap the advantages of higher prices without themselves joining a marketing association or reducing their output.[48]

---

[47] Hamilton, *New Day to New Deal*.
[48] Hamilton, *New Day to New Deal*. Also see Mordecai Ezekiel oral history, CUOH.

The faltering of Hoover's program and the deepening of the Depression opened the way for alternative proposals from the agricultural economists and land use specialists of the BAE. Though they shared Hoover's commitment to building a more efficient farm sector through voluntary and nonbureaucratic methods, the economists did not share his faith in cooperative marketing. Farmers, they believed, did not suffer from an organizational or managerial void; what they lacked was information and competent technical guidance. Furthermore, neither Hoover nor the McNary-Haugen types considered the likelihood that the country had overinvested in agriculture, or that national policies should address the presence of a substantial class of poor farmers.[49]

L. C. Gray and BAE bureau chief Nils Olsen seized the opportunity to advance land use planning as the proper response to the farm crisis. They linked poor land utilization to a problem that many of their colleagues, including the Farm Board and Hugh Bennett, now perceived as the primary difficulty facing U.S. agriculture: overproduction. Gray claimed that crop surpluses, low prices, and low farm incomes indicated the general maladjustment of American agriculture. Whereas in the early 1920s Gray had advised a cautious approach to farm development, by the end of the decade he urged the country to "liquidate" the results of agricultural overexpansion. National land classification efforts and a "discriminating extension policy," Gray believed, should encourage the abandonment of poor land and promote agricultural reorganization in areas fit for continued occupancy. In addition, Gray maintained that the government should launch programs to purchase submarginal land and guide displaced farmers to new agricultural or industrial employment. Gray and Olsen sought greater publicity for their ideas and befriended Arthur Hyde, Hoover's secretary of agriculture. Although Hyde was reluctant to endorse a full-fledged BAE land classification program, he did agree to sponsor a national land utilization conference in the fall of 1931.[50]

From the conference emerged several land use advisory bodies intended to formulate policy and to submit legislation to Congress. In 1932, Gray's Division of Land Economics threw itself into the preparation of many of the research reports issued by these committees. "These releases," Gray remembered, "preached the doctrines that the long reign of individualism

[49] Hamilton, *New Day to New Deal*.

[50] Kirkendall, "L. C. Gray"; Hugh H. Bennett, "What to Do With Surplus Land," September 1931, HBP, NA RG 114, Entry 21, Box 4; L. C. Gray and O. E. Baker, *Land Utilization and the Farm Problem* (GPO, 1930); L. C. Gray, "National Land Policies in Retrospect and Prospect," *Journal of Farm Economics* 13 (1931).

had created widespread social and economic maladjustments in the use of land, [and that] each acre of land has a socially best use, which must be discovered through the process of land planning." But the endless research did not bring about a comprehensive new land policy or a new system of agricultural planning. Rather than crafting legislation giving farmers incentives to cooperate, the committees continued to recommend expanded programs of agricultural extension and technical guidance.[51]

Not all farm and land utilization advocates, however, found themselves at such a loss for ideas. In particular, former BAE employee and Montana State University economist M. L. Wilson entered agricultural policy circles with a set of proposals designed to break the impasse. As the Depression deepened, as farm prices dropped, and as international trade fell victim to fits of economic nationalism, Wilson concluded that the problems facing American farmers demanded a two-part solution: first, emergency measures designed to reduce domestic crop surpluses and to raise farm income immediately; and second, the implementation of agricultural planning machinery to bring about proper land adjustments over the longer term, including the abandonment of marginal land. Wilson now turned his attention to the promotion of a "Voluntary Domestic Allotment Plan," a measure he believed had the potential to bring about both short-term and long-range goals.[52]

The domestic allotment plan, which proposed to raise commodity prices without dumping crops abroad and without raising domestic production levels, entered farm policy discussions in the late 1920s as an alternative to the McNary-Haugen bills. The plan would require processors of agricultural products, such as flour millers, to purchase certificates issued to farmers on the basis of their "domestic allotment," or the share an individual farmer contributed to the total amount of a commodity bought and consumed within the country. Wilson became intrigued by the allotment proposal because it offered immediate assistance and could therefore serve as the first phase in a program of agricultural recovery.

[51] *Proceedings of the National Conference on Land Utilization* (GPO, 1932); "Recommendations of the National Conference on Land Utilization," 23 November 1931, WP 2100, 23:21; "Land Use Problems Attacked by Two Committees in Four-Day Meet," Hoover Cabinet Papers, Agriculture, Land Use Studies, 1930–1932, HHL; Purcell, "Quarter Century of Land Economics"; Gray, "Evolution of the Land Program"; Hamilton, *New Day to New Deal*, 178–80.

[52] Hamilton, *New Day to New Deal*, 180–5; Richard S. Kirkendall, *Social Scientists and Farm Politics in the Age of Roosevelt* (1966), 20–4. Also see William D. Rowley, *M. L. Wilson and the Campaign for Domestic Allotment* (1970).

However, because the allotment plan might bind farmers even more closely to their existing crops, it would be necessary to join it with plans for long-term agricultural and land use adjustments.[53]

In his subsequent quest to publicize the allotment plan, Wilson found a close ally in Mordecai Ezekiel, an economist with the Farm Board. Like Wilson, Ezekiel had concluded that the abysmal state of international trade demanded a purely domestic approach to the farm problem: emergency measures to reduce crop surpluses coupled with long-term agricultural planning. Under Wilson and Ezekiel, the allotment plan metamorphosed into a "smokescreen" for the "heavy artillery on agricultural planning." A processing tax would replace the certificates, thereby providing the federal treasury with money to pay farmers willing to reduce production voluntarily. Representatives from the land-grant colleges and the Extension Service would participate in the administration of the program, but only through local committees composed of farmers, bankers, and community leaders. Wilson theorized that this decentralized committee system, with its potential for local and democratic decision making, would provide the foundation for long-term shifts in local and regional agricultural strategy.[54]

Flawed in retrospect, this deference to voluntarism and local conditions nonetheless reflected a genuine belief that decision making at the grass-roots level would translate into informed and equitable policy. Little did the framers of the allotment plan sense the weakness of noncoercive measures or the limits of local planning bodies, which could be easily overtaken by elite interests and become an impediment to reform. A pity, because long-term reform is what the framers had foremost on their minds. The central component of Wilson's strategy was not the short-term reduction of surpluses or the immediate infusion of cash into farmers' pockets – these measures, though necessary, were intended to be temporary – but a long-range national program of land utilization and soil conservation.

Wilson agreed with Gray that the nation's unrestricted homestead policies had created human and environmental maladjustment in rural

---

[53] Hamilton, *New Day to New Deal*, 182–92; Ezekiel to Tugwell, 20 October 1939, WP 00003, 7:8; Wilson oral history, CUOH.

[54] The idea that Wilson and Ezekiel wanted to use the allotment machinery to build "administrative capacities" at the local level is elegantly developed in Hamilton, *New Day to New Deal*; Wilson's description of the allotment plan as a "smokescreen for agricultural planning" comes from a letter he wrote to Ezekiel in April 1932, quoted in Hamilton, *New Day to New Deal*, 192.

America. The federal government, Wilson argued, should sponsor a
national land inventory and should assume the leadership in a program of
land use research and policy. Programs in mountainous areas and in
cutover regions might include reforestation, wildlife and game management, and recreational activities, while programs in the desert and public
domain states might address rangeland rehabilitation, vegetative cover,
and stock water development. Wilson also recommended that the federal
and state governments purchase submarginal lands. Such acquisitions, he
claimed, would consolidate public holdings for forests, parks, and watershed protection, and would remove from private ownership lands that
could not be used profitably without human hardship and soil degradation. As an example of land utilization in action Wilson pointed to the
program in New York State, where Governor Roosevelt had launched
an ambitious land classification and land purchase scheme. But Wilson
went further than Gray in an attempt to link these new land proposals with concrete measures to discourage crop surpluses and to balance
production with domestic demand. Wilson understood that the problem
of overproduction was not confined to marginal land but that surpluses
also emanated from good land and from farms and farmers considered
"supermarginal" in the terminology of land economics. Therefore Wilson
insisted that some form of the domestic allotment plan should accompany
the land program.[55]

As did most farm economists, Wilson expected the future would hold
larger farms, fewer farmers, and the revival of overseas markets. Still, such
a vision depended on employment opportunities for displaced farmers,
opportunities sorely lacking during the Depression. Would the farmers
released from poor agricultural lands, he asked, join the already overcrowded ranks of the urban unemployed? Wilson answered with a firm
negative. Agricultural and industrial policy could both rehabilitate American farming and restore "balance" to the rural-urban relationship. "There
is a twilight zone between industry and agriculture," he wrote, "where
higher standards of living are available which are consistent with industrial employment on the one hand and better use of the land on the
other." Echoing the Giant Power proponents, Wilson argued that industrial decentralization could bring manufacturing jobs to the country, and
that small-farm "subsistence homesteads" could combine factory work

---

[55] M. L. Wilson, "Land Utilization," 16 April 1932, Economics Series Lecture No. 25,
University of Chicago Press; Wilson, "A Land Use Program for the Federal Government,"
Journal of Farm Economics 15 (1933).

with part-time agriculture. Another possibility was the resettlement of displaced farmers onto viable lands, possibly even onto well-planned and self-financing irrigation projects.[56]

Wilson and Ezekiel purposely combined such land use adjustment proposals with the domestic allotment plan to win over the more traditional farm organizations, and they often employed the language of parity to defend what they hoped would be a temporary measure to raise farm income directly. "Land-use planning must be the foundation for any farm-relief program," Wilson declared in a 1932 radio address. "At the same time, neither this nor any combination of plans can be successful with a wobbling monetary system that forces farmers to pay their obligations with three times the amount of farm produce that the obligations represented when they were contracted." Coupling the two programs, however, lost them the president's support. Wilson and Ezekiel attempted to secure Hoover's approval, but he expressed great disdain for the domestic allotment plan. Agricultural recovery, Hoover claimed, depended not on any system that paid farmers directly to reduce production but on the generous expansion of short-term credit to farm cooperatives and some individual farmers such as that provided through the Federal Reserve, the new Reconstruction Finance Corporation, and a reorganized system of federal land banks. "There is no relief to the farmer by extending Government bureaucracy to control his production and thus curtail his liberties, nor by subsidies that only bring more bureaucracy and ultimate collapse," Hoover declared before the Republican Convention of 1932.[57]

Yet Hoover was somewhat amenable to the goals of the land utilization movement, and he approved a land leasing measure put forward by Secretary Hyde in response to the domestic allotment plan. Hyde proposed that the federal government levy a small processing tax to lease marginal

---

[56] Wilson, "Land Utilization"; Wilson, "A Land Use Program for the Federal Government"; Wilson, "A New Land-Use Program: The Place of Subsistence Homesteads," *Journal of Land and Public Utility Economics* 10 (1934); Wilson, "Planning Agriculture in Relation to Industry," *Rural America* (December 1934), 4; Wilson oral history, CUOH; P. K. Whelpton, "The Extent, Character and Future of the New Landward Movement," *Journal of Farm Economics* 15 (1933); "Back-to-Land Movement Needs Safeguards, National Committee Says," 8 April 1932, Hoover Cabinet Papers, Agriculture, Land Use Studies, 1930–1932, HHL; Gray, "National Land Policies." Also see Kirkendall, "L. C. Gray"; and Conkin, *Tomorrow a New World*.

[57] Wilson, "Land Utilization"; Hamilton, *New Day to New Deal*, 195–215; Wilbur and Hyde, *Hoover Policies*, 152–80; *Public Papers of the Presidents: Herbert Hoover*, 369–70, quoted in Hamilton, *New Day to New Deal*, 207.

lands, with an option to purchase. "This would fit into a general land utilization program," Hyde argued, "whereby the government eventually would take over much of the poor land now being used for raising crops and plant it to trees or convert it into public parks." Hyde claimed that the leasing proposal was "less harmful" than the domestic allotment plan because it would cost less and would not require intricate bureaucratic machinery. He also maintained that the least productive and most marginal land would be automatically retired, as farmers making the lowest profits would submit the lowest bids. "The low cost producer on fertile lands would not be disturbed," Hyde explained, "[and] this is as it should be." By 1933, however, most farm advocates agreed that the low-cost producer on fertile lands was part of the overproduction problem. Hoover and Hyde resolutely refused to entertain Wilson's contention that farm policy would first require emergency measures to restore balance between the nation's supply and demand for farm products (paying all farmers to reduce crop surpluses) *before* steps to build a long-range program of land retirement and crop adjustments could be instituted. Wilson, for his part, dismissed the leasing proposal as a conservative measure backed by millers and food packers who wanted to avoid the higher processing tax; he had little faith in Hyde's assurance that the Hoover administration would eventually purchase marginal land and put it to proper "public use."[58]

Nor did Hoover and Hyde suggest what might become of the displaced farmers. The government, they said, would naturally allow the families to remain on the leased land and to raise food and "garden stuff" for their own use. But was mere subsistence a permanent solution or, more to the point, a politically viable one? If, as Hoover conceded, the federal government should begin to take marginal land out of production, he never acknowledged Wilson's corollary – that the government must also create alternate employment opportunities in rural areas. Hoover, in fact, offered scant support for the single "resettlement" proposal of the early Depression: a scheme for planned farm communities in the South. As if on cue, Hoover indicated that such programs were best left to local initiative, perhaps with a small amount of financial assistance from the Farm Board.[59]

[58] "A Hyde Farm Plan," 30 December 1932, and "Statement by Secretary of Agriculture Arthur M. Hyde," 18 February 1933, Hoover Papers, President's Subject File, "Farm Matters – Hyde Farm Plan 1933," HHL; Wilson oral history, CUOH.

[59] "A Hyde Farm Plan." Documents concerning the southern settlement bills are contained in Hoover Papers, President's Subject File, "Rural Development," HHL. Hoover's reaction is recorded in Patterson to McRae, 25 April 1930, in the same file.

Despite his engineering and humanitarian credentials, Hoover disappointed the rural advocates associated with the New Conservation. His approach to the electric power and the farm relief issues revealed that he thought industrial organization and private (though public-spirited) cooperation would ultimately benefit rural Americans. Cheaper electricity, efficient farming, and proper land use would somehow flow out of the streamlined system. To sell power to the final consumer or to raise the price of farm products directly would bankrupt the government, morally and financially. Hoover's prescriptions, however, were at odds with the latest developments in conservationist thought. Reformers such as Morris Cooke, George Norris, and Franklin Roosevelt did not agree with him that abundant, inexpensive electricity would inevitably flow to the farm from a more efficiently organized utility industry. And other analysts such as M. L. Wilson and Mordecai Ezekiel did not believe that individual farmers, pinned between low commodity prices and few employment alternatives, would be able to cooperate with a national land utilization program without tangible incentives and the administrative capacity to do so. In the end Hoover simply disagreed with the bedrock principle of the New Conservation – that the farm problem directly reflected maladjustments in resource distribution and resource use. If he had agreed, Hoover might have regarded rural conservation measures as one way out of the Depression, rather than as a reward to be earned in the event of citizen self-organization and economic recovery.

FDR: GOVERNOR AND CANDIDATE

Franklin Roosevelt entered the presidential campaign of 1932 with a considerable background in the new rural conservation. While governor of New York, he responded to the state's astonishing rate of farm abandonment – approximately three hundred thousand farms ceased operations during the 1920s – with a set of proposals designed to stabilize the agricultural population by means of better conservation planning. Roosevelt claimed that improper land use was the primary economic reason for the relative decline of the state's rural areas. "We have come to realize," he explained before a Cornell audience in 1930, "that many thousands of acres in this State have been cultivated at a loss, acres which are not under modern conditions suitable for agriculture." In addition, Roosevelt continued, New York had "used many thousands of acres for growing crops unsuited to the particular soil." Rural areas also faced unfairly high taxes, inadequate marketing processes, poor schools, poor health care, and the absence of a "socially interesting" farm life. Roosevelt argued that the problem therefore demanded a two-part solution: reforesting acres unfit for cultivation, and helping those engaged in farming suitable land to remain under more favorable and more profitable conditions. Regional planning, he explained, could "from the economic side make possible the earning of an adequate compensation, and on the social side the enjoyment of all the necessary advantages which exist today in the cities."[60]

The first farm legislation passed during Roosevelt's term as governor reduced rural taxes and shifted the cost of schools and roads from the local to the state government. Roosevelt and his agricultural advisers also requested prompt completion of the state's land and soil survey. "When the study is completed," Roosevelt informed the legislature, "accurate data will be at hand to indicate definitely which lands of the State can profitably be continued in cultivation, which lands of the State should be devoted to reforestation, and which lands of the State should be used for industrial purposes." New York voters subsequently approved a constitutional amendment authorizing a multimillion-dollar bond issue to finance the reforestation of abandoned farmland. While most of the purchased land would be earmarked for future timber supply, the forests within the Adirondack and Catskill preserves would remain untouched. At the higher elevations, Roosevelt argued, the restored forests would also regulate stream flow, help prevent floods, and provide more dependable sources of water for villages and cities.[61]

New York's land program formed a critical part of Roosevelt's larger regional vision, especially after the onset of the Depression. He hoped that urbanites might find relief from hunger, joblessness, and congested conditions by moving into the countryside, and that the agricultural

---

[60] "Address at State College of Agriculture," 1930, *PPA*, 140–3; "Annual Message to the Legislature," 1929, *PPA*, 81; "Address Before the Conference of Governors," 1931, *PPA*, 485–94. Also see Fusfeld, *Economic Thought*. Statistics on farm abandonment in New York are included in Bernard Bellush, *Franklin D. Roosevelt as Governor of New York* (1955), 91–2.

[61] "A Proposal for a Survey of Soil and Climatic Conditions," 1929, *PPA*, 477–9; "A Message to the Legislature Formulating a Land Policy for the State," 1931, *PPA*, 480–5; "Annual Message to the Legislature," 1932, *PPA*, 119; Salter, *A Critical Review*, 130–3; "Radio Address on the Conservation of Natural Resources," 1930, *PPA*, 521–5; "Radio Address Urging Voters to Support the Reforestation Amendment," 1931, *PPA*, 526–31; "Address Before the Conference of Governors," 1931, *PPA*, 485–94. For a critical assessment of New York's land program see Salter, *A Critical Review*; and E. Melanie DuPuis, "In the Name of Nature: Ecology, Marginality, and Rural Land Use Planning During the New Deal," in E. Melanie DuPuis and Peter Vandergeest, eds., *Creating the Countryside: The Politics of Rural and Environmental Discourse* (1996).

population once residing on marginal lands might locate employment within the state's better farming regions or in small industrial plants established in rural areas. "Hitherto we have spoken of two types of living and only two – urban and rural," he explained. "I believe we can look forward to three rather than two types, for there is a definite place for an intermediate type between the urban and the rural, namely, a rural-industrial group." To be sure, this picture of small factories nestled into the upstate hills reinforced Roosevelt's romantic attachment to the back-to-the-land movement and justified his proposals to provide unemployed city dwellers with subsistence homesteads in the country. But his commitment to a more balanced distribution of population translated into concrete efforts to redistribute the state's economic resources and to raise rural incomes. "Remember please that land and its proper use is still the basis of the prosperity of a State," Roosevelt reminded his fellow New Yorkers in 1931. "I want to build up the land as, in part at least, an insurance against future depressions."[62]

Roosevelt also promised to provide New York with inexpensive electricity from state-developed hydropower facilities on the St. Lawrence River and from a strengthened program of utility regulation. "In the brief time I have been speaking to you," he declared in his inaugural address, "there has run to waste on their paths to the sea enough power from our rivers to have turned the wheels of a thousand factories, to have lit a million farmers' homes." He pledged that the government would forever retain title to the state's power sites, and that electricity would be distributed at the lowest possible cost. Roosevelt left open the possibility that private enterprise might play a role in the distribution of the power, though he warned against a "too hasty assumption that mere regulation is, in itself, a sure guarantee of protection of the interest of the consumer."[63]

A few months later the governor followed up his cautionary advice with an admonition aimed directly at the utility companies: his administration would consider public transmission and distribution of the power if private interests proved unable or unwilling to provide service at reasonable rates. Roosevelt also suggested to a national audience in *Forum* magazine that public generation and distribution of hydropower in key locations such as Muscle Shoals, Boulder Dam, and the St. Lawrence River

[62] "Address Before the Conference of Governors," 1931, *PPA*, 487; "Address Before the American Country Life Conference," 1931, *PPA*, 503–15; "Speech by Roosevelt to the Citizens of the State of New York," 26 October 1931, *FDRC*, 98.
[63] "First Inaugural Address as Governor," 1929, *PPA*, 77–8.

might serve as a useful "yardstick" with which "to measure the cost of producing and transmitting electricity" in general. Underlying the governor's power proposals was his belief that private companies discriminated against domestic consumers and small users. Roosevelt compared New York's electric rates unfavorably with those just across the border in Canada, where the provincial legislature had set up a public commission to produce and distribute hydroelectric power at cost to the farms, villages, and towns of southern Ontario. Roosevelt, however, brandished the Ontario rates as an example of areawide coverage at reasonable rates, not yet as an argument for public distribution as well as public generation. He still wanted to give the utility companies a chance to cooperate.[64]

In 1931 the state legislature established the New York Power Authority and charged it with developing hydroelectric energy from the St. Lawrence. The authority would build dams and powerhouses and make agreements with private firms for the transmission and distribution of the electricity. Power rates would be fixed by contract to ensure that rural and domestic consumers received inexpensive electricity at nondiscriminatory prices. Roosevelt appointed several experienced utility regulators to the Power Authority, including Morris Cooke of Pennsylvania. Along with Roosevelt, Cooke claimed that private companies overcharged small users, and he argued that lower power rates combined with areawide coverage would increase the consumption of electricity. He concluded that just one successful example of public regulation at the state level might well inspire similar experiments across the nation, and he traveled to New York excited at the prospect of demonstrating once and for all how "regulation by contract" could bring about fair retail rates.[65]

The Power Authority at once began to conduct technical studies on how best to generate and distribute electricity. Its members and staff began this process with a willingness to cooperate with private industry, but they gradually altered their views because one newly formed company, the Niagara-Hudson, controlled much of the state and occupied a monopolistic bidding advantage. Negotiations with Niagara-Hudson proved unsuccessful, and Cooke suggested that the state consider building its own transmission lines. He and other members of the authority also

---

64 "Plan for the Development of the Water Power Resources of the St. Lawrence," 1929, *PPA*, 172; Roosevelt, "The Real Meaning of the Power Problem," *Forum* (December 1929), cited in Fusfeld, *Economic Thought*, 139; "Campaign Address," 1930, *PPA*, 419–26.

65 *PPA*, 163; Fusfeld, *Economic Thought*, 141; Cooke to Frankfurter, 19 December 1932, NFRS, Box 8.

recommended to Roosevelt in late 1931 that municipalities and farm cooperatives be permitted to construct their own distribution systems. Early
the following year the governor indeed asked state lawmakers to approve
a law allowing municipalities to form utility districts, but the legislature
turned down this proposal. Roosevelt's plans suffered an equally devas-
tating setback when the Hoover administration rebuffed his attempts to
involve the Power Authority in diplomatic negotiations with Canada over
the development of multipurpose works on the St. Lawrence.[66]

Despite the failure of Roosevelt's regional program to materialize during his term as governor, he never abandoned his vision of a rural renais-
sance built upon the proper use of land and the availability of inexpensive
hydroelectric power. The Depression, in fact, only strengthened these commitments. Unlike Hoover, who insisted that farm recovery depended on
general economic recovery, Roosevelt wanted to raise rural living standards directly. During the presidential campaign of 1932, he embraced
rural conservation policy as a weapon in the struggle for economic recovery and as a political device to distinguish him from his competitor.
Though Roosevelt recognized that no single factor would bring immediate prosperity to the agricultural population, he linked the Depression
to the absence of farm purchasing power and claimed that low rural
incomes kept factories idle and urban workers unemployed. "Our economic life today is a seamless web," he explained. "If we get back to the
root of the difficulty, we will find that it is the present lack of equality
for agriculture." Though he saw the need for "quick-acting remedies"
such as surplus reduction, he claimed that permanent farm relief required
national agricultural planning in general and land use planning in particular. Roosevelt also viewed rural electrification as part of this overall
strategy to restore buying power to the farmer. He claimed that the country had been unable to reap full advantage from its natural resources
because selfish utility interests refused to establish rates low enough to
encourage widespread electrical consumption. "We are backward in the
use of electricity in our homes and on our farms," he declared. "Low
prices to the domestic consumer will result in his using far more electrical
appliances than he does today."[67]

---

[66] PPA, 163–6; Christie, Morris Llewellyn Cooke, 100–5; Cooke to Frankfurter, 19 December 1932, and Cooke, "Informal Memorandum on Governor Roosevelt's Power Record,"
n.d. (ca. 1932), NFRS, Box 51; "A Recommendation for Legislation Permitting Municipalities to Build Their Own Power Plants," 1932, PPA, 202–3.

[67] Franklin D. Roosevelt, Looking Forward (1933), 125–36, 147–54.

Roosevelt's concern with "homes" as well as "farms" points to his developing sense of government responsibility for all those hit hard by economic decline, not just farmers too isolated to receive lines or low electric rates, but also industrial workers out of work or too poor to buy appliances or electric service. As governor, Roosevelt had addressed the question of the urban poor by instituting work relief and welfare benefits for the unemployed, anticipating the similar programs of the New Deal as well as the federal government's recognition of organized labor. Still, the underconsumptionist model of the Depression that Roosevelt initially adopted cast the farm sector as the primary problem, with the low purchasing power of the working class a complementary concern. A small group of academics and advisers known as the Brain Trust pushed Roosevelt to endorse this analysis of agricultural underconsumption and to translate it into a political strategy.

During the spring of 1932, as Roosevelt was preparing for the presidential race, the Brain Trust met regularly at the governor's request to hammer out a set of organizing principles for the campaign. Raymond Moley, the group's founder, recalled that as of April no "Roosevelt program" existed, only the governor's "policies, near-policies, and mere leanings." The governor's power program, Moley reported, was foremost among these interests. Not only did Roosevelt claim that the sources of waterpower belonged to the American people in perpetuity (a position taken by his uncle Theodore), but he also insisted that the government had a duty to see that the power was produced and distributed to the people at the lowest possible cost. In addition, the candidate's advisers understood that his power plan was only part of a larger vision of rural rehabilitation and regional development. "Roosevelt," Moley remembered, "had advocated reforestation, land utilization, the relief of farmers from an inequitable tax burden, and the curative possibilities of diversifying our industrial life by sending a proportion of it into the rural districts." Though Roosevelt was vaguely interested in short-term farm relief measures such as the McNary-Haugen plan, he impressed his advisers with the idea that long-term agricultural prosperity was linked to the use and availability of land and water resources. Roosevelt, Moley emphasized, essentially saw "the central problem of agriculture – the paradox of scarcity in the midst of plenty" – as a problem of conservation.[68]

Accordingly, the Brain Trust listed "Agriculture" (under the larger heading of "Conservation") as the campaign's top priority. The group

[68] Raymond Moley, *After Seven Years* (1939), 12–13.

knew that Roosevelt intended to address the nation's farm crisis and that he also hoped to tempt the discontented Republican yeomen of the Midwest across party lines. But their candidate had not yet linked his desire to win votes, to relieve human misery, and to bring about a permanent rural life with a more general approach to fighting the Depression. Therefore his advisers recommended that Roosevelt repackage his inclination to address the country's agricultural troubles. The Depression, they argued, was not simply industrial in character; it had begun in the farm sector. It followed that national economic recovery depended on agricultural recovery and that programs to assist the farmer directly would help the nation as a whole. "The obvious beginning of our discontent in this country," Moley explained, "was the persistence of the delusion that the nation could prosper while its farmers went begging."[69]

The primary architect of the campaign's farm strategy was Rexford Tugwell, a young professor at Columbia University. Tugwell, whom Moley described as a "first-rate economist who had pushed beyond the frontiers of stiff classicism," was an institutionalist who believed that planning (or "social management," a term he preferred) could shape economic and technological forces into instruments for the common good. Tugwell argued that the Depression originated in the domestic economic imbalances of the preceding decade. Production costs had fallen rapidly, and workers produced more per man-hour than ever before, but businesses failed to pass on these gains in efficiency as higher wages to workers or as lower prices to consumers. Instead, they retained the profits as protective reserves or built more plants. The result, Tugwell reasoned, was an imprudent increase in productive capacity (overproduction) without a commensurate increase in purchasing power (underconsumption). At a particular disadvantage were the nation's farmers, who suffered from the "deranged" exchange relationship between farm and industrial goods and who lacked sufficient purchasing power to buy their share of manufactured products. City workers, in turn, found themselves on the unemployment lines when the factories shut down. Because urban unemployment was related to low agricultural incomes, Tugwell believed that the government should reestablish the "exchangeability" among groups. "It was a downright economic necessity that [farmers] should be consumers," Tugwell declared at the Roosevelts' supper table. "To keep the economy

---

[69] Moley, *After Seven Years*, 14–5; Rexford Tugwell, *The Brains Trust* (1968), 12–22. Also see Gertrude A. Slichter, "Franklin D. Roosevelt and the Farm Problem, 1929–1932," *Mississippi Valley Historical Review* 43 (1956).

going," he insisted, "everyone must be able to buy and sell to everyone else."[70]

Tugwell criticized the Hoover administration's recovery program for dispensing emergency aid only to financial institutions and production facilities at the top of the economic pyramid. He therefore looked approvingly upon Roosevelt's promises to provide assistance to the bottom as well as the top. And largely owing to Tugwell's influence, Roosevelt began to justify farm relief as part of a general approach to economic recovery. "One-half of our population, over 50 million people, are dependent on agriculture," he declared after accepting the Democratic nomination. "And, my friends, if those 50 million people have no money, no cash, to buy what is produced in the city, the city suffers." Roosevelt urged that steps be taken to restore the purchasing power of rural Americans, and that the country accept a new picture of group cooperation. "This Nation is not merely a Nation of independence," he affirmed. "If we are to survive, [we are] bound to be a Nation of interdependence – town and city, and North and South, East and West."[71]

Tugwell not only helped Roosevelt formulate this theory of rural underconsumption; he also shared the governor's (and the New Conservationists') conviction that the farm crisis was ultimately a problem for natural resource policy. Echoing the analysis of BAE economists such as L. C. Gray and M. L. Wilson, Tugwell argued that the country had not yet cultivated a permanent agriculture; most of the nation's farmers had not yet progressed beyond a pioneer stage of primitive and transient cultivation. World War I had further encouraged irresponsible expansion, leading directly to the agricultural depression of the 1920s. Individual interests, Tugwell claimed, had run contrary to the social interest, resulting in soil erosion, butchered forests, rising rates of tenancy, and widespread rural depression. To make things worse, none of the farm relief proposals in Congress required any actual change in the practice of farming. "Agriculture was to be made profitable," he complained in 1929, "and this was to be done uncritically and with no attempt to gauge the future or to penalize inefficiency or anti-social techniques." Tugwell instead insisted that the federal government should perform two functions as part of any

[70] Moley, *After Seven Years*, 15; Bernard Sternsher, *Rexford Tugwell and the New Deal* (1964), 15–25; Tugwell, "The Responsibilities of Partnership," 27 June 1934, and Tugwell, "Address Before the Consumers' League of Ohio," 11 May 1934, LVF; Tugwell, *Brains Trust*, 16, 24–5.
[71] Sternsher, *Rexford Tugwell*, 26–39; "The Governor Accepts the Nomination for the Presidency," 1932, PPA, 647–59.

farm program: it should withdraw marginal land from production and convert it into public forests, parks, and grazing reserves; and it should require that farmers maintain "continuous productivity" on private land by adopting improved practices such as plowing on the contour, planting more legumes, and replacing erosion-inducing row crops with grasses and trees. The fact that farmers were begging for relief, Tugwell suggested, gave the "expert his chance" to couple long-term conservation and land use adjustment measures with financial assistance. "We had been mining our soil for a long time," he expressed to a sympathetic Roosevelt, "but we were now doing something even worse, we were exploiting our people, using up their savings and their capital goods and reducing their levels of life." Tugwell advised the presidential hopeful that the desperate situation was now his opportunity.[72]

As for a specific agricultural program, both the candidate and his Columbia adviser believed that it should combine production control with the nation's interest in conservation. Neither Tugwell nor Roosevelt approved of the export-dumping proposals in circulation like McNary-Haugen, for these would have subsidized producers without bringing about necessary changes in farm practice. Restricting production in the midst of widespread depression, Tugwell argued, was not as heartless or as half-baked as its detractors made it sound. It would involve not a net decrease in food supplies but shifts in land use: replacing the soil-destroying staples (cotton, corn, and wheat) with soil-building grasses, soybeans, and alfalfa. Still, Roosevelt found it necessary to court the major farm organizations, and he suggested to the American Farm Bureau Federation, the National Grange, and the Farmers' Union that he would accept any proposal they agreed upon together. However, behind the scenes he encouraged Tugwell to search for a better plan, one that combined production control and conservation with direct assistance so that compliant farmers might see their incomes rise immediately.[73]

Through Mordecai Ezekiel, Tugwell heard of one proposal – the domestic allotment plan – that met both of those conditions, though it provided for administrative machinery less coercive than perhaps Tugwell might have preferred. He traveled to a farm economics conference in Chicago to meet with M. L. Wilson, the plan's chief publicist, and to hear from

[72] Tugwell, "Farm Relief and a Permanent Agriculture," *Annals of the American Academy* 142 (1929); Tugwell, "The Place of Government in a National Land Program," *Journal of Farm Economics* 16 (1934); Tugwell, *Brains Trust*, 205, 207.

[73] Tugwell, *Brains Trust*, 205–8; Michael V. Namorato, ed., *The Diary of Rexford G. Tugwell, 1932–1935* (1992), 42; Kirkendall, *Social Scientists and Farm Politics*, 42.

other proponents, such as Henry A. Wallace, an influential agricultural editor, and Howard Tolley, an advocate of agricultural planning who had worked with the BAE. Tugwell was impressed with Wilson and with his specific set of policy proposals, and he convinced the Montana professor to book a ticket for Albany, New York, to meet with the Roosevelt camp.[74]

Wilson and Ezekiel had begun their efforts to publicize the domestic allotment plan in a spirit of neutral bipartisanship, but they faced opposition from the Hoover administration, which held the line against raising prices directly. They also drew the criticism of many farm leaders, who wanted some combination of inflation and increased prices without meddlesome administrative interference. So by his July conference with the Democratic candidate, Wilson was ready with a new political pitch. The meeting went quite well; the governor especially warmed up to the professor when Wilson praised New York's land program. They also found themselves in total agreement about the need for submarginal land retirement and industrial decentralization. "Well now, M. L., let's get straight on this," Roosevelt said, slapping his knee, "have you got my plan, or have I got your plan?" Still, Wilson warned that a land program would go only so far. Farmers, he explained, were in such a state of mind that they wanted something done quickly. Midwesterners, traditionally Republican, were now ready to vote for a Democrat if he offered quick relief. Wilson insisted the governor could win those farm votes by promising aid without being too specific.[75]

In this final push to promote the domestic allotment plan, Wilson and Ezekiel also found help from the soon-to-be secretary of agriculture – Iowa farm editor Henry A. Wallace. A self-taught market statistician and plant geneticist, and the scion of a much-beloved family of agricultural journalists and professional farm advocates, Wallace was a devout agrarian fiercely devoted to progressive causes. His father, a Theodore Roosevelt Republican who had served as secretary of agriculture under Harding and Coolidge, supported the congressional farm bloc and sparred famously with Commerce Secretary Herbert Hoover over farm policy. Wallace had also absorbed his family's agricultural fundamentalism and its conception of the farmer as God's chosen servant and environmental steward. To be

---

[74] *Diary of Rexford G. Tugwell*, 42–45; Hamilton, *New Day to New Deal*, 210–11; Kirkendall, *Social Scientists and Farm Politics*, 41–6.
[75] Hamilton, *New Day to New Deal*, 198–201; Tugwell, *Brains Trust*, 449; Wilson oral history, CUOH.

a farmer meant that one must curb one's greed, for the land and the soil limited the full flowering of the profit motive. In the words of Wallace's grandfather, those who cultivated the earth had "a sacred duty to maintain the stored energy of the farm." The grandson pursued this theme off and on throughout his career, writing a college thesis on soil fertility and pleading with farmers during the 1920s to address overproduction by planting "Less Corn, More Clover." As secretary of agriculture during the New Deal, Wallace would visualize conservation policy as a tool working both to preserve and to modernize the family farm, his agrarian and abstemious background always stopping him short of a genuine confrontation with the full-fledged capitalist energy that modernized farming could indeed inspire.[76]

Still, conservation was but one route to farm recovery in Wallace's mind. During the farm crisis of the 1920s, and especially after the onset of the Depression, Wallace had become convinced that only government intervention could solve the problem of overproduction. The ideal solution, in his view, would have been to eliminate the odious tariff that protected corporate interests and allowed industry to raise prices and restrict production. Since tariff reform was a political impossibility, and because family-sized farms were unable to employ industrial tactics to tame competition, he supported the McNary-Haugen bills during the 1920s and even broke with the midwestern Republican tradition to campaign for Democratic candidate Al Smith in 1928. During Hoover's presidency, Wallace watched the Farm Board fail – indeed, he predicted it would – and added his support to the domestic allotment plan. By the early 1930s, Wallace had become the leading voice of former McNary-Haugenites who now supported the domestic allotment plan, and he served as a critical intermediary between the academic agriculturalists who formulated the plan and traditional farm leaders and congressmen.

Roosevelt courted Wallace and brought him into the 1932 campaign. Along with M. L. Wilson and Rexford Tugwell, Wallace crafted the candidate's September farm address delivered in Topeka, Kansas. Roosevelt took Wilson's advice to promise aid without being too specific, and he basically outlined the allotment plan without mentioning its name, without calling for acreage reduction, and without even outlining a specific

[76] The sketch of Wallace comes from Lord, *Wallaces of Iowa*; Edward L. Schapsmeier and Frederick H. Schapsmeier, *Henry A. Wallace of Iowa: The Agrarian Years, 1910–1940* (1968), 6; and John C. Culver and John Hyde, *American Dreamer: The Life and Times of Henry A. Wallace* (2000).

method of farm payments. Nevertheless, Roosevelt deftly allied himself with the farmer by once and for all removing the taint of special-interest legislation from the idea of agricultural assistance. He alleged that poverty existed in the midst of abundance: farmers struggled just within reach of incomparable natural resources. And at the heart of the Depression was the farmer's falling share of the national income. Without his buying power, Roosevelt claimed, factories would remain closed and workers would remain idle. "This Nation," he declared, "cannot endure if it is half 'boom' and half 'broke.'" He called for permanent measures such as a program of national agricultural planning, a national policy of land utilization, and efforts to decentralize industry. However, Roosevelt granted that these "slow-moving" proposals had to be complemented by more "quick-acting remedies." An emergency farm plan, he said, must give benefits to agriculture that were equal to the tariff protection enjoyed by industry. Additionally, any such legislation should increase prices without increasing production; it should finance itself; and it should be voluntary. Wilson was thrilled with Roosevelt's sly approach. "Curiosity is a great means for developing and introducing ideas," he wrote Ezekiel. "It will be very easy for him after election to announce that the voluntary domestic allotment plan as embodied in such and such a bill completely fulfills his expectations."[77]

Roosevelt had less need for such stealth when formulating a position on electric utilities and rural service. As Moley indicated, the governor had lavished most of his attention on this issue, developing a combative regulatory philosophy that coupled T. R.'s emphasis on public ownership of waterpower sites with a new insistence on widespread distribution and nondiscriminatory pricing. Roosevelt had furthermore indicated that government-owned hydroelectric plants might usefully serve as a "yardstick" for setting private rates, and had supported George Norris's attempt to include long-distance transmission authority within the Muscle Shoals legislation. Like the New Conservationists, Roosevelt believed that rural electrification would uplift agricultural regions and provide farmers with a higher standard of living.[78]

---

77 Moley, *After Seven Years*, 41–5; Slichter, "Franklin D. Roosevelt"; "Roosevelt's Farm Adviser Tells His Plan," *Chicago Sunday Tribune*, 2 October 1932; "Campaign Address on the Farm Problem," *PPA*, 693–711; Wilson to Ezekiel, 8 October 1932, WP 00003, Box 6.
78 Ernest Gruening, "Power as a Campaign Issue," *Current History* 37 (1932); King, "Power Records."

During the campaign Roosevelt also embedded his utilities proposals within the underconsumptionist analysis of the Depression. The industrial slump, as he and his advisers ceaselessly claimed, was linked to insufficient demand and low purchasing power. Raising farm income directly with the allotment plan was one part of the solution, but another step toward increasing consumption was to lower industrial prices. Here, as Tugwell argued, public utilities were the worst offenders, for they "refuse to require lowered rates because of declining income, not realizing that the reason for declining income is the refusal to reduce rates." Roosevelt repeated this assertion in his campaign address on power policy in Portland, Oregon, taking aim at the "selfish interests" who failed to see that lower prices would encourage widespread public use. Though Roosevelt made it clear he did not support government ownership of the utility industry, he set down two exceptions to that rule. First, he believed that any community not satisfied with its electric service could set up its own system. Second, he invoked the federal government's sovereignty over the nation's waterpower resources to propose the public development and distribution of electricity from the Colorado, Tennessee, St. Lawrence, and Columbia Rivers. "Each one of these," he declared, "will forever be a national yardstick to prevent extortion against the public and to encourage the wider use of . . . electricity."[79]

Roosevelt distinguished himself from Hoover not simply by promising relief to farmers and unemployed workers. Bolstered by a view of the Depression that traced its origins to the lack of consumer buying power, Roosevelt saw direct assistance and rural resource programs as essential to recovery. He had always felt that rural Americans would see their standards of living rise when they used their land properly and when they had the opportunity to purchase electricity at low rates. But he now argued that these things would help farmers become consumers. Unlike Hoover, who did not accept the tenets of the New Conservation, Roosevelt regarded rural electrification, soil conservation, and reforestation as measures to lift the Depression, rather than as rewards to be earned only after the economy had recovered. And his thinking was not only reflected in his farm and power policies: it also underlay his famous campaign promise to put a million men to work restoring marginal and abandoned lands. "It is clear," he explained, justifying this proposal for what

---

[79] *Diary of Rexford G. Tugwell*, 36–7; "Campaign Address on Public Utilities," 1932, *PPA*, 727–42.

would become the Civilian Conservation Corps, "that economic foresight and immediate employment march hand in hand." Roosevelt's position was unmistakable: permanent recovery required the immediate marriage of human and natural resources.[80]

Concerned by the steady depopulation of the countryside and by low standards of living in rural areas, two sets of reformers crafted a New Conservationist agenda during the 1920s. Electric utility regulators and public power proponents argued that the benefits of interconnection and hydropower development should be shared equitably and distributed at equal cost to rural consumers. Land economists linked farm distress with imprudent agricultural expansion onto marginal lands and claimed that land use planning might remedy unprofitable operations, market instability, and soil degradation. A desire to bring "balance" and "permanence" to rural areas animated both sets of reformers; they believed that creating a settled and cultivated rural life required both that farmers replace the agricultural systems of the pioneers with more sustainable and profitable operations and that the benefits of urban centers – modernized homes and alternate employment opportunities – be available to farm families.

The public and political life of the new rural conservation had local, regional, and national dimensions. On the state level, a few eastern governors attempted to bring power resources under a single regulatory umbrella, requiring that the benefits of long-distance transmission lines and industrial interconnection be shared with sparsely settled and densely populated regions alike. In the Upper Midwest, state officials applied the ideas of land economics to the cutover regions, and in the process of doing so set forward an influential model for a national land program. Still, the New Conservation's political center remained in Washington, where utility reformers worked to strengthen federal control over hydropower developments, and where farm advocates demanded a national solution to the deepening agricultural crisis.

After 1930, when commodity prices bottomed out and when jobs dried up in the cities, the recommendations of the rural electrification and land utilization movements – the New Conservation's two "policy tributaries" – coalesced into a set of emergency and long-range policy possibilities. In the short term, rural recovery demanded an immediate

---

[80] "The Governor Accepts the Nomination for the Presidency," 1932, *PPA*, 654; "Senator Norris's Appeal to Break 'Party Regularity' for Election of Roosevelt," *New York Times*, 18 October 1932.

injection of income assistance, quickly followed by the introduction of less wasteful agricultural practices, the retirement of marginal land, and perhaps even the creation of better-planned farming communities and subsistence homesteads. In the long term, the voluntary administrative machinery created to implement the emergency measures might then be transformed into a vehicle for comprehensive yet equitable agricultural readjustment. Inexpensive rural electricity, meanwhile, would immediately improve farm lives and farm output, while eventually bringing industries and employment opportunities to rural areas.

The New Conservation, however, did not develop within an ideological vacuum, but rather emerged as a political counterpoint to the associational character of the 1920s and to the decade's most committed associationalist – Commerce Secretary and President Herbert Hoover. Though he was a committed conservationist of the Progressive-era variety with a sincere desire to help rural Americans, Hoover did not believe that rural electrification or the farm crisis required "interest-group" solutions or expanded regulatory systems. Convinced to the last that a streamlined industrial system and state-sponsored voluntary and private initiatives would benefit all, Hoover missed an opportunity to capitalize on what by the early 1930s had become a significant new extension of conservationist thought. Not even in the changed context of the Depression, Hoover avowed, would government transmission of power or government-supported farm prices justify the resulting blows to economic liberty and individual opportunity. Nor would the promise of long-range adjustments justify direct intervention in agricultural markets or the ill-considered sponsorship of new farm colonies.

Hoover's attitude may have been warranted in part by the New Conservation's conflicted and opportunistic thinking. It is true that a few planners elegantly reconciled emergency measures to rehabilitate existing farmers and to build new rural communities with their knowledge that the end result could only be a smaller farm population. What may have been an entirely rational set of proposals was also a clever appeal to many different interest groups and a ready-made justification for a sweeping array of programs. Anyone who favored multipurpose water projects, for example, or the reclamation program, rural electrification, industrial decentralization, subsistence homesteads, marginal land retirement, soil conservation, reforestation, park expansion, or the "back-to-the-land" movement could place that vision somewhere within the initial framework. But how would the government, or even the most dedicated public servants, adjudicate between these often contradictory interests? Was the goal to keep farmers on the land or to encourage them to find employment elsewhere? How exactly would short-term income assistance evolve into long-range conservation adjustments?

Such tensions point to the inherent conflicts at the heart of the New Conservation. These reformers hoped that farms could be made more efficient while the rural communities surrounding them were made more equitable; they thought farming could yield substantially increased incomes while land use remained sustainable and responsible; and they felt confident that decentralized forms of administration would protect gains in efficiency, equity, and sustainability. In other words, the ideological characteristics that made the New Conservation such a potent political force – its conflicting commitments to raised living standards, environmental balance, economic justice, and noncoercive measures – also reduced its potential for meaningful reform. How would government administrators demand that farmers limit their exploitation of the land (and consequently their material wants) once conservation had been presented as an income-generating tool? How could they enforce the equitable distribution of opportunity on the land once newly modernized farmers resisted the competition of smaller producers and organized to retain the advantages of bigness?

In 1932, such worries lay in the future. Franklin Roosevelt enthusiastically embraced the precepts of the New Conservation and placed rural development policy at the forefront of his strategy to combat the Depression.

2

Poor People, Poor Land

The River, Pare Lorentz's 1937 documentary film on the Mississippi
Valley, opens with a trickle of water high in the mountains. The trickle
turns into a small brook; the brook runs into a rushing stream, the stream
into a river, and the river into the mighty Mississippi. This grand drainage
system, the narrator informs the audience, empties two-thirds of the
American continent, carrying water "from as far west as Idaho and as
far east as Pennsylvania." But all is not well. In time, the peaceful movement of the tributaries is replaced by images of surging floodwaters. The
Mississippi – the nation's very lifeblood – has gotten badly out of joint.
Up and down the valley, miners and foresters have lopped off the tops of
the mountains, and farmers have plowed up the slopes and wrecked the
soil. These resources, the audience hears, built the nation, but at too great
a cost. Water has rushed and swirled over the denuded land, fueling more
violent floods and leaving behind a generation of destitute farmers who
face a life of disease and drudgery. "Poor land makes poor people," the
narrator intones, "and poor people make poor land."[1]

No statement could have served as a more fitting précis for the agrarian conservation of the New Deal. For the first time, policymakers took
as their starting point the central premise of the New Conservation: that
rural living standards would improve with proper use and fair distribution of natural resources. Exploitation must cease, they demanded, but
not simply because the profligate nation faced a resource shortage. Conservation must now avert human tragedy. "The throwing out of balance
of the resources of Nature throws out of balance also the lives of men,"

[1] Pare Lorentz, *The River* (Resettlement Administration, 1937).

Franklin D. Roosevelt declared. "We find millions of our citizens stranded in village and on farm because Nature cannot support them in the livelihood they had sought to gain through her."[2] Poor land created poor people – the association carried social as well as environmental implications. Resource policy now had a dual purpose: the restoration of the land and the rehabilitation of its inhabitants.

In the presidential election of 1932, after a campaign that promised a marriage between this new rural conservation and economic recovery, Roosevelt carried the South and the West, swept the farm states, and polled his largest majorities in the farm regions. Accompanying the incoming president were the largest majorities congressional Democrats had ever known: 60–35 in the Senate and 311–116 in the House. Many of these were new congressmen, voted in by formerly Republican districts. Though such conditions by themselves did not mean Congress automatically followed Roosevelt's initiative, they did provide the president with a remarkably agreeable atmosphere during the first legislative session of his term. Pressured by constituents at home to do something quickly, Congress willingly submitted to executive leadership and engaged in a remarkable flurry of legislative energy.[3]

Five key measures passed during the Hundred Days established the basis of New Deal rural resource policy: the AAA, CCC, FERA, NIRA, and TVA. The first of these, the Agricultural Adjustment Act, was a bill that combined the recommendations of the agricultural planners and the McNary-Haugen forces. The legislation embodied the Brain Trusters' underconsumptionist analysis, which traced the causes of the Depression to the farmer's lack of purchasing power (the AAA's full title was *An Act to Relieve the Existing National Economic Emergency by Increasing Agricultural Purchasing Power*). The AAA established the years from 1909 to 1914 as the base period for calculating the ideal exchange relationship between farmers and other producers, and it named seven commodities as "basic" – cotton, wheat, field corn, hogs, rice, tobacco, and milk. The law also authorized the secretary of agriculture to determine the rate of processing taxes and to use the tax proceeds for adjustment operations and for the removal of agricultural surpluses. The secretary could deploy a variety of weapons to accomplish these tasks, including direct payments

---

[2] "Roosevelt to the Congress," 1935, *FDRC*, 342.
[3] Theodore Saloutos and John Hicks, *Agricultural Discontent in the Middle West, 1900–1939* (1951); William E. Leuchtenberg, *Franklin D. Roosevelt and the New Deal* (1963); James T. Patterson, *Congressional Conservatism and the New Deal* (1967); David M. Kennedy, *Freedom from Fear: The American People in Depression and War* (1999).

for acreage reductions, options on commodities stored by the government, rental contracts, and marketing agreements.[4]

After an initial period of uncertainty and conflict, production control soon became the primary focus of the Agricultural Adjustment Administration (AAA). The principal mechanism was the price-support loan: the government paid farmers a set amount for what they agreed to produce, such as ten cents a pound for cotton or forty-five cents a bushel for corn. The farmer could keep the money he had been lent, repaying the government only if the price rose above that of the loan. Participation was voluntary and depended on consent. While the USDA Extension Service advertised and promoted the AAA, production committees established by local election held the power to administer programs and to check compliance among those who had signed on. The framers of the domestic allotment plan finally saw their ideas put into action, and along with Henry Wallace, the new secretary of agriculture, and Rexford Tugwell, the new assistant secretary, they held out high hopes for cooperation between the AAA's planning division and these local committees. Administrators and conservationists also believed that farmers would finally have the cash to replace the most destructive field crops with grasses and legumes, and that the AAA could coordinate the short-term payments with a long-term land utilization plan.[5]

Following up on his promise to provide immediate unemployment assistance, Roosevelt also asked Congress for an emergency conservation corps, for relief grants to the states, and for a program of public works. He secured all three, each containing provisions that created new rural resource responsibilities for the federal government. The Emergency Work Conservation Act authorized the president to provide young men

---

[4] David E. Hamilton, *From New Day to New Deal: American Farm Policy from Hoover to Roosevelt, 1928–1933* (1991); Richard S. Kirkendall, *Social Scientists and Farm Politics in the Age of Roosevelt* (1966).

[5] Anthony J. Badger, *The New Deal: The Depression Years, 1933–1940* (1989); Ezekiel to Tugwell, 20 October 1939, WP 00003, 7:8; "Background and Summary of Legislation Relating to Agricultural Adjustment, Conservation, Crop Insurance, and Price Control," 15 August 1946, Clinton Anderson Papers, Box 14, HSTL; Economic Research Service, *History of Agricultural Price-Support and Adjustment Programs, 1933–84* (GPO, 1984); Howard R. Tolley, "The Program Planning Division of the Agricultural Adjustment Administration," *Journal of Farm Economics* 16 (1934); Chester C. Davis, "The Grass Revolution," 19 November 1935, WP 2100, 7:40. By emphasizing the role of state actors and policy intellectuals in crafting and administering the AAA, I am not arguing that they acted alone or apart from other social forces; see Jess Gilbert and Carolyn Howe, "Beyond 'State vs. Society': Theories of the State and New Deal Agricultural Policies," *American Sociological Review* 56 (1991).

with jobs reforesting public lands, preventing soil erosion, and improving the national parks and forests. This legislation created the Civilian Conservation Corps (CCC), which soon became one of the New Deal's most popular programs. The CCC cooperated with other federal agencies and provided a plentiful source of manpower for demonstration and restoration work on private as well as public lands. Congress next approved an emergency relief measure, which established the Federal Emergency Relief Administration (FERA) to direct and coordinate relief grants for the rural poor. FERA soon tailored a large portion of its relief efforts to rural areas and coordinated the work of state rural rehabilitation corporations with the land utilization program.[6]

Finally, the National Industrial Recovery Act provided the basis for what became a public works fiefdom under Harold Ickes, the new interior secretary. The legislation established the ill-fated National Recovery Administration (NRA), an attempt to regulate production, prices, wages, and hours; its famous Section 7(a) gave industrial workers the right to unionize. The act also contained key rural resource provisions and was intended to complement the farm recovery program. Title II authorized the federal government to build subsistence homesteads to redress "the overbalance of population in industrial centers," and Roosevelt assigned this task to the Interior Department. Most important, Title III appropriated $3.3 billion for a Public Works Administration (PWA), an agency Roosevelt also assigned to Ickes. The PWA soon financed the construction of large hydroelectric dams and public transmission systems, along with soil conservation work and submarginal land purchases. The theory was that public works money would operate alongside the AAA's cash benefits to increase the total number of purchases nationwide, while the NRA saw to it that labor and capital shared the fruits of recovery.[7]

Scattered throughout several departments and strewn across the executive landscape, these rural resource programs fell under the aegis of no single agency or bureau. The exception to this rule was the Tennessee Valley Authority (TVA), a government corporation created during the Hundred Days to uplift the impoverished Tennessee Valley. Vetoed twice

---

[6] FDRC, 138–48; Sidney Baldwin, *Poverty and Politics: The Rise and Decline of the Farm Security Administration* (1968); P. K. Hooker, "The Land Utilization Program: A Chronology," 1942, Records of P. K. Hooker, NA RG 114, Entry 35, Box 3.

[7] T. H. Watkins, *Righteous Pilgrim: The Life and Times of Harold L. Ickes* (1990); "General Information Concerning the Purposes and Policies of the Division of Subsistence Homesteads," 15 November 1933, Department of the Interior, LVF; Kennedy, *Freedom from Fear*, 151–2.

by Republican presidents, Senator George Norris's Muscle Shoals bill had finally found its home. Roosevelt embraced Norris's call for public operation of the idle hydropower facilities and for government transmission of electricity. The president also saw a singular opportunity to create a single conservation entity charged with the joint rehabilitation of human and natural resources.

Granted such a sweeping set of legislative mandates and furnished with a range of new action agencies, Franklin Roosevelt brought the New Conservationists into his administration and provided this policy community a remarkably free hand in crafting and administering the rural resource programs. The personal and professional connections forged during the 1920s grew in strength and number during the New Deal, now protected by "the sunshine of presidential favor" and nourished by congressional appropriations and the president's emergency funds.[8] These organizational networks provided ideological unity and accounted for the federal conservation agencies' overlapping goals and personnel. The New Dealers drew sustenance from their informal alliances while they attempted to build rural conservation constituencies. Holding the members of the policy community together was their concern for farm people and their belief that conservation adjustments would restore balance to a diseased economic system.

More specifically, the new programs rested on a particular set of assumptions about the American economy. Farm and conservation advocates, including many members of Congress, believed that the nation's prosperity rested on an agricultural base. As the farmers fared, so fared the country. They interpreted the Depression as an industrial emergency, to be sure, but they believed that the farm depression of the 1920s had foreshadowed the economic collapse and that insufficient rural income had prolonged and intensified it. "No idea pulsed more vibrantly at the very heart of the New Deal in 1933," as David Kennedy explains, "than the conviction that on the success [of the effort to raise] farm incomes rode the hopes not only of the nation's farmers but of the nation itself."[9]

Ubiquitous invocations of the moral superiority of the American farmer manifested this thinking. In reality, the agrarianism of the New Deal was a big tent. It could accommodate those who touted rural life as the solution to America's urban and industrial ills, as well as those who simply

---

[8] L. C. Gray, "The Evolution of the Land Program," 22 March 1939, LVF.
[9] Kennedy, *Freedom from Fear*, 200.

wanted greater balance between agricultural and industrial standards of living. For all of these politicians and administrators, conservation became a weapon in their struggle to retain and rebuild the country's farm population. They were certain that the proper use and fair distribution of a region's natural resources would create stable, permanent communities. This rural security, in turn, would thwart future depressions. No longer, they hoped, would the differential between farm and factory incomes send the country over the economic edge.

This underconsumptionist analysis often blended with a more pointed critique of the rural-urban relationship. Greatly influenced by the distinctive social and environmental history of the South, many New Dealers had concluded that industrial and metropolitan centers kept the resource-rich hinterlands in a colonial state of underdevelopment by drawing off their raw materials, rather than developing these resources for the permanent use of the area's inhabitants. This, they argued, resulted in two interlocked and impoverishing forms of exploitation: the monopolistic extraction of natural resources, and the unsustainable abuse of land, woods, and water. Eliminating the difference between farm and factory incomes therefore entailed that the agricultural regions retain the right to their own resources, and that they use those resources properly.

No single initiative better embodied this thinking than TVA. Created to restore and develop the resources of an entire watershed area, TVA constructed multipurpose dams, transmitted hydroelectric power to farms and towns, and began the slow process of healing the region's damaged forests and eroded soils. In so doing, it sought to raise the incomes and living standards of the South's overwhelmingly rural population. Almost immediately, TVA captured the national limelight and set the initial direction of rural conservation policy. Unlike the other programs, TVA was united both geographically and administratively. The AAA, the PWA, and FERA had missions other than resource development, but TVA represented the full embodiment of the New Conservation from the start. For the first time, Congress stipulated that small and domestic consumers, especially farmers, would be considered the special beneficiaries of federal hydropower installations, and TVA pioneered the use of rural cooperatives to bring electricity to the countryside. The agency also helped farmers repair their land and halt soil erosion. Together, rural electrification and land restoration worked to strengthen TVA's influential philosophy of decentralization. Resource policy, the agency's planners believed, could keep farmers in place because the authority would help southern industry "grow on the land."

Still, the Tennessee Valley Authority represented only a portion of the New Deal's offerings. It continued to serve as the most potent symbol of the new rural conservation, but owing to a limited sense of internal mission it never experimented as deliberately as the other agricultural and conservation agencies. TVA never reached the poorest farmers and tenants of the region; it never purchased very large areas of eroded and deforested land for restoration; and it never created new communities for farmers left homeless by its reservoirs. Such experiments, however, did take place beyond the borders of TVA, where several overlapping yet conflicting philosophies of rural reconstruction vied for dominance.

An initial approach, exemplified by the subsistence homestead projects and some of the reclamation ventures, bore the influence of the back-to-the-land movement. These New Dealers not only wanted to rehabilitate existing farmers, they also intended to create entirely new rural communities. This strategy drew criticism from others who argued that it was foolish to create *more* farmers in the midst of an agricultural depression. One such rejoinder was launched by Rexford Tugwell's Resettlement Administration, which purchased large blocks of abandoned or submarginal land, converted it to parks, preserves, and grazing areas, and attempted to resettle some of the former inhabitants onto better farms. The Resettlement Administration was tolerated in areas where large stretches of land lay abused and forsaken, but the agency's philosophy proved quite unwelcome in areas where crop farmers had been fairly successful in the immediate past and where they intended to become successful again. Massive land retirement, especially if followed by government ownership, proved intensely unpopular and politically unworkable. Instead, farmers accepted and demanded conservation techniques that promised them help in staying put. They found such assistance from the AAA, the Rural Electrification Administration, the Soil Conservation Service, and – for a while – the rural rehabilitation programs and the Farm Security Administration. Representatives from these agencies argued that neither landowners nor tenants would need to relocate if given ample credit and agricultural guidance, and they set out to help as many farmers as possible remain on the land. By 1938, this approach had gained the upper hand, thereby strengthening the national appeal of agricultural conservation policies designed to remedy rural distress by helping farmers to stay in place.

Helping farmers remain on the land represented neither a romantic throwback nor an escapist evasion of reality. The Depression had dramatically changed the rules of the game, and the New Dealers faced an economic emergency unprecedented in its scope and duration. Hardly anyone predicted a quick recovery or an expansion of industrial employment. It appeared to these new rural conservationists that economic balance could be achieved only after all farmers, rich and poor, obtained equal access to the natural resources that surrounded them and after they were helped to use those resources sustainably. In building support for their programs, therefore, the New Conservationists established the political justification for an expanded federal role and laid the groundwork for a transformation in liberalism. The nation's strength, they argued, depended on the vitality of rural America; all farmers needed help because the country required their prosperity and because its endangered resources required their stewardship. Agrarian conservation policy fueled government expansion by explicitly assigning to the state the responsibility for rural welfare.

This expansion of the state, however, required a critical compromise – one that revealed both the potential and the limits of the liberal conservation regime. To gain widespread political acceptance, conservation could not be unduly coercive. Despite the popular perception that the New Deal instituted a distant bureaucracy of out-of-touch experts, its rural programs were largely voluntary, and those that threatened local prerogatives or local power arrangements often withered as a result. Conservation also had to yield immediate benefits. And it often did: electrification, for example, brought instant rewards; so too could soil improvement and water control measures. But these compromises privileged short-term goals over longer-term adjustments. Rarely would farmers sacrifice yields or income in the short term to institute conservation practices that promised restored landscapes (or a more equitable division of agricultural opportunity) over the long term.

The end result would be a form of government intervention that ultimately served to increase the value of private property without requiring much else. Thus the genuinely redistributive and restorative effects of agrarian conservation must be balanced by the knowledge that it would eventually be forced to operate within a restricted set of social and environmental parameters. Given the voluntary nature of the programs, farmers' own desires to take care of perceived needs and wants, and a distribution of political power tilted in favor of landowners, it is difficult to imagine a different outcome. The fallout from these compromises would not be immediately apparent, however, and during the early New Deal policymakers struggled to realize the potential of the New Conservation. They first turned their attention to TVA.

THE TENNESSEE VALLEY AUTHORITY

To a large degree, TVA owed its existence to the persistence of George Norris. Throughout the 1920s and early 1930s, he successfully battled a series of Republican-led attempts to dispose of the federal Muscle Shoals facilities (a hydroelectric dam and two nitrate plants). Allied with a national network of public power advocates, he instead proposed that the government retain ownership of the site, expand its operations, and transmit electricity to rural communities and municipalities. Norris cleverly cast this proposal first as a flood control and navigation measure, and only second as a power scheme. In doing so he articulated the guiding principle of the multiple-purpose idea: "We should commit an economic sin, a folly," he insisted, "if we built large dams to control floods or improve navigation ... without utilizing the water to produce electric power." Still, even though power production was to be a "by-product" of multipurpose development, it was far from an afterthought in the minds of Norris and his allies. The government, they argued, should distribute that electricity to those without power, and to others at prices far lower than they had been compelled to pay.[10]

Norris also emphasized the guiding principle of the New Conservation: poor land made poor people. No private corporation ever organized, he argued, was large enough to handle the conservation of every natural resource, nor did private interests take as their mission the rehabilitation of a region's human inhabitants. "Already the winds whipping against the hillsides, the rains beating down, the floods churning through its valleys, had carried away much of the fertile soil of the Tennessee region," Norris lamented. "I thought I could look ahead to a time when thousands of people would be compelled either to abandon the land entirely, or to live in the utmost squalor and poverty." Norris believed TVA would now demonstrate the benefits of conserving and developing a watershed region as one system: controlled floods, restored soils, reforested hillsides, improved shipping, and electrified farms, towns, and factories.[11]

The Muscle Shoals controversy was a national battle, with national implications. Norris, Roosevelt, and other power progressives saw an opportunity to expose the exorbitant rates of the "power trust," as well

---

[10] George W. Norris, *Fighting Liberal* (1945), 268. Also see Richard Lowitt's three-volume biography: *George W. Norris: The Making of a Progressive, 1861–1912* (1963); *George W. Norris: The Persistence of a Progressive, 1913–1933* (1971); *George W. Norris: The Triumph of a Progressive, 1933–1944* (1978).

[11] Norris, *Fighting Liberal*, 249, 262–8.

as to uplift a river valley and its people. But TVA was not simply a national undertaking; it was also a specifically southern project. Its framers thought in terms of regional as well as national reconstruction. In particular, they drew most heavily on the idea of the South as a colonial economy, rich in resources and raw materials but institutionally and technologically under-developed. If the South, the poorest and most rural region of the country, could be integrated into the national economy, the methods that accom-plished this feat might work the same miracle elsewhere. Thus the south-ern stage would perform two functions for the New Dealers: TVA would both represent the New Conservation and operate as a distinctive articu-lation of it.

The most influential formulations of southern underdevelopment had emanated from Chapel Hill, North Carolina. There a group of young academics worked at the university's Institute for Social Science Research with its founder, Howard Odum, the paterfamilias of southern sociol-ogy. In the 1920s, Odum first painted the picture of a South overflowing with primary wealth but deficient in social and technological organiza-tion. "There was abundant evidence," he concluded, "to indicate that the southern states, because of their incredibly rich resources, were capable of almost unlimited development provided they could eliminate the stu-pendous economic and social waste which kept them drained to poverty levels."[12]

Odum's student Rupert Vance presented a more pointed critique of the South's colonial status. After an exhaustive review of the region's phys-ical environment, he also concluded that neither geography nor biology accounted for the South's poor economic position. Instead, Vance claimed that the answer lay in the region's history. Like the rest of America, the South began as a colonial economy: it exported the wealth of soils, forests, and minerals to a mother country for fabrication, and bought them back. But rather than escaping from these tentacles as did the North, the South perpetuated its colonial status. The plantation system, with its single crop of cotton, was dependent on the industrialized areas, and southern farmers mined the fertility of the soil in increasingly desperate efforts to maintain the balance of trade with Europe and the Northeast. Slavery and the cot-ton culture retarded the accumulation of capital and the development of

---

[12] Howard W. Odum, "Regionalism vs. Sectionalism in the South's Place in the National Economy," *Social Forces* 12 (1933). Also see Baldwin, *Poverty and Politics*, 40–1; and Bruce J. Schulman, *From Cotton Belt to Sunbelt: Federal Policy, Economic Development, and the Transformation of the South, 1938–1980* (1991), 41–2.

high-wage industry. The plantation's postbellum descendant, cotton tenancy, only repeated the region's antebellum blunders. Now, at the end of the 1920s, the South's economy lagged behind. The average income per capita of the thirteen southern states was just under half the national average. Agriculture remained the main source of income for most of the South's population, though southern farmers earned only half as much as farmers elsewhere.[13]

Vance believed that two interlocked forms of exploitation explained southern conditions. "Destructive exploitation," or man's devastation of his natural environment, had viciously joined with "absentee exploitation," or the region's colonial-debtor status. The task of regional planning, then, was to transform the South's extractive, unsustainable cropping and mining economy into one of self-contained development. Conservation measures, such as hydroelectric development, reforestation, and more permanent forms of cultivation, would help the South accumulate capital and raise its standards of living without denigrating its resource base.[14]

Vance also argued that the South needed to rectify its poor rates of urbanization and industrialization. He took aim, however, at the local "Chamber of Commerce" efforts to entice new industries from already developed areas. This haphazard and uncoordinated development had led to overproduction, demoralization among wage workers, and the resurgence of sectional antagonism. Vance also denounced the escapist program of the Southern Agrarians, who envisioned southern renewal as a return to regional and agricultural autarky. What the South needed, he insisted, was a middle way between the forces of "Neo-Mercantilism" and the "Neo-Confederacy." There was no turning back from industrialism, he maintained; there was only the hope that the agrarian sector could be saved from exploitation. Electricity might bring about a diffused pattern of towns and factories, which in turn would allow farmers to diversify their output and work part-time for higher paychecks. Indeed, despite their criticism of the "neo-Confederate" platform, Vance and his colleagues shared more with the agrarians than they realized. Regionalists of all stripes agreed that the South could industrialize slowly without urban congestion and unemployment, the ills that plagued the North.

---

[13] Rupert B. Vance, *Human Geography of the South: A Study in Regional Resources and Human Adequacy* (1932).

[14] Vance, *Human Geography*; Vance, "What of Submarginal Areas in Regional Planning?" *Social Forces* 12 (1933).

Southern development would build upon, even nurture, the region's rural character and its rural way of life.[15]

The TVA Act, the result of legislative bargaining rather than academic discussion, incorporated the concrete concerns of Norris and the power progressives but nonetheless gave voice and opportunity to the ideas of the regionalists. The act assigned to a three-member board of directors the corporation's primary tasks: providing for the navigability and flood control of the Tennessee River, restoring and reforesting marginal lands, and coordinating the agricultural and industrial development of the valley. It gave the board the power of eminent domain and the power to acquire real estate for the construction of dams, reservoirs, transmission lines, powerhouses, and navigation structures on the river and its tributaries. "To avoid the waste of water power," TVA was also authorized to generate electricity and to transmit and market it to certain preferential customers, all nonprofit: states, counties, municipalities, and cooperative organizations of citizens or farmers. The act specified that TVA encourage "the fullest possible use of electric light and power on farms" and that it sponsor "the wider and better use of electric power for agricultural and domestic use, or for small or local industries." To carry out this mission, TVA was given the authority to construct transmission lines to farms and small villages "not otherwise supplied with electricity at reasonable rates," and to see that the sale and distribution of such electric power was "just and equitable." To further clarify this power policy, the legislation required that the authority's projects be considered "primarily for the benefit of domestic and rural consumers . . . and accordingly that sale to and use by industry shall be a secondary purpose, to be utilized principally to secure a sufficiently high load factor and revenue returns which will permit domestic and rural use at the lowest possible rates."[16]

As to regional and land use planning, the legislation paid much less attention to either, embedding TVA's planning duties within two comparatively weak sections of the bill. Sections 22 and 23 gave the president the power to conduct surveys and to develop plans for the region in order to foster the "orderly and proper physical development" of the valley. These powers, which Roosevelt promptly assigned to TVA, included the

[15] Vance, *Human Geography*; Vance, "Is Agrarianism for Farmers?" in John S. Reed and Daniel J. Singal, eds., *Regionalism and the South: Selected Papers of Rupert Vance* (1982), 62; T. J. Woofter, "The Tennessee Valley Plan," *Social Forces* 12 (1933), 332; Odum, "Regionalism vs. Sectionalism," 354; Edward Shapiro, "The Southern Agrarians and the Tennessee Valley Authority," *American Quarterly* 22 (1970).

[16] Tennessee Valley Authority Act, 73rd Cong., 1st sess. [HR 5081], May 1933.

authorization to recommend legislation for several purposes: the maximum amount of power production consistent with flood control and navigation; the proper use of marginal lands and the proper methods of reforestation; and finally, the "economic and social well-being of the people living in the river basin." Though the act's preamble indicated that TVA should reforest and restore marginal lands while providing for the agricultural development of the region, its strongest statutory powers with regard to land use and the prevention of soil erosion were linked to its authority to manufacture and distribute fertilizer.[17]

The infant agency faced a daunting set of human and environmental conditions. With the help of other government departments, especially the USDA and the state agricultural colleges, TVA administrators compiled reams of data on the Tennessee Valley. The region was overwhelmingly rural: 78 percent as opposed to the national average of 44 percent. Over half the valley's population depended directly on farming for its livelihood. The region's agriculture, however, presented no uniform pattern. Cotton farming dominated the uplands of northern Alabama, northeastern Mississippi, and West Tennessee; a more diversified grazing and cropping economy characterized the Appalachian valleys; and low-level subsistence farming prevailed at the higher elevations and within the more isolated bottomlands. Despite these differences, average farm values and farm incomes remained a fraction of their national counterparts. Forestry, a once-thriving industry, provided jobs for less than 1 percent of the valley's workforce. Mining opportunities also petered out after the onset of the Depression. In 1930, the region's per capita income was lower than that of every state except South Carolina. In 1934, rural relief rates in the Appalachians and northern Cotton Belt were among the very highest in the country.[18]

---

[17] Tennessee Valley Authority Act; Earle S. Draper testimony to Congress, *TVAH*, 3704–5. Also see Lawrence L. Durisch and Robert E. Lowry, "The Scope and Content of Administrative Decision – The TVA Illustration," *Public Administration Review* 13 (1953); Paul K. Conkin, "Intellectual and Political Roots," in Erwin C. Hargrove and Paul K. Conkin, eds., *TVA: Fifty Years of Grass-Roots Bureaucracy* (1983); and Erwin C. Hargrove, *Prisoners of Myth: The Leadership of the Tennessee Valley Authority* (1994).

[18] *Economic and Social Problems and Conditions of the Southern Appalachians* (GPO, 1935); Tugwell, "Report on That Part of the Tennessee River Basin Above Muscle Shoals," 1933, cited in Michael J. McDonald and John Muldowny, *TVA and the Dispossessed: The Resettlement of Population in the Norris Dam Area* (1982); Earle S. Draper, "Statement of Department of Regional Planning Studies," *TVAH*, 3701–28; Daniel Schaffer, "Environment and TVA: Toward a Regional Plan for the Tennessee Valley," *Tennessee Historical Quarterly* 43 (1984); Federal Emergency Relief Administration, *Six Rural Problem Areas* (GPO, 1935).

Government observers pinpointed environmental degradation as the chief cause for the Tennessee Valley's rural poverty. An extractive, colonial economy had squandered the region's rich inheritance. Uncontrolled lumbering and unwise clearing depleted the forest resources, while the cultivation and abandonment of sloping land scarred and ruined the soil. In addition, Appalachian farmers clung to traditional agricultural methods. Unrestrained row cropping of corn, cotton, and tobacco exhausted the land and exposed it to damage from wind and rain. By one estimate, erosion had damaged over four-fifths of the region's cultivated acreage, irreparably gullying a fifth of that land. These conditions provided scant opportunity for the notoriously dense Appalachian population. While area farmers had previously escaped by migrating outward in search of urban or factory work, the Depression forced thousands to return home, to clear more land, and to start the destructive cycle anew. Despite its agricultural character, the valley's rural population was not fully employed. The region faced a closing pair of Malthusian scissors – there were too many people trying to make a living from a rapidly dwindling resource base.[19]

All was not lost. The land might be restored: the uplands reforested, the soils replenished and protected. Additionally, the region's water resources held tremendous potential. The Tennessee River traveled a 650-mile course, tracing a deep crescent-shaped curve from where its two major tributaries joined in Knoxville, Tennessee, to Paducah, Kentucky, where it finally met the Ohio. The watershed, which covered nearly all of Tennessee and portions of six additional states, drained the highest rainfall area in the East, yielding a water volume comparable to the Ohio or the Missouri. A sharp drop in northern Alabama at Muscle Shoals prevented profitable navigation, and had for a long time delayed dreams of linking Knoxville to the country's bustling inland waterways. That same obstacle, however, offered the second-greatest hydroelectric potential in the eastern part of the country (Niagara Falls formed the greatest). Dams to tame the shoals for shipping might also produce kilowatts upon kilowatts of power. Indeed, by the early 1930s the U.S. Army Corps of Engineers had completed a series of Tennessee River surveys setting out several such

---

[19] Hugh H. Bennett, "Relation of Soils and Soil Conditions in the Tennessee Valley to Needed Adjustments in Land Use Practice," Records of the SCS Research Division, NA RG 114, Entry 21, Box 2; *Economic and Social Problems and Conditions of the Southern Appalachians*; Draper, "Statement of Department of Regional Planning Studies"; Schaffer, "Environment and TVA"; McDonald and Muldowny, *TVA and the Dispossessed*.

multiple-purpose possibilities. With the political fight over the disposition of the Shoals completed, TVA set out to tap the valley's goldmine and to distribute this natural wealth to its people.[20]

This task fell to the three quarrelsome members of the TVA Board. The chairman, Arthur E. Morgan (A. E.), came to TVA from Ohio, where he had engineered a series of successful flood control dams and served as the president of Antioch College. When A. E. arrived in Tennessee, he adopted the prevailing portrait of the region as one rich in natural resources but now suffering from environmental degradation. Like the southern regionalists, A. E. also warned against development that only perpetuated existing inequalities. "It isn't enough that we increase production," he explained; "that does not necessarily mean an increase in the general welfare." Regional independence, he claimed, would punch the valley's ticket to economic security. New commercial channels forged within local communities would allow the area to break away from the outside financial and industrial centers that preyed upon it. A. E.'s theory of self-sufficiency, however, was not an isolationist philosophy. He believed that regional development would allow the Tennessee Valley to assume its rightful place in the national economy as an equal, not a stepchild.[21]

A. E. agreed with the government reports that far too many people were trying to make a living from the land. As he saw it, one part of the solution was to treat the land: to halt the soil erosion, to educate the farmers (perhaps even by confiscating their property), and to replant the forests. But another, equally important strategy was to develop small, local industries. These businesses would employ the marginal population without necessitating rural out-migration or urbanization. "We do not want merely to duplicate here the industrial set-up that has broken down in Detroit and Pittsburgh and the other cities," A. E. explained. "Industry should furnish a market for local agriculture, should largely supply local needs, and should add a cash income." He pinned his hopes on the development of high-skill craft cooperatives that employed regional talent and local resources. He wanted the Tennessee Valley to emulate France and

---

[20] Conkin, "Intellectual and Political Roots"; Donald Swain, *Federal Conservation Policy, 1921–1933* (1963), 101–2.

[21] Roy Talbert, Jr., *FDR's Utopian: Arthur Morgan of the TVA* (1987); A. E. Morgan, "The Tennessee Valley Project as a Great National Experiment," *Planning Problems* (October 1933), 109; Morgan, "Bench-Marks in the Tennessee Valley: The Strength of the Hills," *SG* (January 1934); Morgan, "Bench-Marks in the Tennessee Valley: Roads to Prosperity in the TVA," *SG* (November 1934). Also see A. E. Morgan, *The Making of the TVA* (1974).

its strong tradition of "character production," rather than to duplicate the congested steel centers of Germany. "America has run to large size and may have greatly overdone mass production," A. E. wrote, in typical anti-industrial fashion. "We are going to develop individuality, we are going to put our character into our products, and not make the region the Ruhr of America."[22]

Harcourt A. Morgan (H. A.) joined the board after a long career in agricultural education and after serving as president of the University of Tennessee. After years of work in the South, H. A. had concluded that its agricultural system had fallen terribly out of balance; erosion, poverty, and malnutrition were the results. Along with Rupert Vance, H. A. blamed the cotton economy, which had been built up to benefit the textile mills and metropolitan centers of the North. "When industrialization is over-concentrated in certain areas," he claimed, "the sections producing raw materials [drain off] their resources and impair the economy for which Nature fitted them...We have neglected soil in pursuit of urban and industrial growth." H. A. had pleaded with area farmers to replace corn and cotton with soil-building pasture crops, such as grasses and clovers. Humans, he believed, must align their operations with the requirements of nature. This was an idea he labeled "our common mooring."[23]

H. A., like A. E., recognized that the South could not remain dependent on farming. Its greatest need remained the establishment of agricultural balance, but the problem was that new conservation practices required greater incomes. Poor farmers, as H. A. complained in the late 1920s, had precious little buying power. He believed that a limited amount of industrial activity could simultaneously increase farm income and save the soil. "Whenever industry has been decentralized and distributed in rural sections," H. A. said, "you find more public revenue available, lower tax rates, increased value of agricultural products and property ... life in every way richer, deeper, better worth the living." H. A. did not have large mass-production factories in mind, nor did he want the region to attract more

[22] Morgan, "Bench-Marks: Roads to Prosperity," 8, 550, 551; A. E. Morgan, Memorandum to TVA Board, 30 July 1933, *TVAH*, 100–2; Morgan, "The Tennessee Valley Project"; Morgan, "Tennessee Valley Becomes Laboratory for Nation," *New York Times*, 25 March 1934; "Report of Arthur E. Morgan to the President on the Activities of the Tennessee Valley Authority," 10 May 1934, LVF. Also see Schaffer, "Environment and TVA."

[23] "The Morgan Story," in Lewis D. Wallace, ed., *Makers of Millions* (1951); H. A. Morgan and Ellis F. Hartford, *Our Common Mooring* (1941), 3, 11; H. A. Morgan testimony, *TVAH*, 272–8.

low-wage textile mills. Rather, he thought industry should be built upon the agricultural resources of local areas – it should "grow on the land." Processing, grinding, packing, refrigeration: these were the methods to bring about much-needed changes in land use and farm income. Electricity, he understood, now made this possible. Throughout the 1920s H. A. backed George Norris's attempts to protect Muscle Shoals from corporate development on the grounds that private developers had little interest in distributing electric power on an areawide basis.[24]

David Lilienthal, the third and youngest member of the TVA Board, joined A. E. and H. A. after a brief but distinguished stint as a utilities regulator in Wisconsin. In 1931, Governor Philip La Follette had called him to Madison, Wisconsin, to help the state's Public Service Commission craft a comprehensive reform program governing the utility industry. In 1917, the state's residents had purchased electricity from 312 companies; by 1930, just 3 holding companies controlled almost the entire power market. Wisconsin faced the same challenge as other states: how to require efficient service and fair rates from a near-monopoly. In the end, the Wisconsin experience, only partly successful, whetted Lilienthal's appetite for national issues. Along with his counterparts in Pennsylvania and New York, he decided that state regulation was ineffectual and concluded that the situation required a federal solution, perhaps even a significant experiment in public ownership.[25]

Echoing one of the New Deal's principal refrains, Lilienthal argued that the country had essentially solved the problem of production. Now, he said, it must adapt itself to this revolutionary change by solving the problem of distribution. He argued that the nation's capacity to produce enough for all derived, in large part, from electric power. No other force promised such high standards of living and such freedom from drudgery. "No wonder, then," he explained, "it is so vital that we maintain the strictest public control over this great natural resource." For Lilienthal and others of his ilk, power production was no ordinary business. It was, in the language of common law, "affected with a public interest." And Lilienthal declared that TVA was now given a special national purpose: it

[24] "The Morgan Story"; Morgan and Hartford, *Our Common Mooring*; H. A. Morgan, "Decentralization of Industry," n.d., TVA Board File, NA RG 142, Curtis-Morgan-Morgan, 001.32, NARA Southeast Region; John P. Ferris oral history, MOH; Ferris testimony, *TVAH*, 1420–2; Barrett Shelton, "The Decatur Story," 1949, LVF.
[25] Steven M. Neuse, *David E. Lilienthal: The Journey of an American Liberal* (1996); Lilienthal, "A Five-Point Program for the Electrification of America," 1933, NFRS, Box 52. Also see Thomas K. McCraw, *TVA and the Power Fight, 1933–1939* (1971).

would lead the way through the "tangle of engineering obstacles and economic difficulties" toward the widest possible use of electricity. Congress had not declared war on private ownership, Lilienthal always assured his audiences. Public operation was simply "a reminder that electricity is a public service and that unless it is exercised by private corporations with fairness ... the public, at any time, may itself assume the function of providing itself with this necessity of community life."[26]

Soon after their first meeting, TVA's board members agreed to carve up the agency's major responsibilities. A. E. took control of engineering and construction, as well as forestry, land, and regional planning (except for agriculture). H. A. assumed responsibility for chemical and agricultural matters, including the fertilizer program, rural life planning, and matters relating to localized industry. Lilienthal acquired the power operations and the task of distributing the electricity. This tripartite setup was less a result of mutual deliberation than a by-product of initial ideological discord. H. A. and Lilienthal were taken aback when A. E. appeared to have made major policy decisions without consulting them. They were equally alarmed by a few of A. E.'s more radical proposals. Particularly irksome to H. A. was his new colleague's suggestion that property be taken away from farmers who abused their land. Lilienthal and H. A. felt that such unorthodox ideas would alienate the very people TVA was attempting to assist. Indeed, they understood the political parameters in which the New Conservation would have to operate: TVA's measures would be presented as a set of options, not as a set of requirements.[27]

Disagreement over two forms of "decentralization" – one political, the other economic – also contributed to the board's lingering divisiveness. The first kind of decentralization underlay TVA's early decision to work with existing state and local institutions whenever possible. H. A., the primary architect (if not the primary popularizer) of this "grass-roots philosophy," did not believe TVA should force a ready-made blueprint upon the valley. Long experience had taught him that farmers and southerners accepted change only slowly, and never involuntarily. Therefore, TVA should work with the familiar institutions that the region's people had already come to trust. A. E., however, had envisioned TVA as a national laboratory for social and economic planning: an experiment in which a

---

26 Lilienthal, "Address Before the Rotary Club of Chattanooga," 1933, NFRS, Box 52; Lilienthal, "A Five-Point Program." For A. E. Morgan's interpretation of these events see *Making of the TVA*.

27 H. A. Morgan testimony, *TVAH*, 102–11; A. E. Morgan, Memorandum to TVA Board; Neuse, *Lilienthal*, 73.

commitment to unhindered reform, not the messy business of building an imperfect constituency, guided the new agency. This meant, in contrast to the decentralized approach that prevailed, that TVA should have been isolated from narrow, local, and elite interests. But A. E. would fight a losing battle. On this matter of deference to existing local arrangements, H. A. found an ally in Lilienthal, who later mythologized the grass-roots concept in his rhetorical masterpiece, *TVA: Democracy on the March*. TVA, Lilienthal argued, would give people the option of exercising their Jeffersonian rights: they now had the tools with which to choose what kind of community and industrial life they desired. What the region, its farms, and its towns decided to do with TVA's tools was up to them.[28]

An equally influential board alliance formed in support of a second type of decentralization. This was the decentralization of industry: the codependence of farms and factories that both H. A. and A. E. held so dear. Though each approached the problem from a separate vantage point (H. A. wanted to preserve the farm, A. E. the small town), both Morgans had concluded that industrial decentralization would rescue the South's natural resources while preserving its rural, unspoiled character. Lilienthal, on the other hand, never really agreed with his colleagues on this point. There could be "no turning back from the machine," he said, "I am against basket-weaving and all that it implies ... We cannot prepare for the second coming of Daniel Boone." But Lilienthal's philosophy did not prevail during the authority's first years; he was too busy protecting the nascent power program from a host of legal and constitutional challenges. It was the combined vision of the two Morgans – with Lilienthal's help at rural electrification, to be sure – that gave TVA its initial decentralized character.[29]

The most visible and photogenic signs of progress were the high dams that TVA built along the Tennessee River and its tributaries. The enabling legislation gave the authority broad powers to construct water control facilities, but it did not specify how many or what type. The Army Corps of Engineers had plotted a series of low navigation dams for the river in

---

[28] Ferris oral history, MOH; Philip Selznick, *TVA and the Grass Roots: A Study in Politics and Organization* (1949); David Lilienthal, *TVA: Democracy on the March* (1944); Lilienthal, "Address Before the Rotary Club"; Shelton, "Decatur Story"; Talbert, *FDR's Utopian*. Also see Hargrove, *Prisoners of Myth*, for an excellent and evenhanded portrait of the TVA "troika."

[29] Ferris oral history, MOH; Lilienthal, "Some Observations on the TVA" (1936), quoted in Hargrove, *Prisoners of Myth*, 36. On A. E.'s lingering resentment of Lilienthal's "basket-making" comments see *Making of the TVA*, 56.

the early 1930s. In 1932, the Corps began construction of a lock at the
Wheeler site in Alabama, and it undertook preliminary investigations at
the Cove Creek area in eastern Tennessee (soon to be named Norris Dam).
TVA assumed responsibility for these two projects in 1933 and unhesitat-
ingly decided that high dams rather than low dams would best serve the
multiple purposes of navigation, flood control, and power production. A
year later the board authorized the construction of a third high dam at
Pickwick Landing, and TVA received appropriations from Congress for
additional dams at Guntersville, Chickamauga, and Hiwassee. In 1936,
Congress also approved TVA's comprehensive statement of intent (*The
Unified Development of the Tennessee River System*), which called for
nine major dams on the Tennessee between Knoxville and Paducah and
three large storage dams on its major tributaries. In just eight years, from
1933 to 1941, TVA completed no fewer than seven dams. The Bureau
of Reclamation designed Norris and Wheeler, the first two, but TVA had
assembled its own staff by the time it began Pickwick in 1934.[30]

The construction program owed its rapid success to A. E., who diligently pulled together a loyal, professional workforce. A. E. also took the
opportunity to put some of his planning theories into action. As provided
under Sections 22 and 23 of the TVA Act, he created a Department of
Land Planning and Housing and a Social and Economic Research Division
(these were combined in 1937 to form the Department of Regional Planning Studies). There existed no body of data on the land and its people
comparable to the Corps surveys of the waterways, so these departments
spent much time surveying the region by foot and by air and collect-
ing information. With help from other federal agencies, especially the
USDA, TVA began a detailed analysis of a sample area – the nine counties
between Knoxville and Chattanooga – and confirmed the agency's belief
that soil erosion posed the primary land use problem. Surveyors found that
70 percent of the area's farm families worked land that was severely and
actively eroding. Such research provided the background for more extensive land classification work. It also strengthened the prevailing sense that
the region required a more diversified economy to halt the waste of both
human and natural resources.[31]

---

[30] C. Herman Pritchett, *The Tennessee Valley Authority: A Study in Public Administration*
   (1943); Durisch and Lowry, "Scope and Content."
[31] Draper, "Statement of Department of Regional Planning Studies"; Earle Draper, "Levels
   of Planning," *Planner's Journal* (March–April 1937), 31. On the soil survey see Carleton
   R. Ball, "A Study of the Work of the Land-Grant Colleges in the Tennessee Valley Area,"
   1939, LVF.

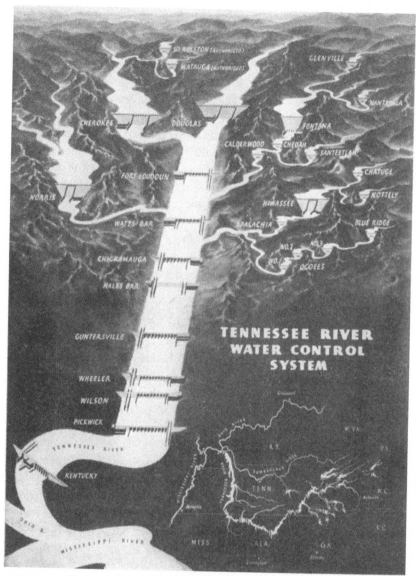

FIGURE 2.1. Tennessee River Water Control System, 1944. Library of Congress, Prints & Photographs Division, FSA-OWI Collection [LC-USW33-015690-2C DLC]

To head the land planning and housing efforts A. E. recruited Earle S. Draper, a prominent town planner who had helped design the small manufacturing center of Kingsport, Tennessee. Though the project was a private venture, Kingsport was widely hailed as an appropriate model for regional development because it attempted to reconcile the interests of area farmers with the need for southern industrialization. Influenced by this experience, Draper came to TVA with the idea that its planners should also work out a balanced combination of agriculture and manufacturing. This, he said, would lift valley incomes and make possible the standard comforts of American life. Draper agreed with A. E. that the authority should cultivate "rural-urban" areas, communities where "people could get their own food from the soil and their other needs from industry in relatively small units." The showpiece of this thinking was the town of Norris, built to house the workforce at the Norris Dam and reservoir site. A. E. and his planning staff decided that Norris would be no makeshift construction camp. Rather, they designed it as a permanent town and laid it out like an English garden city, with individual home plots surrounded by a belt of farm and forest land. They built low-cost, fully electrified houses, and each family had access to a four-acre subsistence garden outside town. Several cooperatives provided groceries and other necessities, and a 580-seat community center was built for religious services and adult education classes. A. E. also established a small ceramics plant in Norris, hoping that valley residents might profit from turning the region's native clay into high-quality porcelain.[32]

As Norris's greenbelt suggested, forestry initially played an important role in TVA's regional planning culture. TVA personnel looked upon the afforestation of marginal and sloping land as necessary to control erosion and to rebuild the region's forests, almost all of which were second growth. They established nurseries and planted trees (mostly native conifers) on private as well as public land. The Civilian Conservation Corps, which operated several dozen camps in the valley, carried out much of this work. The "CCC Boys" controlled erosion and runoff not only by reforestation

---

[32] Draper, "Statement of Department of Regional Planning Studies"; Draper oral history, MOH; Draper, "Levels of Planning"; Draper, "Regional Planning and the Development of Land and Water Resources," *Proceedings and Addresses of the Oregon Planning Council* 2 (July 1935); A. E. Morgan, "Bench-Marks in the Tennessee Valley: Planning for the Use of the Land," *SG* (March 1934), 237; Talbert, *FDR's Utopian*, 116–21; Morgan, *Making of the TVA*, 67–9.

but also by planting grasses, building check dams, and helping farmers construct terraces.[33]

The Forestry Department took the most pride in its public operations on TVA-owned land. When TVA purchased land for reservoirs, it also purchased a "protective strip" around the perimeter of the shoreline. At Norris Dam, this strip of land extended outward for over a quarter of a mile. The planners and foresters argued that siltation, which shortened the lifespan of the reservoir and the navigation structures, could best be prevented if TVA controlled the land surrounding the lake. They also claimed that demonstrations in regional planning and land use adjustments necessitated public ownership. In 1935, the Forestry Department took 117,000 acres of this land by the Norris reservoir to use as an example of sustained-yield management. A. E. and Chief Forester Edward C. M. Richards intended to create "a complete forest economy" for the Norris Lake Forest. Greatly influenced by European models of community-owned forests, they drew up plans to settle a trained workforce first at Norris and then in other parts of the region. A. E. believed that many areas of the valley were large enough to support a small community with forest work, small-scale farming, and craft-based industries such as cabinetmaking. Forest areas and lakeside views also offered recreational possibilities and the opportunity for communities to increase their incomes with tourist dollars.[34]

A. E. similarly attempted to create a more balanced economy by encouraging producers' cooperatives. With federal relief funds, he founded the Tennessee Valley Associated Cooperatives (TVAC) in 1934 to establish and promote the development of cooperative enterprises. The Norris Town Stores received TVAC help, as did craft associations that produced and distributed textiles and wood products (such as the baskets that prompted Lilienthal's ridicule). Most of TVAC's work, however, focused on helping small farmers process and prepare foods for regional

[33] Earle Draper, "Forestry and Regional Planning," *American Forests* (April 1935); "Organization and Scope of Forestry Department," *TVAH*, 1505–11; Thomas D. Clark, *The Greening of the South: The Recovery of Land and Forest* (1984).

[34] Draper, "Forestry and Regional Planning"; "Organization and Scope of Forestry Department"; Clark, *Greening of the South*; Daniel Schaffer, "Ideal and Reality in 1930s Regional Planning: The Case of the Tennessee Valley Authority," *Planning Perspectives* 1 (1986); Edward C. M. Richards, "The Future of TVA Forestry," *Journal of Forestry* 36 (July 1938), 649; Morgan, *Making of the TVA*, 59–72. Also see Brian Black, "Organic Planning: Ecology and Design in the Landscape of the Tennessee Valley Authority," in Michel Conan, ed., *Environmentalism in Landscape Architecture* (2000).

markets. "In the mountains where people lived in deep poverty," A. E. later explained, "there were many small valleys with fertile tracts too small for modern large-scale corn or wheat culture but large enough for truck farming." A. E. recruited an experienced canner, who canvassed the hills, built three small canneries, and taught farmers how to raise beans. Other cooperatives sold poultry and dairy products, potatoes, canned fruits, and locally milled grains.[35]

Many of these small, farm-based enterprises could not have existed without TVA electricity. Lilienthal, in charge of distributing TVA power, agreed with A. E. on the value of rural electrification. The two directors, however, could not agree on much else. From the start, Lilienthal wanted the cooperatives to use more TVA power, to employ more people, and to introduce new manufacturing and industrial opportunities to the area. It took several years, however, before Lilienthal's vision prevailed. In the meantime, he battled with A. E. and the private utility industry over the scope and content of the authority's power program.

The TVA Act had stipulated that the authority was to provide electric power at the lowest possible rates, but it did not indicate exactly how this "yardstick" was to be created. Several pressing questions remained – whether TVA would sell retail as well as wholesale power, how large an operating area it would create, and what its relations with the region's private utilities should be. The major private interest in the area was the Commonwealth and Southern Corporation (C&S), a holding company directed by Wendell L. Willkie. A. E. wanted to cooperate with Willkie by agreeing to confine TVA's operations to a single but representative rural-urban area. "To build two paralleling and competitive power systems in a region is an economic waste," A. E. insisted. Lilienthal, little interested in cooperation, argued against any such restrictions. He responded that the authority should never agree to stay out of an area that requested government power.[36]

In late August of 1933, A. E. and Lilienthal agreed that TVA would restrict its initial operations to the areas near Wilson and Norris Dams, but that future circumstances might warrant its expansion. This gave Lilienthal a period of relative calm to construct an electric power market, while at the same time it left the utilities to wonder what the authority

---

[35] *TVAH*, 4562, 4566–7; Morgan, *Making of the TVA*, 72–3.
[36] Jordan Schwartz, *The New Dealers: Power Politics in the Age of Roosevelt* (1993), 222; Thomas K. McCraw, *Morgan vs. Lilienthal: The Feud Within the TVA* (1970), 3; "Memorandum from A. E. Morgan," 14 August 1933, NFRS, Box 52; Lilienthal, "Memorandum in Opposition to Proposal of Chairman A. E. Morgan," NFRS, Box 52.

really intended. In setting rates, Lilienthal relied on the advice of Llewellyn Evans, former manager of the municipally owned power company in Tacoma, Washington, and a forceful proponent of the idea that low rates translated into high consumption. He also consulted with members of New York's Power Authority, such as Leland Olds and Morris Cooke, who had conducted some of the first distribution studies in the country. The resulting rate structure that Lilienthal announced in September was based on a combination of hard data and heartfelt intuition, but the cheap prices inspired many communities, including some outside the agreed-upon area, to ask for TVA power. Lilienthal negotiated TVA's first wholesale contract with the town of Tupelo, Mississippi, home of Congressman John Rankin, who had sponsored the TVA bill in the House. Tupelo agreed to sell TVA power at rates set by the authority. Lilienthal also encouraged other municipalities who did not already own their own public distribution systems to apply for loans and grants from the Public Works Administration (PWA). Willkie, his hand finally forced by the PWA's threat to duplicate private lines with public money, agreed to sell C&S properties in northern Alabama, northern Mississippi, and parts of Tennessee.[37]

Though Willkie had relinquished only the Mississippi properties by 1934, this area served as the proving ground for the TVA yardstick. In Tupelo, average power usage increased immediately, and residents were repaid with even lower rates. In Mississippi, Lilienthal also launched TVA's first experiment in rural electrification. Compared to a national average of around 11 percent, only 3 percent of farmers in the Tennessee Valley had electricity. Following up on its promise to serve farms with rates equal to those of towns, TVA helped farmers living near Corinth organize the Alcorn County Electric Cooperative. Corinth's residents had been served by C&S, but the area's farmers had not. After extending a loan to the Alcorn cooperative, TVA sold electricity to Corinth at rates 50 percent below the old C&S rate, and the town then extended power to the co-op without a service charge. The Alcorn co-op proved quite a success, and it repaid its debts more quickly than expected. Most important, its financial solvency demonstrated the feasibility of the cooperative as a means of bringing about areawide electric service to rural regions. As TVA expanded its operations into Georgia, Alabama, and Tennessee,

---

[37] Neuse, *Lilienthal*, 78–82; A. E. Morgan, "Bench-Marks in the Tennessee Valley: A Birch Rod in the National Cupboard," *SG* (March 1934); Leland Olds testimony, *TVAH*, 5837–9; McCraw, *TVA and the Power Fight*; Wendell Willkie testimony, *TVAH*, 4245–6.

other farmers duplicated the Alcorn organization. By 1937, TVA served a total of nineteen rural cooperatives, and from 1934 to 1937 the rate of increase in farms receiving electricity in TVA states almost doubled the national average. Some farmers received TVA power not from co-ops but from towns like Knoxville and Dayton that extended service outside the city limits. After 1935, TVA loans for rural service were supplemented and then eclipsed by those from the Rural Electrification Administration (REA).[38]

In Mississippi Lilienthal also pioneered a program to get electric appliances into the hands of potential consumers. Low power prices, he understood, were only half the solution; TVA must also create demand for power. Lilienthal reasoned that there would never be a widespread use of electricity without large-scale distribution of low-cost appliances. "The crux of the whole matter is a lack of purchasing power in the hands of the people," he wrote. He believed that prices for appliances such as refrigerators, electric ranges, and water heaters were far too high. Manufacturers, he claimed, borrowing a metaphor often used to criticize the private utilities, had "skimmed the cream" off the appliance market.

To reverse this stalemate Lilienthal founded the Electric Home and Farm Authority (EHFA) with NIRA funds in January 1934. The EHFA cooperated with manufacturers in the development of lower-priced appliances, and it extended credit so that consumers might purchase these items. While not entirely successful, the program strengthened TVA's political and symbolic image. The EHFA was also extended nationally in 1935 with a generous infusion of cash from the Reconstruction Finance Corporation. That the residents of northern Mississippi purchased only a limited number of "TVA-approved" appliances was beside the point. They used more electricity nonetheless. Lilienthal's gamble had paid off: he had demonstrated that consumers in town and on the farms would use more power if they did not have to pay as much for it.[39]

The dams that generated the electricity Lilienthal labored so hard to distribute also powered the fertilizer plants that formed the basis of

---

[38] McCraw, *TVA and the Power Fight*; D. Clayton Brown, *Electricity for Rural America: The Fight for the REA* (1980), 35–40; Julius A. Krug testimony, *TVAH*, 5230–1, 5260–81.

[39] Lilienthal testimony, *TVAH*, 824–7; Lilienthal, "A Five-Point Program"; Lilienthal, "The TVA Points Ahead," *Christian Century*, 7 October 1936, cited in Schwartz, *The New Dealers*, 237; Lilienthal, "TVA Appliances," *Business Week*, 17 March 1934, 10–11, cited in Gregory B. Field, "'Electricity for All': The Electric Home and Farm Authority and the Politics of Mass Consumption, 1932–1935," *Business History Review* 64 (1990), 35; Neuse, *Lilienthal*, 78.

H. A. Morgan's agricultural program. The TVA Act assumed that the chemical facilities at Muscle Shoals would produce nitrates, as provided under the munitions legislation passed during World War I. H. A., however, interpreted the fertilizer provisions of the act as a broader authorization to improve the valley's soils, and he spearheaded the decision to produce phosphate rather than nitrate fertilizers. This decision constituted nothing less than a repudiation of the area's traditional agricultural practices. H. A. claimed that indiscriminate use of cheap nitrates on clean-tilled row crops would never improve the land. The South had historically consumed most of the nation's fertilizer, but its soils remained exhausted and its land impoverished. Southern farmers had applied tons of fertilizer to their cash crops as growth stimulants, assuming that soil fertility was simply a matter of adding certain chemical nutrients. Fertility, H. A. argued, also depended on the physical conditions of the soil, on its humus and other organic matter. Such conditions in turn derived from a program of soil management that included rotations, cover crops, and other conservation practices. H. A. insisted that farmers had no need of more nitrates; nature had already provided them with legumes. Legumes not only transferred nitrogen from the air to the soil, they also encouraged crop rotations and farm-system adjustments. Tests at the agricultural college and at the experiment stations had indicated that soil-protecting legumes and pastures grew most quickly after researchers prepared the land with phosphate and lime. Because lime was plentiful, the limited amount of phosphorus in the valley's soils was the limiting factor in the region's agricultural development. And so H. A., supported by the TVA Board, made the decision to produce and demonstrate new forms of concentrated phosphate.[40]

H. A. dreamed of replacing the valley's scrub pine, broom sedge, and poverty grass with clover, alfalfa, lespedeza, and bluegrass. With the addition of phosphate and lime, areas that had produced only carbohydrates and cellulose (corn and cotton, for example) could be made to produce mineral-rich protein food and feed. In essence, H. A. hoped to substitute livestock and green meadows for row crops and gullies. He also linked the fertilizer program to TVA's primary goal: the multipurpose control of the valley's water resources. "Just 1 inch of rainfall on 1 acre of land weighs about 113 tons," H. A. always reminded an audience. "Multiply that by averages of 40 or 50 inches per year and consider that that rain is

---

[40] Norman I. Wengert, *Valley of Tomorrow: The TVA and Agriculture* (1952), 20–9; Wallace, *Makers of Millions*, 48–9; H. A. Morgan testimony, *TVAH*, 272–4.

falling upon millions of sloping, tilled acres, and we can gain some conception of the vast forces of Nature with which we are concerned." Preventing floods and protecting navigation required that water be retained and controlled where it fell; and guarding the land against erratic runoff entailed a program of phosphate fertilizers and vegetative ground cover.[41]

Because of his intimate relationship with the University of Tennessee and with the Extension Service, H. A. proposed that TVA's agricultural program be carried forward in cooperation with the land-grant colleges of the region. This decision epitomized H. A.'s philosophy of administrative decentralization. It was, to be sure, as Philip Selznick has demonstrated, a politically expedient strategy. With TVA facing an uncertain future, this "grass-roots" approach appeased the valley's agricultural establishment, which included not only the colleges but also their traditional base of support: the powerful American Farm Bureau Federation (AFBF), composed of the area's mostly white, well-to-do farmers.[42]

Such initial political compromises, however necessary, could easily have set the stage for social and environmental consequences at odds with the New Conservationists' intent. A reliance on existing institutions favored farmers already served by those arrangements and bolstered a constituency that sought to preserve its favored status. The small farmer, though initially held up as the model aid recipient, would prove unable to compete politically with an ideology that sanctified economic consolidation. Equity would yield to efficiency. Furthermore, the use of demonstration work and noncoercive measures associated conservation adjustments almost exclusively with economic gain: everyone involved assumed that no farmer willingly adopted new practices if not out of self-interest. H. A. Morgan was correct in his assessment that grassed pastures would serve agriculturalists better than eroded and exhausted cropland, both in the short and in the long run. But real environmental stewardship – such as the ability to resist the ecologically destructive chemical inputs introduced after World War II, to take just one example – would require an outlook other than income maximization. Sustainability would also yield to efficiency.

Still, for all its weaknesses, the grass-roots philosophy did represent an understandable decision not to duplicate resources and personnel. The colleges possessed highly trained research and education specialists – experts who had long endorsed the values of conservation and field

[41] Wengert, *Valley of Tomorrow*, 28; H. A. Morgan testimony, *TVAH*, 273.
[42] Selznick, *TVA and the Grass Roots*.

diversification – and they owned equipment, laboratories, and experimental farms. Most important, the extension agents had been preaching H. A.'s particular doctrines of land adjustment long before TVA came along, though limited funds had prevented this message from taking hold. Now, H. A. believed, TVA could give the research and extension program the extra help it had always needed. One extension agent agreed wholeheartedly. He explained that he had been trying to get assistance for twenty years before TVA funded twelve demonstration farms in his area. "Now when I want to tell the men about how to develop a permanent pasture, I hold a meeting with them *on* one," he said. "A man can stick his fingers into what I'm telling him about."[43]

Specifically, TVA disseminated its "phosphate philosophy" by means of two types of test demonstrations. On farm-unit demonstrations, TVA and its cooperating staff worked with an agricultural community to select a representative farm from the area. The landowner and the agricultural specialists worked out a farm plan that provided for the gradual replacement of soil-depleting crops with cover crops. TVA supplied the fertilizer, and it often provided machinery (such as terracing or contouring equipment) to hold down the soil mechanically. Unit demonstrations frequently aroused the interest of their neighbors, many of whom used their AAA payments to purchase legume seed and fertilizer on their own. Farmers surrounding the unit demonstration could also ask TVA to establish something called an area demonstration. The area demonstrations, which replicated the unit demonstrations across a small subwatershed, usually included between thirty and seventy-five farms. By 1938, almost 15 percent of the valley's farmland was in either unit or area demonstrations. These farms covered 5,775 square miles, an area slightly larger than the size of Connecticut.[44]

The area demonstrations also reflected H. A.'s commitment to community development and industrial decentralization. H. A. intended any new commercial activity to fortify rather than to vitiate the region's agricultural base. He established an Agricultural Industries Department and gathered a staff to help him formulate an industrial policy for TVA. One of these assistants was John P. Ferris. H. A. and Ferris believed TVA could foster small enterprises peculiarly suited to the region, such as those using

[43] Ball, "A Study of the Work of the Land-Grant Colleges"; Wengert, *Valley of Tomorrow*; John C. McAmis oral history, MOH; George C. Stoney, "A Valley to Hold To," *SG* (July 1940), 393.

[44] McAmis testimony, *TVAH*, 1406–7; Wengert, *Valley of Tomorrow*; Stoney, "A Valley to Hold To"; Ball, "A Study of the Work of the Land-Grant Colleges."

local raw materials and serving nearby markets. Equitable power rates now meant that rural communities could enjoy the benefits of a more balanced economy without having to send their people away from the farm.[45]

H. A.'s specific industrial strategy grew out of the agricultural program's conservation work. TVA's first responsibility, controlling water on the land, depended on the expansion of cover crops. However, Ferris and H. A. reasoned that farmers needed to earn more income before they could manage their land, terrace their property, or purchase legume seeds, fertilizers, and equipment. And increased rural income, Ferris explained, depended on "new crops, better marketing of existing crops, and adding value to some of the farm products by processing them before they go to market." To these ends TVA helped the colleges and experiment stations develop community refrigerators, cold storage units, feed grinders, improved curing techniques, and new quick-freezing processes. Most of these activities were intended to help farmers shift at least part of their operations from crops to pasture and livestock. Dairying and meat production, for example, were enterprises made possible only with rural refrigeration and better animal feed. Agricultural planners also wanted the region's farmers to earn more money from the bottomlands so that they would not need to plow the slopes. To take just one example, a single acre of strawberries, quick-frozen for export, yielded far more cash than many acres of cotton or corn.[46]

H. A.'s activities dovetailed ideologically with A. E. Morgan's views on industrial decentralization and small-scale, cooperative enterprise. However, the two directors and their supporting staffs clashed viciously over the direction of TVA's land purchase policy. The regional planners and foresters who worked with A. E., such as Earle Draper and Ned Richards, represented a conservation tradition that stressed public ownership and scientific forestry. Taking their cue from the U.S. Forest Service, which acquired and afforested thousands of acres of submarginal and tax-delinquent land during the Depression, TVA foresters initiated the authority's overpurchase of reservoir lands and hoped to steer the agency in the direction of more such purchases. Their intent, to be sure, diverged from simple utilitarian conservation. Experiments such as the Norris Lake

---

[45] H. A. Morgan testimony, *TVAH*, 275; Ferris oral history, MOH; Ferris, "Memorandum for H. A. Morgan on Suggested Policy Concerning Industry," 1933, TVA Board File, NA RG 142, Curtis-Morgan-Morgan, 950.01, NARA Southeast Region.

[46] Ferris oral history, MOH; Ferris testimony, *TVAH*, 1418–35; Ball, "A Study of the Work of the Land-Grant Colleges"; McAmis oral history, MOH.

Forest and the town of Norris indicated that the planners hoped to combine land purchases with social and economic reform. A. E., for example, eventually wanted forests to be placed in the hands of communities rather than corporations. TVA forestry also broke with the tradition of public ownership by formulating a program to reach private landowners directly and to distribute seedlings and assistance free of charge.[47]

H. A. and his agriculturists wanted none of this. They, too, represented a conservation tradition, but theirs was agricultural conservation that stressed education and direct aid to private landowners, not public ownership. The "agricultural group," as H. A.'s forces came to be known, wanted to displace as few farmers as possible. They were saddened to see the precious bottomlands taken up for reservoirs, especially in hilly areas such as East Tennessee, where the small river valleys supplied the only farmland level enough to grow crops permanently. These agrarians knew that reservoirs had displaced almost forty-two hundred families during TVA's first four years, and that many of those families had to leave because of the overpurchase policy. While they saw the necessity for reforesting the steepest slopes, the agriculturalists had little confidence that forestry or forest communities could employ enough rural people. Poor land, they felt, would yield high incomes and high living standards when restored to pasture, not when planted with trees. The agricultural group exerted intense pressure upon the regional planners, who officially lost power along with A. E. Morgan in 1938. TVA gradually restricted land purchases around the reservoirs and eventually sold off much of the land that was purchased in its early years. The TVA forestry activities were also rerouted through the Extension Service.[48]

In its first five years, TVA gave vivid illustration of the promises of the New Conservation. In doing so, it established an influential set of

[47] Selznick, *TVA and the Grass Roots*; Schaffer, "Environment and TVA"; Schaffer, "Ideal and Reality in 1930s Regional Planning"; Thomas K. Rudel, "Did TVA Make a Difference? An Organizational Dilemma and Reforestation in the Southern Appalachians," *Society and Natural Resources* 8 (1995); William E. Shands and Robert G. Healy, *The Lands Nobody Wanted: Policy for National Forests in the Eastern United States* (1977); Draper oral history, MOH; Richards, "The Future of TVA Forestry"; Morgan, *Making of the TVA*, 63.
[48] Draper oral history, MOH; Schaffer, "Ideal and Reality in 1930s Regional Planning"; Selznick, *TVA and the Grass Roots*; M. Harry Satterfield, "The Removal of Families from Tennessee Valley Authority Reservoir Areas," *Social Forces* 16 (1937); Durisch and Lowry, "Scope and Content"; McAmis testimony, *TVAH*, 1404–5; Willis Baker testimony, *TVAH*, 1504–11. On the real, but limited, forms of assistance offered to displaced families, see Ball, "A Study of the Work of the Land-Grant Colleges"; and McDonald and Muldowny, *TVA and the Dispossessed*.

principles that guided rural development efforts in the rest of the country. Most important was the idea that the federal government should help rural areas in general, not just the South, to escape from their colonial status. No longer should distant utility companies stake a monopolistic claim to a region's rivers, nor should farmers mine the soil in order to purchase goods manufactured far away. Rural resources must now benefit an area's most immediate inhabitants. Linked to this colonial analysis was the effort to equalize rural and urban incomes. And farm incomes, the TVA experience suggested, rose when hydropower projects sent cheap electricity to rural cooperatives and when soil restoration efforts returned the gullies to grass or, in some cases, to trees. TVA also helped pioneer the strategy of industrial decentralization. Its planners believed that farmers would not need to migrate to cities for work if they switched to more sustainable agricultural methods and if they earned more money from each product before shipping it out. The desire to help rural people remain on their land motivated TVA's efforts to diversify farmers' fields as well as the economies of their rural towns.

TVA also revealed the political advantages of agricultural conservation. The struggle between the regional planners and the agriculturalists was not a fight between the "real" conservationists and the unthinking servants of the establishment, as has often been portrayed. Rather, it was an argument between two separate conservation traditions, and therefore an argument about conservation itself, about whom it should serve, and about what it should accomplish. By the end of the 1930s, the forces of agricultural conservation had prevailed. No more farmers than absolutely necessary would lose their property, and no longer would the authority acquire large parcels of nonreservoir land to manage as it saw fit. But neither would TVA accomplish much more in the realm of rural planning than what was justified under its mandate to produce and distribute fertilizer to private landholders. As one journalist quipped in 1940, "It seems like another case of 'to him that hath shall be given'... The TVA folk know about this, too, and they ask in all honesty, what can be done? Their job is stop erosion, no matter on whose land it might occur."[49]

"To him that hath shall be given": a fitting summary of the compromises required of liberal policy. Halting erosion and bringing about necessary conservation adjustments required deference to existing local arrangements, noncoercive methods, and the demonstration of immediate returns. It also required relationships almost exclusively with landowners.

[49] Stoney, "A Land to Hold To," 395.

Of course landowners deserved such assistance. Many were desperately poor, and given historians' understandable attention to class differences within agriculture it is altogether too easy to forget just how many farmers – even landowners of some stature – lived on the margins. TVA benefits helped prepare many of these citizens for a more equitable relationship with their urban counterparts. Still, TVA never attempted to reach the "bottom third" – the poorest farmers, the tenants, or the landless. Ultimately, the failure to find secure places on the land for everyone and the inability to reduce rural inequality would underscore the weaknesses of national conservation policy and precipitate a shift in its overall direction. But not yet. More experimental efforts to remedy the twin evils of poor people and poor land were taking shape elsewhere across the United States.

BEYOND TVA: LAND UTILIZATION AND RURAL REHABILITATION

In the winter of 1935, L. C. Gray of the Resettlement Administration's Division of Land Utilization addressed his colleagues at an annual meeting of farm economists. For more than a decade, Gray had worked in the U.S. Department of Agriculture as a land analyst committed to government involvement in farm and conservation planning. As a contributor to the New Conservation of the 1920s and early 1930s, he had argued that improper land use created instability and increased tenancy in the agricultural economy, and that comprehensive land utilization would stabilize agricultural prices, preserve soils and forests, and repair the fabric of rural society. Now, flush with the early successes of New Deal programs aimed at precisely these ends, Gray proudly announced the advent of a new conservation era. "The single most distinctive characteristic of the innovations in land policy," he declared, "is the more direct concern with social and human problems." Gray argued that earlier conservationists had made considerable progress in protecting forests and parks but that they had overlooked the human and environmental needs of inhabited rural areas. Now, he claimed, "land is being opened or closed to settlement by these programs not only to conserve physical resources, but more particularly to improve the economic opportunities and social well-being of the groups of families utilizing them."[50]

---

[50] L. C. Gray, "The Social and Economic Implications of the National Land Program," *Journal of Farm Economics* 18 (May 1936), 258. Also see Gray, "The Government's Approach to the Problems of Poor Land," Elco Greenshields Papers, Box 23, HHL; and Gray, "A National Policy for Land and Water," 1935, LVF.

Gray also advanced the economic worldview that underlay the rural resource and farm reconstruction programs of the New Deal: he blamed the Depression on the imbalance between rural and urban incomes. If national distress could be traced to the farm depression, then efforts to rehabilitate rural economies would redound to the benefit of the country as a whole. Rural conservation, as Gray's ally M. L. Wilson explained it, "will make the cities and industries dependent upon agriculture permanent and lasting." Gray agreed: "It is evident," he asserted, "that our national safety lies in the direction of making it possible for a larger proportion of our population to find a secure foothold on the land."[51]

Even though many New Dealers shared the same economic presuppositions, they hardly worked together in harmony. Indeed, contemporary observers divided the New Deal's agricultural personnel into three ideological camps, and scholars have continued to find the groupings useful. First there were the more conservative and business-minded men such as the AAA's first director, George Peek, former head of Moline Plow Company, and Cully Cobb of the AAA's Cotton Section. Chosen to placate commercial farm interests and the Farm Bureau, these men promoted the AAA insofar as it benefited their upper- and middle-class constituents. A second faction, clustered around Rexford Tugwell and Jerome Frank ("boys with their hair ablaze," in Peek's famous words), became known as the "urban liberals" owing to their Ivy League ties and eastern connections. Despite their cosmopolitan backgrounds, however, these reformers were sensitive to the issues of rural poverty and racial oppression, and they labored not simply to raise farm prices but to distribute the benefits fairly. The urban liberals were political centralizers, confident that an activist and more coercive state might bring about the transformations required for social justice. Men such as Henry Wallace, M. L. Wilson, and L. C. Gray composed a third, middle group, sometimes labeled the "agricultural pragmatists" or the "midwestern farm boys." These agrarian intellectuals, to borrow sociologist Jess Gilbert's term, were reared on family farms, attended land-grant colleges, and wanted to restore and modernize the middle-sized farms of their youth. Because of their upbringing in the less class-stratified regions of the country, the agrarian intellectuals had more confidence in local planning and gradual, voluntary change.[52]

[51] Gray, "A National Policy for Land and Water"; M. L. Wilson, "Dust Storms and Rural Rehabilitation," 1935, WP 00003, 6:23; Gray, "Large-Scale Regional and Rural Land Planning," *Planning Problems* (October 1933).

[52] Theodore Saloutos, *The American Farmer and the New Deal* (1982); Jess Gilbert, "Eastern Urban Liberals and Midwestern Agrarian Intellectuals: Two Group Portraits of Progressives in the New Deal Department of Agriculture," *Agricultural History* 74 (2000).

While both the urban liberals and the agrarian intellectuals held pro-gressive commitments, the differences in their backgrounds and tem-peraments culminated in sharp policy disagreements, most notably over the question of southern landlord-tenant relations. Nevertheless, the two groups had much in common, favoring national economic planning and social democracy secured by a resurgent agrarian wing.[53] The urban liber-als and agrarian intellectuals also united in their commitment to the New Conservation and the belief that permanent farm prosperity required rural resource adjustments. Unlike the more conservative farm advocates or the American Farm Bureau, which sought merely to elevate farm prices, both groups of agricultural progressives viewed the AAA as a temporary mea-sure. With the support of President Roosevelt, they launched a variety of rural conservation programs to supplement the AAA. These programs developed not just within the AAA and the Agriculture Department, but also within FERA and the Interior Department. Insofar as these other activities attempted to reach the poorest farmers, they stretched the pos-sibilities of liberal reform.[54]

One such effort took shape as the Land Utilization Program, through which the federal government purchased large sections of submarginal, eroded, and abandoned land and provided funds for its conversion to grazing, forestry, wildlife, and recreation areas. The administrators hoped that such purchases would help the land's occupants as well as the land itself. They concentrated their efforts in areas with the highest rural relief loads: the Cotton South, the Appalachian South, the cutover regions of the Lakes states, and the northern and southern plains. The land program's designers viewed poverty and soil erosion as flip sides of the same coin: tax delinquency and farm distress, they argued, reflected misguided settlement patterns and improper land use, not individual failure. This thinking grew out of the land utilization movement of the 1920s and out of the efforts by individual states, such as Wisconsin and New York, to remove poor land from cultivation. Roosevelt's submarginal land policies in New York, in fact, provided the technical model for the national program.[55]

---

[53] Gilbert, "Eastern Urban Liberals and Midwestern Agrarian Intellectuals," 178–9.

[54] Henry Wallace, "Land Use: Toward a Unified Land Policy," *Planning Problems* (Octo-ber 1934); Kirkendall, *Social Scientists and Farm Politics*. Also see Tim Lehman, *Public Values, Private Lands: Farmland Preservation Policy, 1933–1985* (1995); and Wilson oral history, CUOH.

[55] Hooker, "Land Utilization Program"; H. H. Wooten, *The Land Utilization Program, 1934 to 1964* (GPO, 1965); Margaret R. Purcell, "A Quarter Century of Land Economics in the Department of Agriculture, 1919–44," October 1945, manuscript in possession of author; Tugwell, "The Place of Government in a National Land Program," *Journal*

The land utilization projects began in a moment of détente between the Departments of Agriculture and Interior, and with a compromise over their traditional bone of contention: the reclamation program. Interior Secretary Harold Ickes, who also directed the new Public Works Administration (PWA), intended to direct some of the emergency funds that Congress had made available in 1933 to the completion of Hoover Dam and to the construction of new irrigation and hydropower projects. Critics of the reclamation program declared it foolish and irresponsible to increase farm production in the midst of low prices and accumulating agricultural surpluses. Although Ickes defended the Reclamation Bureau and would continue to do so, he agreed that federal land policy required a more coordinated approach. With the help of L. C. Gray and M. L. Wilson, an interdepartmental committee recommended that public works money fund the retirement of marginal and submarginal land to offset any increases in cultivated acreage from new irrigation projects. In December 1933, Ickes released $25 million for such purposes.[56]

The submarginal land program supplemented the Taylor Grazing Act of 1934, which closed the remainder of the public domain to further settlement. By this time the land still open for homestead entry was restricted to the arid and semiarid portions of the West, areas characterized by overgrazed and deteriorating land. This poor land, in the eyes of the agricultural economists who helped draft the legislation, simply could not support more farm families. The act's formulators also intended to halt the environmental degradation of the open, unregulated range by empowering the Interior Department to create self-governing grazing districts and to manage a grazing permit system. Yet environmental protection was not the program's only rationale: it was also intended to raise prices for stock growers. This hopeful combination of sustainability, profitability, and local control mixed a classic New Deal concoction, the conflicting pressures of whose goals were kept in check only briefly by the stagnant economy and the strong arm of Secretary Ickes.[57]

of *Farm Economics* 16 (1934); FERA, "Six Rural Problem Areas"; "Land Utilization Projects," Records of P. K. Hooker, NA RG 114, Entry 35, Box 7.

[56] Wooten, *Land Utilization Program*; Hooker, "Land Utilization Program"; Joint Committee to Harold Ickes, 1933, Records of P. K. Hooker, NA RG 114, Entry 35, Box 4; Purcell, "Quarter Century of Land Economics"; Mordecai Ezekiel oral history, CUOH.

[57] Richard Lowitt, *The New Deal and the West* (1984), 68, passim. On the public domain and the Taylor Act, also see Roy M. Robbins, *Our Landed Heritage: The Public Domain, 1776–1936* (1950); and E. Louise Peffer, *The Closing of the Public Domain: Disposal and Reservation Policies, 1900–1950* (1951).

If the Taylor Act signaled the end of the homestead era, the land utilization program marked its reversal. For the first time, the federal government purchased property with the belief that farmers had settled poor land unknowingly and that they were now pinned by economic and environmental forces beyond their control. Planners in the Agriculture Department applauded the land purchase program because they believed it symbolized the federal government's new attention to the twin evils of rural poverty and resource degradation. At the close of the New Deal's first year, Rexford Tugwell hoped that the government would perform two functions with respect to the land: that it would obtain and administer areas "not effectively operated under private ownership," and that it would require individuals to maintain "continuous productivity" on private holdings.[58]

Because administrators like Gray and Tugwell intended land purchases to relieve rural distress, the land utilization program quickly merged with other federal relief efforts. In 1934, the land program joined forces with the Federal Emergency Relief Administration (FERA), an independent welfare agency under the direction of Harry Hopkins. FERA was established to assist unemployed workers across the nation, and at first Hopkins made no distinction between the rural and the urban poor. However, he soon discovered that the farm situation required a more coordinated plan of attack. In 1934, he announced the formation of a Division of Rural Rehabilitation to promote self-support among farm families. This division administered rural assistance "in place," or on the family's own land, but it also provided rehabilitation "on the wing" for others uprooted by crop failure, foreclosure, or government buyout of submarginal land. Under Gray's direction, the Land Policy Section of the AAA selected lands to be purchased, as well as lands onto which the displaced farmers might be resettled. FERA then worked with the individual farmers, most often through state rural rehabilitation corporations financed by the federal government.[59]

The land program received an unexpected shot in the arm from a major drought that settled over the western states in the summer of 1934. While crops withered and livestock starved, FERA added 550,000 additional farm families to its relief rolls. Lorena Hickock, Harry Hopkins's traveling

[58] Kirkendall, *Social Scientists and Farm Politics*; Tugwell, "The Place of Government," 55.
[59] Hooker, "Land Utilization Program"; "History of the Farm Security Administration," n.d., LVF; Purcell, "Quarter Century of Land Economics"; Kirkendall, *Social Scientists and Farm Politics*; Baldwin, *Poverty and Politics*; Paul E. Mertz, *New Deal Policy and Southern Rural Poverty* (1978).

investigator, reported from Williston, North Dakota, that 95 percent of
the area's farmers had gone bankrupt. "Those whose wheat crops were
ruined by drought or grasshoppers or hail – and there are a lot of them –
are destitute," she wrote, "and the livestock men are not getting enough
for their products to carry them through winter." Roosevelt asked the
Congress for special relief funds to address the emergency, and Congress
appropriated an additional $5 million. A new federal agency, the Drought
Relief Service, coordinated the work of the AAA, the USDA, and FERA,
and purchased livestock in danger of dying from heat and starvation.
Many New Dealers, including the president, interpreted the emergency as
a confirmation of their belief that these arid areas should never have been
settled so densely in the first place. "Many million acres of such land must
be returned to grass or trees if we are to prevent a new and man-made
Sahara," declared FDR. A journalist following the drought for *Survey
Graphic* concurred: "If nature regularly kept a non-agricultural grassland
in a certain region, it is not an act of God if we go there to begin farming
and fail for want of rain." It seemed that the only permanent solution
must involve purchasing submarginal land and relocating willing families
elsewhere. "Human knowledge," Roosevelt proclaimed, "is great enough
today to give us assurances of success in carrying through the abandonment of many millions of acres for agricultural use and the replacing of
these acres with others on which at least a living can be earned."[60]

Roosevelt followed up these statements by appointing a National
Resources Board (NRB) to prepare a report. Chaired by Interior Secretary
Harold Ickes, the board included Agriculture Secretary Henry Wallace and
Relief Administrator Harry Hopkins. In just five months, the NRB assem-
bled the first comprehensive inventory of the nation's land, water, and
mineral resources. M. L. Wilson and L. C. Gray directed the NRB's Land
Planning Committee, which also included Hugh H. Bennett, chief of the
Soil Erosion Service, and Mordecai Ezekiel, now an economic adviser to
Henry Wallace. Echoing the land utilization reports of the 1920s and early
1930s, the Land Committee blamed the epidemic of farm abandonment,

[60] Martha B. Bruère, "Lifting the Drought," *SG* (November 1934); Hickock to Hop-
kins, 1933, in Richard Lowitt and Maurine Beasley, eds., *One Third of a Nation:
Lorena Hickock Reports on the Great Depression* (1981); R. Douglas Hurt, *The
Dust Bowl: An Agricultural and Social History* (1981), 106–7; J. Russell Smith, "The
Drought – Act of God and Freedom," *SG* (September 1934), 412; Harry Hopkins,
Work Relief Administration Press Conference, 1934, New Deal Network, http://newdeal.
feri.org/workrelief/hop06.htm, posted 7/14/02; Roosevelt to the Congress, 1934, *FDRC*,
290.

bankruptcies, and foreclosures on the cultivation of marginal and erodable land. It recommended that the federal government acquire some 75 million acres of land, mostly in the South and the Great Lakes states and on the Great Plains. Such purchases, the Land Committee believed, would relieve the mounting distress of farm occupants and rural communities. It also believed submarginal land purchases would allow a more permanent and prosperous rural culture to develop. The committee members hoped that the industrial economy might recover, but they assumed that most of the present and future farm population must remain on the land. Therefore they recommended that federal land policy should help farmers steer a "middle course" between total self-sufficiency and extreme forms of commercial agriculture.[61]

The NRB Land Report, issued in December 1934, sanctioned the land purchase projects and rehabilitation schemes initiated a year before. The land utilization program, however, did not remain long under FERA jurisdiction. In 1935 it moved to the Resettlement Administration, and it traveled from there to the Bureau of Agricultural Economics and to the Soil Conservation Service, where it reached its final resting place in 1938. Still, despite this persistent reshuffling, the land program's administrators faced the same questions throughout the decade: what to do with the purchased land and what to do with the land's inhabitants. To address the first question, a submarginal land committee composed of representatives from the AAA's Land Policy Section, the National Park Service, the Bureau of Biological Survey, and the Office of Indian Affairs decided whether each purchase area would become an agricultural rehabilitation site, a recreational park, a wildlife preserve, or a Native American project. They then turned the land over to the relevant department or agency, which generally employed members of the Civilian Conservation Corps (CCC) and local unemployed workers to restore the land and to build new infrastructure, such as roads and recreational facilities. By 1938, land utilization projects covered portions of just about every state. In North Carolina, for example, fifteen thousand acres of worn-out cotton land were transformed into the William B. Umstead State Park. Large sections of clear-cut land in the Florida panhandle were replanted with trees and added to the Apalachicola National Forest and the St. Marks Migratory Waterfowl Refuge. And on the western plains, the Cimarron,

[61] Purcell, "Quarter Century of Land Economics"; National Resources Board, *A Report on National Planning and Public Works* (GPO, 1934), 105. Also see Lehman, *Public Values, Private Lands.*

Thunder Basin, Kiowa, and Comanche National Grasslands began as land utilization projects designed to provide relief to victims of drought and dust. By 1946, when Congress halted further land purchases, the federal government had acquired over 11 million acres, a figure far short of the recommended 75 million but significant nonetheless.[62]

The rehabilitation and resettlement of the land's occupants posed a different set of difficulties. Two separate agencies initiated the New Deal's rural community projects outside the Tennessee Valley: FERA's Rural Rehabilitation Division and the Interior Department's Division of Subsistence Homesteads. The subsistence homesteads program, as authorized by Title II of the National Industrial Recovery Act, aimed to provide for "the redistribution of the overbalance of population in industrial centers." This language reflected the legislation's primary intent: to relieve industrial, not necessarily rural, distress. After the onset of the Depression, many jobless and newly impoverished workers had sought refuge and security in the country. From 1930 to 1934, more people migrated to the country than to the city, and the number of farms increased to an all-time high. Though the back-to-the-land movement occurred across the country, it was concentrated in the heavily industrialized areas of New England, the Mid-Atlantic, and the Far West. Many reformers and politicians, including the president, viewed this migration as an appropriate response to the industrial emergency. They hoped that the government might inaugurate a more decentralized society by guiding and directing the development of self-sufficient and part-time farming communities. By executive order Roosevelt assigned this task to the Interior Department and recruited M. L. Wilson from the AAA to serve as its director.[63]

Wilson had first caught Roosevelt's attention as the public architect of the voluntary domestic allotment plan (the AAA), but the two men soon found themselves in agreement on the need for a long-range program of submarginal land retirement and industrial decentralization. Wilson accepted that the "engineered agriculture" of the future would require

[62] Wooten, *Land Utilization Program*; Hooker, "Land Utilization Program"; "History of the Farm Security Administration"; Phoebe Cutler, *The Public Landscape of the New Deal* (1985), 71–3; Michael Carlebach and Eugene F. Provenzo, Jr., *Farm Security Administration Photographs of Florida* (1993), 18–19; R. Douglas Hurt, "Federal Land Reclamation in the Dust Bowl," *Great Plains Quarterly* 6 (1986).

[63] "General Information Concerning the Purposes and Policies of the Division of Subsistence Homesteads"; Edmund de S. Brunner and Irving Lorge, *Rural Trends in Depression Years* (1937); Paul K. Conkin, *Tomorrow a New World: The New Deal Community Program* (1959); Wilson, "A New Land-Use Program: The Place of Subsistence Homesteads," *Journal of Land and Public Utility Economics* 10 (1934).

fewer workers and larger farms. Certainly, his experiments with large-scale wheat farming during the 1920s had pointed in this direction. "It has been estimated that we could easily release two million of the six million families now on the land," he remarked in 1932. However, the onset of the Depression had shaken Wilson's confidence and had propelled him to the center of New Deal efforts to help farmers remain on the land – where else could the supposedly "releasable" farmers find employment? "How can these two million families ... be fitted into the walks of life without great human sacrifice?" he asked. "This comes very near to the crux of the agricultural problem."[64]

Echoing A. E. Morgan and H. A. Morgan of TVA, Wilson argued that agricultural and industrial policy could both rehabilitate submarginal farmers and restore balance to the rural-urban relationship. He believed in the potential for building a "twilight zone" between industry and agriculture: new factories in rural areas would provide manufacturing jobs, and small subsistence homesteads would allow farmers to combine some wage work with part-time farming. TVA, Wilson claimed, had already embraced this philosophy with its plans for the model town of Norris; A. E. Morgan, in fact, offered Wilson help and encouragement. Wilson also had the support of Secretary of Agriculture Henry Wallace, who declared that "the human waste on poor land is even more appalling than the soil waste" and predicted that America's "new frontier" might consist of "thousands of self-subsistence homestead communities properly related to decentralized industry."[65]

Though Wilson usually emphasized the relationship between subsistence homesteads and submarginal land purchases, the program attempted to serve populations other than stranded farmers. It initiated several experiments: workers' garden homesteads near small industrial centers; projects for stranded industrial workers such as coal miners; programs for the elimination of "rural slums" on submarginal land; and projects undertaken in cooperation with the Bureau of Reclamation to resettle unsuccessful dry farmers onto irrigation sites. Though Wilson managed to begin

---

[64] Russell Lord, "The Rebirth of Rural Life: Part II," *SG* (December 1941), 687; Wilson oral history, CUOH; Wilson, "Planning Agriculture in Relation to Industry," *Rural America* (December 1934), 4; Wilson, "A New Land-Use Program."

[65] Wilson, "Decentralization of Industry in the New Deal," *Social Forces* 13 (1935); Wilson, "The Place of Subsistence Homesteads in Our National Economy," *Journal of Farm Economics* 16 (1934); Henry A. Wallace, *New Frontiers* (1934), 242–3, 286. Also see Henry Wallace to Frances Perkins and Harold Ickes, 5 April 1933, Suggestions for Economic Recovery, 1933, NA RG 48, Entry 767, Box 1.

thirty-two projects, the program was plagued by legal and administrative difficulties. Officials had little luck persuading industries to relocate, and pro-business members of Congress blocked efforts to fund such enterprises with public money. Interior Secretary Ickes also felt beleaguered by a program he neither requested nor desired, and he tightened federal controls over the local groups and private individuals who sponsored and developed the homesteads. After a managerial dispute with Ickes, Wilson resigned in June 1934 to accept a new post as assistant secretary of agriculture. However, Wilson's departure did not signal the end of his faith in the subsistence homesteads idea; he continued to believe that poor farmers might find greater security on better land and within "rurban" communities.[66]

FERA's Division of Rural Rehabilitation became the second New Deal agency to plan and to build rural communities. At the end of 1933, FERA announced that a million farm families, over 5 million people, drew all or part of their livelihood from federal relief checks. Further analysis revealed the highest rural relief loads concentrated in the Appalachian-Ozark region, the Cotton South, the Lakes states cutover, and the wheat sections of the Great Plains. Federal administrators believed that the problems of each area stemmed from disparate sources. The Appalachian-Ozark hills and the Lakes states cutover, they claimed, suffered from the "too rapid" development of small farms on marginal land and the loss of forestry and mining income. The problems of the wheat areas arose from a destructive combination of drought and unwise agricultural expansion in an arid region, and the welfare situation of the cotton areas reflected the "Negro problem" and the breakdown of the sharecropping and tenant system. Acknowledging these differences, FERA analysts nonetheless asserted that rural distress shared the same root cause everywhere: a frontier mentality of reckless individualism and heedless environmental destruction. "The frontier philosophy," a FERA report declared, "led to the present dilemma of stranded communities, bankrupt farmers, and widespread unemployment...[T]he rapid and heedless exploitation

[66] "Government Testing Value of Subsistence Homesteads," *New York Times*, 11 February 1934; "Misuse of the Nation's Land Leads Toward a New Policy," *New York Times*, 11 November 1934; "General Information Concerning the Purposes and Policies of the Division of Subsistence Homesteads"; Conkin, *Tomorrow a New World*; Kirkendall, *Social Scientists and Farm Politics*. Also see Donald Holley, *Uncle Sam's Farmers: The New Deal Communities in the Lower Mississippi Valley* (1975); and Harry C. McDean, "Social Scientists and Farm Poverty on the North American Plains, 1933–1940," *Great Plains Quarterly* 3 (1983).

of the human and natural resources in these areas bears tragic witness to the fruits of such a philosophy." It followed from such notions that attempts to assist poor farmers would also address the problem of poor land.[67]

Lawrence Westbrook, who headed FERA's Division of Rural Rehabilitation, intended to eliminate the need for direct relief by providing farmers with the means for self-support. Under Westbrook's direction, the division developed three assistance strategies. First, it acquired L. C. Gray's land retirement program and continued the process of selecting and purchasing submarginal lands. It also developed a community-building program similar to that of the subsistence homesteads division. Westbrook shared M. L. Wilson's belief that the federal government should guide and supervise the back-to-the-land movement. He thought that unemployed and distressed farmers could become self-supporting when helped to build and to purchase small subsistence plots within planned rural communities. The end goal, Westbrook stressed, was not to create competition for the AAA's reduction program by increasing the acreage of staple crops but to equip needy farmers to produce their own food and feed. He argued that additional cash income could be earned from village-based industries or part-time work on construction projects. The third, and largest, rural rehabilitation effort was the administration of "supervised credit" for farmers already located on productive land. Though these loans largely paid for livestock and farm supplies, they were also intended to help poor farmers, especially tenants, improve the land and protect it from further erosion. Though FERA intended to create a national program, the vast majority of its rehabilitation clients were located in the South.[68]

While the back-to-the land movement influenced FERA's activities, its rural rehabilitation efforts departed substantially from the subsistence homesteads model. First, FERA did not initiate projects for city dwellers; its clients consisted entirely of rural relief recipients. As Lorena Hickock wrote to Harry Hopkins from South Carolina, FERA's intent was not to move industrial workers into the country but to take "people who are already on the land – thousands of share-croppers, tenant farmers, farm hands, who are existing in tumbledown shacks ... cluttering up farms where there is no employment for them," and to provide them with

---

[67] "History of the Farm Security Administration"; Wilson, "Rural Rehabilitation," 1935, WP 00003, 6:24; FERA, "Six Rural Problem Areas," 7.
[68] Baldwin, *Poverty and Politics;* Conkin, *Tomorrow a New World;* Wilson, "Rural Rehabilitation"; Mertz, *New Deal Policy.*

modest credit and supervision. Though FERA did initiate several community projects, the lion's share of the relief funds went to individual clients.[69]

A different approach to rural economic diversification also separated the original subsistence homesteads concept from FERA's strategy. Conceived as part of the omnibus industrial recovery measure, the subsistence homesteads division had hoped to persuade industries to locate in rural areas. But the division never had much success in doing so. After M. L. Wilson left Subsistence Homesteads to become the assistant secretary of agriculture, he supported an alternate approach embraced by FERA and Westbrook: the encouragement of permanent part-time work in village- and farm-based industries. Along with A. E. and H. A. Morgan of TVA, Wilson argued that farming alone could not support all of the country's rural occupants, and that alternate employment opportunities could be found in supplemental activities linked closely with farm and forestry work. In 1935, he proudly claimed that work centers located near rural relief projects had provided FERA clients with jobs in food and feed processing, in forestry and wood-products work, and on soil conservation projects. Wilson also justified these efforts with an appeal to the underconsumptionist analysis of the Depression. Rural rehabilitation and conservation, he declared, built up farmers' buying power and contributed to national industrial recovery.[70]

FERA planned and initiated a total of twenty-eight projects: fifteen in the South, ten in Nebraska and the Dakotas, and one each in Minnesota, Arizona, and New Mexico. Some of these were all-rural farming communities, others experiments in village and industrial planning. FERA built its largest farm community in Mississippi County, Arkansas. W. R. Dyess, the state's relief administrator, purchased a swamp and cutover timberland with federal funds, drained the swamp, built roads and bridges, and constructed hundreds of cottages. When the formal dedication of Dyess Colony took place in May 1936, the community contained five hundred farms, ranging in size from twenty to forty acres. One of the most publicized rural-industrial projects, Pine Mountain Valley, was created in Harris County, Georgia. Relief administrators there planned for settlers to grow specialized truck crops and to work in small industries. They

---

[69] Conkin, *Tomorrow a New World*; Hickock to Hopkins, 5 February 1934, quoted in Mertz, *New Deal Policy*, 65–6.
[70] Wilson, "Rural Rehabilitation."

built three hundred homesteads, a church, an electric power system, and a cannery, fish hatchery, dairy, sawmill, and vineyard.[71]

As Donald Holley argues in his study of the farm projects of the Lower Mississippi Valley, the New Deal farm communities initially won the support of key southern congressmen such as Joseph Robinson, Theodore Bilbo, Pat Harrison, and Wilbur Mills. In 1936, a Gallup poll even showed over 80 percent of respondents from Arkansas, Mississippi, and Louisiana in favor of federal legislation to assist farm tenants. But FERA's work in the South soon encountered fierce opposition. Lacking the clear congressional mandate enjoyed by the AAA, its relief projects drew criticism from landowners who wanted a seasonal supply of inexpensive labor and from the American Farm Bureau, which accused FERA of responding to socialistic and communistic influences. The efforts to serve black clients alongside whites also raised southern hackles. Even though the New Deal administrators proceeded extremely cautiously – some would say far too cautiously – in limiting racial mixing and in restricting the use of "Negro personnel," many southerners feared that the New Dealers ultimately intended to overturn Jim Crow. "I know that the aim of this Administration is to force racial equality on us here in the South," wrote one Mississippi woman, "and the farm program is the biggest weapon they have."[72]

The criticism of FERA and the early New Deal relief efforts was not confined to racists or the Farm Bureau; it also came from the left and from groups like the Southern Tenant Farmer's Union. Rural rehabilitation programs helped only a limited number of clients and rarely touched the most impoverished farmers. Furthermore, the AAA consistently exacerbated relief problems in the South by distributing parity payments to landowners while doing little to enforce the requirement that tenants and sharecroppers share those benefits. By the beginning of 1935, the USDA progressives agreed that adequate administrative instruments for coping with rural poverty did not yet exist. The AAA had begun to balance farm and urban incomes, but it did not assist those near or at the bottom of the agricultural ladder. The Subsistence Homesteads Division, while an interesting experiment, had mixed up the urban with the rural unemployed and had not developed a consistent approach to the needs of

---

[71] Conkin, *Tomorrow a New World*; Holley, *Uncle Sam's Farmers*; Roosevelt to Brown, 1938, FDRC, 276–7.

[72] Holley, *Uncle Sam's Farmers*, 175–89; Ruby Pugh to George Mitchell, 1941, quoted in Holley, *Uncle Sam's Farmers*, 185.

poor farmers. The land purchase program and FERA's Division of Rural Rehabilitation, these planners believed, contained the most promising approaches.[73]

BURIED IN DIRT: THE RESETTLEMENT IDEA AND
THE FUTURE OF THE GREAT PLAINS

By the spring of 1935 New Dealers recognized that no single agency was prepared to do battle with chronic farm poverty. At that moment quintessential urban liberal Rexford Tugwell took up the cause. Frustrated by daily reminders that the AAA penalized poor farmers, and disillusioned by the haphazard and uncoordinated strategy of the country's rural programs, Tugwell decided that the time was ripe for a new approach. This new approach, he hoped, would be based upon the single premise that rural rehabilitation must begin with land retirement. Tugwell believed that government purchase of submarginal land offered the only permanent solution to the problem of low-income farmers. Such lands should never have been farmed and they should be restored to a condition that "nature would tolerate." Much of this land, he recognized, already lay abandoned; poor and drought-stricken farmers had simply picked up and moved on. If left to itself, the misused and abandoned land would further compound the problems of erosion and floods. Moreover, it would continue to tempt new settlers when conditions improved, thereby restarting the vicious cycle of agricultural expansion, economic contraction, and farmer entrapment. The heart of his conception, Tugwell explained, "was the simultaneous attack on the wastage of people and the inefficient use of resources, each of which was so much the cause of the other that they were inextricably linked."[74]

Tugwell discussed these ideas with M. L. Wilson, Henry Wallace, and the president. In April, Roosevelt established an independent agency, the Resettlement Administration (RA), by executive order and with funds from the congressional relief appropriation of 1935. The order named Tugwell as the RA's director and gave the new agency the authority to purchase land, to undertake conservation and land restoration projects,

---

[73] Mertz, *New Deal Policy*; Kirkendall, *Social Scientists and Farm Politics*; Baldwin, *Poverty and Politics*.

[74] Baldwin, *Poverty and Politics*; Bernard Sternsher, *Rexford Tugwell and the New Deal* (1964); Will W. Alexander oral history, CUOH; Resettlement Administration, *America's Land* (GPO, 1936); Tugwell, "The Resettlement Idea," *Agricultural History* 33 (1959), 160.

to build resettlement communities, and to make rural rehabilitation loans. The RA absorbed the subsistence homesteads program, FERA's rural projects, and FERA's rural rehabilitation division. It also acquired L. C. Gray's two land planning offices: the Land Planning Section of the BAE and the Land Policy Section of the AAA. In short, Roosevelt and Tugwell had a created a new administrative entity devoted to the twin problems of poor people and poor land, but one independent of the USDA, the AAA, and the federal relief establishment. The brief experiment would throw into sharp relief the political and environmental boundaries of liberal policy.[75]

The RA's Land Utilization Division selected and purchased submarginal land and converted it to pastures, forests, wildlife preserves, and parks. It also cooperated with the Works Progress Administration (WPA) in coordinating the employment of stranded families on the restoration projects – planting trees and grasses, building dams, and constructing roads. The Resettlement Division carried out the work of relocation. It inherited the projects begun by Subsistence Homesteads and FERA, and initiated more community farming projects and camps for uprooted and migratory families. The Rehabilitation Division took over FERA's standard loan program and operated several additional lending programs.[76]

By the end of 1936, the RA had purchased over 9 million acres, more than half of which were tax-delinquent, and had begun restoration with the help of the Soil Conservation Service, the Forest Service, the CCC, and federal relief labor. It had completed nineteen rural resettlement projects, built over twenty-five hundred rural homes, and begun construction on forty-four additional rural communities. It had made supervised loans to almost four hundred thousand farm families and distributed emergency grants to almost eight hundred thousand families. The RA's director, however, did not view these activities as equally important. In particular, Tugwell took a dim view of rehabilitation in place. Permanent reform, he believed, must always begin with the deeper malady: poor land use. Therefore he stressed submarginal land purchases and farmer relocation. A longtime critic of the back-to-the-land movement, he also scorned what he saw as the romantic escapism of subsistence farming. When the RA took over projects begun under FERA or the Subsistence Homesteads

---

[75] Kirkendall, *Social Scientists and Farm Politics*; Sternsher, *Rexford Tugwell*; Hooker, "Land Utilization Program"; Gray, "The Social and Economic Implications of the Land Program"; "History of the Farm Security Administration."

[76] "History of the Farm Security Administration"; Resettlement Administration, *America's Land*; Hooker, "Land Utilization Program."

Division, it often consolidated the small plots into larger and more mechanized units, and often dropped the emphasis on part-time work in village industries.[77]

Tugwell certainly hoped that New Deal policy might jumpstart the manufacturing and service sectors, and he believed that industrial recovery would eventually provide more choices to both farmers and rural planners. In the meantime, however, he worked with the RA to help farmers stay in farming. Tugwell's assumption that rural living standards were linked to the availability and use of natural resources established his credentials as a New Conservationist and linked him to the policy community of rural resource planners. When this network was first forged during the 1920s, its members had agreed that submarginal land retirement and farmer relocation might be necessary to address the unfortunate consequences of agricultural overexpansion. The land purchase and rural resettlement programs represented the culmination of this line of thinking: the federal government would add more land – erodable and deteriorating land that should never have been farmed in the first place – to a protected public domain. This strategy, however, posed predictable difficulties: which communities, which farmers, would bear the sacrifice?

Just as the South, and later the Far West, would play the primary roles in establishing the social limits of liberal conservation policy (insofar as planners would hit resistance to further efforts to assist the small farmer and the minority poor), the western plains would establish the environmental boundaries of New Deal agricultural policy. Plains farmers and their political representatives did not want to hear that the grassland should never have been plowed, or that the government intended to obtain and retain large chunks of it. "[When] the New Deal really tried to become new and innovative," as Donald Worster argues in his study of the Dust Bowl, "plainsmen turned hostile."[78] As a result, a different strain of the New Conservation – rehabilitation in place – would gain ground. Propelled by the western drought, and by instances of local resistance to land purchases and to the resettlement idea, the New Dealers helped institute voluntary strategies to help farmers remain on their own land and to see immediate returns.

---

[77] Resettlement Administration, *What the Resettlement Administration Has Done* (GPO, 1936); Alexander oral history, CUOH; Lehman, *Public Values, Private Lands*; Conkin, *Tomorrow a New World*; Sternsher, *Rexford Tugwell*; Rexford Tugwell, *The Brains Trust* (1968).

[78] Donald Worster, *Dust Bowl: The Southern Plains in the 1930s* (1979), 28.

Indeed, no one series of events more influenced this direction in agrarian conservation policy than the western drought and the Dust Bowl. While much of the country experienced unusually dry weather during the 1930s, the central plains states bore the brunt of repeated droughts. Though plains farmers everywhere faced withered crops and starving livestock, the residents of the southern plains suffered from dust storms and severe wind erosion. For the most part they had arrived in the years following World War I, pushing onto arid lands where success was far from certain and hoping to cultivate large sections of wheat with the aid of gasoline tractors and combine harvesters. As wheat prices dropped in the 1920s, the settlers borrowed money for more machinery and broke sod for more wheat. They used a new form of agricultural technology – the one-way disc plow – because it broke the sod and destroyed weeds faster. It also laid bare large stretches of erodable soils that were particularly vulnerable to overcropping. Drought, preventing the wheat from growing and holding the soil intact, first appeared in the summer of 1931, when one-third of the Panhandle area of Oklahoma, Texas, western Kansas, southeastern Colorado, and northeastern New Mexico was plowed under and the soil exposed. Strong winds whipped the dirt into dust clouds that wreaked havoc for the next several years. Federal officials estimated that a single dust storm in May 1934 carried away 300 million tons of fertile topsoil, some of it as far as the Atlantic Ocean. A 1936 survey of fourteen Dust Bowl counties disclosed that 54 percent of the land planted to grain had been blown out. That same year nearly 20 percent of the cropland in forty-five counties lay idle, and one out of every four farm homes had been abandoned.[79]

The western drought and the Dust Bowl highlighted the problem of soil erosion and drew the nation's attention to the plight of those caught in its vise. Many Dust Bowl residents, weighted with poverty and desperation, left their homes. However, as R. Douglas Hurt has shown, most farmers remained in the area and profited from government relief and reconstruction programs. The Dust Bowl area, in fact, received more federal funds per capita than any other agricultural region. And in the plains states as a whole, drought-stricken farmers benefited immediately from AAA payments, emergency cattle purchases, emergency listing funds, soil conservation programs, relief grants, crop and seed loans, and jobs with

---

[79] Works Progress Administration, *Areas of Intense Drought Distress, 1930–1936* (GPO, 1937); Hurt, *Dust Bowl*; Carl C. Taylor, Helen W. Wheeler, and E. L. Kirkpatrick, *Disadvantaged Classes in American Agriculture* (GPO, 1938). Also see Worster, *Dust Bowl*.

the WPA and the PWA. The tragedy also provided a new opportunity for a number of federal officials to denounce the "pioneer psychology" that had resulted in such degradation. "Not until the frontier had dissolved into the Pacific did we realize that the opportunity to abandon worn-out land for new was gone," wrote Henry Wallace at the end of 1935. "Recent dust storms," he continued, "shook us out of this lethargy, warned us dramatically . . . that practically all the better lands have been occupied for agriculture, that much formerly fertile land has been ruined or greatly impoverished, and that considerably more land will go the same way unless we take steps to save it."[80]

Exactly which "steps" would save the Great Plains was a matter of some dispute. In 1934, the Land Committee of the National Resources Board had recommended the withdrawal from cultivation of some 75 million acres of crop and pasture land. While the committee lauded efforts to control both wind and water erosion, it insisted that a large proportion of recently settled land should be devoted to other uses. In particular, the Land Report targeted large regions of Oklahoma, Colorado, Wyoming, the Dakotas, and Montana as places to encourage permanent farm retirement. The report and its policy corollary, the land utilization program, provided one possible answer to the problem of the plains: resettlement and restoration. It also formed the basis for the president's declaration in June 1934 that much of the arid plains should be returned to grass, and for Rexford Tugwell's hope that land retirement might serve as one of the region's primary reconstruction strategies.[81]

Between 1933 and 1946, the federal government acquired over 7 million acres on the northern and southern plains and in the Southwest. Though land purchases became quite controversial, many plains residents asked to be relieved of tax-delinquent and submarginal land. Many farmers also begged for the opportunity to move to a resettlement project; applications for each project far exceeded the openings available. Mayme and Bert Stagner, for example, had settled on a Colorado plains farm in 1930 but had suffered "total disaster" two years later when drought ruined their crop. Bert attempted to find work as a day laborer on some of the more established farms in Baca County, but the wind storms, as his wife recalled, had piled up sand and dust, wiping out "everything for

[80] Hurt, *Dust Bowl*; David B. Danbom, *Born in the Country: A History of Rural America* (1995), 225; Lowitt, *New Deal and the West*, 39; Wallace, "Report of the Secretary of Agriculture," *1935 Yearbook of Agriculture* (GPO, 1936), 60.
[81] National Resources Board, *A Report on National Planning and Public Works*, 175–77; Roosevelt to the Congress, 1934, FDRC, 290; Tugwell to Roosevelt, 1935, FDRC, 519.

everybody." Federal officials soon designated much of southeastern Colorado as submarginal and planned a land utilization project for the area. In 1936, Mayme heard that the government was planning to construct a resettlement community in the San Luis Valley for families from the Colorado plains, and she wrote to President Roosevelt asking for a chance to get out, "to have a home and live a decent life."[82]

What enticed many of these plains farmers to their new homes on resettlement projects was the promise of water. Some residents whose land had been slated for retirement received letters informing them of resettlement opportunities where they might "purchase farms and homes where the rainfall is more plentiful... or where it is possible to irrigate the land." Such rosy promises inspired more than a few families to pack their bags. Selah and Nellie Converse had worked a four-hundred-acre dry farm in Montana for seventeen years, but suffered from crop failure nine years in a row. When they heard of the community planned for Fairfield Bench, Montana, Nellie declared that she would trade the dry farm for "anything as long as there was plenty of water." Indeed, many resettlement communities, particularly in the Mountain West, were constructed as irrigation projects with the assistance of the Bureau of Reclamation, the PWA, and the WPA.[83]

While the federal government helped many farmers displaced by land purchases to become irrigation farmers, it also attempted to transform plains agriculture into a ranching economy by regrassing and reseeding submarginal lands and by consolidating some of the land utilization purchases into public grazing districts. Ranching, in the eyes of the land analysts, formed a less risky endeavor, and one more suited to the arid environment. Unlike growing crops, which exposed soils to wind and water erosion, grazing required farmers to maintain and protect a permanent vegetative cover. For the Milk River project in northern Montana, one of the largest land utilization and resettlement schemes in the nation, the government purchased almost 1 million acres of abandoned farmland and overgrazed pasture, restored the grass, and built check dams

[82] Wooten, *Land Utilization Program*; Hurt, "Federal Land Reclamation"; Mayme Stagner quoted in Brian Q. Cannon, *Remaking the Agrarian Dream: New Deal Rural Resettlement in the Mountain West* (1996), 20–6.

[83] Cannon, *Remaking the Agrarian Dream*, 2, 29, 57–72. Donald J. Pisani also makes the point that historians often overlook the smaller reclamation projects owing to the enormous publicity given to the high dams of the New Deal: see *Water and American Government: The Reclamation Bureau, National Water Policy, and the West, 1902–1935* (2002), 151–2.

and stock-watering ponds. The RA helped some of the impoverished dry farmers relocate onto irrigated tracts by the river, but set up most as stock raisers organized into grazing associations.[84]

Despite such examples, neither the RA agenda of land retirement and farmer resettlement nor the New Deal's initial attempt to "lower expectations" by encouraging a shift from cropping to grazing represented the ultimate direction of New Deal agricultural conservation.[85] All these measures tested the limits of American farmers' willingness to cede authority to the public sphere and to federal experts. More important, permanent land restrictions aggravated farmers and community boosters who wanted to get on with the more profitable business of growing wheat. They accepted relief, not reform.[86] Relief came to the plains with a set of conservationist remedies that began alongside the RA agenda but eventually eclipsed it: technical and noncoercive measures to halt soil erosion and to increase the productivity of private cropland. These remedies would ultimately characterize the liberal conservation regime, its limits along with its accomplishments.

Hugh H. Bennett, chief of the Soil Erosion Service, embodied this approach. During the 1920s, Bennett had drawn the nation's attention to the "national menace" of soil erosion, arguing that sheet and gully erosion explained lost fertility and decreased farm income. In 1929, Congress passed legislation authorizing several erosion experiment stations, and in 1933 Interior Secretary Harold Ickes allotted Bennett $10 million from the PWA for additional conservation work. Like the Tennessee Valley Authority, the Soil Erosion Service (SES) established demonstration projects and helped farmers implement voluntary conservation measures such as contour plowing, terracing, strip cropping, pasture building, and stock-watering ponds. The SES supplied technical direction as well as the machinery, seed, shrubs, and trees. It also worked with the Civilian Conservation Corps to supplement labor furnished by farm owners. By the fall of 1934, the SES operated thirty-one demonstration projects in twenty-eight states. In Greenville County, South Carolina, for example, the SES helped farmers replant eroded slopes and diversify their crop mixes; in Jewell County, Kansas, the SES showed residents how to increase grain

---

[84] Hurt, "Federal Land Reclamation"; Mary W. M. Hargreaves, *Dry Farming in the Northern Great Plains: Years of Readjustment, 1920–1990* (1993); Wooten, *Land Utilization Program;* Resettlement Administration, *America's Land;* Cannon, *Remaking the Agrarian Dream.*

[85] Lowitt, *New Deal and the West,* chapters 3 and 4.

[86] Worster, *Dust Bowl,* 129.

yields and to prevent gullies by terracing their land and plowing on the contour.[87]

The SES – renamed the Soil Conservation Service (SCS) under the Department of Agriculture in 1935 – established several wind erosion demonstration projects in the Dust Bowl area. Farmers signed on to the program, agreeing to cooperate with the SCS for five years. The benefits of the most basic soil-preserving measure, contour plowing, were appreciated by 1936, when a group of skeptical Texas farmers watched in surprise as one of their neighbors grew 160 acres of feed on his contoured land. The SCS also emphasized the utility of terracing, arguing that a two-inch rain could be converted into a seven-inch rain with the aid of terracing and contouring. In addition, conservation officials promoted the strip cropping of drought-resistant, soil-holding feed crops. Superior wheat and sorghum yields on the demonstration farms, along with a reduction in soil blowing, illustrated the benefits of such methods throughout the 1930s. By the end of the decade, 80 percent of farmers under SCS contracts attributed increased net farm incomes to the conservation program, 89 percent attributed increased land values to the program, and a full 95 percent aimed to continue the conservation methods after their contracts ended.[88]

When M. L. Wilson, assistant secretary of agriculture and chairman of the NRB's Land Planning Committee, traveled through the drought states in 1935, he applauded all this contouring, terracing, and listing (listing works the surface of the soil, leaving it in alternating ridges and furrows, better able to withstand the wind). Yet, with one foot still in the land retirement camp, he warned that emergency tillage operations could never become a permanent solution. Wilson believed that the region must first jettison its high-stakes gambling mentality and retire its marginal land. Far too much light and erodable soil had been put under the plow to grow wheat and corn, Wilson claimed, and he doubted that any soil conservation methods would prevent wind erosion over the long term. Such lands must be taken out of private cultivation and made "the common property" of the people. Understanding political realities, however,

[87] Douglas Helms, ed., *Readings in the History of the Soil Conservation Service* (GPO, SCS Economics and Social Sciences Division, Historical Notes No.1, 1992); Hugh H. Bennett, "Huge Waste by Soil Erosion: The Nation Begins a Survey," *New York Times*, 14 May 1933; Soil Erosion Service, Memorandum for the Press, 5 October 1934, HBP, NA RG 114, Entry 21, Box 8; Neil Maher, "'Crazy Quilt Farming on Round Land': The Great Depression, the Soil Conservation Service, and the Politics of Landscape Change on the Great Plains During the New Deal," *Western Historical Quarterly* 31 (2000).

[88] Hurt, *Dust Bowl.*

Wilson also advised that cash cropping could and should continue in areas where farmers diligently employed techniques such as strip farming, contouring, terracing, and stubble retention.[89]

In essence, Wilson crafted his recommendations to appeal both to those conservationists who felt the plains should have never been plowed and to the farmers and community boosters who thought plains farmers could continue to raise cash crops. USDA officials such as Wilson found they had to steer this more cautious course because many drought-area residents and their political representatives feared that the administration ultimately intended to "depopulate" the plains. Indeed, the underlying philosophy of the RA – that land purchase and rural resettlement constituted the only sure long-term prescriptions – offended crop farmers who believed that drought alone was to blame for their difficulties. Most alarmingly for plains residents, the president himself appeared to be part of this conspiracy to return the cultivated fields to grass. At a press conference in early 1936, Roosevelt had declared that much of the plains should never have been plowed and that the dust storms were the result of using land for the wrong purpose. "Instead of using it for pasture," he asserted, "we are using it for wheat." Such statements provoked howls of indignant rage; Senator Morris Sheppard of Texas was so incensed he wrote to Roosevelt to remind the president that "hundreds of thousands of acres of wheat have been successfully cultivated in the Panhandle for the past quarter of a century." Sheppard enclosed a telegram signed by several of Amarillo's "prominent citizens" who wanted assurance that the value of Panhandle investments would not be destroyed and the people "transported to a land selected by others for them."[90]

Indeed, opposition to the land purchase program often occasioned local protests. In Musselshell County, Montana, and Perkins County, South Dakota, groups of settlers challenged the county commissioners' decision to sell tax-delinquent land to the federal government. They circulated petitions and showed up in large numbers at public meetings to express their dissatisfaction. One Perkins County farmer even vented his anger in verse:

> Submarginal land is here they say
> and should be taken right away . . .
> Far better leave us folks alone
> we'll struggle through and save our home.[91]

---

[89] Wilson, "Dust Storms and Rural Rehabilitation"; C. W. Warburton, Memorandum for M. L. Wilson, 1935, WP 00003, 6:26.

[90] Press Conference, 1936, *FDRC*, 469; Sheppard to Roosevelt, 1936, *FDRC*, 471.

[91] Hargreaves, *Dry Farming in the Northern Great Plains*, 122–3.

Faced with resistance to land purchases and to the idea of resettlement, the president and other conservation officials moderated both their rhetoric and their program. In July 1936, Tugwell attempted to reassure anxious plains residents that adjustment did not entail the complete abandonment of dry farming. "It is all too easy to conclude that all land subject to blowing or easy run-off ought to go back to grass or trees," he said; "it is not only impractical, but unnecessary." The president concurred: "Nobody," he insisted, "ever had any idea in their sane senses of depopulating the country." That summer Roosevelt appointed a Great Plains Drought Area Committee to study the drought area and to make recommendations on the most efficient use of the natural resources of the plains. It reported back by the end of August and counseled that soil conservation and the efficient use of water resources were basic to any long-range adjustment program. Though the committee did recommend that certain submarginal lands should be taken out of commercial production, it also took care to endorse the technical and engineering solutions that would increase the value of private land: contour plowing, listing, strip cropping, terracing, water spreading, and small dam construction.[92]

Following a late summer inspection trip through the drought area, Roosevelt spoke about his experience in a Fireside Chat and reiterated the Drought Committee's recommendations. The president took the opportunity to praise the resilience and determination of the farm families with whom he spoke on the tour, and to reiterate the message that nothing he witnessed "meant depopulating these areas." The people, he declared, were ready to use new methods "to meet changes in Nature" – soil and water conservation methods would enable more and more farmers "to maintain themselves on the land." Once again drawing upon the underconsumptionist analysis of the Depression, the president argued that the welfare of city workers depended on the security of the agricultural population. Helping farmers to remain on the land, he asserted, would strengthen the national economy. "We are going to conserve soil, conserve water, and conserve life," Roosevelt announced. "We are going to have a farm policy that will serve the national welfare."[93]

Shortly after his radio address, Roosevelt asked the Drought Committee's chairman, Morris Cooke of the Rural Electrification Administration, to direct a follow-up committee to report back on a long-term

[92] Tugwell, "Down to Earth," *Current History* 44 (July 1936), quoted in Hargreaves, *Dry Farming in the Northern Great Plains*, 120; Press Conference, 1936, *FDRC*, 539–40; Roosevelt to Cooke, 1936, *FDRC*, 541; "Great Plains Drought Area Committee Report," 1936, *FDRC*, 557–9.
[93] Speech by Roosevelt, 1936, *FDRC*, 568–71.

program for the plains. This new effort also included L. C. Gray of the Resettlement Administration and Hugh Bennett of the Soil Conservation Service, as well as personnel from the National Resources Committee, the Corps of Engineers, the Bureau of Reclamation, and the Works Progress Administration. Knowing that the committee might need to downplay land purchases and farmer resettlement for its conclusions to be accepted in the region, the president asked that Cooke and his colleagues "leave no stone unturned" in exploring how a reasonable standard of living could be obtained for the largest possible farm population.[94]

The committee submitted its report, *The Future of the Great Plains*, before the start of the new year. The report began, ominously enough, with a denunciation of the pioneering ethos. It declared that the present situation was the result not of a permanent change in climate but of man-made modifications to the environmental conditions of the plains. "There is no evidence," it asserted, "that in historic times there was ever a severe enough drought to destroy the grass roots and cause wind erosion comparable with that which took place in 1934 and 1936; that phenomenon is chargeable to . . . plowing and overcropping." The report argued that as range and croplands deteriorated, the tenancy rate rose, more farms were abandoned, and the region suffered from "a marked decline in the quality of living." Such conditions, in turn, led to a high degree of dependency; federal relief payments in some counties totaled as much as two hundred dollars per capita.[95]

Though the Great Plains Committee recommended the continuation of the land purchase program, it took pains to demonstrate an overarching commitment to the development of private property. The report emphasized that the lands to be purchased would consist only of "scattered" croplands, not large tracts, and that in many cases the prevention of "uneconomic and undesirable" farm occupancy could be made possible with means other than federal purchase. When urging further federal acquisition and government control of grazing land, for example, the report claimed that the government's role would be one of merely assisting cooperative and farmer-led grazing districts to develop a "manageable

[94] Roosevelt to Cooke, 1936, *FDRC*, 575–6.
[95] Great Plains Committee, *The Future of the Great Plains* (GPO, 1936), 2, 6. Also see Worster, *Dust Bowl*, 192–7; Lowitt, *New Deal and the West*, 44–6; and Gilbert F. White, "*The Future of the Great Plains* Revisited," *Great Plains Quarterly* 6 (1986). For a fascinating look at Dust Bowl historiography as postmodern puzzle, see William Cronon, "A Place for Stories: Nature, History, and Narrative," *Journal of American History* 78 (1992).

ownership pattern within their boundaries." Government credit, the report also argued, could help private operators enlarge their farms. Taking a similarly cautious approach to the issue of resettlement, the report noted that the resettlement program should be retained as an emergency relief program, but that the need for such stopgap measures would diminish as a long-term regional plan was put into place.[96]

Taking its cue from the president's initial directions, the Great Plains Report included a lengthy presentation of recommendations for improved water and soil conservation techniques. "The greatest natural handicap of the Great Plains," the report declared, "is the lack of sufficient rainfall." The report downplayed the feasibility of large-scale irrigation and reclamation projects, and it suggested that the federal government and the Bureau of Reclamation develop medium- and small-sized water projects, such as tributary storage reservoirs or pumping plants on major streams. It also encouraged local and state entities to assist farmers in constructing wells, farm ponds, and small reservoirs. Stressing the relationship between soil and water conservation, the report mentioned how soil conservation measures like listing and terracing captured rainfall and runoff for the growth of grass and cash crops. The report also highlighted other erosion control measures such as contour plowing, strip cropping, and crop diversification, and it included SCS photographs to illustrate these methods.[97]

All in all, despite its critical analysis of plains agriculture, *The Future of the Great Plains* concluded with an optimistic message for the region. The dust storms may have signaled an imbalance between man and nature, but a fail-safe set of methods and techniques would ensure both farm security and adequate standards of living. Furthermore, the report advised, a host of local, state, and federal agencies would help farmers retain, even expand, their foothold on the land.

Forged in large part on the western plains, this reorientation in conservation strategy signaled the beginning of the end for government land acquisition and farmer resettlement. The strategy of government ownership, more representative of the old Progressive conservation than the New Conservation, faced organized resistance when applied to rural areas where crop growing had been successful in the recent past and where it might be again. Farmers wanted help not only in remaining farmers but also in rebuilding the communities where they lived. Liberal conservation

---

[96] *Future of the Great Plains*, 71–8.
[97] *Future of the Great Plains*, 76–89.

policy had to operate within the political interstices provided by farmers' distress, their abused land, and their desire to shore up and expand their private operations. Four other kinds of aid soon overshadowed the land utilization and the resettlement projects: rural electrification, soil conservation, water control, and – for a brief moment – tenant assistance.

RURAL ELECTRIFICATION, SOIL CONSERVATION,
WATER CONTROL, AND FARM SECURITY

The optimistic concluding message of *The Future of the Great Plains* reflected the influence of Morris Cooke, the committee's chairman and the first director of the Rural Electrification Administration. As one of the leading contributors to the New Conservation during the 1920s and early 1930s, Cooke had worked with Governor Gifford Pinchot of Pennsylvania on an unsuccessful statewide plan to extend electric service to rural areas, and he served on New York's Power Authority at the request of Governor Franklin Roosevelt. Cooke maintained that the utility companies discriminated against small and domestic consumers, especially farmers, and he believed that rural electrification would remedy the economic imbalance between the country and the city, thereby correcting what he called the "uneven progress of industry and agriculture." Cooke and Roosevelt agreed that the country had been unable to reap full advantage from its natural resources because selfish utility interests refused to establish rates low enough to encourage widespread electrical consumption. Rural electrification would uplift agricultural regions and provide farmers with an "American" standard of living.[98]

In 1933 Cooke set up headquarters in Washington, D.C. He was thrilled with the Tennessee Valley Authority Act, the very first piece of national legislation requiring that electricity from federal hydropower projects be distributed for the particular benefit of domestic and rural consumers. The act also authorized TVA to construct transmission lines to farms and small villages in order to promote the fullest possible use of electricity. While Cooke saw great possibilities in the formation of TVA, he also conceived of the Depression as an opportunity to bring power to the rest of rural America. In June 1933, he sent off a memo to the president entitled "Electrify Rural America Now," in which he declared that "the real problem of rural electrification, reaching the dirt farmer, has barely been

[98] Cooke, "Electricity Goes to the Country," *SG* (September 1936), 506–10; Jean Christie, *Morris Llewellyn Cooke, Progressive Engineer* (1983), 115–20.

touched." Cooke recommended the formation of a committee to get the facts, and he mentioned that the new Public Works Administration (PWA) might serve as the ideal "modus operandi." Satisfied that the administration was indeed gearing up to study the possibilities, Cooke wrote to his friend David Lilienthal at TVA that he and Lilienthal were "stressing two ends of the same problem."[99]

Indeed, Harold Ickes's PWA served as the vehicle for Cooke's official influence within the New Deal. Pressured by the emergency to start spending right away, Ickes divided the PWA allocations into federal and nonfederal programs. "Federal" monies were channeled immediately to existing departments and agencies, such as Interior's own Bureau of Reclamation and the U.S. Army Corps of Engineers. States and municipalities, on the other hand, could apply for "nonfederal" grants and loans to initiate projects after PWA review of their requests. Almost immediately, applications poured in for assistance with projects for flood control, irrigation, improved navigation, and electric power production. So many requests emanated from the Mississippi Valley region that Ickes appointed Cooke to chair a committee to sort the requests. However, Ickes asked the Mississippi Valley Committee (MVC) to do more than review the project applications; he also commissioned a "plan" for the Mississippi Valley. Though Ickes conceded that farmers in the valley suffered from "hard times," he declared that the primary causes of rural decline were "a failing water supply, decreased soil fertility, and lack of electric power which would enable the farmer to share in a rising standard of living."[100]

The MVC submitted its report at the end of 1934. It surveyed the valley's subregions and proposed that the federal government coordinate and finance a unified program of water control, multipurpose river development, power generation, and rural electrification. Arguing that land and forest resources were intimately related to water control, the report also devoted considerable attention to the problems presented by soil erosion and forest depletion. Guiding the committee's work was its overarching belief that the nation's economic security was dependent on its physical security. "The people cannot reach the highest standard of well-being unless there is the wisest use of the land and water," the report declared. "Engineering does not exist for its own sake . . . It is of little

---

[99] "Electrify Rural America Now," Cooke to Roosevelt, 5 June 1933, NFRS, Box 51; Cooke to Lilienthal, 11 December 1933, NFRS, Box 52.
[100] Jeanne Nienaber Clarke, *Roosevelt's Warrior: Harold L. Ickes and the New Deal* (1996), 65–6, 160; Christie, *Morris Llewellyn Cooke*, 133; Ickes, "Saving the Good Earth: The Mississippi Valley Committee and Its Plan," *SG* (February 1934), 53.

use to control rivers if we cannot thereby improve the quality of human living."[101]

The PWA infused money into river development and conservation projects all over the country. Just about every multipurpose dam built during the New Deal received a PWA loan or grant; federal public works money, for example, made possible the completion of Hoover Dam and provided the seed money for what became the massive Central Valley Project of California. The PWA helped many communities purchase or construct public distribution systems for electric power, and pressured private utilities to cede territory to the federal government. Public works money also financed land utilization purchases, underwrote Hugh Bennett's Soil Erosion Service, and helped the Park Service restore its holdings and expand its territory.[102]

After his work with the MVC, Morris Cooke resumed his crusade to electrify the countryside. In 1935, just 11 percent of American farms received electricity from private or public utilities. Cooke compared the United States unfavorably with France, where 90 percent of rural communities received electricity, and with New Zealand, where two-thirds of the rural population was served. In May 1935, the president responded to pressure from Cooke, from other members of the administration, and from the major farm organizations, and established the Rural Electrification Administration (REA) as a relief agency. Roosevelt's executive order directed the REA to extend loans to private companies, associations, or cooperatives. Cooke hoped to cooperate with the private utilities; in fact, he believed that there was little demand in America for public ownership, only the demand that the supply of electricity be "plentiful, widely distributed, and cheap." However, the private utilities proved unwilling to lower rates, and they remained suspicious of the REA owing to the New Deal's other ventures into the power arena, such as TVA and legislative efforts to dismantle holding companies. Cooke then turned to consumer-owned cooperatives, as TVA had first done in Mississippi. In 1936, Senator George Norris and House Speaker Sam Rayburn sponsored a bill to make the REA a permanent agency, and the president signed the Rural Electrification Act that May. The act gave the agency authorization to operate for

---

[101] *Report of the Mississippi Valley Committee* (GPO, 1934), 3.

[102] Ickes, *Back to Work: The Story of PWA* (1935); Clarke, *Roosevelt's Warrior*, 155–75; Linda J. Lear, "Boulder Dam: A Crossroads in Natural Resource Policy," *Journal of the West* (1985); McCraw, *TVA and the Power Fight*.

ten years with Treasury and Reconstruction Finance Corporation funds, and it provided for two types of loans: loans for the construction and operation of generating plants and electric distribution systems, and loans to help individuals purchase wiring, electrical equipment, and appliances. Private companies would be able to borrow from the REA, but preference was to be given to public entities, such as states and cooperatives, rather than to corporations.[103]

At the heart of Cooke's conception of the REA was his belief that the security of the nation rested on "the strength, vitality, and living standards of rural America." Rural electrification, he maintained, would correct the economic imbalance between the city and the country by making farm life more stable and more profitable, thereby checking migration from farm to farm, and from farm to city. Accordingly, the REA operated under the assumption, largely proven by TVA, that the consumption of electricity would rise when farmers had the opportunity to purchase power at low rates. By the end of 1937, the REA had granted loans to a total of 373 projects, only 5 percent of which were operated by private utility companies. The REA projects served almost 230,000 new customers with just under 65,000 miles of new lines. By the beginning of 1939, one out of every five American farms received electricity, in contrast to the 1935 ratio of one farm in ten.[104]

Also guiding Cooke's efforts was his conception of rural electrification as a vehicle for water and soil conservation. He argued that farm electrification justified public hydroelectric projects by providing a new market for almost unlimited quantities of power. He also claimed that rural electrification would make possible the regulation of smaller, single-purpose structures on the headwaters and tributaries where large

[103] Morris Cooke, "Forecast of Power Development," *American Economic Review* 27 (1937), 236–7; Morris Cooke, "The Early Days of the Rural Electrification Idea," *American Political Science Review* 42 (1948); Mark Cordell Stauter, "The Rural Electrification Administration, 1935–1945: A New Deal Case Study" (Ph.D. diss., Duke University, 1973); Christie, *Morris Llewellyn Cooke*; Brown, *Electricity for Rural America*; "The Rural Electrification Act of 1936," *REN* (November 1935). Also see H. R. Person, "The Rural Electrification Administration in Perspective," *Agricultural History* 24 (1950); Philip J. Funigiello, *Toward a National Power Policy: The New Deal and the Electric Utility Industry, 1933–1941* (1973); and Schwartz, *The New Dealers*.

[104] Cooke to Norris, 14 November 1935, *REN* (November 1935); Cooke, "Electricity Goes to the Country"; "Costs Come Down – Lines Go Up," *REN* (October 1936); "Who Sponsors REA Projects?" *REN* (December 1937); "Statement by Secretary Wallace on REA," *REN* (August 1939).

multipurpose projects could not be built. Equally important for Cooke's formulation of electrification as an agent of resource conservation was his fear of land degradation. A fierce partisan of soil conservation and an ardent supporter of his friend Hugh Bennett, Cooke argued that the United States had "twenty years of grace" to defeat soil erosion, that "insidious enemy." The drama of the dust storms, he wrote, had made the nation "erosion-conscious," but erosion plagued the entire country. Cooke praised methods such as contour plowing, strip planting, and pasture seeding, and he argued that a "permanent agriculture" was the "first step in a long ecological chain of causes and effects which leads to the solution of all our water problems." In addition to preserving the precious layer of topsoil, better farming practices would also prevent dams from becoming clogged with silt. In turn, the electricity produced by the dams would help farmers increase their income, diversify their fields, and implement yet more soil conservation practices. New types of pumping, for example, could build up water reserves on or below the surface, thereby irrigating soil-holding grasses or crops. As in the Tennessee Valley, rural electrification would also allow farmers to switch from cropping to dairying, and from erosion-inducing plowing to permanent pastures. In essence, Cooke believed that electricity would promote agricultural intensification and make the countryside capable of permanently supporting more people.[105]

Hugh Bennett, Cooke's friend of many years and his colleague on the Great Plains Committee, had a similar vision. In April 1935, as dust from the plains swirled about Capitol Hill, Bennett pointed dramatically to the scene outside and persuaded Congress to pass the Soil Erosion Act. This legislation made permanent the Soil Erosion Service, moving it to the USDA and changing its name to the Soil Conservation Service (SCS). Bennett secured the authority to extend the agency's work beyond the demonstration projects and to support a nationwide conservation program based on direct assistance to farmers. The SCS encouraged the states to pass legislation permitting farmers to establish by referendum special soil conservation districts. The soil conservation districts, like the AAA committees, followed from M. L. Wilson's commitment to voluntarism and participatory planning. While these districts did not constitute units

---

[105] Cooke, "Forecast of Power Development," 242, 241; Cooke, "Electricity Goes to the Country"; Christie, *Morris Llewellyn Cooke*; Cooke, "Twenty Years of Grace," *SG* (June 1935), 277; Cooke to Roosevelt, 10 April 1935, NFRS, Box 51.

of local government like cities or counties, they possessed authority to conduct research, manage demonstration projects, acquire property, and enforce land use regulations mutually agreed upon. Like TVA, the SCS helped districts acquire conservation machinery such as grass seeders and spriggers. The SCS also assisted farmers in drawing up individual conservation plans, developing water facilities, filling gullies, and planting trees.[106]

The soil conservation program proved emblematic of the era. "The New Deal's symbolic worker," as Alistair Cooke famously observed, had a will "to take up contour plowing late in life." Americans learned about soil conservation through government publications like Russell Lord's *To Hold This Soil*, and through lavishly illustrated works for the general reader such as Lord's *Behold Our Land*.[107]

The conservation agencies also teamed up to publicize what they saw as their combined mission. In 1935, the SCS, the Rural Electrification Administration, and the Resettlement Administration together produced *Little Waters*. The pamphlet declared that the farmer could increase his productivity and assure his security on the land by converting sloping land from cropland to pastureland and forests, by terracing and contour plowing, and by building farm reservoirs. Complementing the land use reforms would be small dams to provide hydropower, protection from floods, and water for supplementary irrigation. Two drawings, the first entitled "Headwaters Uncontrolled" and the second, "Headwaters Controlled," expressed the overarching message of *Little Waters* – that resource conservation techniques could rehabilitate rural regions and even amplify their carrying capacity.[108]

Still, despite the cooperation between the SCS, the REA, and the RA on *Little Waters*, Morris Cooke and Hugh Bennett had developed a set of conservation possibilities more politically resilient than Rexford

[106] Douglas Helms, "Conservation Districts: Getting to the Roots," in *Readings in the History of the Soil Conservation Service*, 25–30; Wayne D. Rasmussen, "History of Soil Conservation, Institutions and Incentives," in Harold G. Halcrow et al., eds., *Soil Conservation Policies, Institutions, and Incentives* (1982). On the origins of the model state law, see Douglas Helms, "The Preparation of the Standard State Soil Conservation Districts Law: An Interview with Philip M. Glick" (U.S. Department of Agriculture, Soil Conservation Service, 1990). Also see Russell Lord, *To Hold This Soil* (GPO, 1938).

[107] Cooke quoted in Badger, *The New Deal*, 170; Lord, *To Hold This Soil*; Russell Lord, *Behold Our Land* (1938). Also see John Opie, *The Law of the Land: Two Hundred Years of American Farmland Policy* (1987).

[108] *Little Waters: Their Use and Relations to the Land* (GPO, 1936).

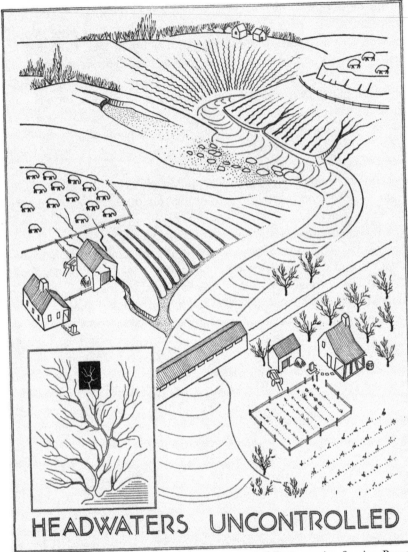

FIGURE 2.2. "Headwaters Uncontrolled." From Soil Conservation Service, Resettlement Administration, and Rural Electrification Administration, *Little Waters* (Washington, D.C.: Government Printing Office, 1936)

Tugwell and L. C. Gray's resettlement ideas. The directors of the REA and the SCS designed technical strategies to keep farmers on the land and to raise the value of their property, not to remove them from it. Unlike the architects of the land utilization and resettlement programs, Cooke and

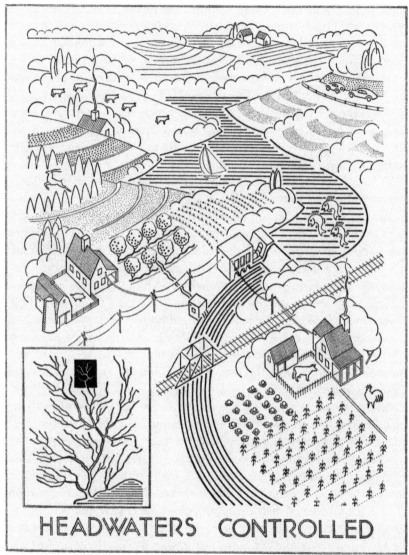

FIGURE 2.3. "Headwaters Controlled." From Soil Conservation Service, Resettlement Administration, and Rural Electrification Administration, *Little Waters* (Washington, D.C.: Government Printing Office, 1936)

Bennett did not insist on government purchase and land retirement as the primary goal of federal conservation policy. Though Cooke and Bennett viewed the SCS and REA programs as complementing land purchases, not necessarily competing with them, soil conservation, water resources development, and rural electrification constituted a set of alternative approaches. These strategies certainly appealed to farmers and to commercial boosters who resented the implication that no amount of skill or pluck could overcome the challenges thrown up by Mother Nature. Furthermore, the land utilization projects took time, while the other techniques could be implemented more quickly. The combined impact of the SCS and the REA (along with the AAA, which also helped farm owners implement conservation methods) was to direct national policy in the direction of a conservation approach geared toward maintaining and supporting farmers on their own land.[109]

Various methods for water control accomplished similar ends. More than anything, residents in the drier areas of the country thirsted for water and dreamed of the return of rain. Heartened only somewhat by the scattered showers that fell after 1936, they were pleased with the Great Plains Committee's suggestions that the federal government develop medium- and small-sized water projects and that it assist individual farmers in constructing wells, farm ponds, and small reservoirs. Congress responded to these pleas and to the recommendations of Morris Cooke and Hugh Bennett. Influenced in large part by the publication of *Little Waters*, the Flood Control Act of 1936 gave the USDA responsibility for providing upstream watershed protection across the nation. The legislation was intended to complement the large projects and the downstream flood control work of the U.S. Army Corps of Engineers by providing conservation assistance to the farmers along the smaller tributaries. A year later, Congress passed the Pope-Jones Act authorizing the Agriculture and Interior Departments to develop water storage ponds, water-spreading facilities, and irrigation works in seventeen western states, a task initiated by the Farm Security Administration (the RA's successor) and directed in part by the SCS. Agricultural officials viewed the Pope-Jones legislation as an essential part of their efforts to permit the largest number of farm families to remain in place. In 1939, the Flood Control Act of 1936 and the Pope-Jones Act of 1937 were supplemented with the Wheeler-Case bill, which directed the interior secretary to construct Water Conservation and Utilization (WCU) projects in the arid and semiarid portions

---

[109] David Danbom makes a similar point in *Born in the Country*, as do Mary Hargreaves in *Dry Farming in the Northern Great Plains*, Richard Kirkendall in *Social Scientists and Farm Politics*, and Donald Worster in *Dust Bowl*. For the idea that many plains residents objected to the land utilization projects not because they rejected the philosophy of the New Deal but because of the perception that they were slowly or unfairly compensated, see Hurt, "Federal Land Reclamation."

of the nation. WCU funding flowed to the Bureau of Reclamation and to the state water conservation boards, which cooperated with the WPA and other federal agencies to construct irrigation works and to serve rural rehabilitation clients.[110]

The experience of farmers in southwestern Kansas illustrates well how rural resource policy shifted from land purchases toward conservation assistance that functioned more explicitly to keep farmers in place. Residents of the Kansas Dust Bowl faced dust storms and severe wind erosion from 1931 to 1939, and during those years they experimented with a variety of possible conservation strategies. Always calling on the federal government for help, Kansas farmers enforced listing regulations and acquired funds to combat soil blowing and to maintain summer fallow on their fields. In 1937, members of the Southwest Agricultural Association even proposed a central authority, "a little TVA for the Dust Bowl region," to coordinate a comprehensive regional plan that would include land retirement, water conservation, and flood control.[111]

Even though they soon dropped the idea of a coordinating authority, the area's farmers did not abandon their pleas for federal assistance. In 1937, they specifically requested federal help in returning submarginal land to grass, and in 1938 they approved the initiation of a land utilization program in Morton County. After less than a year, however, Morton County farmers asked for the cessation of the project. The purchases, they claimed, were emptying out the towns and forcing families onto relief. Residents also argued that the government was acquiring good land along with the bad, and local authorities worried that the county would lose its tax base. Responding to these concerns, the federal government halted purchases in 1939 and concentrated on reseeding and managing the 107,000 acres of land it had acquired. Meanwhile, Kansas farmers installed pumping and irrigation equipment in larger and larger numbers after 1940.

---

[110] Douglas Helms, "Small Watersheds and the USDA: Legacy of the Flood Control Act of 1936," in *Readings in the History of the Soil Conservation Service*, 96–105; Rasmussen, "History of Soil Conservation, Institutions and Incentives," 11–12; Hugh H. Bennett, "Field Memorandum SCS #769," 25 March 1939, Records of P. K. Hooker, NA RG 114, Entry 35, Box 13; Wilson to Carl Hayden, 14 March 1938, Records of P. K. Hooker, NA RG 114, Entry 35, Box 5; Hargreaves, *Dry Farming in the Northern Great Plains*, 130–6; Michael C. Robinson, *Water for the West: The Bureau of Reclamation* (1979), 59.

[111] The discussion in this paragraph and the next comes from Pamela Riney-Kehrberg, "From the Horse's Mouth: Dust Bowl Farmers and Their Solutions to the Problem of Aridity," *Agricultural History* 66 (1992).

Indeed, all over the Great Plains, federal money paid for irrigation equipment and the electricity to operate it. To be fair, the REA did not view the new irrigation methods simply as a way for farmers to avoid implementing conservation practices, though of course this is what soon occurred. Initially, the REA followed TVA's example and promoted electricity not as a replacement for conservation, but as its handmaiden. Supplementary water, pumped from nearby streams or underground sources, could help farmers diversify their agricultural pursuits. Irrigation, for example, would allow farmers to maintain permanent cover crops such as alfalfa. Raising poultry and managing dairy herds would be possible with electricity, and expanding livestock holdings meant that more acres could be put to pasture and fewer to the plow. Electricity also allowed farmers to process, dry, or can agricultural products before shipping them out, thereby increasing local income and providing farmers with the funds to implement yet more conservation methods. Like TVA, the REA hoped to keep farmers in place by helping them diversify their fields as well as the economies of their local towns.[112]

A final illustration of the national shift to rehabilitation in place was the cessation of large-scale government land purchases. Though the federal government continued to purchase and restore submarginal land well into the 1940s, the land utilization program underwent a significant transformation after 1937. This transformation, which complemented and paralleled the establishment of the Farm Security Administration in 1937, underscored the strength of the appeal of leaving farmers in place, yet also demonstrated that liberals still struggled with the question of the rural poor.

In 1937, USDA Secretary Henry Wallace conceded that previous government land purchases had been "blocked in rather solidly to effectuate the use of the areas as forests, game preserves, and recreational areas." Now, he declared, the most important consideration for the land program would be given "to whether the occupants' opportunity for making a living can be best improved by such purchases or by leaving them where they are and enabling them to make certain adjustments in their farming economy." Essentially, Wallace agreed that too much good land had

---

[112] Robert Dailey, "Rural Electrification's Aid Sought to Fight Drought in South Dakota," *REN* (March 1937); R. L. Cochran, "Electrification Ushers in New Era of Prosperity," *REN* (August 1938); "REA Electricity Pumps Water for Irrigation in Colorado," *REN* (October 1938); "Diversification Hits the Plains," *REN* (June 1942); "The Soil-Saving Becks Know Power's Value," *REN* (December 1942); "Power Along the Platte," *REN* (December 1942).

indeed been purchased with the bad, and that more attention would be given to helping farmers remain in place. Under the authorization provided to him by the Bankhead-Jones Farm Tenant Act of 1937, the secretary transferred the land program to the Bureau of Agricultural Economics, where it was agreed that the purchases would "furnish a maximum number of families with an improved basis for making a living." Future projects would no longer be established primarily for parks or wildlife reserves, but for farms and farm families. This shift, well under way by the end of the year, was cemented when the Soil Conservation Service assumed control of the land utilization projects in the fall of 1938. The SCS directed the program toward conservation adjustments that would bring about an improved agricultural economy: "more economic farm and ranch units, better living conditions, better government services, and facilities."[113]

The transformation of the land utilization program accompanied the demise of the Resettlement Administration and the formation of its replacement, the Farm Security Administration – the successor agency that officially redirected rural rehabilitation policy away from resettlement and toward rehabilitation in place. While still director of the RA, Tugwell had initiated the change after he faced resistance to land purchases and resettlement in the Great Plains. Indeed, rural rehabilitation loans – not funds for submarginal land purchases and farmer relocation – had always comprised the largest portion of the RA budget. Nonetheless, Tugwell had continued to believe that there would be no permanent solution for low-income farmers until they were moved off submarginal land.[114]

Stung by criticism of the RA's model communities, however, and battered by charges that the agency intended to "socialize" America's land and "collectivize" its people, Tugwell resigned in December 1936. Wallace transferred the RA to the USDA and appointed the RA's deputy administrator, Will Alexander, as Tugwell's successor. Alexander was a southerner committed to improving the conditions of the poor farmers, black and white, of his native region. While he agreed that poor land contributed significantly to rural poverty, Alexander had concluded that Tugwell's equation was somewhat of an oversimplification. Much more emphasis, he believed, should be placed on helping people at the bottom acquire

---

[113] Hooker, "Land Utilization Program," 33, 40; Bennett, "Field Memorandum #769." Also see Wooten, *Land Utilization Program*; and Melissa G. Wiedenfeld, "The Development of a New Deal Land Policy: Fergus County, Montana, 1900–1945" (Ph.D. diss., Louisiana State University, 1997).

[114] Alexander oral history, CUOH. Also see Tugwell, "The Resettlement Idea."

security of income and tenure on the farms where they already lived. Better equipment, more credit, expert guidance and advice – these were the rural rehabilitation tools that Alexander thought should guide the federal government's approach. Most important, Alexander was committed to a much larger assault on farm poverty, one to be sanctioned this time by legislative action rather than by executive decision.[115]

In this thinking Alexander was not alone. Despite indications that commodity prices had risen and that farm surpluses had been reduced, even that the national economic emergency in general might be receding, it was clear the problem of chronic rural poverty remained. Plains farmers still faced drought and foreclosure, and in class-divided regions such as the South and the Far West, the AAA had further entrenched the wealthier farmers and harmed tenants, sharecroppers, and migratory laborers. While many New Dealers, including Alexander, analyzed rural poverty in its various guises, most discussions of the problem focused on tenancy as the primary impediment to rural security. A crusade against tenancy, and for farm ownership, held far more mainstream appeal than the collective or cooperative experiments of the Resettlement Administration; the family farm, after all, better reflected the American yeoman ideal. An emphasis on the problem of farm tenancy also carried a conservation dimension: rural advocates often argued that tenants had few incentives to institute long-range conservation adjustments. Beginning in 1935, Senator John H. Bankhead and Representative Marvin Jones had begun to introduce tenant-purchase legislation in Congress and in 1936, at Morris Cooke's suggestion, the president appointed a Special Committee on Farm Tenancy to recommend the "most promising ways" of addressing the problem. "The growing insecurity of many classes of farm tenants, frequently associated with soil depletion and declining living standards," Roosevelt wrote to Wallace, "presents a challenge to national action which I hope we can meet in a thoroughly constructive manner."[116]

[115] Baldwin, *Poverty and Politics*, 106–31; Alexander oral history, CUOH. Also see Wilma Dykeman and James Stokely, *Seeds of Southern Change: The Life of Will Alexander* (1962).
[116] Baldwin, *Poverty and Politics*, 132–92; Jess Gilbert and Alice O'Connor, "Leaving the Land Behind: Struggles for Land Reform in U. S. Federal Policy," in Harvey M. Jacobs, ed., *Who Owns America? Social Conflict over Property Rights* (1998), 114; Chris Rasmussen, "'Never a Landlord for the Good of the Land': Farm Tenancy, Soil Conservation, and the New Deal in Iowa," *Agricultural History* 73 (1999); President's Committee on Farm Tenancy, *Farm Tenancy* (GPO, 1937), 6; Saloutos, *American Farmer and the New Deal*, 165; Roosevelt to Wallace, 1936, in *Farm Tenancy*, 25.

The committee released the Farm Tenancy Report in February 1937, in time to influence the passage of legislation in Congress. The report drew attention to the poor conditions of many groups of farm families – tenants, croppers, laborers, and farmers stranded on submarginal land – and argued that this insecurity was a "threat to the integrity of rural life." One in four farm families, the report declared, occupied a precarious position in the nation's social and economic structure that "should not be tolerated." Central to the report's view of farm poverty was its analysis of the relationship between poor people and poor land. It argued that insecure tenure conditions yielded "a downward spiral" of soil and human erosion, while secure tenure conditions raised living standards and provided farmers with incentives to terrace their lands, to improve their pastures, and to plow along the contour. The report recommended measures to facilitate farm ownership and to help existing owners retain their farms, as well as measures to increase the security and living conditions of farm laborers. It suggested that a new "Farm Security Administration" guide this unified assault on farm poverty and concluded with a call to action: "action to enable increasing numbers of farm families to enter into sound relationships with the land they till and with the communities in which they live."[117]

The Bankhead-Jones (Farm Security) Act, passed by Congress in July, included many of the report's recommendations. In September, Wallace created the Farm Security Administration (FSA) within the USDA as successor to the Resettlement Administration. As provided by Title I of the enabling act, the FSA loaned money to help tenants become owners. Under its largest program, Rural Rehabilitation, the FSA extended rehabilitation grants and loans to higher-risk families, mostly in the South, and combined this help with technical guidance and conservation assistance. Rehabilitation loans also helped farmers reduce their debts, acquire medical services, and join cooperative enterprises. By 1943, one in nine American farmers had received a loan or grant from the FSA. The agency also administered the resettlement projects and model communities inherited from FERA and the RA, and it operated camps for migratory farm workers in California (memorialized by John Steinbeck in *The Grapes of Wrath*) and in South Florida. Though the FSA never acquired the funds or the political support to wage a full-scale war on rural poverty, its existence indicated the country's willingness, at least for a time, to experiment with

[117] *Farm Tenancy*, 4, 9–11, 20.

remedies for poor people and poor land, and to confront economic and political inequality in the countryside.[118]

When Franklin Roosevelt took office in 1933, he pledged to support a new philosophy of agricultural rehabilitation and rural resource development. Convinced that rural living standards would improve with the proper use and fair distribution of natural resources, Roosevelt embraced the principles of the New Conservation and brought its chief proponents into his administration. The president and these rural advocates believed that the economic health of the nation depended on the welfare of the country's farm population, and they embedded their plans to save the nation's deteriorating land and to bring cheap hydropower to the countryside within an analysis of the Depression that viewed insufficient farm income as its primary cause. Believing rural areas to be the victims of two interlocked forms of exploitation – the corporate extraction of natural resources, and the unsustainable abuse of those resources – the New Dealers crafted and administered programs designed to address the related ills of poor people and poor land, and to bring the farmer a standard of living equal to that of his urban counterpart.

While farmers were neither the most important nor the most enduring element of the new Democratic political coalition (that honor belonged to the urban working class), rural support, often nonpartisan, lay behind liberal policy designed to equalize rural and urban living standards. In the first few years of the New Deal, Roosevelt had the key support of the Southern Democrats who controlled Congress. "Whatever their ideological convictions," Anthony Badger writes, "southern congressmen, both leaders and rank and file, were acutely aware of the desperate need of their constituents for relief from rural devastation." Even notorious Negrophobes like John Rankin and Theodore Bilbo understood the political importance of securing rural electrification and price-support legislation.[119] Roosevelt also had the initial advantage of a divided Republican Party. Its more progressive, largely western wing – composed of congressmen like Nebraska Senator George Norris, Hiram Johnson of California, and Bronson Cutting of New Mexico – was willing to go along with the farm and conservation legislation, even to sponsor some of it. Finally, the

---

[118] "History of the Farm Security Administration"; Baldwin, *Poverty and Politics*, 193–230; Wooten, *Land Utilization Program*; Carlebach and Provenzo, *Farm Security Administration Photographs*; Gilbert and O'Connor, "Leaving the Land Behind," 115.

[119] Badger, *The New Deal*, 261, 270.

New Deal programs did succeed in raising agricultural incomes immediately, and many rural residents appreciated the help despite frustrations with bureaucracy and red tape. Few observers were surprised when the election of 1936 yielded a farm landslide in Roosevelt's favor.[120]

The New Deal's efforts to retain and to rebuild the nation's farm population acquired a twofold character. Within the Tennessee River Valley, TVA constructed multipurpose dams for power generation, flood control, and improved navigation. As the first federal undertaking authorized to produce and transmit power specifically for the benefit of rural and domestic consumers, TVA also distributed electricity to small towns and to rural cooperatives. Its forestry program purchased submarginal lands for restoration, and its agricultural program worked directly with farm owners to halt soil erosion and to diversify their agricultural and economic pursuits. Similar goals characterized the federal programs beyond the Tennessee Valley, though these efforts attempted to assist those whom TVA had not – the poorer farmers, the tenants, and the landless.

Despite these differences between the Tennessee Valley and the rest of the country, all of the programs underwent a similar transition. After experiments with large land purchases, the resource agencies nationwide adopted conservation policies designed primarily to help farmers remain on their land. Within TVA, the triumph of its agricultural personnel over its regional planners and foresters and the curtailment of the authority's overpurchase policy sealed this direction. No longer would TVA displace more farmers than absolutely necessary to build its reservoirs, or give serious consideration to the idea that cooperative forest communities could enjoy standards of living equal to those of crop and dairy farmers. Beyond the Tennessee Valley, the demise of Tugwell's RA signaled the transition to rehabilitation in place. A host of technical assistance strategies – soil conservation, rural electrification, irrigation, and flood control – replaced the idea that addressing rural distress ultimately meant moving people away from poor land.

New Deal policy operated within the contours set by the Depression. While many New Dealers predicted that the economy would soon recover, few signs of industrial expansion had appeared by the end of the 1930s. Because farmers could not expect job opportunities elsewhere, their welfare was presumed to be linked to their opportunities on the land. Even if many administrators and lawmakers believed that a brighter economic

[120] For a discussion of the election of 1936 see Saloutos, *American Farmer and the New Deal*, chapter 16.

future would necessarily bring with it a vastly decreased farm population, they hoped the rural resource programs would help farmers find immediate security by remaining farmers, not by migrating to the cities to become factory workers. However short-lived it would soon prove to be, this agrarian mindset was midwife to a new social contract: government responsibility for rural welfare.

Of course, agrarian thinking also postponed efforts to tackle the tensions inherent in the New Deal farm policies: if the conservation measures served mostly to help the more well-to-do farmers increase their yields, what, in the end, would happen to poor farmers and to the smaller producers? Would they really have the opportunity to earn incomes equal to their more commercial neighbors? Was it possible both to preserve and to modernize the family farm? Such questions prompted one politician from rural Texas to embrace the New Deal's agrarian policies fully, and then to direct them toward an industrial future.

1. Morris Cooke, chairman of Drought Committee, at abandoned farm near Guymon, Oklahoma, 1936. Photo by Arthur Rothstein. Library of Congress, Prints & Photographs Division, FSA-OWI Collection [LC-USF34-005232-E DLC]

2. Rexford Tugwell and farmer of Dust Bowl area in Texas Panhandle, 1936. Photo by Arthur Rothstein. Library of Congress, Prints & Photographs Division, FSA-OWI Collection [LC-USF34-005249-D DLC]

3. President Roosevelt visits farmer who is receiving drought relief grant, Mandan, North Dakota, 1936. Photo by Arthur Rothstein. Library of Congress, Prints & Photographs Division, FSA-OWI Collection [LC-DIG-fsa-8b28231 DLC]

4. Erosion south of Franklin, Heard County, Georgia. 1941. Photo by Jack Delano. Library of Congress, Prints & Photographs Division, FSA-OWI Collection [LC-USF34-04385 9-D DLC]

5. Eroded land on a tenant's farm, Walker County, Alabama. 1937. Photo by Arthur Rothstein. Library of Congress, Prints & Photographs Division, FSA-OWI Collection [LC-USF346-025121-D DLC]

6. Tennessee Valley Authority's original caption: "The meter on the wall of the rural shack indicates that it now receives its share of electricity from the power carried overland by the huge TVA transmission line" (n.d., created between 1933 and 1945). Library of Congress, Prints & Photographs Division, FSA-OWI Collection [LC-USW33-015606-ZC DLC]

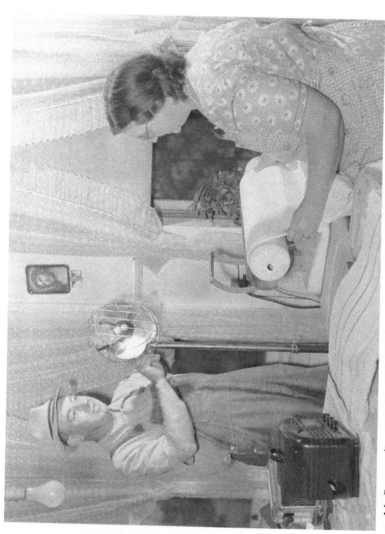

7. Mr. Bacon adjusts an electric fan for his wife, who is using an electric iron, Knox County, Tennessee (TVA), 1942. Photo by Arthur Rothstein. Library of Congress, Prints & Photographs Division, FSA-OWI Collection [LC-USW3-004061-D DLC]

8. Grand Coulee Dam on the Columbia River, Washington, 1941. Photo by U.S. Bureau of Reclamation. Library of Congress, Prints & Photographs Division, FSA-OWI Collection [LC-USW33-035035-C DLC]

3

"The Best New Dealer from Texas"

The Hill Country forms both the physical and the psychological heart of Texas. The proper geographical name for this area is the Edwards Plateau, a rocky region that rises to the west of Austin and San Antonio. Crisp air and superb views surprise the visitor accustomed to the humid pine forests and swampy lowlands of East Texas, or the dry prairies of West Texas. In spring the scrub oaks and cedar (actually juniper, but Texans dub it "cedar") fill with songbirds, and prickly pear cactus poke through fields of wildflowers. Clear streams weave along limestone beds, often dropping into deep blue pools framed by willow trees.

Today, the Hill Country is best known for its recreational opportunities and retirement living. The mountains overlook a string of sparkling man-made reservoirs, jammed full each weekend with Jet Skis and motorboats. Expensive Italianate villas share the view with clusters of stucco condominiums, and bed-and-breakfasts offer nostalgic weekend retreats complete with log cabins, fly fishing, and goat milking. But for much of its history the Hill Country remained isolated, an unforgiving landscape of poor land and even poorer farmers. Lured there in the nineteenth century by the region's lush grass and clear streams, settlers soon found that cattle grazing exposed the thin layer of topsoil. Heat and drought scorched the bare earth, and streams dried to a trickle. Flash floods carved gullies into the hillsides and washed away the land's illusive fertility. Cedar brakes and tenacious hardwood brush took over the eroded hills. Dreams of riches dashed, Hill Country residents lapsed into a marginal existence running goats and sheep in the hills and raising cotton, corn, and sorghum in the scattered bottomlands.[1]

Everything changed in the 1930s. Federal agricultural programs reduced surplus livestock and raised incomes. Farmers also received payments for terracing their land, removing cedar, and planting soil-building crops on their fields and pastures. Most important, the state of Texas authorized an independent agency, the Lower Colorado River Authority (the LCRA), to develop comprehensive plans for the Colorado River (the Colorado rises in the northern part of the state, runs south through the Hill Country, through the city of Austin, and drains into the Gulf of Mexico). The LCRA, along with the federal Bureau of Reclamation, the Public Works Administration, and private contractors, built a series of dams along the river to provide flood control, hydroelectric power, water for irrigation, and reservoirs for recreation.

The region would never have experienced such dramatic change had it not been for a rising political star. Perhaps because of his own origins along the Pedernales River in the Hill Country, Lyndon B. Johnson identified with the tough circumstances of farm life and labored to uplift the rural population of his district. Johnson worked tirelessly to secure federal programs for the Hill Country after he was elected to Congress in 1937, and the experience of bringing the string of six dams, farm programs, and work relief to his constituents shaped his career and liberal outlook. He labored intimately with LCRA officials, and he knew the USDA county agents and soil conservation officers of his district by their first names. He cultivated friendships with prominent liberals in Washington, requesting autographed photos and plying them with Texas grapefruit, pecans, and Christmas turkeys.[2]

Johnson's early career highlighted the new political and environmental order of the 1930s. Many New Dealers maintained that an imbalance

[1] 1925 Agricultural Census: Burnet, Williamson, Blanco, Hays, and Llano Counties; Hugh H. Bennett, *The Soils and Agriculture of the Southern States* (1921), 231–32; John Graves, *Hard Scrabble: Observations on a Patch of Land* (1974); John Graves, *Texas Heartland: A Hill Country Year* (1975); Robert A. Caro, *The Years of Lyndon Johnson: The Path to Power* (1982), 8–14.
[2] "Pedernales" is pronounced "Purr-denales." "Arthur Goldschmidt," in Katie Louchheim, ed., *The Making of the New Deal: The Insiders Speak* (1983), 249–50. Also see individual correspondence records: Thomas Corcoran, Harold Ickes, Abe Fortas, and Henry Wallace, House Papers (HP), Lyndon Johnson Library (LBJL). The chapter's title comes from a Thomas Corcoran quip quoted in Robert Dallek, *Lone Star Rising: Lyndon Johnson and His Times* (1991), 170.

between the country and the city triggered the Depression – an imbalance between the prices farmers received and the prices they paid, an imbalance between the income of rural areas and the income of city dwellers. The solution, then, lay in a concerted effort to uplift the agricultural areas with soil and range conservation, multipurpose river development, rural electrification, and recreational opportunities. The policy architects believed that if a region's natural resources were both owned by the people closest to them and distributed fairly, the imbalance between farm and factory incomes could be corrected. As the previous chapters have demonstrated, rural development thus entailed not only raising the buying power of the farmer (though of course many New Dealers used that language exclusively), but also rebuilding rural communities on the basis of sustainable and equitable use of water, power, and land.

Not yet explored is how exactly this New Conservation allowed the New Dealers to mobilize and to build local constituencies. While the Tennessee Valley Authority provided much of the ideological inspiration and most of the legal precedents for the New Deal's rural resource initiatives, and while it certainly had the support of many area politicians, TVA ultimately represented assistance dispensed from above. Not all of the rural rehabilitation efforts and farm support programs fit that top-down model, however, even when initiatives were designed and made available by national figures and national agencies. Regional leaders found they had to maneuver strategically to secure New Deal benefits, and a satisfying outcome was by no means assured. Even though New Deal conservation never became a movement from below, it required the active and committed involvement of local officials. Furthermore, these public servants often set out to protect the interests of the poor and the middling classes of farmers along with the more well-to-do.

Indeed, Lyndon Johnson's experience illustrated how one could build a political strategy upon the New Deal's expanded definition of conservation. As a dedicated liaison between Washington and the farmers of the Tenth District, Johnson articulated two rationales for rural development: first, that farmers must receive their "fair share of the national income"; and second, that Texans must take control of their destiny by harnessing their own natural resources. These two goals intersected most prominently, for example, in the campaign for electric power and rural electrification. LBJ waged a successful battle to sell LCRA power not to private utilities but to farm cooperatives and municipalities, with financing from the federal government. "Texas towns," he exclaimed in a 1938 radio address, "have dried up and blown off the map because Texas has always been so busy giving its natural resources like this cheap power away...Let's keep Central Texas money at home."[3]

This experience shaped Johnson's liberalism, his unwavering belief that an activist government could create prosperity. By expanding the range of agricultural assistance measures, by linking the electric power from the river with the homes in the fields, and by building an infrastructure for economic development, Johnson made the land and water into political allies. In so doing, he bypassed the traditionally conservative arena of state politics and cemented his district's relationship with the federal government. "All of our rich topsoil was wasting away," he later reflected in a television interview.

And so we started to do something about it. We had to dig some wells. We had to terrace our land. We had to remove some of the small cedars and trees...We built six dams on our river. We brought the floods under control. We provided our people with cheap power...That all resulted from the power of the government to bring the greatest good to the greatest number.[4]

Johnson fervently believed that the government had indeed brought the greatest good to the greatest number of people. Surveying the vast environmental and economic changes that had come to the Hill Country since 1933, he could take much pride in his role in that transformation. Still, what his later reflections overlooked was that despite his good intentions the New Deal resource programs often bypassed the very poorest farmers and tenants, and that the benefits of rural development predominantly flowed to those farmers most able to remain on their land and to profit from government largesse. For the most part, Central Texas residents received conservation assistance not from the relief or resettlement programs designed specifically for tenants and sharecroppers but from the federal agencies that worked with farm owners: the Extension Service, the Agricultural Adjustment Administration, the Rural Electrification Administration, and the Soil Conservation Service. To be sure, Johnson worried about class differences within agriculture, and he worked to bring the grants and loans of the Farm Security Administration to the tenants of his district. However, the young politician understood the primary dilemma of the agrarian liberal: if government programs worked to make some farmers more secure and more productive, was the best

---

[3] LBJ radio address, HP Box 166.
[4] *The Hill Country: Lyndon Johnson's Texas*, NBC News television program, 9 May 1966, transcription in Reference File "Hill Country," LBJL.

policy really to keep everyone on the land? Sensing that long-term trends did not augur well for small and marginal farmers, Johnson seized the opportunity provided by World War II to test a new approach. Rather than formulating more programs to keep the very poorest farmers on the land, Johnson worked to build an industrial infrastructure based upon cheap hydropower from the LCRA's newly completed set of dams. By the end of World War II, the congressman had decided that the nation required fewer farmers but more factories, more wage workers, and more city dwellers. In effect, Johnson's career straddled the agrarian and the industrial New Deals.

THE HILL COUNTRY SETTING

Johnson's battle to improve the lives of rural Texans emerged from his family's own experience in Central Texas. His father, Sam Johnson, attempted to establish a large farm on the Pedernales after World War I, but the family's fate was ultimately tied to the Hill Country environment, with its unpredictable rainfall, its floods, and its thin, eroded soils. A cousin recalled in detail how Sam's struggle with a single gully symbolized the hardship. The gully, a winding gash creeping down through the fields and to the river, yawned "deep enough to walk elephants in." The more the gully widened and deepened because of wind and rain, the less cotton the farm could yield. So Sam set out to conquer the thing, to fill it up with rich soil from the bottom of the river. Twice he filled the wound, and two times flash floods, "gully-washers" both, swept down from the hills. Not once did the cotton seeds he planted have a chance to sprout and hold the fill in place. Still Sam struggled and struggled on the farm, plowing the thin layer of topsoil and the hardpan underneath it after every rain. But the "land all drained toward the river," the cousin remembered. "It kept getting washed away in the rains. If you left it alone, it would have very slowly built up ... After Sam started to plow it ... you could see the topsoil running down the hills."[5]

What crops the floodwaters left, the dry summer of 1920 and the world market in cotton finished off. Sam had expected to sell some cotton at fifty or sixty cents a pound, but the price fell to eight cents per pound in the fall. He never recovered financially from this loss; Sam Johnson stayed in debt the rest of his life. Residents of Johnson City remembered that the family never had enough to eat; Sam took to running up grocery bills in several

[5] Caro, *Path to Power*, 85–9.

different towns at a time. Lyndon often invoked his father's troubles when speaking of the need for permanent farm measures. "My interest in such legislation," he declared, "wasn't just theoretical or academic. It came right out of the bottom of my own experience. My own father struggled for years to save his farm when I was a boy. He lost that farm. It was a family tragedy I never want to see duplicated."[6]

Lyndon also observed the demanding lives of Hill Country women. In a time before running water and electricity, endless chores sucked the youth from farm wives and left them in a permanent state of weariness. Water for washing, cooking, cleaning, and drinking had to be lugged from the outside pump in a four-gallon, thirty-two-pound bucket. Wood for heating and cooking also needed carrying into the house. On washday (literally lasting an entire day) clothes were boiled outside over open fires in huge vats and scrubbed for hours. Canning fruits and vegetables, preparing meals for the family and the farmhands, and tending to the chickens filled even more hours with drudgery. "At last I realized," Johnson's mother later reflected, "that life is real and earnest and not the charming fairy tale of which I had so long dreamed."[7]

Not only the Johnsons suffered during the 1920s; the Depression hit the Hill Country, as it did other rural areas, early and hard. With commodity prices falling, parents sent children, girls as well as boys, "off the farm" to earn meager cash wages. "We had a sense of insecurity," a resident remembered. "You go ten, fifteen miles east of Austin and you begin to see black soil and prosperous cotton farms, and big houses on the farms. But there was no black soil around us. And there were no big houses. I had a feeling even as a boy: in this town, there were no opportunities." The 1920s, roaring and dynamic and urban, passed by Blanco County, where in 1925 fewer than 2 percent of the farms even owned a radio. For his part, Johnson escaped as a teenager, spending time in California before returning home to attend college. In 1931, while teaching high school in Houston, he secured a job as a legislative secretary with Richard Kleberg, the new U.S. representative from the Fourteenth Congressional District. After an interview in Corpus Christi, both Johnson and Kleberg boarded an afternoon train to Washington, D.C.[8]

---

[6] Caro, *Path to Power*, 89–94; *Brenham Banner-Press*, 23 September 1937.
[7] Doris Kearns, *Lyndon Johnson and the American Dream* (1976), 20; Caro, *Path to Power*, 50–3, 116; Dallek, *Lone Star Rising*, 28–9; Memoir quoted in Caro, 53.
[8] Emmette Redford, quoted in Caro, *Path to Power*, 116; 1925 Agricultural Census: Blanco County; Kearns, *Lyndon Johnson*, 42–70; Dallek, *Lone Star Rising*, 58–93.

The onset of the Depression profoundly shaped Johnson's experience as congressional secretary. Each day the post brought bags overflowing with letters from farmers and veterans pleading for assistance. In the early spring of 1933, a third of the farmers in Nueces County faced the prospect of losing their land. In years before, they might have obtained relief from local organizations, but in February the Corpus Christi Salvation Army revealed that its funds would run out in May. On 25 February, a dour gathering of fifteen hundred armed farmers vowed to block foreclosure proceedings. Representative Kleberg viewed any relief initiatives with suspicion and pronounced most of the New Deal legislation dangerously "socialistic." Johnson, on the other hand, had watched Hoover's ineffectual handling of the crisis with great unease and cast his lot with Roosevelt. He threatened to resign if Kleberg did not vote for the Agricultural Adjustment Act, pointing out that the mail ran thirty-to-one in its favor. Kleberg stuck to his principles by voting against TVA and FERA, but gave in on the AAA.[9]

The AAA would have passed without Kleberg's vote, but the farmers of the Fourteenth District would not have fared so well without his secretary. Because Kleberg evinced little interest in the program, Johnson and his small staff worked vigorously to promote the AAA. One source of much initial confusion and delay was the spring plow-up campaign, in which farmers applied to receive payments for having reduced their crops. Johnson spent hours talking with the USDA county agents and individual farmers. Often pretending to be "Congressman Kleberg – from the Agriculture Committee," he gained valuable telephone time with important AAA officials to streamline the bureaucratic process. He waited for applications from his farmers to arrive at the AAA and saw to it that they found their way to the top of the processing stacks. He also helped arrange a large set of farm refinancing agreements from the Federal Land Bank in Houston, and in the fall of 1933 the Fourteenth District of Texas was the first of the country's 435 congressional districts to have all of its AAA loan applications approved.[10]

This is not to say that Johnson spent each hour of every day on agricultural affairs. He also captured the leadership of the Little Congress, curried the favor of senior politicians, and found time to woo Claudia ("Lady Bird") Taylor, his steadfast, lifelong partner. But despite (or maybe because of) his striking successes in political networking, he yearned

---

[9] Caro, *Path to Power*, 251; Dallek, *Lone Star Rising*, 108.
[10] Caro, *Path to Power*, 255–60.

for a more independent position. When Roosevelt created the National Youth Administration (NYA) in June 1935, Johnson used his connections to acquire the post of Texas state director. The NYA aimed to help young people, boys and girls between the ages of sixteen and twenty-five, either to stay in school or to acquire trade skills by working in carefully selected public projects. Johnson, the youngest state director in the country, worked with district officials, coordinating school assistance, public works projects, and opportunities for employment in private firms.[11]

Nothing but praise for the Texas NYA issued from the press. Still, Johnson always kept an eye out for other opportunities, carefully building political contacts all over Texas. He considered running for a spot in the Texas Senate in 1936, but correctly surmised that a young New Dealer would have no easy time in state politics. Johnson, like other determined southern liberals, understood he had to make an "end run" around his state capital and link his ambition to the federal government.[12] There, Johnson knew he could find assistance from a host of like-minded planners and policymakers who labored to transform the South's politics, its economy, and its rural environments.

The opportunity of a lifetime presented itself when James B. Buchanan, the congressman representing Johnson's own district, died of a heart attack on 22 February 1937. Buchanan had spent over two decades in Washington, and now, as chairman of the House Appropriations Committee, he was a widely respected figure at the height of his career. Buchanan had taken a particular interest in the development of the Colorado River, which ran through the center of his district. Indeed, the attempt to build flood control works and hydroelectric facilities on the Colorado had defined Buchanan's role in the House, as it would Lyndon Johnson's.

HISTORICAL DEVELOPMENT OF THE COLORADO RIVER

The Colorado River flows through several geographical regions of Texas. From its source near the New Mexico border, the waterway travels down through the plains of West Texas. The central portion of the river cuts through the Edwards Plateau (Hill Country) at San Saba, Llano, Burnet, and Travis Counties. From the city of Austin, located in Travis County at the eastern edge of the hills, the river winds its way over a coastal plain to

---

[11] Carol A. Weisenberger, *Dollars and Dreams: The National Youth Administration in Texas* (1994), 60–1.
[12] Bruce J. Schulman, *Lyndon B. Johnson and American Liberalism* (1995), 17.

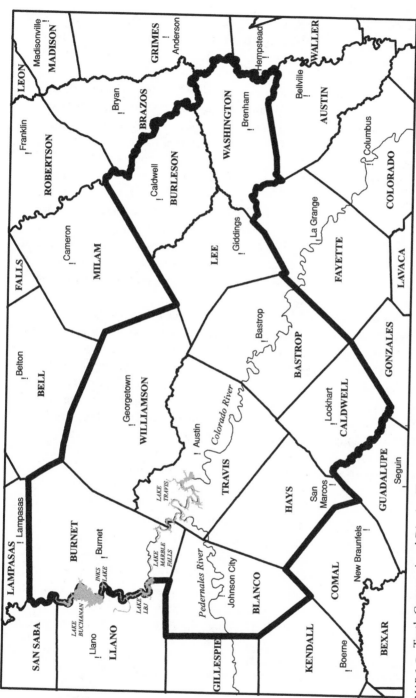

MAP 3.1. Tenth Congressional District, Texas, 1938. Courtesy of Charles Eckstein, Texas Legislative Council

Matagorda Bay at the Gulf of Mexico. Rainfall on the watershed ranges from fifteen inches at the source to forty inches at the mouth, and the total basin area is 41,530 square miles, a bit larger than the Tennessee River watershed.[13]

Flooding plagued the settlers along the Colorado. Most of the downstream flooding originated (and still comes) from the central Edwards Plateau. The region's steep slopes, canyons, and shallow, nonporous soils were simply unequipped to cope with the area's violent seasonal downpours. Efforts to dam the river and to clear the channel of debris proceeded sporadically until after four major floods in the first quarter of the twentieth century. In 1917, the state of Texas approved an amendment to the Texas Constitution that authorized the legislature to conserve, preserve, and develop the state's natural resources. In 1919, the Army Corps of Engineers, pressured by landowners along the river, issued an influential report calling for a set of multipurpose dams north of Austin and levees below the city to manage the river for flood control, hydroelectric power, irrigation, and municipal water.[14]

The most important new development, however, was the effort and subsequent failure of private firms to construct dams in the highlands in the late 1920s. Martin J. Insull of Chicago, the very symbol of the "power trust," played a significant part in these initial corporate efforts. Influenced in part by the 1927 Mississippi flood and the commencement of Hoover Dam, Insull's Middle West Utilities Company began surveys of the Colorado above Austin. These efforts garnered a fair bit of support, especially downstream, where residents looked forward to flood control and water for irrigation in addition to hydroelectric power. After shelling out $1.5 million for water rights and the surveys, Insull pulled out in 1928, caught between warring factions of upstream and downstream interests.[15]

A local attorney named Alvin J. Wirtz took an active interest in the affairs of the Colorado River. No one individual was more crucial to the development of the Colorado, and later to Lyndon Johnson's early career, than Wirtz. A practicing lawyer from a small town south of Austin, Wirtz served as state senator and closely linked his legal career with efforts to develop water and power resources along the rivers of southern Texas. He persuaded a Chicago firm to finish the surveys initiated by the Insull

---

[13] John A. Adams, Jr., *Damming the Colorado: The Rise of the Lower Colorado River Authority* (1990), 4; LCRA, "Development of the Lower Colorado River Authority," 1954, LCRA Box 3C, 10–11.

[14] LCRA, "Development of the LCRA," 11–12; Adams, *Damming the Colorado*, 9–13.

[15] Adams, *Damming the Colorado*, 16.

interests and to acquire land and water rights at six sites. Work on the first project, a hydro plant to be named Hamilton Dam, began in 1931. But confusion ensued when in November of that year the firm sold out to a subsidiary of Insull's Middle West Utilities, and when five months later the Insull kingdom collapsed. The assets and records went to the receivership of Wirtz.[16]

At the time, the favored method for developing river resources was the creation of river authorities or reclamation districts, authorized by Texas constitutional law to coordinate water supply, flood control, and power generation. Wirtz had served as special counsel to the Brazos River Conservation and Reclamation District (formed in 1929), and helped develop the Guadalupe-Blanco River Authority (formed in 1933). Often representing private interests such as the Insulls, he fought for acquisition rights and power facilities along the waterways.[17]

In theory, the river authorities were to occupy a "middle realm of government" between the local and state levels.[18] But by the 1930s, Wirtz and his close Washington friend, Representative Buchanan of the Tenth District, sensed that the New Deal could create primary relationships between local projects and the federal government. In turn, regional conservation efforts might achieve a certain power and independence based on strong links to Congress and the executive agencies. In short, Wirtz and Buchanan understood that federal money had become available on an unprecedented scale through agencies such as the Bureau of Reclamation and the Public Works Administration (PWA), both under the direction of powerful Interior Secretary Harold Ickes. At Wirtz's suggestion, Buchanan and officials of the Colorado River Company (the firm cobbled together by Wirtz after Insull's collapse) met with Ickes and his staff in Washington. Ickes directed Elwood Mead, commissioner of reclamation, to give full support to investigations of the project. Buchanan ensured that the engineering studies received ample funding, and even petitioned the president for aid in completing Hamilton Dam after earlier appeals for funds had been turned down. As the (probably apocryphal) story goes, Buchanan informed Roosevelt that he wanted a birthday present. "What do you want, Buck?" said the president. "My dam," answered Buchanan. "Well then, I guess we'd better give it to you, Buck," Roosevelt replied as he phoned Ickes with the order.[19]

[16] Arthur E. Goldschmidt/Elizabeth Wickenden oral history, LBJL; Max Starcke/Mrs. Max Starcke oral history, LBJL; Adams, *Damming the Colorado*, 17–25.
[17] Adams, *Damming the Colorado*, 24–5, 34.
[18] Robert H. Boyle, John Graves, and T. H. Watkins, *The Water Hustlers* (1970), 41.
[19] Adams, *Damming the Colorado*, 33–4; Caro, *Path to Power*, 378.

Whether or not this tête-à-tête actually occurred, the acquisition of federal patronage proved much more complicated. The first PWA grant had been made with the proviso that Texas create the appropriate public entity (such as a river authority) to receive funding. This was easier said than done. It is true that up to that time four such authorities (the Brazos, Guadalupe-Blanco, Valley, and Lower Neches districts) had been established in Texas. But efforts to launch a Colorado River Authority proceeded with difficulty. Investors and state legislators wanted the project in private hands. Buchanan, however, reminded residents that ample funds would come only after a public agency was established. Addressing an excited crowd at the construction site of Hamilton Dam, he vowed that the project would become "the hydroelectric power center of Texas" and "the biggest thing next to the TVA." Texans subsequently referred to the structure as "Buchanan Dam" after the congressman, in direct contradiction of a federal law prohibiting the naming of a dam for a living figure.[20]

Buchanan enlisted the help of Representative Joseph J. Mansfield, a fellow Texan from a Colorado River district who chaired the House Rivers and Harbors Committee. Wirtz arranged for a formidable Washington group including Buchanan, Mansfield, and the chief counsel of the PWA and Interior Department to testify over a period of weeks before the state legislature. Interests in favor of the authority included not only those who desired flood control, power, water, and jobs for the area, but also rice farmers and irrigators of the lower valley and investors who wanted to recover assets ponied up for the Insull project. On 17 September 1934, the state senate passed the Lower Colorado River Authority Bill, but the legislation failed in the house, where it met fierce opposition from a coalition of private utilities and West Texas ranchers. The bill passed later that year in a special session after Buchanan pressured the legal division of the PWA to support a water rights amendment desired by the state's western ranchers.[21]

Thus, in 1934, the LCRA came into being as a nonprofit conservation and reclamation district, a "government agency, body politic and corporate of the State of Texas" that included the ten counties of the river's lower basin. The bill directed the governor to appoint a board of twelve

---

[20] Adams, *Damming the Colorado*, 34–6.
[21] Comer Clay, "The Lower Colorado River Authority: A Study in Politics and Public Administration" (Ph.D. diss., University of Texas, 1948), 177–8; Adams, *Damming the Colorado*, 36–9.

directors subject to confirmation by the state senate. Notably, the LCRA was not empowered to levy or collect taxes, though it could issue revenue bonds.[22]

Buchanan recognized that the mere existence of a public agency would not guarantee PWA approval, so in early 1935 he labored to secure funds from Ickes and to remove two potential problems. First, the LCRA (unlike TVA or the Colorado Compact that governed the construction of Hoover Dam) exercised jurisdiction only within the state of Texas. A federal grant would mean the "first precedent in the development of intrastate rivers for any purpose other than navigation." Second, the LCRA promoters had championed the possibilities of flood control and irrigation, keeping the hydroelectric power question in the background. From the beginning, they proceeded with the multipurpose project while keeping their intent to generate electricity under wraps. Not fooled, the Texas power interests, especially Texas Power and Light, continued to fight the LCRA, taking as their model similar efforts to suspend government-financed competition in the Tennessee Valley.[23]

Still, the funds came through. Although Ickes and his staff understood the difficulties, the president approved a $20 million allotment to the LCRA in May 1935. Of this amount, $5 million came as a grant from the Bureau of Reclamation for flood control, and $15 million came as a combination PWA loan and grant arrangement to finance those aspects of the project not specifically dedicated to flood control. This $20 million in public works financing was third only to that awarded Hoover Dam ($38 million) and Grand Coulee ($23 million). Job creation formed another justification for the Texas allocation; Ickes acquired Texas relief statistics for a fifty-mile radius around the half-complete dam, and believed that the project would alleviate the misery of 95,422 relief recipients in the area.[24]

The LCRA planned four dam projects – completion of Buchanan, the start of Roy Inks and Marshall Ford, and the rebuilding of the Austin Dam destroyed during the 1935 flood. At this point the private power companies, understanding the hydroelectric potential of the projects, sued in federal court to prevent construction of these facilities. The Texas utilities

[22] LCRA, "Years of Progress at the LCRA," 1965, LCRA Box 3B; "Development of the Lower Colorado," 1–7.

[23] Buchanan to Engelhard, 10 November 1934, quoted in Adams, *Damming the Colorado*, 39; Adams, *Damming the Colorado*, 39–40, 54–5.

[24] Roosevelt to Secretary of the Treasury, 2 July 1935, HP Box 166; Adams, *Damming the Colorado*, 41–4.

claimed that the Supreme Court's 1935 decision in *Ashwander*, a decision that upheld TVA's right to sell whatever power it produced from its first dam, should not apply to intrastate river authorities. For their part, LCRA and Reclamation officials, continuing their strategy to conceal the power question, insisted the dams were solely for flood control and irrigation. Meanwhile, with continued PWA assistance, construction on Buchanan and Roy Inks moved at fever pitch. Then, when the Supreme Court handed down further decisions establishing the legality of PWA-financed power projects operated in competition with private business, the LCRA openly declared its intention to produce inexpensive hydropower. Buchanan pledged to secure the final funding for Marshall Ford when Congress reopened in January 1937.[25]

Enough money remained from an earlier appropriation to begin construction of the Marshall Ford Dam. The site was located eighteen miles northwest of Austin in a remote, hilly area, and the LCRA and Bureau of Reclamation approved plans for improved roads, a railspur, a field headquarters, and a workers' camp. Buchanan successfully enticed Harold Ickes to speak at an on-site dedication, and the secretary proudly lauded the country's conservation accomplishments before igniting a ceremonial fuse. Buchanan, unable to attend the event owing to his Washington schedule, succumbed to a heart attack three days later.[26]

CONGRESSMAN JOHNSON

On the afternoon of 22 February 1937, Alvin Wirtz received a visit from Lyndon Johnson. Wirtz had come to know the fellow Texan when Johnson worked for Congressman Kleberg. While representing the LCRA on visits to Washington, Wirtz marveled at the young secretary's ability to schedule appointments with important officials. One LCRA board member who accompanied Wirtz on one of these jaunts recalled that Johnson "knew Washington ... he could get you in to any place."[27]

Now Johnson had come to ask for Wirtz's support in a long-shot bid to fill Buchanan's seat. Foremost in Wirtz's mind was the future of the LCRA. Could Johnson step in where Buchanan had left off? Wirtz believed that he could, that with his formidable operating skills Johnson would successfully direct federal dollars to the LCRA system. Johnson announced his

[25] PWA press release, August 1937, HP Box 166; Adams, *Damming the Colorado*, 52–66.
[26] Adams, *Damming the Colorado*, 66–70.
[27] Caro, *Path to Power*, 285, 392; Weisenberger, *Dollars and Dreams*, 60; Abe Fortas oral history, LBJL.

intentions early, thus discouraging Buchanan's widow from the race. Eight other contenders also threw their hats into the ring. With ten thousand dollars in cash wired from Lady Bird's father, Wirtz (now the campaign manager) began the task of introducing his candidate to the district.[28]

By any reckoning, the campaign should have been lost before it began. Hardly anyone had heard of Lyndon Johnson. He hailed from Blanco County, the least populated county in the district, and was seldom recognized on the streets of Austin. Only twenty-eight years old, Johnson faced competition from a fearsome set of seasoned politicians. But Wirtz hit upon a strategy to set him apart from the other candidates, insisting Johnson present himself as the "total Roosevelt man." In 1936, FDR had carried the Tenth District by nine to one, and polls in 1937 found that voters overwhelmingly supported the president's controversial Supreme Court reorganization plan. Sam Fore, a friend from the Kleberg days, put it this way: "Lyndon, look, the important thing about this race is FDR. People like him, and he's in hot water over that Court-packing thing. He needs our help and we are going to come out loud and clear for him. There's not going to be any halfway stuff."[29]

Johnson embraced this advice, positioning himself as the only candidate 100 percent behind the Roosevelt program. "What good can come," he explained, "of having plans for controlling a Colorado River, Brazos River, or the Blanco and Guadalupe River, if in the end the Supreme Court shall say that these plans are not within the province of the government and the people themselves?" "There is *only one issue* in this campaign," he hollered. "Are you *for* the President, or *against* him?" Johnson campaigned fiercely, driving through every town in the district and instructing his wife not to let him back in the house before dark. He let loose a barrage of newspaper ads, mailings, and radio speeches. Concluding he had a slim chance to woo voters in Austin, Johnson concentrated his efforts in the areas outside the capital. A cousin remembered that on his first campaign Lyndon went everywhere: "to the blackland belt, to the sandyland people, to the people on the forks of the creeks." He stopped at each filling station to pump a gallon of gas, shook hands in every business district, and leapt over fences to meet farmers at work.[30]

Johnson promised a program of rural relief and rural development. He pledged to complete Marshall Ford and the Brazos flood control projects,

---

[28] Caro, *Path to Power*, 393; Dallek, *Lone Star Rising*, 146.
[29] Sam Fore, quoted in Dallek, *Lone Star Rising*, 147.
[30] *Austin Statesman*, 6 March 1937; Dallek, *Lone Star Rising*, 149–55; Caro, *Path to Power*, 409, 422.

to continue work programs, to increase farm income and decrease interest rates, and to support tenant-purchase legislation. "I'm a farmer like you," he would say. "I was raised up on a farm. I know what it's like to be afraid that they're going to take your land away." And he persuasively linked Roosevelt with these campaign promises. "Didn't you just tell me you was goin' under when the soil conservation program came in, and they started paying you to let your land lie out? Well, whose program is that? Roosevelt's. Didn't you tell me your boy's doin' terracing over in Kerrville? Well, whose program do you think the CCC is? Roosevelt's."[31]

On election day, only 29,948 people (out of an estimated population of 264,000) cast their votes, and of those only 8,280 persons voted for Johnson. Amazingly, however, he beat his closest opponent by 3,200 votes. In the end, Johnson won the election with the support of only 3 percent of the district's population. Later, when Robert Caro analyzed the election returns, he found that Johnson's support had come from the western hill counties, from the remote, poor precincts where Johnson had visited each farmer and rancher individually. At the time, Johnson's cousin certainly wasn't surprised: "[Lyndon] told them: 'I *know* what you people are up against. Because I'm one of you people.' And it wasn't the people of the cities who elected him."[32]

Franklin Roosevelt quickly learned that an ardent supporter had been elected to fill Buchanan's seat. On 11 April, the president received a telegram from the mayor of Brenham noting that Johnson's success was a "fine victory and high testimonial of your great leadership... [The] reorganization of the Supreme Court was made the main issue... with Johnson the most outspoken for you."[33] When Roosevelt met Johnson in Galveston the next month, the president was quite impressed with the "uninhibited pro" and later directed White House assistant Thomas Corcoran to "help him with anything you can."[34]

The first issue at hand, of course, was securing adequate funds for the Marshall Ford Dam and other LCRA projects. By coming all out for the president's court-packing scheme, Johnson and Wirtz had indeed hit upon a brilliant strategy. Johnson killed two birds with one stone: first,

---

[31] *Brenham Banner-Press*, 23 September 1937; Caro, *Path to Power*, 416–17. Caro reconstructed these impromptu tidbits by combining interview and newspaper material with Johnson's known manner of speaking. While Johnson may not have spoken these phrases verbatim, the sentiments expressed do reveal his actions and beliefs.

[32] Caro, *Path to Power*, 437–9.

[33] 11 April 1937, MF-LBJ.

[34] Dallek, *Lone Star Rising*, 161.

he convinced the voters that he was "their man" in Washington, and most important, he won valuable allies in the Roosevelt administration. Several people who worked in Washington at the time remembered that after the election (and after Roosevelt's directions to Tom Corcoran) Johnson gained entrée to powerful officials. Arthur Goldschmidt, who worked in the power division of the PWA, remembered that the election "put [Johnson] in immediate friendly relations with Ickes, who was very strong on the court issue." Even the president himself appreciated this new protégé. Oscar Chapman, assistant secretary of the interior, recalled that "Johnson's support of public power led him right straight into the White House doorway." With court suits piling up against the PWA, the executive branch appreciated the newest Roosevelt partisan.[35]

Johnson hardly secured funds for the LCRA on his own. In this effort he was assisted by Texas Senators Tom Connally and Morris Sheppard and by Congressmen J. J. Mansfield and Sam Rayburn. Mansfield (chairman of Rivers and Harbors) especially played a crucial role in drafting legislation for the money Representative Buchanan had intended to secure. But Johnson worked diligently to negotiate an agreement between the city of Austin and the LCRA to rebuild the Austin Dam, and he arranged critical meetings between Washington officials and LCRA personnel. The Department of the Interior finally approved an allotment for $5 million on 21 July 1937, and Roosevelt issued the executive order releasing the funds.[36]

At the end of his first term Johnson proudly boasted of his initial achievements. Newspapers all over the district expressed similar satisfaction with his record, especially the $5 million obtained for the LCRA. They also praised Johnson's commitment to farmers, conservation, and work relief. Because the Supreme Court had struck down the first AAA, Johnson fought to extend low-interest rates to farmers and to pass an emergency subsidy and commodity loan on the 1937 cotton crop. He also urged that the country pass new, more permanent farm legislation. In addition, he arranged for the retention of CCC camps, and for studies of federal fish hatcheries in the new LCRA reservoirs.[37] "I don't need to tell

[35] Oscar L. Chapman oral history, LBJL; Goldschmidt/Wickenden oral history, LBJL
[36] Adams, *Damming the Colorado*, 72–81; *Austin American*, 26 July 1937.
[37] *Brenham Banner-Press*, 15 July 1937; *Texas Observer*, 19 July 1937; *Houston Post*, 23 July 1937; *Austin American*, 26 July 1937; *Williamson County Sun*, 6 August 1937; *Elgin Courier*, 19 August 1937; *Bastrop Advertiser*, 26 August 1937; *Williamson County Sun*, 9 September 1937; *Austin American*, 10 September 1937.

you what has been done," Johnson claimed one evening to a jam-packed courtroom in Brenham.

You know how the unemployed have vanished from our streets, how they have gone onto public projects . . . You have seen our boys and girls return to the schools and colleges. You have seen our conservation and flood control projects slowly rising where before there were only eroding lands and diminishing resources. You know all about the refinancing of our homes and farms. You know about the end of breadlines, the conquest of fear and doubt, and the ascent of hope.[38]

Johnson also laid out his long-term vision for the district with an elaborate metaphor, comparing the Depression to a deluge. "You know," he said, "I like to think of America at work on its problems – its farm problem, for instance – in the light of a bunch of strong, hearty men down on the levee fighting back a great onrush of floodwaters. Maybe you've been down there yourself, and can follow me, step by step, in the picture."

He continued:

Here is all our fine farmland at the mercy of a river which has gone berserk . . . The storms raging for weeks up in the hills have piled up an unprecedented head of water and it is tumbling down to destroy us . . . We snatch up sacks, shovel sand into them, toss them into the breaches . . . [W]hen we have at last rescued our homes and our precious but poor little possessions, then what do we do? I'll tell you. We figure out some way to stop the next flood before it becomes a flood.

In order to protect the country from future "floods" (depressions), Johnson sought a comprehensive program of rural development. He called for permanent solutions, something besides the sandbags at the last moment, something sounder than the "policy of rocking along."[39] Not that emergency measures designed to alleviate immediate suffering were unimportant; Johnson supported stopgap farm credit and crop loans, and he sponsored work projects carried out by the WPA, CCC, and NYA in his district. But Johnson rarely spoke of relief or recovery without also mapping out plans for reform.

In his quest for rural uplift, Johnson insisted that the security of the nation depended on the well-being of the farmer. For the new congressman, as well as for many other New Dealers, this vision embraced more than the familiar economic trope that agriculture must receive its "fair share of the national income." It was an agrarian position rooted in the Jeffersonian vision of an independent, virtuous rural culture as the nucleus

[38] *Brenham Banner-Press*, 23 September 1937; *Tri-County News*, 30 September 1937.
[39] *Brenham Banner-Press*, 23 September 1937.

of American society. "Whether you are a banker, a merchant, a business man, a barber, a waitress, a clerk, a doctor, [or] a lawyer," he maintained time and again, "your future is bound up in the future of the farmers who live all around you."[40] Such thinking underpinned the more tangible approaches to the Depression adopted by Johnson and promulgated by national planners – conservationist policies designed to develop rural areas.

The farming systems in Johnson's district corresponded with geographic conditions and soil types. Though small strips of alluvial deposits along the Colorado River provided some excellent farmland, the thin stony soils of the Edwards Plateau and Llano Uplift covered much of the western and northwestern counties. Deeply eroded and dessicated, most of the Hill Country in Blanco, Burnet, and Hays Counties was dedicated to grazing and browsing livestock: mostly goats and sheep, but also some cattle. As one traveled east and south toward the prairies, the average farm size decreased while the acreage devoted to field crops jumped dramatically. The deeper, richer soils of the rolling "blacklands," and the area's large African American population, contrasted sharply with the rough hills and predominantly white faces of the upper region.[41]

Texans were by no means unaware of the need for soil conservation before the 1930s. In fact, several measures taken to address erosion before the New Deal prepared the ground for more extensive programs. In 1929, LBJ's predecessor, James Buchanan, had pronounced soil erosion a master criminal. Speaking in favor of a congressional measure to establish conservation experiment stations, Buchanan concluded that "uncontrolled surface water is the enemy of man. Controlled, it is a priceless blessing."[42]

In May 1931, the Texas legislature passed resolutions directed at financial institutions, "asking for cooperation of all agencies in preventing erosion." It requested that banks, farm mortgage institutions, and farm credit agencies use conservation measures as criteria in making farm loans, to

[40] *Brenham Banner-Press*, 23 September 1937.
[41] 1925 Agricultural Census: Bastrop, Blanco, Burleson, Burnet, Caldwell, Hays, Lee, Washington, and Williamson Counties; Extension Service Annual Narrative and Statistical Reports, microfilm series T-890, NA RG 33: 1934 Annual Extension Report: Blanco County; Paul H. Rigby, "A Statistical Study of the Lower Colorado River Authority's Soil Conservation and Farm and Ranch Improvement Program" (Ph.D. diss., University of Texas, 1952), 18–32.
[42] Quoted in Hugh H. Bennett, "Uncle Sam Takes Thought of Soil Productivity," HBP, NA RG 114, Entry 21, Box 4.

the end that "our soils may be conserved and that moisture be controlled, and fertility maintained and restored by terracing." The same legislation provided for the use of county-owned road machinery in terracing farmland.[43]

Throughout the 1920s, the USDA Extension Service had also demonstrated the beneficial effects of terracing and soil building in several Central Texas counties. Some agents had decried the "one crop system of cotton farming" and made diligent efforts to encourage diversification, crop rotations, green manuring, and fertilizing. They also warned that pastures were far too overstocked.[44] But their reports, filed annually in Washington, indicated that improved techniques never took root until New Deal agricultural programs supplied real financial incentives.

When the Extension Service began to administer the AAA programs, agents in Tenth District counties signed up participants in the spring plow-up campaign, and for cotton and corn-hog contracts. Even more important in the hilly northwestern counties, the federal government's 1934 stock-purchase plan bought animals in danger of dying as a result of severe drought conditions. In Blanco County (Johnson's home), farmers and ranchers received a total of $107,223 for their goats, sheep, and cattle. This huge sum constituted almost 93 percent of total AAA benefits to the county in 1934. In the flatter, more prosperous parts of the district, farmers benefited more from cotton and corn-hog payments. They planted sudan grass on pastures newly obtained from reducing crop acreage, and terraced land still in crops because terracing entitled the producer to more income from the AAA.[45]

The extension agents saw immediate benefits from the AAA: an instantaneous infusion of cash used to pay long-standing debts and taxes; the reduction of grazing animals on dry, eroded pastures that desperately needed rehabilitation; and diminished acreage devoted to row crops, an adjustment that the agents had been advocating for some time. They also noticed an important shift in perception – farmers had developed new

---

[43] "Resolutions Asking for Cooperation of All Agencies in Preventing Erosion," passed by Texas Legislature and signed by Governor, May 1931, and circular letter from J. E. McDonald to the bankers of Texas, 11 June 1931, Correspondence of Director of Soil Erosion and Moisture Conservation Investigations, HBP, NA RG 114, Entry 18, Box 3; Hugh H. Bennett, "Federal Land Bank Rates Topsoil As Farmer's Principal Capital," HBP, NA RG 114, Entry 21, Box 2; "Texas Passes High Mark in Terracing," HBP, NA RG 114, Entry 21, Box 8.

[44] 1928 Annual Extension Reports: Blanco, Hays, and Burnet Counties.

[45] 1934 Annual Extension Reports: Blanco, Travis, Hays, and Washington Counties.

attitudes about the role of the federal government. "Confidence in the government and in Extension work is much stronger as a result of the program," a satisfied Blanco County agent reported. "For a while, farmers had about lost hope; they could not make a living and no one seemed to be doing anything about it." But "as a result of the AAA programs, everything has changed; prices are beginning to near normal and farming and ranching has a future." Rural Texans, the agent concluded, had learned their lesson. "Farmers have found that they must cooperate to secure results."[46]

When Johnson campaigned for Congress in 1937, he operated with this altered worldview in mind. To be sure, the more affluent eastern counties profited much more from the early AAA programs than the western hill counties.[47] Still, almost everyone had benefited in some small way, and many residents were now receptive to the idea that the government should alleviate suffering and promote better forms of land management. In 1937, Johnson outlined a long-term agricultural program that included production control, improved transportation and product research, soil conservation, and a tenant-purchase program to attack "one of the greatest enigmas in agriculture."[48]

Johnson kept his promises. He helped secure passage of the Bankhead-Jones Act in 1937, which established the Farm Security Administration. The Texas FSA offered loans to selected tenants so that they might become landowners and made grants to farmers in emergency situations (such as those inundated in a flood or faced with foreclosure). Johnson saw to it that both types of aid came to his district. By way of emergency measures, Johnson announced that FSA money would be available in the summer of 1938 for victims of the 1938 Colorado flood. In December of that year, he also organized FSA loans for farmers without collateral in his district. As for the tenancy provisions, in 1937 he arranged for the inclusion of Williamson and Washington Counties in the tenant-purchase program. These two counties suffered from some of the highest tenancy rates in the district, and Washington County contained the largest number of black farmers, most of whom worked land they did not own. The program was extended to Blanco County in 1940. While it would be difficult to isolate the FSA's influence (technology, markets, and migration to factory work also played large roles), tenancy rates in the Tenth District fell. In 1925,

[46] 1934 Annual Extension Reports: Blanco, Travis, Hays, and Washington Counties.
[47] Caro, *Path to Power*, 497–8.
[48] *Brenham Banner-Press*, 23 September 1937; *Tri-County News*, 30 September 1937.

tenants accounted for almost 60 percent of farmers in the area; by 1950 the percentage hovered around half that number (Table 3.1).[49]

Johnson also maintained that the country needed a "sane, safe, and economically logical" system of crop control, "one that works on our farm flow of production as gates and valves control the flow of waters from a storage lake." To this end, he backed the farm legislation destined to become the new AAA of 1938. Notably, Johnson called for a graduated system of benefit payments "so that the big corporation farmer will not be paid in accordance with his bigness, while the little farmer, struggling along with his 40, 60, or 100 acres is assisted only in proportion to his littleness." While such a progressive system of payments never materialized, the new legislation worked on a tilled-acre basis, rather than a yield basis, and provided for the continuation of the soil conservation program. To ensure market outlets, Johnson also secured aid for paved farm-to-market roads (constructed as WPA projects) and federal support of cotton-products research.[50]

While terracing proceeded apace in all the counties, and while many farmers earned their soil-building allowances by including green manures and winter legumes in their crop rotations, the most far-reaching agricultural conservation development in the late thirties occurred on the range. Under the AAA's Range Conservation Program, farmers received payments for cutting down certain species of brush, improving pastures by deferred grazing or artificial reseeding, contouring and terracing, and digging tanks or wells. Johnson took particular interest in this program, most likely because he was familiar with the tough juniper "cedar" brush of the Hill Country, the ubiquitous, tangled thickets that covered the fields and sucked up the moisture. The congressman called county agents frequently and sent mailings directly to constituents, and he arranged funds for the Blanco County agent to hire cedar-choppers to clear one farm as a demonstration. Because Johnson also arranged for AAA payments of five dollars for each acre cleared, the cash-strapped Hill Country farmers could afford to clear their own cedar as well.[51]

---

49 Letter from AAA Administrator, College Station, Texas, HP Box 169; *Dallas News*, 5 August 1938; Caro, *Path to Power*, 498–9; *Austin American*, 14 September 1937; *Tri-County News*, 16 December 1937; 1925 Agricultural Census: Washington County; 1940 Annual Extension Reports: Washington and Blanco Counties.

50 *Brenham Banner-Press*, 23 September 1937; *Tri-County News*, 30 December 1937; *Bastrop Advertiser*, 27 December 1937; Dallek, *Lone Star Rising*, 170–1.

51 The Range Conservation Program began in 1935 and was extended to all Texas counties in 1937. 1938 Annual Extension Reports: Blanco, Travis, Washington, and Burnet Counties; *Caldwell News*, 28 April 1938; Caro, *Path to Power*, 499–500; B. F. Vance to Johnson, 21 November 1945, F. H. Whitaker to Johnson, 1 January 1946, HP Box 265.

TABLE 3.1. Tenancy Rates (%) in Tenth District Counties, White and Black

County	1925			1945			1950		
	White	Black	Combined	White	Black	Combined	White	Black	Combined
Blanco	34.4	40.0	34.6	19.2	0	18.7	16.2	0	16.0
Burnet	52.0	75.0	52.2	35.0	100.0	35.2	23.3	—	23.3
Hays	67.9	65.2	67.7	25.4	31.3	25.6	22.2	10.7	21.9
Travis	70.2	88.1	74.8	35.9	64.8	39.4	29.4	57.6	32.4
Williamson	65.3	88.8	67.2	50.0	77.3	51.5	45.0	78.9	46.1
Caldwell	76.8	68.5	75.5	39.3	33.2	38.4	35.2	33.0	34.9
Bastrop	62.7	79.2	68.9	30.7	36.5	32.6	24.8	32.0	26.5
Lee	45.9	63.1	51.0	26.5	34.8	28.5	23.9	27.1	24.6
Burleson	52.1	82.1	66.2	36.2	41.6	37.7	26.0	33.4	27.9
Washington	43.8	77.3	58.2	38.6	58.7	44.5	30.2	45.0	34.4
AVERAGE†	59.5	78.2	66.0	36.7	49.6	38.9	30.6	43.9	32.4
Texas	57.1	75.7	60.4	35.7	52.0	37.6	29.2	40.7	30.4

Note: "White" includes Mexicans (all years).
† Excluding Blanco, Burnet, and Hays, whose small black populations skew results (see Table 3.7).
Source: Agricultural Census.

All over Blanco County, residents repeated near-miraculous benefits after ridding their land of prickly pear cactus, mesquite, lechuguilla, and especially cedar. A Cypress Hill farmer declared that his heavy cedar section would not carry one cow to thirty acres before cutting and burning the cedar, and that he now ran one cow every five acres. Another fellow from Johnson City said his range had improved 500 percent and that "an old spring is now flowing in the area of the burn that was never known to be more than a damp spot... it is running now, notwithstanding the fact that the county is experiencing a 9 month drought." Other ranchers witnessed springs "break forth" after the brush was cleared; on the morning of 10 August 1938, for example, one of these springs supplied the water for "12 cattle, 5 deer, and a flock of about 20 turkeys... and [the owner] said the spring was never known to flow during the 75 years the ranch was owned by his grandfather, father, and him." The residents might be forgiven the biblical language of springs "breaking forth." After all, it could not have seemed anything but astounding when moisture increased and verdant grass grew after the simple, albeit laborious, task of clearing the brush.[52]

Soil conservation in the district received an added boost after the 1938 reorganization of the Bureau of Agricultural Economics to emphasize local, participatory agricultural planning. Land use planning committees were formed in several counties, and local leaders, along with representatives from the Extension Service, the Soil Conservation Service (SCS), the FSA, and the Farm Credit Administration, worked to compile planning maps and set goals. They consistently included soil and water conservation projects – cedar eradication, terracing, contouring, pasture seeding, and tank construction – on the list of priorities. The AAA partially underwrote these tasks, continuing to remit payments for such practices. In 1944, one agent proudly reported that "a person can travel any highway or county road... and see old farm lands with new terraces, tanks, and acreage planted to winter legumes." All in all, despite evidence at the national level that the Extension Service and the AAA county committees harbored reservations about the SCS-sponsored soil conservation districts, the Central Texas reports from the early 1940s indicate a genuine spirit of cooperation and mutual support. For example, the county committees, extension agents, and SCS personnel helped organize and distribute county-owned machinery for building terraces, and they

[52] 1938 Annual Extension Report: Blanco County; B. F. Vance to Johnson, 21 November 1945, F. H. Whitaker to Johnson, 1 January 1946, HP Box 265.

TABLE 3.2. *Percentage of Farmland Used as Pasture in Tenth District Counties and State of Texas*

County	1925	1945	1950
Blanco	79.4	93.2	90.7
Burnet	66.6	85.2	82.8
Hays	73.1	87.0	82.0
Travis	45.2	74.0	62.5
Williamson	23.6	49.1	44.7
Caldwell	22.5	68.9	68.0
Bastrop	48.5	77.1	78.9
Lee	67.0	77.4	75.6
Burleson	49.3	72.2	73.5
Washington	41.5	66.0	68.6
AVERAGE	51.7	75.0	72.7
Texas	68.4	76.8	75.3

Source: Agricultural Census.

worked together on a 504-acre demonstration plot just outside Johnson City.[53]

Data from the agricultural census demonstrate that federal agricultural programs had far-reaching effects in Central Texas. Land utilization planners had long viewed grazing as a more sustainable form of land use than cropping, and they designed the AAA and other USDA measures not only to reduce market-clogging surpluses but also to take marginal and damaged lands out of cultivation. And from 1925 to 1950, the acreage used for crops in Texas's Tenth District dropped by half, from 40 to 20 percent of the farmland. Concomitantly, the acreage devoted to pasture climbed from 52 to 73 percent of the farmland (Tables 3.2 and 3.3). These averages mask some particularly dramatic examples; for instance, in Bastrop County the percentage of farmland in crops fell from 45 to 14, and the percentage of farmland used as pasture in Caldwell County increased from 23 to 68. This shift from cropland to pasture reflected two trends: first, the total acreage in farms increased between 1925 and 1950, and most of that new land was dedicated to cattle, sheep, and goats; and second, acreage that had been used for growing annual crops became pastureland.

[53] 1940 Annual Extension Reports: Travis, Blanco, and Washington Counties; 1942 Annual Extension Reports: Travis, Washington, and Bastrop Counties; 1944 Annual Extension Reports: Washington, Travis, Blanco, and Bastrop Counties.

TABLE 3.3. *Percentage of Farmland Used for Crops in Tenth District Counties and State of Texas*

County	1925	1940	1945	1950
Blanco	10.0	6.3	6.1	5.6
Burnet	15.3	12.4	13.0	11.2
Hays	25.0	14.5	10.8	10.9
Travis	49.7	29.6	22.3	25.5
Williamson	73.0	46.9	47.0	48.2
Caldwell	56.9	41.2	26.6	25.7
Bastrop	45.1	22.1	15.2	13.9
Lee	28.8	23.6	19.2	18.7
Burleson	47.4	31.2	24.9	20.9
Washington	52.3	37.4	29.3	24.0
AVERAGE	40.4	26.5	21.4	20.4
Texas	25.8	20.4	20.0	19.3

Note: Data for 1925, 1940, and 1945 include acreage for cropland harvested and crop failure; 1950 data include only cropland harvested. Figures do not include idle or fallow cropland, or plowed pasture.
Source: Agricultural Census.

Unfortunately, the agricultural census does not record the number of terraces built or cedars removed, but acreage planted in legumes – a similar indicator of soil conservation practice – also increased (Table 3.4).

LCRA EXPANSION: RURAL ELECTRIFICATION, RECREATION, AND WARTIME GROWTH

While Johnson encouraged the agricultural extension and improvement programs, he also played an important role in coordinating LCRA expansion. As he settled into his congressional routine during the winter of 1937–8, he kept a close watch over LCRA affairs in Washington and continued to work on the details involved in completing Marshall Ford Dam. In January, he announced a grant from the WPA to clear timber from the Marshall Ford basin, a job that afforded seven months' work for 433 men. At Wirtz's suggestion, he secured an agreement from Reclamation Commissioner John Page later that spring that exempted the LCRA from repaying the government as required under federal reclamation law. Page concurred that Marshall Ford was primarily for flood control, that the project would only indirectly benefit downstream irrigators, and that the bureau had in any case served only as an "agency for construction."

TABLE 3.4. *Percentage of Cropland Planted in Legumes in Tenth District Counties and State of Texas*

County	1925	1940	1945	1950
Blanco	.01	7.2	1.7	1.4
Burnet	.009	2.6	1.6	2.5
Hays	0.5	1.0	0.2	3.8
Travis	.05	0.3	0.2	1.5
Williamson	.02	0.5	0.3	0.7
Caldwell	0.2	2.6	1.9	3.4
Bastrop	0.2	8.7	5.2	7.4
Lee[†]	0.5	19.3	22.6	20.2
Burleson	0.2	8.7	4.5	4.4
Washington	.06	3.6	0.5	0.7
AVERAGE	0.2	5.5	3.8	4.6
Texas	0.5	5.7	3.9	3.8

Note: Figures for legumes include both annual field crops (peanuts, soybeans, cowpeas, other miscellaneous beans) and hay crops (alfalfa, timothy, or clover).
[†] Large increase owing almost entirely to peanuts.
Source: Agricultural Census.

All seemed to be proceeding smoothly until Ickes, concerned about the increasing cost of the dam, informed Johnson that only a low dam would be completed, not the high dam the LCRA expected. Ickes felt confident the existing structures could handle flood conditions, if the Buchanan and Marshall Field reservoirs were lowered in advance of flows from the highlands. However, Ickes did add that the low dam could be raised if "experience" demonstrated "the need."[54]

Experience indeed demanded a high dam in the summer of 1938. After Wirtz and Johnson maneuvered inconclusively to reinstate funds from Washington, Central Texas suffered its worst flooding in over a hundred years. Ten days of pounding rain covered the entire watershed, and the runoff overwhelmed the two operating dams (Buchanan and Inks). Water swept away homes, crops, and livestock in several downstream counties, and the river, at a level forty-two feet above normal, covered parts of downtown Austin for three days. Preliminary reports indicated that the

[54] *Austin American*, 29 January 1938; Wirtz to Johnson, 28 February 1938, HP Box 167; Engelhard to Mansfield, 23 February 1938, HP Box 169; Ickes to Johnson, 1 March 1938, LBJA Famous Names Box 5, LBJL; Engelhard to Mansfield, 2 March 1938, HP Box 169; Adams, *Damming the Colorado*, 81–4.

flood had taken twelve lives and left over four thousand people home-less.[55]

Outrage erupted over the LCRA's seeming incompetence. Evidence emerged that the dam operators had possibly failed to manage the reservoir levels properly, that they should have lowered the lakes in preparation for containing the floodwaters. Sensing a political opportunity, the power companies argued that the dams could not be managed for both flood control and power production; "an empty dam cannot run generators," said the president of West Texas Utilities Company, "and a full dam cannot store floodwaters." A cursory Interior Department investigation cleared the LCRA of gross negligence, but the Texas senate conducted a more extensive investigation during the summer. In the end, an understanding emerged about the role of the LCRA: Wirtz agreed that the LCRA would manage the dams at a "maximum efficiency for flood control, consistent with the production of revenue through the manufacture and sale of electric current." That is, the LCRA did not have to keep the dams dry, which was what maximum flood control would require; it could retire its bonds by selling power. In Washington, Johnson continued to pressure federal officials for the high dam, and by the summer of 1939 the Reclamation Bureau allocated the funds for Marshall Ford (renamed Mansfield Dam after Congressman Mansfield in 1941). Only the Central Valley and Grand Coulee projects collected a larger portion of the reclamation budget.[56]

During the late 1930s Johnson also began a movement to electrify the surrounding farm areas. Despite its public condemnation of the projects, Texas Power and Light expected to purchase wholesale power from the LCRA once the hydroelectric facilities came on-line. In Johnson's mind, however, it made little sense to have come so far and then to sell all the power to a private company that had little interest in transporting the power to the farms. "Is this great stock of power, generated by the flood-water forces which heretofore have raged through our district, going to be put to the use of bettering the lives and economic situations of our farmers," he asked, "or are we going to let it get away from us, into private hands?" In contrast, Johnson advocated the development of publicly owned distribution systems, rather than private utilities, as the final link in a program of rural development. Understanding the significant extension

---

[55] See folder on 1938 flood, HP Box 169; Adams, *Damming the Colorado*, 85–8.

[56] See folder on 1938 flood, HP Box 169; Adams, *Damming the Colorado*, 87–95. A picture of Marshall Ford appeared on the cover of the April 1939 issue of *Reclamation Era*.

of conservationist thought initiated by FDR and legally enshrined in the TVA Act of 1933 – that now all farms and farm areas must be considered the special beneficiaries of federal power projects – Johnson set out to bring this assistance to Central Texas. Rural cooperatives and municipal facilities, he argued, should distribute inexpensive hydroelectric power from the dams to the farms and the towns. As one LCRA associate remembered, "This was all tied in together into one package, so that actually he could see this dream with the LCRA and then the co-ops working in the selling of power and the electricity to the farms as [an economic program] that would help the agricultural areas."[57]

Through the influence of USDA county agents, many Texas farmers had already grown quite interested in the federal program of rural electrification, which in 1935 was expanded beyond TVA to a new Rural Electrification Administration (REA) intended to serve regions outside the Tennessee Valley. In March of 1938, Johnson urged farm groups in Central Texas to link their desire for electrification with the LCRA. At the same time, he directed the LCRA's general manager to put an engineer consultant in the field and asked that the LCRA make a survey of potential rural customers, just as the authority was doing with respect to potential city outlets for power distribution. "There are hundreds of farm homes all over Central Texas," Johnson wrote, "where the smoky lantern and the stifling kerosene lamp are still the chief sources of illumination, and elbow grease is still the principal motive power. There are dozens of small towns, farm communities, and little cities which have no light and power at all."[58]

In April, Johnson invited the LCRA Board of Directors to a conference in Washington. Rather than praising their successes, however, the brash congressman issued a stern lecture on the board's failure to complete the power survey. "We ought to have drawn a circle around those dams," he admonished, "and there should have been a yes-or-no answer from every potential customer!" After all, the reason the LCRA "was given a chance to exist" was "the control of disastrous floods and the turning of their power into the channels of a better life for our farmers and ranchers and the residents of smaller cities." Johnson informed the board that to sell power to the private companies would bring the LCRA well-deserved

---

[57] *Blanco County News*, 24 March 1938; Dorothy Palmie in Starcke/Starcke oral history, LBJL.
[58] "Short History of the Development of the Pedernales Electric Cooperative," McWilliams to Johnson, 26 August 1939, HP Box 173; *Austin American*, 20 March 1938; *Blanco County News*, 24 March 1938.

criticism. "The single disposal of the majority of the prime power to private utilities is a crazy idea," he asserted. "I tell you that if we come to such an eventuality we are all likely to be run out of the state."[59]

Johnson defended this position by arguing that the LCRA would create a monopoly by selling power to Texas Power and Light (TP&L). He reminded the board members about TVA Chairman Arthur E. Morgan's disastrous attempt to cooperate with the power companies in the Tennessee Valley. In January of 1937, Morgan had announced in the *New York Times* that he would find "common ground with the utilities" through "reasonableness, fair play, and open dealing."[60] This sentiment, at odds with the expectations of TVA proponents, had provoked a debate about the authority's mission and direction. Wanting to take advantage of the similarity between TVA and the LCRA, Johnson read from an anti-Morgan speech delivered the previous year in Congress by Democratic Senator Kenneth McKellar of Tennessee. "If Chairman [Morgan]," McKellar had said (and Johnson quoted), "If Chairman Morgan has cold feet on the aims and purposes of the Authority, if he has reached the conclusion that it can only properly succeed by combining and confederating with the power companies in restraint of trade... then it seems to me he would wish to retire from the Authority." As if this sentiment didn't seal his case, Johnson also reminded his listeners that Harold Ickes himself had warned of the devious intentions of the private utilities when he dedicated Buchanan Dam in 1937. At that ceremony, Ickes had declared that the government could put the nation's resources to work for the common good, but that all Americans needed to be wary of the private power companies who intended to "fry the fat out of the profits from sale of the power" and become monopolies.[61]

Johnson had reason to worry. If the LCRA could not find other customers for the power generated at Buchanan and Inks Dams, it would be forced to sell it all to TP&L. But getting power to rural customers was tricky. Federal guidelines stipulated that a region must include three farms per mile of transmission line to receive an REA loan, a requirement that the sparsely settled counties of the Hill Country could not meet. Thus the situation had reached an impasse: the private utilities were unwilling to

[59] "Statement of Lyndon Johnson at a Conference with Members of the LCRA Board," 12 April 1938, LCRA Box PB 26.

[60] "Dr. Morgan Pleads for 'Cooperation' with the Utilities," *New York Times*, 17 January 1937, quoted in Steven M. Neuse, *David E. Lilienthal: The Journey of an American Liberal* (1996), 99.

[61] "Statement of Lyndon Johnson," 12 April 1938.

string lines to the farms, and the farms were unable to receive aid from the REA.

Johnson spoke several times with the director of the REA but found that the agency "wasn't going lend any money down there where there were only one and a half customers per mile." So in June 1938 Johnson decided to appeal directly to the president. At the advice of Tom Corcoran, he showed Roosevelt pictures of Buchanan Dam, the transmission lines, and the house of a tenant farmer. "Water, water everywhere, not a drop to drink!" Johnson exclaimed. "Power, power everywhere, but not in a home on the banks of these rural rivers!" While Johnson waited, Roosevelt placed a telephone call and asked the REA director to approve the loans. "I know how you've got to have guidelines," the president said, "but you just go ahead and approve this for me – charge it to my account."[62]

Roosevelt was most likely receptive to Johnson's pleas because of his and his administration's heightened concern with the South. At the president's request, a group of southern liberals had compiled a *Report on Economic Conditions of the South* in the spring and summer of 1938. Influenced in large part by the thinking of southern regionalist Howard Odum, the group had depicted the South as a colonial economy, rich in resources but economically and institutionally underdeveloped. As a result of the *Report*, Roosevelt's attention turned toward what he labeled the "Nation's No. 1 economic problem – the Nation's problem, not merely the South's." Owing to the Democrats' newly consolidated working-class support in the North, Roosevelt was beginning to feel less beholden to Southern Democrats in Congress. As Bruce Schulman has shown, the president and the southern advocates clustered around him now felt the time was ripe for a more coordinated attempt to raise southern living standards and to integrate the laggard region into the national economy. "It was not so much that the New Deal withered after 1938," Schulman argues, "as that it headed south."[63]

Lyndon Johnson became acquainted with the *Report on Economic Conditions* through his friend Tex Goldschmidt in the PWA. Goldschmidt, who was working with the REA on the Central Texas situation, advised Johnson to connect the power issue with the report by emphasizing "(1)

[62] White House memo, 3 June 1938, MF-LBJ; "Lady Bird Johnson," in Louchheim, *The Making of the New Deal*, 304–5; Dallek, *Lone Star Rising*, 179–81.

[63] Bruce J. Schulman, *From Cotton Belt to Sunbelt: Federal Policy, Economic Development, and the Transformation of the South, 1938–1980* (1991), 3, xii. The *Report on Economic Conditions* has recently been reprinted as Peter A. Coclanis and David L. Carlton, eds., *Confronting Poverty in the Great Depression* (1996).

the ownership of the power industry outside of the South and (2) use of [the] natural resources of the South to the advantage of the people of the South."[64]

After this advice, Johnson's rhetoric concerning rural electrification took a new turn. He emphasized the conundrum involved in raising southern standards of living:

What the South needs is power to stimulate its progress and growth, [but] because it is agricultural, its income level is low [and] electricity is costly. Therefore, the South cannot have electricity until it lifts its income. Since such a stalemate cannot be solved without first raising the income rate of the South, rural electrification has tackled it from the other end.

Johnson also sought to inflame historic anxieties about the domination of northeastern capital. Reaching back to the region's Populist and Confederate traditions, he exhorted his constituents to see that "every resource Texas has ever had has attracted the attention of outside financiers. It was so with our oil and gas...with our sulphur...with our lumber. It is what has happened to our soil, wasted and depleted and washed and worn away by one-crop quick-money farming methods to fatten some outsider's bankroll." Like the national New Dealers, Johnson fervently believed that the government could help the South harness its resources for its own people.[65]

Now that he could put aside a few worries about REA financing, Johnson turned his attention to convincing towns and rural cooperatives to establish their own distribution services. Each town or co-op would need to apply to the REA or PWA for loans in constructing such systems, but the mechanics of gathering membership fees, organizing the committees, and electing the boards proved daunting. Johnson and Wirtz persuaded the editor of the *Austin American* to promote rural electrification, and they hired a professional operations manager to assist individual communities in sorting out their options.[66]

Johnson put most of his energy into the unincorporated parts of the countryside, convincing farm groups to establish their own cooperative distribution systems. In this effort, Johnson worked closely with the USDA

---

[64] Goldschmidt/Wickenden oral history, LBJL; Goldschmidt to Johnson, 13 August 1938, HP Box 170.

[65] "LCRA Light REA Story," 1938, HP Box 166; "Colorado River Authority Interview with Congressman Lyndon Johnson," 1938, HP Box 166.

[66] "Short History of the Development of the Pedernales Electric Cooperative"; Starcke/Starcke oral history, LBJL; Clay, "Lower Colorado River Authority," 205–6; Dallek, *Lone Star Rising*, 181.

county agents in organizing the Pedernales Electric Cooperative (PEC). Though some insisted that the "country folk" would stubbornly hold on to the ways of the past, Johnson "had a standing offer to buy any man a Stetson ... who found a farmer or rancher refusing to pay the price of bringing electricity to his place."[67] At meetings Johnson cited TVA studies showing the benefits of low electric rates. Addressing rallies in Blanco and Johnson City, the congressman asked:

What does rural electrification mean? The LCRA has developed a flood control, reclamation, and conservation program, and incidental to this program is a large supply of hydroelectric power ... Cheap rural electricity from the REA means that there are many new fields open to Texas farmers. They can pump water cheaply. They can light their barns at night. They can churn with it, milk their cows with it, refrigerate their milk and foods, shell their corn with it, gin their cotton ... The farm wife, roasting herself over a cookstove on washday, can heat her iron with electricity. Instead of scrubbing her life away on a washboard, she can own a washing machine ... She can have a vacuum cleaner, an electric toaster, an electric percolator, an icebox, even an electric stove.[68]

By the early fall of 1938 the co-op's initial membership had risen to thirty-five hundred, and in September the REA allotted almost half a million dollars to construct 1,830 miles of rural lines in the PEC's ten-county area. Johnson also secured REA funds to build the cooperative's headquarters in Johnson City. Architects from TVA collaborated with a local firm to plan the design of native limestone, and a group of Mexican-American youths from the NYA assisted in its construction. The Johnson City *Record Courier*, duly impressed with the lightning speed at which the PEC came into being, suggested that the town celebrate a "Congressman Johnson Day" to observe "the outstanding accomplishments of this matchless young congressman of whom we are all justly proud." The next year, another cooperative formed – the Lower Colorado River Electric Cooperative (LCREC). The LCRA signed contracts with both cooperatives, agreeing to carry out the accounting and construction work at cost.[69]

---

[67] 1938 Annual Extension Report: Blanco County; Edwin C. Bearns, "Resource Study: Lyndon B. Johnson and the Hill Country, 1937–1963" (Santa Fe: Division of Conservation, National Park Service, Southwest Cultural Resources Center, 1984), 5.

[68] "LCRA Light REA Story," HP Box 166.

[69] "Short History of the Development of the Pedernales Electric Cooperative"; Bearns, "Resource Study"; Kellam to Johnson, 29 August 1939, HP Box 171; "P.E.C.: Serving the Hill Country," *LCRA News*, December 1947; *Johnson City Record Courier*, 5 May 1939; "NYA Boys Erect Building for REA Co-op," *REN* (July 1939), 12–13; Clay, "Lower Colorado River Authority," 214.

In the case of towns and cities, local elections determined whether a municipal system would be established. The elections pitted representatives of TP&L against the LCRA public relations machine. While TP&L sent notices to customers to vote against municipal systems, arguing that the LCRA intended only to duplicate existing lines, editorials in favor of public facilities argued that "you are going to buy and pay for [L]CRA power one way or another. You are going to buy it from yourself, to pay for your projects with your revenues at half the present cost, or you are going to buy it at any price the New York bankers tell you." Johnson traveled from town to town, giving speeches and radio addresses on behalf of public power. His efforts were successful – twenty-five out of twenty-six cities decided in favor of public power, and six towns received PWA loans and grants in the fall of 1938 for municipal systems. "You must be a very happy man," wrote a doctor from Bastrop, Texas, thanking Johnson for his help, "wanting to do so much good and being in a position to do it."[70]

To plan the retail rates, LCRA personnel consulted TVA and REA reports. Still, it was one thing to supply electricity to the countryside, but quite another to ensure that customers for that power materialized. The economic rationale for rural electrification was the idea that as electric rates went down, consumption would rise, thus enabling the public distribution systems to pay their debt out of increased revenue. But since the rural areas were poor and incomes low, how would farmers buy the new machines and appliances to take advantage of low power rates? As the TVA experience had demonstrated, there needed to be promotion and financing for electric equipment. Johnson worked with the Electric Home and Farm Authority (EHFA, established to finance electric equipment purchases in the TVA area, later expanded nationally) to market appliances, and with county agents in assessing demand for cold storage lockers to preserve marketable perishables. By April of 1939, Johnson had arranged REA funds for a cooperative refrigerating station in San Marcos. In 1940, he helped organize three appearances of an "Electrical Magic Circus," sponsored jointly by the REA, PEC, LCREC, and LCRA. Drawing around fifteen thousand people, these autumn circuses showcased appliances and farm machinery, urging attendees to "Use Electricity Extensively." LCRA reports indicate that generous lending practices on

---

[70] TP&L letter addressed "To Our Customers," HP Box 166; editorial prepared in Johnson's office, HP Box 166; Dallek, *Lone Star Rising*, 182; *San Antonio Light*, 20 November 1938; Bryson to Johnson, 23 October 1938, HP Box 172.

the part of both public agencies and private concerns helped appliance and equipment sales proceed smoothly.[71]

There still remained the issue of how to manage the relationship with the region's private utilities. Much like the utilities in the Tennessee Valley region, TP&L faced a delicate situation after the success of the LCRA and the municipalities in acquiring funds from the PWA. The utility justifiably asserted that the LCRA would just as soon duplicate existing lines, as a recent Supreme Court decision in favor of PWA power projects had upheld that very practice. Sensing the need to cooperate, TP&L offered to sell its properties at $7.4 million, but the LCRA rejected the initial offer as too high. Complicating matters was also TP&L's stipulation that it be able to purchase surplus power from the LCRA. Johnson feared that this would raise rates, and at one point he even told the president of TP&L to "take a running jump and go straight to hell." At Wirtz's suggestion, Johnson toned down his rhetoric and they worked out a successful agreement. In 1939, the LCRA bought the properties at $5 million and agreed to sell surplus power to TP&L until demand in the LCRA service area called for "recapture" of the power. The Reconstruction Finance Corporation (RFC) provided loans to the LCRA for the purchase.[72]

The White House was pleased with the outcome. In July of 1939, PWA counsel Benjamin Cohen wrote to the president that Johnson "has done an admirable job in working out the problems of Texas' little TVA...cooperation between public and private power is not impossible." Later that month, Roosevelt invited Johnson to serve as the new director of the REA. Johnson turned down the job, explaining that "my own job now is a contract with the people of Texas." Roosevelt's gesture was most likely a symbolic one, as Tom Corcoran had informed Johnson that Roosevelt preferred to have him in Congress. Still, the offer indicated a genuine demonstration of the president's appreciation for the young congressman's work. "I was very sorry you did not accept," he wrote to Johnson a few days later, "but I do think I ought to tell you that very rarely have I known a proposed candidate for any position receive

---

[71] *Austin American*, 29 September 1938; Johnson to Goldschmidt, 15 September 1938, HP Box 170; *Dallas News*, 9 October 1938; McDonough to Johnson, 24 February 1939, HP Box 170; Johnson to *Austin Statesman*, 27 May 1939, HP Box 175; Miller to Johnson, 24 July 1939, HP Box 171; McWilliams to Johnson, 26 April 1940, HP Box 182; "Electrical Magic Circus" pamphlet, HP Box 182; 1940 Annual Extension Report: Blanco County.
[72] Adams, *Damming the Colorado*, 103; Dallek, *Lone Star Rising*, 182–3; Cohen to Roosevelt, 18 July 1939, MF-LBJ; Johnson to Wirtz, 23 August 1940, HP Box 182.

such unanimous recommendations from sources as was the case with you."[73]

Johnson was not above posting these words all over the Tenth District, or above advertising his and the LCRA's accomplishments far and wide. In October, he mailed a letter to six thousand constituents addressed "My Dear Friend" in which he declared that "you are now getting the benefits of cheap public power," and he included a chart detailing those low rates. He asserted that "before we put our river to work" they were paying one dollar for ten kilowatt-hours, but now they paid seventy-five cents for fifteen kilowatt-hours, thus keeping "Tenth District money in the Tenth District, instead of paying big fees and dividends to officers and holding companies east of the Alleghenies." Johnson also sent duplicates of the letter and power chart to many Washington officials, enclosing the copies with fawning notes of appreciation. His message to Roosevelt was typical: "Except for your unflagging interest, it is unlikely we could ever have sent out the enclosed letter and chart. I am sending them to you that you may see tangibilities as they arise from your hopes and plans."[74] Johnson's boasts proved justifiable; in 1940 (the first year for which data are available), only 22 percent of Tenth District farms used electricity; by 1950 that percentage had quadrupled (Table 3.5).

Though flood control and power activities dominated the initial affairs of the LCRA, some hoped that the LCRA's mission, like TVA's, would also include more general conservation objectives, especially recreational opportunities and tourist facilities. An editorial prepared in Johnson's office read, "Harness the river and stop the floods! Stop the washing away of our topsoil, our most precious resource! Fill lakes full of blue water to laugh at droughts and bring tourists from all over America!" In 1934, the legislature had written a recreational mandate into the LCRA act, directing the authority to acquire land on opposite sides of Lake Buchanan for parks. The act also required that the LCRA retain a strip of land bordering the lake for public access to the water if it ever sold land around the reservoirs. In 1935, the authority even adopted a seal embodying this more expansive view of its mission. The seal, a five-point star spelling out TEXAS with one letter on each of the points, displayed

[73] Cohen to Roosevelt, 19 July 1939, Wallace to Roosevelt, 19 July 1939, MF-LBJ; Johnson to Roosevelt, 29 July 1939, Roosevelt to Johnson, 2 August 1939, HP Box 174; *Austin Statesman*, 7 August 1939; Dallek, *Lone Star Rising*, 183–4.
[74] Johnson to Roosevelt, 4 October 1939, MF-LBJ. Also see Johnson to Slattery, Corcoran, Ickes, and Cohen, HP Box 169.

TABLE 3.5. *Percentage of Farms with Electricity in Tenth District Counties and State of Texas*

County	1940	1945	1950
Blanco	55.9	73.7	89.1
Burnet	30.5	69.5	92.0
Hays	20.9	52.0	88.2
Travis	32.9	60.9	84.0
Williamson	34.7	61.1	91.2
Caldwell	12.8	32.5	73.2
Bastrop	4.5	27.0	69.5
Lee	4.8	34.7	79.5
Burleson	12.6	25.8	68.9
Washington	9.8	33.8	73.6
AVERAGE	21.9	47.1	80.9
Texas	22.4	40.9	78.7

Note: No figures available for 1925–40.
Source: Agricultural Census.

symbols representing generation of power, electric light, forestation, reclamation, and conservation of fish life.[75]

Key to attracting tourists to the "highland lakes" was an ample supply of fish and game. In 1938, Johnson began working with the Federal Bureau of Fisheries to open fish hatcheries. He understood that when the LCRA construction program was complete, there would be five brand new lakes, but no nearby state or federal facilities with the ability to provide stocks of fish. In the middle of April, Johnson conducted negotiations to open a hatchery near Roy Inks Dam, and later that month the LCRA voted to deed sixty-three acres of land to the U.S. government for that purpose. The Bureau of Fisheries provided the supervision, equipment, and materials; an NYA camp supplied the labor. The hatchery at Roy Inks and a second facility built later below Austin Dam kept the lakes and nearby streams well supplied with bass, crappie, bluegill, and bream. The Agriculture Department set up hunting opportunities in the area, and county agents reported progress in wildlife conservation. In Hays County, for example, the agent reported the success of an eighty-two-thousand-acre game conservation area on which wildlife specialists held quail breeding demonstrations. The LCRA also attempted to increase the deer population on the lands surrounding Lake Travis, the reservoir created by Mansfield

[75] "LCRA Light REA Story," HP Box 166; Clay, "Lower Colorado River Authority," 178, 232–3.

Dam. They wrapped an eleven-hundred-acre "restoration area" in deer-proof fence and closed it to hunting for a period of ten years.[76]

Johnson also took an interest in the development of park facilities. In November 1937, he blocked the scheduled abandonment of a CCC camp in Longhorn Cavern State Park so that the CCC could construct a scenic parkway connecting the caverns to Inks Dam. "Secretary Ickes has just approved retention of Longhorn Camp," he informed Burnet County residents, "and it is being retained because of my personal plea to the Secretary, in which I gave him assurance that a five-hundred foot parkway from Cavern to Inks Dam to be selected by the Park Service would be donated to the State Parks Board." The Burnet newspaper spoke ecstatically about the possibilities. "When this parkway is completed," the *Bulletin* raved, "many points of interest may be visited from Burnet without going over the same route twice ... The lakes are being stocked with fish and we will not attempt at this time to tell about this and additional attractions to vacationists when fishing and motor boating times come next year." The LCRA donated land to the state for a park at Inks Dam to complete the picture, and Johnson worked with the National Park Service to develop this property, later called Inks Lake State Park, with the labor of the Longhorn CCC.[77]

The advent of World War II, however, shifted LCRA policy dramatically. The war demonstrated that cheap electric power and plentiful natural resources could attract industry to nonurban areas, thus aiding the war effort and providing higher-paid factory and defense work. Even before Pearl Harbor, Johnson saw that the LCRA might supply power for the war effort. In the spring of 1940, he met with the LCRA in Austin on the matter, proposing airplane factories, but Wirtz (now interior undersecretary) later wired back to him that Austin would be a more suitable place for munitions factories, owing to its close proximity to raw materials such as cotton, sulphur, and chemicals. Later that year Johnson requested a deficiency appropriation to finish Marshall Ford, casting the project in terms of its value to national defense. "Completion is further desirable in order to provide a supply of power," he wrote the president, "a part of which will be distributed in connection with the national defense program

---

[76] *Temple Telegram*, 10 April 1938; *Austin American*, 19 April 1938; *Round Rock Leader*, 21 April 1938; *Burnet Bulletin*, 28 April 1938; 1938 Annual Extension Report: Hays County; Gabrielson to Johnson, 15 March 1945, HP Box 275; Clay, "Lower Colorado River Authority," 234–5.

[77] *Burnet Bulletin*, 1 December 1937, 30 December 1937; Johnson to Wirth, 9 October 1939, HP Box 166.

in the San Antonio area where a large part of the Government's military activities are centered, and in industrial areas around Houston and Dallas where war industries are now and will be located." Apparently Roosevelt found Johnson's reasoning persuasive; eight days later he transmitted the appropriation request to the Speaker of the House.[78]

Johnson also appealed directly to Secretary of War Henry Stimson, arguing that Texas's central location protected it from long-range bombing, and to White House assistant James Rowe, pointing out that steel and chemical plants in the area "should make the location of a defense industry in the Austin Area even more advantageous." Such efforts dovetailed perfectly with the Roosevelt administration's commitment to locating defense industries in the South in order to catalyze the development of high-wage manufacturing and bring southern wages into line with those of the rest of the country.[79] Johnson's exertions paid off; officials remembered that he was instrumental in bringing the Naval Air Base to Corpus Christi, the Naval Air Training Station near Dallas, and shipbuilding factories to southeastern Texas. Power from LCRA dams kept most of these facilities running, along with magnesium plants, gun factories, oil fields, refineries, and graphite mines. The authority even boasted that one war plant alone consumed more electricity than the entire city of San Antonio. "The Dams You Built Help Protect the Land You Love," proclaimed one wartime publicity pamphlet.[80]

The nation also mobilized its farm resources to feed soldiers and allies during the war, and USDA County War Boards organized by the Extension Service set out to fulfill production goals established in Washington. County land use planning committees morphed into "County Agricultural Victory Councils" and organized "Food for Freedom" campaigns that promoted community activities such as victory gardens and scrap rubber collections. Earlier concerns with land use and resource conservation were placed on the back burner, while farmers and agents grappled with problems of labor and equipment shortages. As the draft and migration to higher-paid factory work drained labor from the rural areas, farmers began planting labor-saving crops and sharing equipment with neighbors. In Bastrop County, for example, the Victory Council spent most of July

[78] Wirtz to Johnson, 18 May 1940, HP Box 182; Johnson to Roosevelt, 3 September 1940, Roosevelt to Johnson, 11 September 1940, MF-LBJ.

[79] Schulman, *From Cotton Belt to Sunbelt.*

[80] Johnson to Rowe, 19 February 1941, Papers of James H. Rowe, LBJL; Dallek, *Lone Star Rising*, 198; LCRA pamphlet, "The Dams You Built Protect the Land You Love"; Clay, "Lower Colorado River Authority," 215–16.

1944 coordinating a combine-sharing scheme. Johnson, along with other southern and western congressmen, also argued that the country should import a sufficient number of Mexican workers to harvest the 1944 cotton crop, and the Extension Service distributed money allocated by Congress for Mexican farm labor.[81]

The war experience convinced Johnson that a new world was emerging, that the war's "silver lining" had been to show "us what we can make out of Texas in the future, in terms of developing our natural resources and channeling them into industry." Out of the soil, he proclaimed, would sprout starch plants for a plastics industry, and the cedar-covered hills would provide a "source for building materials in view of wood hardening chemicals developed by war chemists."[82] But Johnson did not abandon the cause of farm improvement, a process he believed still vital to rural uplift. While the war had demonstrated the benefits of factories to the region's economy, it had also revealed transformations in the farm sector: a shortage of machinery and equipment, and the drift of tenants and farm laborers to higher-paid industrial jobs. This labor shortage prompted Johnson's far too expedient support for the importation of poorly paid Mexican workers to pick cotton in the lower counties. Still, the war had convinced him that a growing industrial sector could provide new jobs while farms and ranches became more productive. Therefore, after the war was over he proposed a renewed program of soil conservation.

The LCRA legislation had directed the authority to engage in erosion prevention activities along the watershed, but until this time flood control constituted the only such conservation effort. (The dams, by preventing floods, protected soils.) In August 1947, Johnson penned a letter to the LCRA's treasurer noting that the authority had "become self-supporting through the sale of hydroelectric power, created incidental to its other broad purposes... [T]he time is ripe to begin work for those broad objectives." In a speech to the board of directors the next month, Johnson reminded them of their legal duty "to restore the fertility of our farm lands" by initiating a program of reclamation and conservation. For starters, he asked that the board authorize the selection of "the most competent man in the country" to direct the work of purchasing and distributing heavy terracing machinery, for terracing more farmland would

---

[81] 1942 Annual Extension Reports: Washington, Bastrop, and Travis Counties; 1944 Annual Extension Reports: Blanco and Bastrop Counties; Bearns, "Resource Study," 33–4.
[82] Johnson quoted in Bearns, "Resource Study," 34.

hold the rainfall where it fell, replenish the underground water table, prevent floods, and retard siltation in the reservoirs. "For proof of what can be done in the Colorado Valley," he declared, "one need but fly over the valley of the Tennessee." The LCRA's balance sheets now showed a profit, Johnson argued, and "the law, and the intent of those who wrote the law, did not contemplate a business for profit." "The LCRA was a mighty weapon for the war effort," he told the directors, "but the war is over. We hope the peace is here to stay. This board can now turn to its legal obligations, lending all of its support and energy to achieving those objectives."[83]

The LCRA thus launched its "Farm and Ranch Improvement Program." Caesar Hohn, extension agent in Washington County, accepted the job of Soil Conservation Supervisor. During the fall of 1947 and spring of 1948, Johnson and Hohn met several times with representatives from the LCRA, the Soil Conservation Service, the Guadalupe-Blanco River Authority, the PMA (Production and Marketing Administration, successor to the AAA), Texas A&M, and the Extension Service to shape the program. Following a trip to the Agricultural Extension Service at the University of Tennessee, Hohn circulated a policy statement on the program's aims. Echoing the TVA idea of "grass-roots democracy," Hohn stressed that the "underlying philosophy of the Authority's program is that it should arise from the people and that it must be a program designed to fit their needs which they, themselves, can conduct." He also made clear that the authority intended to supplement, not duplicate, existing programs. From the very beginning, Johnson had emphasized the need to work with the Extension Service and the recently established soil conservation districts, which he thought were "handicapped for lack of appropriations and would be happy to cooperate." Therefore he and Hohn went out of their way to reassure the agricultural agencies that the LCRA intended only to provide services (namely, machinery rented at cost through county conservation committees) that the existing programs approved.[84]

---

[83] Johnson to Faubion, n.d., LCRA Papers Box 6 (date established in Rigby, "A Statistical Study," 40–1); Johnson, speech to the LCRA Board of Directors, n.d., LCRA Box 111 (date established in Rigby, 41).

[84] Hohn to Johnson, 2 October 1947, 11 February 1948, 15 February 1949, LCRA Box 111; Hohn to Extension Service Office, University of Tennessee, 17 March 1948, LCRA Box 112; Caesar Hohn, "The LCRA Conservation Program: Purpose," HP Box 176; Johnson, speech to the LCRA Board; Rigby, "A Statistical Study," 41–6. The SCS was quite concerned about jurisdictional obligations and initially opposed the LCRA's

Over the next seven years, the farm and ranch program provided heavy machinery (motor graders for terracing and drainage work, bulldozers for brush clearing and spreader dam construction, and drag lines for drainage ditches) and small equipment (such as fertilizer spreaders, seed drills, pulverizer-packers, subsoilers, and grass spriggers) to the county committees. It also aggressively removed cedar from its own property and initiated a series of sixteen Example Farms, in which the farmers participated with agricultural specialists in "whole farm improvement" – a program that included remodeled kitchens and living rooms as well as brush eradication, pasture reseeding, stock tanks, crop rotations, drainage ditches, and ventilated chicken houses.[85] An independent analysis of the authority's farm and ranch activities concluded that they were mainly benefiting the median-size farmers and increasing the "technological efficiency" of the ten-county area. "The project will be of help," the study tellingly predicted, "as the inefficient and marginal producers will be unable to keep up with increases in the efficiency of production as developed by the more energetic and ambitious people who benefit from the program."[86]

This assessment of the LCRA's postwar farm and ranch improvement program illustrates well the ultimate outcome of the rural New Deal. By intending both to preserve and to modernize the family farm, policymakers found themselves privileging the sort of "energetic" and "efficient" folk who already had a foothold on the land and could remain there with government help. Given that these newly secure rural citizens never relinquished their claim to rising living standards (or their perceived postwar entitlement to a slice of the expanding economic pie), the hope that the fair distribution of waterpower and the proper maintenance of soil would both preserve and retain the farm population proved a chimera. Farm assistance in general, and conservation aid in particular, was never intended to force the farm population into a rough equality positioned below that of urbanites or factory workers; it was intended to equalize incomes across the board by raising farm income immediately. To jump ahead of the story, farm support had a chance; farm equity did not. For

---

program. It eventually decided to cooperate, working with the county councils and the LCRA's demonstration farms. Consult Hohn to Starcke, 15 April 1948, LCRA Box 106; and SCS folder, LCRA Box 108.

[85] LCRA, "Designs for Improvement: The Story of the Example Farms of the LCRA," March 1954, LCRA Box 105. Also see Soil Conservation Progress Reports, LCRA Box 106; General Manager's Files, LCRA Box 109; and Max Starcke's Confidential Files, LCRA Box 115.

[86] Rigby, "A Statistical Study," 170.

Johnson, of course, conservation meant abundance, not abstinence; and he certainly wasn't alone in thinking that rural resources, properly used and wisely maintained, promised a future secure of ruinous depressions. This is why he labored so hard to divert a significant portion of those resources into industry and urban areas.

Indeed, after World War II the LCRA stepped up its emphasis on power production and flood control. It had acquired the Comal Plant in 1942, a lignite-powered facility, and it continued construction on two additional hydroelectric plants, both finished in the early 1950s. Revenue bonds, not federal funds, financed these final dams (the LCRA sold its RFC securities to private investors in 1943). Johnson continued to channel REA funds to Central Texas, and by 1955 the authority provided wholesale power to thirty municipalities and eleven rural cooperatives, serving a total of thirty-three counties. In 1956, the LCRA set its sights on "new horizons," expanding activities in flood control, electric distribution to agriculture and industry, barge transportation facilities, and a new thermal (steam) plant completed in 1965. The flood control efforts paid off when in 1952 and again in 1957 the dams impounded floodwaters that would have surpassed the levels of the 1938 deluge. The number of electric consumers increased by almost 20 percent between 1956 and 1965, and industries supplied by the LCRA in the early 1960s included chemical companies, airplane manufacturing plants, refineries, textile mills, furniture factories, meat processors, mines, and quarries.[87]

The political and environmental history of Lyndon Johnson's Hill Country revealed the newness of New Deal conservation. Before the 1930s, "conservation" essentially meant the acquisition and management of a public domain, but the Depression ruptured this sharp divide between public and private. New Dealers instituted novel ways of assisting, financing, even compelling cooperation with a nationwide vision of resource use and general rural development. Implicit in this faith was the view that the federal government possessed a developmental function – a role both in correcting market failures and in helping individuals increase the value of private property.

The most important new mechanism was the subsidy. Aggressive government lending created direct relationships between the federal

[87] *Austin American*, 17 February 1945; LCRA, "Development of the LCRA"; LCRA, "Years of Progress at the LCRA." Also see HP Boxes 303–7 and 316–26 on the REA in the 1940s. Flood statistics are contained in LCRA Box 6.

government and local conservation projects. In Central Texas, public entities for the wholesale and cooperative distribution of hydropower emerged only because the Bureau of Reclamation and the PWA guaranteed grants and loans for dams and transmission facilities. Financial incentives also underlay agricultural adjustment in the Tenth District – farmers sold their starving livestock, reduced crop acreage, and improved overgrazed and undernourished pasturelands because they got paid to do so. Furthermore, they received low-interest loans to string power lines to their property, wire their homes and barns, and buy stoves, washing machines, electric irons, and milking machines. In essence, federal conservation policy sponsored the transformation of farmers from a producing to a consuming class. This, after all, was the intent – to correct the crippling imbalance between the city and the country. "Our rural population," Johnson declared on the Senate floor some twenty years later, "has been brought out of the dark ages and the whole country has prospered."[88]

Like the national planners, Johnson saw the conservation of natural resources (water, waterpower, and land) as key to raising rural incomes and rural productivity. A rough way of articulating these interlocking relationships might read: dams impounded the water that prevented the floods and invited the tourists, and in the process of doing so transmitted electricity to the farmers who worked with the dams to hold the topsoil in place. There is no doubt that Johnson saw this as a complete package for uplifting the countryside. "We had a revolution," he declared, "a revolution with soil conservation, with water power, with rural electrification, with better management practices...I believe that land is our greatest source of wealth and a man who understands it and appreciates it would better understand democracy itself."[89]

To be sure, LBJ's early career encompassed more than farm programs and the LCRA – his other activities in housing, in youth programs, on behalf of African and Mexican Americans, and in military affairs marked him, in Henry Wallace's words, as a "well-rounded New Dealer."[90] But the LCRA, electrification projects, and commitments to agricultural improvement made Johnson's reputation and defined his political niche in Central Texas. In 1951 he reclaimed the family place on the Pedernales, and the ranch became a way for the canny career politician to maintain this

---

[88] "Statement by Senate Democratic Leader on the Twentieth Anniversary of the Rural Electrification Administration," 11 May 1955, Reference File "Rural Electrification," LBJL.

[89] *The Hill Country: Lyndon Johnson's Texas.*

[90] Henry Wallace to Franklin Roosevelt, 19 July 1939, MF-LBJ.

TABLE 3.6. *Average Farm Size (in acres) in Tenth District Counties and State of Texas*

County	1925	1940	1945	1950
Blanco	521.6	668.9	624.6	730.0
Burnet	319.6	464.8	447.9	545.3
Hays	222	323.2	358.8	403.8
Travis	94.1	194.3	210.4	220.3
Williamson	121.5	164.9	165.0	183.7
Caldwell	87.3	148.3	158.8	212.3
Bastrop	92.9	179.7	157.1	245.9
Lee	126.4	145.5	167.9	188.9
Burleson	81.3	134.7	155.7	186.5
Washington	72.5	81.6	103.9	119.3
AVERAGE	173.9	250.6	255.0	303.6
Texas	235.5	329.4	367.1	438.5

Source: Agricultural Census.

country mystique. He presided over enormous barbeques, frequently donned Stetson hats, and never refined his Texas twang. He also used the farm as a touchstone for conservationist beliefs refined during the New Deal – he continued to implement conservation plans by filling gullies, reseeding hillsides, and building check dams. As president, he even occasionally announced environmental policy initiatives from the ranch. In essence, Johnson had attempted to revise the western frontier tradition: with land ownership, he thought, had also come an obligation of stewardship: to conserve, to protect, and to develop the land's resources for the benefit of its closest inhabitants.[91]

Johnson also recognized that the developments he promoted changed far more than land use and appliance sales. From 1925 to 1950, the average farm size in the Tenth District increased by almost half, and the region lost over a third of its farmers (Tables 3.6 and 3.7). While it would be inaccurate to trace these developments entirely to federal programs, the statistical evidence combined with the qualitative evidence indicates that the government's influence cannot have been inconsequential. To embrace farmers as the nucleus of the nation's economic life entailed their uplift, but rural uplift – and the resulting increases in efficiency – meant that fewer and fewer farmers met the nation's needs. There was naught for a politician to do but to equate efficiency with equity, and to champion

[91] Bearns, "Resource Study"; *The Hill Country: Lyndon Johnson's Texas*.

TABLE 3.7. *Farmers in Tenth District Counties and State of Texas, White and Black*

County	1925			1945			1950		
	White	Black	Total	White	Black	Total	White	Black	Total
Blanco	649	30	679	653	21	674	561	6	567
Burnet	1,617	8	1,625	1,296	2	1,299	1,054	0	1,054
Hays	1,628	92	1,720	1,055	32	1,087	899	28	927
Travis	3,566	1,231	4,797	2,442	330	2,772	2,024	238	2,262
Williamson	4,166	356	4,522	3,855	216	4,071	3,624	123	3,747
Caldwell	2,583	502	3,085	1,575	256	1,831	1,300	191	1,491
Bastrop	2,318	1,390	3,708	1,737	823	2,560	1,428	430	1,858
Lee	1,450	602	2,052	1,478	469	1,947	1,316	358	1,674
Burleson	1,618	1,431	3,049	1,552	580	2,132	1,382	476	1,858
Washington	2,066	1,554	4,620	2,316	950	3,266	2,097	832	2,929
TOTAL	21,661	14,392	29,857	17,959	3,679	21,639	15,685	2,682	18,367
Texas	383,920	81,726	465,646	339,027	45,950	384,977	297,052	34,515	331,567

Note: "White" includes Mexicans (all years).
Source: Agricultural Census.

this triumph of production: "The amount of work that went into America's food and fiber was high and productivity per man hour was low," said Johnson in 1956, on the twentieth anniversary of the REA. "Under determined leadership, a bold attack was made upon the evil forces that beset America...We have fewer farmers today, but they are producing more food and fiber."[92] Of course, the average figures conceal the drastic racial and class consequences of government-channeled rural development, which hit tenants and black farmers the hardest. The region lost over 80 percent of its black farmers, but just under 30 percent of its white farmers, and tenancy rates among African Americans always remained higher than for white farmers. When looking at the numbers, especially racial differentials, it is hard to escape the conclusion that the rural New Deal in Central Texas, as in the South more generally, served white rather than black, rich rather than poor, place rather than people. It would be equally futile to deny that the goal of efficiency overwhelmed that of equity. In other words, New Deal rhetoric aside, it proved easier to heal the most mistreated land than to heal all of its people.[93] But the numbers do not reveal all: in particular, they do not reveal the universalist intent of New Deal development, however conceptually and politically limited that intent would prove to be. The policy architects hoped that conservation and the equitable distribution of natural resources would yield a better life for those who remained on the land and for those who left.

Nor do the numbers reveal that many of the landowners who benefited from government involvement were far from well-to-do. While certainly in business to make a profit, Hill Country farmers and ranchers were not the envoys of a rapacious capitalist order, nor were they representatives of the agribusiness elite. Whatever the failings of federal policy, the inescapable fact is that many of the poorer and middling farmers of Central Texas became more integrated into the consumer economy, more a part of the American mainstream. "You can't sell the American farmer on communism," Johnson remarked to a public electric association in 1952. "He's too busy listening to the radio while he drives his family

---

[92] "Statement by Senate Democratic Leader."
[93] See Paul E. Mertz, *New Deal Policy and Southern Rural Poverty* (1978); Pete Daniel, *Breaking the Land: The Transformation of Cotton, Tobacco, and Rice Cultures Since 1880* (1985); Pete Daniel, *Standing at the Crossroads: Southern Life Since 1900* (1986); Schulman, *From Cotton Belt to Sunbelt*; and Anthony J. Badger, *The New Deal: The Depression Years, 1933–1940* (1989).

down to the REA co-op in his four-door sedan."[94] And, Johnson might have added, too busy voting for the farm programs and for the politicians who upheld them. For even the Republican Party grudgingly adjusted to this political reality, bowing to the institutional legacy of the New Deal and to the postwar liberal coalition.

Still, the sobering statistics reveal that New Deal rural planners had not resolved – indeed, had never squarely faced – the critical economic and moral question: what would happen to the "marginal" farmers after improvement programs, land use adjustments, and rising economic expectations made their existence unnecessary? Given farmers' desire for improved living standards and their new inclination to vote for those politicians who delivered the goods, were there resources enough to support everyone on the land? For a while, rehabilitation programs such as Subsistence Homesteads, Resettlement, and Farm Security, which were committed (however insufficiently) to serving those at the bottom of the agricultural ladder, complemented assistance to landowners and better-off farmers. But policymakers of the agrarian stripe would soon be squeezed between a rock and a hard place. On one side, poor rural migrants – many decisively ejected from the farm by the government's own policies – continued to flood the roads and the relief rolls, their sad figures casting doubt upon the efficacy of the whole agrarian policy project. On the other side, conservatives in Congress, buoyed by a growing anti-Roosevelt coalition, soon sharpened their knives to slice away the tiny portions of aid dispensed to the very neediest rural citizens. In Washington and in the field, New Dealers continued to wrestle with the problem of farm poverty and with the resistance of politicians who refused to address it. As the experience in Central Texas foreshadowed, wartime conditions and the accompanying industrialization of the countryside would provide the context for a permanent shift in liberal philosophy.

[94] Lyndon Johnson, speech before the Rio Grande Electric Cooperative, 11 October 1952, Statements File, LBJL.

4

The Industrial Transition

During the 1930s, Lyndon Johnson embraced the agrarian policies of the early New Deal. Labeling farmers the backbone of the nation, the young congressman funneled newly available land, water, and power programs to the rural inhabitants of his district. In so doing, Johnson not only laid the foundation for his own spectacular rise but also helped create a new national landscape: a political and environmental order explicitly linked to the premise that government action should arrest economic decline by creating a constituency for rural conservation assistance. But Johnson's career also revealed the limitations of agrarian policy: rural development programs really aided those most able to stay on their farms and to expand their operations with government help. When the country began to mobilize for war, the adept politician therefore seized the opportunity to expand his region's industrial infrastructure and its urban centers. In effect, World War II provided Johnson with the opportunity to build an industrial future upon Central Texas's agrarian base.

The country as a whole navigated the same transformation. As the Depression lingered and farm incomes remained stagnant, economic thinkers and New Deal administrators revised their prescriptions for recovery. They worried that the agricultural modernization and conservation programs did not address farm poverty sufficiently, nor raise agricultural incomes uniformly. They also began to argue that only industrial jobs yielded high incomes, and that poor and marginal farmers would be best served by policies that encouraged out-migration, urbanization, and industrialization. The onset of World War II provided the opportunity to test these new assumptions. Indeed, during the war many

Americans flocked to the cities to take advantage of defense employment, and large industries also moved to rural areas to take advantage of cheap hydropower. In turn, defense employment appeared to provide an answer to the question that had vexed rural planners from the very beginning – how to rehabilitate the poor farmer after assistance programs strengthened his more affluent neighbors.

Conservation strategy played a key role in this industrial transition. The early 1940s began with an ambitious Bureau of Agricultural Economics planning initiative to coordinate resource and rehabilitation policy in the interest of all farmers, rich and poor. This attempt represented the culmination of the agrarian pragmatist program. But the expectation that proper use and fair distribution of a region's natural resources would allow every farmer to find security on the land disintegrated in the face of the insurmountable political difficulty of reconciling the needs of the smaller producers with the interests of their wealthier, more commercially oriented, and much better organized neighbors. During World War II, the agrarian policy options – community-controlled land planning, rural conservation work, and farm security programs – capitulated to a conservative congressional coalition and its Farm Bureau allies. Many liberals, of course, fought to rescue the Farm Security Administration and the BAE's planning program. Because the war had precipitated truly generous commodity-support programs at levels that far exceeded those of the 1930s, they also asked whether federal policy should really help the larger and better-capitalized farmers gain advantages over small producers, and they questioned the wisdom of a war that sacrificed agricultural democracy at home to battle fascism abroad. Despite such heroic rhetoric, the experience revealed that the New Deal had succeeded in creating a permanent constituency of middling and well-to-do farmers, not poor ones.

The demise of agrarian policy did not spell the doom of federal engagement, however, because liberals embraced an alternate set of conservation tactics to address the problem of farm poverty. Inspired by the examples of the Rural Electrification Administration and the Tennessee Valley Authority, wartime planners and regional boosters declared that multipurpose river projects and factory jobs provided the answer to low rural incomes. The Interior Department and the Corps of Engineers led the way in the West, where recently completed dams on the Columbia and the Colorado powered munitions plants and military research. The industrial liberals did not abandon the cause of agricultural conservation and land use adjustments, but they did foresee a future in which federal resource policy supported a growing manufacturing sector along with a declining but more prosperous farm population. In the end, World War II reinforced and expanded public commitments to rural resource development, and the New Conservation guided this shift from agrarian to industrial liberalism. Like Lyndon Johnson, the New Dealers now concluded that the war's "silver lining" had been to show Americans what government action could make out of the country in the future, "in terms of developing [its] natural resources and channeling them into industry."[1]

The background for this shift in strategy was the taste of economic recovery that came with war mobilization. For the New Conservationists, the Depression had offered an unprecedented opportunity: the presence of such widespread despair and economic stagnation allowed for a moment when the nation's attention could be focused on the twin problems of poor land and poor people. Rural reformers could make the case that the nation's health required both social and environmental reform; it called for attention both to the damaged landscape and to the sociopolitical inequalities that perpetuated and exacerbated rural impermanence. But their program depended on the Depression context, a context in which it was not uncommon for Americans in general to question the national faith in unlimited expansion. To explain the puzzling new stagnation, for example, some analysts had even wondered whether the idea of a "mature economy" might not describe the country's predicament; perhaps it was time to come to terms with an economy that had reached the limits of its capacity to grow. As Franklin Roosevelt had famously put it in 1932, perhaps the nation's task was no longer "discovery, or exploitation of natural resources, or necessarily producing more goods ... [but] the soberer, less dramatic business of administering resources and plants already in hand ... of adjusting production to consumption, of distributing wealth and products more equitably."[2]

The New Conservation, and more particularly, its agrarian wing, operated in this brief, unprecedented, and historically singular political space. Americans had an obligation to help farmers remain on the land because, well, farmers had nowhere else to go. Now World War II changed the moral, political, and economic calculus. Industrial jobs beckoned. All of a sudden policymakers grappled with the issues of commodity shortages,

---

[1] Edwin C. Bearns, "Resource Study: Lyndon B. Johnson and the Hill Country, 1937–1963" (Santa Fe: Division of Conservation, National Park Service, Southwest Cultural Resources Center, 1984), 34.
[2] "Address to the Commonwealth Club," 1932, *PPA*, 751–2.

rising prices, and a labor deficit in the countryside – a sharp turnaround from the earlier questions of overproduction, low prices, and a potentially permanent labor surplus. A powerful conservative coalition in Congress restrained attempts to preserve the New Deal's most progressive programs. And under these new circumstances the unresolved tensions at the heart of the New Conservation – the tensions among the goals of efficiency, equity, and sustainability – broke into open conflict. Efficient production for the war effort edged out concerns for intrarural equity and environmental sustainability, values that appeared quaint and outmoded in the rush toward maximum output.

The agrarians, in other words, were extremely vulnerable when the Depression relaxed its hold over the American psyche. With improved economic conditions, policy programs that had overshadowed the agrarians' programs before the Depression – those helping farmers to get big or to get out, and those assuming that the marginal should find wage work elsewhere – returned to the forefront. But these older and perhaps more resilient ideas did not return in the same form. Behind them now stood the full force of the developmental state, committed to government-sponsored commodity support and government-sponsored industrial expansion. The New Conservation, transformed but still potent, left in its wake a lasting set of institutions and attitudes. While brief, the agrarian moment had laid the foundation upon which the industrial liberalism was built.

THE RESURRECTED AAA AND THE BAE'S COUNTY PLANNING EXPERIMENT

In 1936, the Supreme Court struck down the Agricultural Adjustment Act of 1933. The AAA had reduced the production of most farm products through voluntary commodity contracts, financing the program by a tax levied on processors. A farmer would agree to grow only so many acres of corn or cotton, for example, or to produce only so many pigs or cows, and at harvest time or at the end of the livestock marketing year he received a payment on the commodities he did produce. To administer the program at the local level, a group of elected committee members served on a county association, which worked with the Extension Service to sign up farmers and to check compliance. In its first years, the AAA contributed to a marked rise in farm income: in 1935, farmers earned over 50 percent more than they did in 1932. The Supreme Court, however, declared in

United States v. Butler that the federal government could not regulate the agricultural economy under its constitutional power to tax.[3]

Butler came on the heels of a string of Court rulings against the New Deal, most notably its decision to strike down the National Industrial Recovery Act and the NRA's program of industrial planning. No New Dealer was better prepared to resurrect his agency's program, however, than USDA Secretary Henry Wallace. In a hastily assembled book he called *Whose Constitution?* Wallace took aim at the Court's misleading assertion that agriculture was a purely local concern. "Were agriculture truly a local matter in 1936," he fumed, "half of the people in the United States would quickly starve." Wallace also reiterated the argument that the general welfare required both secure farm incomes and improved soil conservation, and asked Americans to accept a system of cooperative control.

> Probably the most damaging indictment that can be made of the capitalistic system is the way in which its emphasis on unfettered individualism results in exploitation of natural resources in a manner to destroy the physical foundations of national longevity... Is there no way for the capitalistic system to develop a mechanism for taking thought and planning action in terms of the general welfare for the long run?[4]

In the wake of the Court's decision, Wallace turned to the AAA's Program Planning Division, which had been drafting an alternate scheme of agricultural adjustment since 1934. Headed by Howard Tolley, the division had been established to direct the AAA's emergency measures toward a long-range plan for agriculture. Tolley was part of the USDA's collection of agricultural pragmatists, a group reared on midwestern farms who, like Wallace, linked their liberal instincts to a deep faith in local planning and cooperative, voluntary change. Much of the original AAA worried Tolley and his colleagues, who were concerned that the program as initially established aided only the wealthier farmers and that the AAA's ultimate mission – regional agricultural adjustments, soil conservation, and rural permanence – had given way to a single-minded focus on high commodity prices. "In the beginning," Tolley recalled, "all of us in the Triple-A

---

[3] Economic Research Service, *History of Agricultural Price-Support and Adjustment Programs, 1933–84* (GPO, 1984); R. Douglas Hurt, *Problems of Plenty: The American Farmer in the Twentieth Century* (2002), 68–84; Tolley oral history, CUOH.

[4] Henry Wallace, *Whose Constitution?: An Inquiry into the General Welfare* (1936), quoted in John C. Culver and John Hyde, *American Dreamer: The Life and Times of Henry A. Wallace* (2000), 160, 162–3.

advocated reduction of production. That was emergency action ... [but] some of us hoped to do something different, and better." Working with such long-term ends in mind, the division's Land Policy Section had initiated the submarginal land projects, and the Rehabilitation Section had helped design the relief programs that were eventually absorbed by the Resettlement Administration and the Farm Security Administration.[5]

But what of the lands that could remain productive? According to Tolley, policymakers had to help farmers reduce certain crops and increase production of others. Because most of the crops in surplus also caused soil damage, the real question was how to encourage more conservation practices. While the first AAA functioned primarily as an emergency commodity program, it did provide economic assistance for soil conservation. In 1934 and 1935, many farmers used their benefit payments to plant soil-conserving grasses and forage crops on land they set aside under the program. One study in Illinois indicated that 80 percent of the contracted acres had been planted to legumes, and in the country as a whole, alfalfa acreage went up by 15 percent, soybeans by 29 percent, lespedeza by 50 percent, and hay by 8 percent. Many of these adjustments also took place because the AAA began introducing payments for replacement crops. Encouraged by these developments, and wanting to coordinate the AAA's program with the conservation programs offered by the Soil Erosion Service and the Civilian Conservation Corps, Tolley and his colleagues came to the conclusion that soil conservation measures alone could hold down surplus production.[6]

The Supreme Court gave Tolley's group its chance. Just eight weeks after the *Butler* decision, the Program Planning Division proposed – and the Congress passed – the Soil Conservation and Domestic Allotment Act. Although the original AAA contracts had encouraged replacement crops and fallowed fields as important by-products of farm adjustment, soil conservation now became the program's principal goal and its primary justification. The new legislation continued to place emphasis on farm income, but sought to maintain high incomes through payments for specific conservation practices. Farmer committees, now called "agricultural

---

[5] Howard R. Tolley, "The Program Planning Division of the Agricultural Adjustment Administration," *Journal of Farm Economics* 16 (1934); Tolley oral history, CUOH, 249. Also see Richard S. Kirkendall, *Social Scientists and Farm Politics in the Age of Roosevelt* (1966), 135–148; and Kirkendall, "Howard Tolley and Agricultural Planning in the 1930s," *Agricultural History* 39 (1965).
[6] Tolley oral history, CUOH; Chester C. Davis, "The Grass Revolution,"19 November 1935, WP 2100, 7:40; Kirkendall, *Social Scientists and Farm Politics*, 136–8.

conservation associations," continued to administer the program at the local level.[7] Tolley later recalled that the new legislation "was hung on the public welfare clause of the Constitution," and he described its provenance in terms that echoed the justification for the New Deal's rural policy as a whole: "It is very easy to rationalize, [for] conserving the land of the United States enhances the national welfare."[8] After the Court's decision, the funds for the new program came not from a processing tax but from the treasury and from a new round of corporate tax hikes meant to raise general revenue.[9]

The president supported Wallace's and Tolley's efforts to redirect the AAA. Roosevelt argued that any farm program should include both soil conservation and farm income assistance. "Tens of millions of acres have been abandoned because of erosion," he declared. "Real damage to the consumer does not result from moderate increases in food prices, but from collapse of farm income so drastic as to compel ruthless depletion of soil...That is the real menace to the nation's food supply." The new legislation, Roosevelt believed, would finally safeguard the national welfare and aid economic recovery by providing for proper land use and the maintenance of farm purchasing power.[10]

The 1936 legislation, however, contained a fatal flaw: it did not hold down production. By the end of the year, AAA officials had become aware of this possibility. "Even though production control and soil conservation are fundamentally related methods for accomplishing the same purpose," warned one member of the Program Planning Division, "no one should conclude that either is an effective substitute for the other." Held back by the droughts of the mid-1930s, crop yields rebounded in 1937, and prospects looked favorable for 1938. Bolstered by a farm majority vote for the Democrats in November, Congress passed a second Agricultural Adjustment Act that steered a middle course between the first AAA of 1933 and the soil conservation legislation of 1936. Using the word "parity" for the first time, the legislation provided for the continuation of acreage reduction, conservation payments, and price-support loans (now on crops stored by the government). Significantly, the 1938 AAA also made the

---

7 "Background and Summary of Legislation Relating to Agricultural Adjustment, Conservation, Crop Insurance, and Price Control," 15 August 1946, Clinton Anderson Papers, Box 14, HSTL; Theodore Saloutos, *The American Farmer and the New Deal* (1982), 236–8.
8 Tolley oral history, CUOH, 367.
9 Culver and Hyde, *American Dreamer*, 161.
10 Statement by Roosevelt, 1935, *FDRC*, 445; Statement by Roosevelt, 1936, *FDRC*, 492.

adjustment program permanent by freeing it from the annual appropriations process.[11]

By 1938, the farm program had acquired the fiscal foundation that would support it for the next half century. The AAA had been successfully resurrected. It had also reconciled, if only temporarily, the need for soil conservation with production control. Still, the new AAA did not – could not – resolve the administrative and ideological tensions that existed within the Department of Agriculture. The New Deal had dramatically augmented the USDA's responsibilities and influence (indeed, it had become the largest federal agency), but the members of this sprawling department did not always agree on its methods and purpose. The new action agencies – the AAA, the Farm Credit Administration (FCA), the Farm Security Administration, and the Soil Conservation Service – locked horns with each other and with the land-grant colleges and the Extension Service, the more established arms of the state agricultural complex. The AAA and the Extension Service primarily served commercially successful farmers and bypassed tenants, sharecroppers, and the landless. Meanwhile, the FSA aimed to assist poor farmers, but fought with the FCA, which accused it of loaning money to incompetent people. The AAA and the SCS served the same clientele, but clashed over how best to bring about land use changes. Finally, the Extension Service and the land-grant colleges resented all of the New Deal agencies for establishing direct relationships with farmers and for circumventing the long-established reliance on the county agents as the sole source of advice and aid.[12]

Appreciating the need for a better system of social and environmental planning, and facing pressure from Interior Secretary Harold Ickes (who threatened to build a Department of Conservation by reclaiming the Soil Conservation Service and by swiping the Forestry Department), Wallace encouraged efforts to draw up a new scheme of interagency coordination. It is often assumed that the New Deal Department of Agriculture lost its intellectual imagination after Wallace's decision to "purge" the urban liberals from the AAA in 1935. These young reformers, incensed

---

[11] "Background and Summary of Legislation Relating to Agricultural Adjustment," 11; "Economic Implications of the Agricultural Conservation Program," 1936, WP 2100, 8:12; Saloutos, *American Farmer and the New Deal*, 242; Hurt, *Problems of Plenty*, 82.

[12] Jess Gilbert, "Agrarian Intellectuals in a Democratizing State: A Collective Biography of USDA Leaders in the Intended New Deal," in Catherine M. Stock and Robert D. Johnston, eds., *The Countryside in the Age of the Modern State: Political Histories of Rural America* (2001), 232–4; Kirkendall, *Social Scientists and Farm Politics*, 150–64; Saloutos, *American Farmer and the New Deal*, 239–40; Tolley oral history, CUOH.

that AAA payments helped southern cotton planters displace black share-croppers, had issued a new rule requiring that AAA beneficiaries retain the same number of agricultural personnel on their farms. Announced in Wallace's absence, the new rule caused a furor among southern congressmen, who demanded that Wallace withdraw the order immediately. Caught between the Southern Democrats whose support the New Deal required and his own personal loyalties, Wallace rescinded the order. This was the moment when paradigmatic urban liberal Rexford Tugwell established the Resettlement Administration as an agency separate from the USDA. However, this version of events obscures the subsequent contributions of the USDA's agricultural pragmatists – the "agrarian intellectuals," as sociologist Jess Gilbert terms them. These liberals, while ideologically more committed to gradual, voluntary change, did understand that emergency production control, while necessary, would not fully address rural poverty and environmental degradation.

Pragmatists Howard Tolley and USDA Undersecretary M. L. Wilson were particularly concerned by the friction between the Extension Service and the newer action agencies. They believed that the extension program overlooked the needs of the poorest farmers, and wanted to encourage a broader understanding of agriculture's social and economic context, both within the department and among its clients. The vehicle for this broader perspective, they thought, should be a new system of local participatory planning to coordinate production decisions, conservation adjustments, and other assistance efforts: an expanded version of the local AAA committees and the soil conservation districts that Wilson had helped to design. In the summer of 1938, representatives of the USDA and the land-grant colleges met in Mt. Weather, Virginia, and agreed that county-level committees composed of farmers and agency officials should combine land use planning with the action programs. In October, Wallace transferred Tolley's Program Planning Division to the Bureau of Agricultural Economics and placed the BAE in charge of the new initiative.[13]

No one was more pleased with this turn of events than M. L. Wilson, who had proposed the domestic allotment plan in 1930 with the idea that the emergency control measures would evolve into a more democratic form of long-range social and environmental planning. Now it seemed

---

[13] Kirkendall, *Social Scientists and Farm Politics*, 150–64; Tolley oral history, CUOH, 139–42, 396–7, 413–14; Saloutos, *American Farmer and the New Deal*, 243–4; Jess Gilbert, "Democratic Planning in Agricultural Policy: The Federal-County Land-Use Planning Program, 1938–1942," *Agricultural History* 70 (1996).

that the Mt. Weather agreement had brought this vision to reality. Along with Wallace and the other pragmatists, Wilson knew that farm policy first had to deal with the problem of overproduction. But he also knew that the AAA working alone would not address the need for intrarural equity, nor would it address the need for conservation. Crop control, it must be remembered, was never understood by its framers as a permanent solution; it was always conceived of as a short-term emergency measure awaiting long-range adjustments at home and the revival of markets abroad.

Wilson now took the opportunity to promote the BAE's planning program as the moment when the domestic half of this transition could take place. Having dealt with overproduction, the nation should turn its full attention to asking what kind of rural society should emerge from the Depression. For Wilson, this society would balance efficiency with environmental sustainability and social equity. Farmers, he warned, must "combine the adjustment of production with proper care for the soil, with the least disturbance of the agricultural personnel ... and above all with the maintenance of farm incomes on a level sufficient at least to sustain the farm home."[14] Here was a picture in which farmers resisted the temptation of maximum short-term gain in order to protect the soil and to help as many neighbors as possible remain on the land. And yet farmers earned incomes "at least" enough to sustain the farm home.

What could achieve these sweeping objectives? Wilson called his answer "democratic collective control." The BAE would sponsor a network of local committees composed of farmers and USDA representatives. Together they would assess conditions and arrive at desirable solutions, the implementation of which would be voluntary. Wilson and his colleagues intended the committees to represent an area's social structure; the needs of the poorest farmers and farmworkers would be integrated with the interests of the most commercially oriented producers. Wilson optimistically concluded that the new planning initiative pointed toward a "great surge of agricultural democracy in which there is both over-all unity and place for different viewpoints, different programs, [and] different patterns."[15] It was a strikingly humane and democratic vision, but one

[14] M. L. Wilson, "Validity of the Fundamental Assumptions Underlying Agricultural Adjustment," *Journal of Farm Economics* 16 (1936), 22, 25.

[15] M. L. Wilson, *Democracy Has Roots* (1939), 198–9; Wilson, "The New Department of Agriculture," 1939, WP 2100, 5:5. Also see Gilbert, "Agrarian Intellectuals in a Democratizing State," and "Democratic Planning in Agricultural Policy."

fated to come into conflict with farmers' desires to earn higher incomes once the opportunity to do so presented itself.

Still, land planning committees sprouted hopefully throughout the nation. By 1942, almost two-thirds of the counties in the nation had established them. The committees normally included twenty-two to thirty persons, with farmers usually making up more than half of the membership. For the most part, officials from the state Extension Service did the organization work, often aided by their colleagues from the experiment stations. Of the federal agricultural agencies, the AAA and the FSA held positions within the largest number of counties, followed by the SCS, the FCA, the Forest Service, and the Rural Electrification Administration. TVA representatives also participated on many committees in the South. The overarching theory behind the committees and their agrarian pragmatist sponsors was that farmers would make socially and environmentally responsible decisions if they had accurate information and the funds to implement them.[16]

A typical county project began with preparatory work, including organization and discussion, and proceeded to the more intensive job of surveying land use, soil fertility, cropping patterns, and socioeconomic conditions. This land classification work formed the basis for long-range adjustment recommendations and finally a third, "unified" stage of implementation. One of the first committees to proceed through the three phases was that of Teton County, Montana, an arid region where farmers earned most of their income from spring wheat, sheep, and cattle. After the community studied land use, farm size, tenure, and soil and range conditions, it concluded that twenty thousand acres of land should be taken out of crop cultivation. It also proposed more strip cropping, deferred grazing on eroded land, water pumping and storage projects, and more secure tenure conditions for those at the margins.[17]

The most dramatic example of a successful unified program took shape in Greene County, Georgia, in the heart of the southern Black Belt. Years

---

[16] Gilbert, "Democratic Planning in Agricultural Policy," 240–1; Bureau of Agricultural Economics, *Land Use Planning Under Way* (GPO, 1940); John D. Lewis, "Democratic Planning in Agriculture, II," *American Political Science Review* 35 (1941), 462–3; C. W. Warburton, Memorandum for the Secretary, 19 December 1939, WP 2100, 1:7; Report of the Inter-Bureau Coordinating Committee on Conservation, "How Can We Get More Conservation in our Agricultural Programs?" Records of the Division of Program Analysis and Development, NA RG 83, Entry 206, Box 1.

[17] Gilbert, "Democratic Planning in Agricultural Policy," 241–3; BAE, "Land Use Planning Under Way," 12–25.

of row cropping had scarred the hills with deep gullies, and during the 1920s a boll weevil epidemic combined with the depleted land to push many people off the farms. Plagued by some of the highest rates of out-migration and tenancy in the country, the area suffered from the combined effects of human and soil erosion. In 1936, Arthur Raper, a student of regionalists Howard Odum and Rupert Vance, painted a bleak picture of the region's social and environmental conditions. In a somber book entitled *Preface to Peasantry*, he argued that the Black Belt's deteriorating plantation economy had left in its wake "depleted soil, shoddy livestock, inadequate farm equipment, crude agricultural practices, crippled institutions, [and] a defeated and impoverished people." Such circumstances, he believed, prepared the land and its inhabitants for the emergence of a shackled peasant class rather than for the "appearance of the traditional independent American farmer." Raper also criticized the programs of the early New Deal for temporarily rejuvenating the South's dying plantation economy by propping up landowners while penalizing the landless. He concluded that the improvement of rural living conditions awaited "a constructive land policy – a use of the land which will serve the people who live on it." A year later, Raper reiterated this link between poor people and poor land more emphatically: "In the long run the plantation system causes gullies by what it does to the man... To stop gullies, we shall need to examine our philosophy of human relations."[18]

Raper returned to Georgia from 1940 to 1942 to evaluate Greene County's unified farm program, a story he published in 1943 as *Tenants of the Almighty*. Conservation planning in the area had begun in the mid-1930s with a series of land utilization projects that transformed 144,000 acres of worn-out cotton fields into pastures, forests, wildlife refuges, and recreational areas. The projects included provisions for resettlement and employment for the uprooted families. In 1939, the state Extension Service worked with the BAE to assemble a county planning committee composed of farmers, extension workers, and representatives from the FSA, the AAA, the SCS, and the CCC. The committee drew up plans for soil improvement, for better landlord-tenant relations, and for provisions to allow more tenants to operate their own farms. As a result of the program, the number of rural rehabilitation clients increased dramatically.

[18] H. H. Wooten, *The Land Utilization Program, 1934 to 1964* (GPO, 1965); Farm Security Administration, *Greene County, Georgia: The Story of One Southern County* (GPO, 1941); Mary Summers, "The New Deal Farm Programs: Looking for Reconstruction in American Agriculture," *Agricultural History* 74 (2000); Arthur Raper, *Preface to Peasantry: A Tale of Two Black Belt Counties* (1936; reprint, 1968), 3, 5–7, 406; Raper, "Gullies and What They Mean," *Social Forces* 16 (1937), 205–6.

In 1938, only 150 families in the county had received rehabilitation loans; by 1940 that number had risen to 586. The AAA, the SCS, and the FSA worked together to help finance new soil conservation practices as well as better housing, barns, farm gardens, wells, schools, and health care. Moreover, blacks received a larger share of these benefits than was usual for federal relief activities in the South. Arthur Raper smiled upon these developments and ended his second study of the region with a prayer of solidarity: "Men and women and children are we, town and country, white and black, landed and landless. Tenants of the Almighty, all of us, as times write on the face of the earth our care of the land, and in our own faces our care of each other." [19]

The BAE's county planning program illustrated how many New Dealers hoped to rectify environmental and social imbalance. The agrarians believed that farm and conservation assistance would halt outmigration and keep people on the land. They also claimed that rural conservation policies had the potential to benefit all: everyone from the very poorest to the most wealthy would gain equally from the growth of local, participatory planning. But Greene County's experience proved the exception rather than the rule. Very few of the county committees enjoyed this apparent harmony of interests, and most of them did not accurately represent the social and racial structure of their surrounding communities. Localism and voluntarism in most cases meant domination of the process by a select few. Not only were blacks and poor farmers absent from the planning process, the more commercial farmers and their Farm Bureau allies normally organized and dominated the committees. (The Farm Bureau's influence stemmed from its status as the legal sponsor of extension work and from its advisory role with respect to the county agent system.) As one disappointed observer put it, the prevalent assumption among the wealthier farmers and the Farm Bureau was that "small tenants, and particularly sharecroppers, are not competent to recognize and protect their own interests, and that their affairs are best left in the hands of others." Continued interagency rivalries exacerbated these problems of representation: the federal agencies, the state colleges, and the extension officials continued to compete for agenda-setting power and policy territory. [20]

---

[19] Wooten, *Land Utilization Program*, 40–2; FSA, "Greene County"; Arthur Raper, *Tenants of the Almighty* (1943), 364.

[20] Lewis, "Democratic Planning in Agriculture," 455; Kirkendall, *Social Scientists and Farm Politics*, 168–92; Tolley oral history, CUOH, 476–7. For an impassioned critique of the Farm Bureau's relationship to the Extension Service, see Grant McConnell, *The Decline of Agrarian Democracy* (1959).

To address these tensions, M. L. Wilson resigned from his post as undersecretary to direct the Extension Service. In this capacity he hoped to steer one of the most conservative arms of the USDA toward broader support for the county planning program and its cooperative mission. In an address before the American Farm Economic Association, later published in *Rural America*, Wilson once again argued that agriculture faced two problems: the overall relationship between commercial agriculture and industry; and the large portion of the agricultural population that remained in poverty. Wilson admitted that in past years the agricultural institutions of research and education had paid little heed to rural poverty, focusing instead on developing competitive systems of farming. But he explained that the Depression had altered this previous mindset: "As we look into the future," he reflected, "and think in terms of the future of democracy, of the kind of rural life that our social philosophy sanctions and of the complexities and difficulties involved, low-income farming becomes our Number One agricultural problem."[21]

Wilson highlighted the critical question facing agricultural planners and policymakers. "The number of family farms is limited," he acknowledged, "and unless they are reduced in size, they cannot accommodate the so-called surplus of farm families on a scientific commercial family farming basis." The county committees invariably found that any program designed to implement the planning recommendations would displace a substantial portion of the agricultural population. "It is when they reach this point," Wilson observed, "that they turn to Washington and ask, 'What assumptions are we to make in our planning work? What is the national policy with respect to the expansion or contraction of the proportion of our population engaged in agriculture?'" In response to this all-important question – just how many farmers should remain on the land? – the new extension director hoped to offer some moral guidance.[22]

Wilson sketched out several possible approaches. The first was what he termed "individualist optimism," or the idea that anyone could be successful. A second social philosophy Wilson dubbed "agrarian self-sufficiency." Its adherents held that American democracy would be preserved only by the widespread development of small, self-sufficient farms. A third worldview Wilson labeled the "Rational Organization of Agriculture and Industry." In contrast to those promoting self-sufficiency, the

[21] Wilson, "The Problem of Poverty in Agriculture," 1939, WP 00003 12:30; Wilson, "The Problem of Poverty in Agriculture," *Rural America* (September 1940), 3.
[22] Wilson, "The Problem of Poverty in Agriculture," *Rural America*, 4, 9.

rational organizers wanted to confine agricultural efforts to those areas best suited for intensive commercial production and to direct the surplus agricultural population toward the factories and the cities. The fourth, and for Wilson the most promising, social philosophy he dubbed "scientific humanism." These thinkers understood the tremendous potential of science and technology, but wanted to encourage a deeper appreciation of nonmaterial values and traditions. Straining to reconcile maximum output with rural stability, Wilson cast his vote for stability. Scientific humanists, he claimed, did not uphold increased efficiency as the nation's cure-all:

> Technological efficiency is important, but many applications of it have created immeasurable misery. I believe that for the present we must keep a much larger number of people on the farms than many agricultural economists would advise. There are values in rural life, even in a rural life without rich material returns, which in my estimation are superior to maximum commercial productiveness.[23]

A scientific humanist, Wilson concluded, would support an expanded Farm Security Administration, a permanent program of rural conservation works, and the development of rural industrial communities so that farmers could work part-time in factories close to home. After struggling his entire career to marry efficiency with equity and sustainability, Wilson now seemed to be saying that efficiency should take the back seat to more modest (but more rewarding) aspirations. Maximum short-term gains should be tempered by the needs of the soil and the needs of other farm people.[24]

Despite his careful distinction between agrarianism and scientific humanism, Wilson's plea for rural cooperation represented the apotheosis of New Deal agrarian thought. He believed that careful, cooperative consideration of a region's natural resources would bring every farmer a better life, in turn increasing the economic well-being of the nation. Developed first during the 1920s, this New Conservationist philosophy had provided the foundation for just about every farm program of the 1930s, culminating with the BAE's county planning initiative. But as Wilson recognized, these county committees came face to face with the intractable difficulty of reconciling the needs of the landed and the landless, the prosperous and the poor. Would the nation's farmers (and their federal representatives) cast votes for rural policies that kept people on the land for apparently inefficient reasons, as Wilson hoped? Would farmers sacrifice short-term

---

[23] Wilson, "The Problem of Poverty in Agriculture," *Rural America*, 6.
[24] Wilson, "The Problem of Poverty in Agriculture"; Wilson, "Beyond Economics," *Farmers in a Changing World: Yearbook of Agriculture 1940* (GPO, 1940).

gains for a vaguely cooperative and more spiritually satisfying future? Not surprisingly, Wilson's optimism and humanism proved misplaced. As the country geared up for war, and as the larger, more commercial producers exercised their political clout, Congress eliminated the New Deal's agrarian programs while the "rational organizers of agriculture and industry" steered a different course for federal conservation strategy.

WORLD WAR II AND THE DECLINE OF AGRARIAN POLICY

By 1941, federal programs generated over one-third of the nation's agricultural income. Most farmers had come to depend on the government for commodity payments, low-interest loans, conservation assistance, and rural electrification. Henceforth farming would become a much less risky occupation. The New Deal, of course, did not solve the farm problem. Federal policy failed to reduce production; it failed to bring per capita farm income anywhere close to nonfarm income; and it failed to assist thousands of poor tenants, sharecroppers, and migrant workers. "The New Deal," as one scholar has argued, "was essentially a holding operation for a large underemployed agricultural labour force."[25] However, its policies did create a powerful new constituency of middling and wealthier farmers who now asked the government to take permanent responsibility for their welfare. Before the Depression, many farmers had doubted the wisdom of government intervention. Now, on the eve of World War II most deemed it a political and economic entitlement. The New Dealers had encouraged – indeed, they had created – this perception: farmers received more direct federal aid than any other economic group.[26]

This dependence did not mean that farmers always welcomed federal regulation. Production control, the AAA's bedrock principle, proved especially irksome. In defending the domestic allotment plan, its chief publicist, M. L. Wilson, had argued that "profit cannot be got for American agriculture . . . by unlimited production."[27] This reasoning often struck farmers as counterintuitive, even un-American. Convinced that they should coax the land to yield as much as possible, many farmers felt underemployed by production restrictions and mocked the weed patches that grew on the acres they set aside. Americans also viewed the AAA's "policy of scarcity" as morally suspect. First introduced to city dwellers in

---

[25] Anthony J. Badger, *The New Deal: The Depression Years, 1933–1940* (1989), 168.
[26] Hurt, *Problems of Plenty*, 93–6.
[27] Wilson, "Validity of the Fundamental Assumptions," 17.

stories of the killing of pigs and the destruction of cotton, production control appeared downright mean-spirited in a world where so many went begging for food and clothing.

Federal aid also challenged the economic and cultural foundations of rural communities. As Catherine M. Stock argues in her study of the northern plains, Dakota society depended on a delicate balancing act of contradictory beliefs: loyalty to cooperation but also to profit; devotion to the community but also to the individual; and faith in both tradition and progress. The Depression shook this foundation, creating a "main street in crisis," but did not fundamentally alter traditional ideas of self-help, autonomy, and local control. No one who survived the foreclosures, drought, scorching heat, bitter cold, dust storms, and plagues of grasshoppers did so without federal assistance – not just from the AAA, but also from FERA, the WPA, the SCS, the CCC, and the REA. Still, Dakotans did not always accept the New Deal eagerly, nor did they welcome bureaucratic meddling. Even though the Depression revealed the limits of neighborly charity and the New Deal saved their farms and towns, Dakotans chafed at production control and skirted its restrictions; they took offense at resettlement plans; they worried about the dole; and they ridiculed the logic of an employment program that would pay men to shovel a road by hand rather than grading it with a team of horses. "In the end," Stock writes, "such a complex interaction left Dakotans feeling two ways at once about the changes in their world . . . they were both thankful for and fearful of outside assistance."[28] After 1938, Dakota voters returned to their former Republicanism, ousting a New Deal governor and choosing two conservative Republican senators over progressive farm Democrats.

Michael Grant's examination of the rural rehabilitation program on the Great Plains similarly reveals the combination of support and unease that greeted the New Deal. Rural rehabilitation, administered first through the Resettlement Administration and then through the Farm Security Administration, offered poorer farmers subsistence and operating credit. These programs did not reach the very poorest farmers, part-timers, or migrants in search of work; rather, the rehabilitation loans and grants were designed for the "borderline": small- to medium-sized farmers, mostly tenants, who owned or managed moderate holdings, and who now had been forced by economic and environmental conditions to occupy a place just between poverty and security. These were the hardworking but unlucky

---

[28] Catherine M. Stock, *Main Street in Crisis: The Great Depression and the Old Middle Class on the Northern Plains* (1992), 98, 120.

folks their neighbors and political representatives called the "stickers." It was accepted that they had the will and the brains to succeed, just not the collateral to secure a loan from a private bank. Throughout the 1930s the region's Democrats and Republicans alike welcomed efforts to recapitalize its borderline inhabitants along with its more secure farmers.[29]

Doubts about the program's aims quickly arose, however, not only among the affluent farmers but also among the rehabilitation clients themselves. The FSA promoted stability and subsistence, not the expansion of cash cropping – the intent, after all, was to help clients adapt to the real, perhaps permanent, environmental and economic conditions of low rainfall and low commodity prices. This was the Dust Bowl region, after all. As a result, the farmer wishing to expand wheat production would be denied credit from the FSA and instead encouraged to adopt a more diversified plan of livestock and poultry, grass pastures, and feed crops. Clients were being asked to forsake the major commodities markets, and they resented this missed opportunity to increase their short-term income. In other words, it was not simply the larger growers who favored efficiency, risk, and commercial competitiveness over stability, or who would voice dissatisfaction with federal policy on these grounds.[30]

Of course, while rural rehabilitation made lots of news on the plains, it was overshadowed by the AAA, which pumped in more dollars and affected more farmers. The original AAA had enjoyed wide popularity. Plains farmers looked at the government checks not as a form of charity but as a right, just as eastern industrial interests benefited from tariffs and restricted trade. Still, they viewed the program as an "adjustment," not as a set of controls, and while they understood the immediate need for acreage reduction, farmers fully intended to increase production in the future. And so, as the New Deal succeeded in saving commercial agriculture, and as economic prospects looked brighter in the late 1930s, plains residents turned their thoughts toward expansion. While they fully accepted the premise of government assistance (and would continue to do so), they wanted to profit individually from the marketplace and sharply criticized the resurrected AAA of 1938, which attempted to discourage excess wheat production and limited both acreage and income.[31] This frustration carried over into the political realm, where few New Deal

29 Michael Grant, *Down and Out on the Family Farm: Rural Rehabilitation on the Great Plains* (2002).
30 Grant, *Down and Out*, 116.
31 Grant, *Down and Out*, 169.

supporters were sent back to Congress after 1936. With the exception of George Norris, the progressive Republicans who had backed the farm programs now expressed unease with Roosevelt and the national Democrats' alliance with southern conservatives, northern labor, and urban voters. By the end of the 1930s, plains representatives and their constituents concluded they could "have the new farm programs without the New Deal."[32]

World War II brought this uneasiness about government controls to the surface, because mobilization required food and fiber, lots of it and quickly. During the 1930s, rural complaints had done little to disrupt the USDA's program, because its officials had firmly linked their agencies to the goals of conservation, surplus reduction, and price support. Fearful that hasty expansion would topple the careful controls the department had constructed, Henry Wallace had even continued to recommend that farmers sign restriction contracts as war clouds began to gather over Europe and as it became clear that the United States would assist the Allied nations. By 1941, however, after the president had declared that the nation would become the world's "arsenal of democracy," and after he had signed the Lend Lease Act, the USDA mobilized for all-out war production. Claude Wickard, the new agriculture secretary, initiated a "Food for Defense" program and established a nationwide system of War Boards organized around the AAA. "We hope to contribute our maximum effort toward the production of the food and fiber needed by this country and her allies," Wickard declared. "To this task, all others must be subordinated."[33]

American farmers lined up behind the administration's production goals and rapidly increased their output of food grains, oil-bearing crops (soybeans, peanuts, and flaxseed), and vegetables for processing. They tore out the weed patches and pushed again onto marginal lands. Surpluses disappeared, and farm prices rose. The conservation agencies, especially Hugh Bennett's Soil Conservation Service, assisted this wartime policy reorientation. "We can't afford conservation as usual," Bennett proclaimed. "What is needed today is *productive conservation*...Unless conservationists can show how to produce *more* and produce it more efficiently, then we have either failed or still are exceedingly ignorant about

[32] Grant, *Down and Out*, 171.
[33] Sidney Baldwin, *Poverty and Politics: The Rise and Decline of the Farm Security Administration* (1968), 326–8; Walter W. Wilcox, *The Farmer in the Second World War* (1947), 35–49; "Secretary Wickard Reorganizes Department for War-Time Effort," 13 December 1941, Correspondence Relating to Participation in the Defense Program, NA RG 96, Entry 3, Box 1.

the subject." Bennett claimed that farmers could only reach production goals through soil and water conservation farming methods. He recommended that they plant all the land suitable for intensive cultivation, and relegate forestry and wildlife protection only to those lands unsuitable for higher-yielding crops.[34]

The call for "productive conservation" revealed well how war mobilization toppled the earlier balance between efficiency and sustainability. To be sure, Bennett's SCS had formed a crucial part of the more dominant "technical assistance" wing of federal conservation policy. By helping farmers stay in place and increase their yields, the SCS operated within the political boundaries ultimately set for New Deal conservation as a whole: the agency's programs were largely voluntary, and the results usually yielded immediate benefits. Still, with prices low and commodity markets sluggish throughout the 1930s, there had been little pressure to expand production dramatically. The war changed the equation. Of course, the critical compromises required of New Deal policy had already been forged. Farmers wanted relief, not reform, and they indeed benefited from technical and noncoercive measures to increase the productivity of private land. Congress and the USDA never required that highly erodable land be permanently retired or that it be managed for long-term ends; the agricultural conservation programs that gained entitlement status relied on financial incentives, not coercion.[35] Soil conservation, in other words, had already been sold as a "new and improved" form of production, not a form of sacrifice. No doubt this set the ideological stage for short-term ends over longer-term adjustments.

The experience of war mobilization exposed this devil's bargain. Despite the New Deal's emphasis on development, especially rural development, its farm policy had rested on the trinity of limited markets, production control, and soil conservation. In the war, with markets restored and the country in desperate need of farm products, efficiency rolled over sustainability. Nowhere is this better illustrated than in the response of westerners to the return of rain. In Kansas, for example, heavier rainfall

---

[34] Wilcox, *Farmer in the Second World War*, 51–2; Douglas Helms, "The Great Plains Conservation Program, 1956–1981," in Helms, ed., *Readings in the History of the Soil Conservation Service* (GPO, SCS Economics and Social Sciences Division, Historical Notes No. 1, 1992); Hugh H. Bennett, "Soil and Water – Basic Wartime Resources," 1942, LVF.

[35] See Donald Worster, *Dust Bowl: The Southern Plains in the 1930s* (1979), Richard Lowitt, *The New Deal and the West* (1984); and Andrew P. Duffin, "Vanishing Earth: Soil Erosion in the Palouse, 1930–1945," *Agricultural History* 79 (2005).

not only made it possible for crop farmers to take advantage of the new conditions, it also allowed the region to envision a future free of drought, depression, and the federal government. In the 1930s, Kansans may have viewed diversified and balanced farming programs as the path to security, but with the lifting of the drought and the installation of irrigation equipment in the early 1940s, farmers could concentrate more exclusively on wheat and free themselves (in the short term) from environmental limits and government interference. The triumph of efficiency over sustainability did not go unnoticed, of course, and many alarmed SCS agents at the local level did try to check the exhuberance. But they found themselves caught in a trap of their own making; having emphasized conservation as a route to economic prosperity during the Depression, they were powerless to ask farmers to exercise restraint in the face of obvious economic opportunities. As one scholar concluded, the old "strategy of encouraging a return to full production and emphasizing dollar earnings from the land was exploding in the technicians' faces."[36]

Generous pricing policy underpinned this wartime agricultural expansion. Despite consumer and urban worries about the rising cost of food, Congress established farm prices at 85 percent of parity in 1941. Farmers argued that city dwellers' wartime wages, not food costs, were the real cause of inflation, and demanded that farm prices be set even higher. Congress responded in 1942 with the Emergency Price Control Act, which created a price floor at an astonishing 110 percent of parity. Consumers again charged that Congress had surrendered to a greedy pressure group, but farmers countered that the end of the war would bring a repeat of the sudden recession that had followed World War I. When the president asked Congress to find a compromise, it set a ceiling at 100 percent but guaranteed price supports after the war ended. The combination of increased production and high prices gave many farmers their first taste of prosperity, and farm income almost tripled between 1940 and 1945. The average increase in farm prices between 1939 and 1945 exceeded the average increase in hourly wages, although average net incomes for agriculturalists always remained much lower than for industrial workers.[37]

Behind the high wartime prices stood the country's largest and most powerful farm organization, the American Farm Bureau Federation. The

---

[36] Worster, *Dust Bowl*, 226. The Kansas material is drawn from Pamela Riney-Kehrberg, *Rooted in Dust: Surviving Drought and Depression in Southwestern Kansas* (1994), 165–75.

[37] Hurt, *Problems of Plenty*, 98–100; Wilcox, *Farmer in the Second World War*, 40–3, 121–7, 249–51.

Farm Bureau, first organized to sponsor the USDA's extension work, represented the larger, more commercial producers. It exerted bipartisan influence in Congress, currying favor with Democrats and Republicans alike. The Farm Bureau supported the AAA, proved critical in unifying southern and midwestern farmers behind the New Deal, and expanded its membership throughout the 1930s and 1940s. But it opposed the FSA and the BAE's county planning program, arguing that these programs kept marginal and inefficient producers in business. During the war, the Farm Bureau championed high farm prices and blocked attempts to distribute war production quotas to small farmers. It claimed that these people should find work in the cities or in war industries. Equity, like sustainability, was also at war with efficiency.[38]

The agrarian liberals did not give up on the "small-farm issue" without a fight. In 1941, BAE chief Howard Tolley warned that high prices alone would not guarantee widespread farm welfare. "The whole parity price concept," he warned, "has little bearing on the incomes or standards of living of that 50 percent of the farm population that operate very small farms or who work as farm laborers." In contrast to the Farm Bureau, Tolley hoped that the war mobilization efforts could distribute gains equitably among all farmers. In 1943, he reiterated these concerns in *The Farmer Citizen at War* and argued that the country had not yet offered the lower one-half of farm families "the equal chance that our democracy should give them." Insisting that poor agriculturists could not simply pick up and move to factory jobs, Tolley recommended an expansion in education, health care, farm credit, and grass-roots planning for low-income people. He also argued that the country's small producers were the most capable of expanding production for the war. "And the Nation will prosper," Tolley concluded, "in such measure as it approaches the goal of giving economic opportunity . . . and political opportunity alike to those of its people who have been less fortunate than others."[39]

Many Americans shared Tolley's concerns. One farmer from Delaware insisted that the country join hands with its "small independent producers" and design an equitable wartime production policy. "There are

---

[38] Christiana M. Campbell, *The Farm Bureau and the New Deal* (1962); Wilcox, *Farmer in the Second World War*; Baldwin, *Poverty and Politics*; Orville M. Kile, *The Farm Bureau Through Three Decades* (1948); Tolley oral history, CUOH; Will Alexander oral history, CUOH. Also see Wesley McCune, *The Farm Bloc* (1943); and McConnell, *Decline of Agrarian Democracy*.

[39] Tolley, "Agriculture and the Parity Yardstick," 1941, Correspondence Relating to Participation in the Defense Program, NA RG 96, Entry 3, Box 1; Howard Tolley, *The Farmer Citizen at War* (1943), 207–8.

not too many farms or too many farmers," he wrote. "If the forces of the large commercial farmers prevail, the common man, the small farmer and farm worker, will be disfranchised... There is a chance that we will build a new agriculture based on permanence and in which there will be a place for the common man to make his life on small farms throughout the land."[40]

The Farm Security Administration took up the cause of the small producer. Allied with the National Farmers Union and the Southern Tenant Farmer's Union, groups far less powerful than the Farm Bureau, FSA Administrator C. B. Baldwin claimed that low-income farmers (those with annual incomes of less than eight hundred dollars) still made up the majority of the country's farm population, and that they could make a significant contribution to the war. If the rural rehabilitation and technical assistance programs were not expanded, Baldwin warned, the country's small producers would be forced to leave agriculture altogether. Though the USDA and the War Production Board initially agreed to expand the FSA's programs along with the defense preparations, such promises proved short-lived. Too many people, ranging from some of Tolley's colleagues in the BAE to the members of the Farm Bureau, believed that the country was oversupplied with farmers. Orville Kile, a Farm Bureau lobbyist, criticized the FSA's "small farm strategy" and later explained the Farm Bureau's wartime position: "FSA clients as a whole produced relatively little over and above their own needs; were the least efficient producers; and in many instances could help the war effort more by going to work in war industry or for more efficient farmers who then needed help so desperately."[41]

As the FSA's experience suggests, it became difficult to sustain agrarian policies that supported small or self-sufficient producers in the new wartime production environment. This altered political landscape also assisted those who wanted to dismantle the FSA and the county planning programs altogether. Since the late 1930s, a conservative coalition of anti–New Deal Democrats and Republicans had been growing in Congress. Alienated by the leftward turn in domestic policy, by FDR's abortive attempts to pack the Supreme Court, and by the president's efforts to purge the Congress of conservative Democrats, this coalition targeted "nonessential" government spending and forced the New Dealers into a rearguard action to stave off budget cuts. Wartime mobilization only

---

[40] P. Alston Waring, "For What Are We Fighting? The Faith of the Small Farmer," *The Land* (Summer 1943), 45–9.
[41] Baldwin, *Poverty and Politics*; Kile, *Farm Bureau*, 272.

strengthened congressional demands for economy, and FDR – unable to risk political support for the war – did not intervene as lawmakers dismantled relief agencies such as the WPA, the NYA, and the CCC. Allied with the Farm Bureau, congressional conservatives also launched attacks on the BAE and the FSA.[42]

The county planning program was the first to go. In 1942, Congress cut funds for the BAE's projects despite Howard's Tolley's impassioned defense of the conservation and land use programs. Helping to orchestrate congressional opposition, the Farm Bureau claimed that the BAE committees unnecessarily duplicated the Extension Service/AAA setup. Even with its action program removed, however, the BAE continued to support the agrarian liberals and the FSA's small-farm strategy, providing statistics to counter the Farm Bureau's assertion that small farmers could not be counted on to produce enough for the war. The BAE's rural sociological work prompted the agency's final dismemberment in 1944. After it produced studies recommending improved race relations in the South and the stricter enforcement of acreage limitations on western reclamation projects, irate southern congressmen and the California Farm Bureau succeeded in persuading Clinton Andersen, the new agriculture secretary, to demote the BAE. No longer serving as the department's chief planning arm, the BAE became the more docile Economic Research Service.[43]

A bitter struggle over the fate of the FSA accompanied the demise of the BAE. From 1941 to 1944, congressional conservatives targeted the agency and put the FSA on their "death list" of New Deal programs. Chaired by Virginia Senator Harry F. Byrd, the Joint Committee on Reduction of Nonessential Expenditures provided a forum for extended and particularly vituperative attacks on the FSA's program and its personnel. The Farm Bureau charged that the FSA intended to socialize American agriculture and that its administrators were attempting to build up a political machine by soliciting clients and paying their poll taxes. Organizations of

---

[42] Baldwin, *Poverty and Politics*; Kirkendall, *Social Scientists and Farm Politics*; McConnell, *Decline of Agrarian Democracy*. On Congress and anti–New Deal sentiment, see William E. Leutchenberg, *Franklin D. Roosevelt and the New Deal* (1963); James T. Patterson, *Congressional Conservatism and the New Deal* (1967); David M. Kennedy, *Freedom from Fear: The American People in Depression and War* (1999); and Richard N. Chapman, *Contours of Public Policy, 1939–1945* (1981).

[43] Kirkendall, *Social Scientists and Farm Politics*, 195–254; Tolley oral history, CUOH; Charles M. Hardin, "The Bureau of Agricultural Economics Under Fire: A Study in Valuation Conflicts," *Journal of Farm Economics* 28 (1946).

large growers from the South and West, such as the Associated Farmers of California and the National Cotton Council, weighed in against the FSA's efforts to mandate wage standards and labor conditions for farm workers. The U.S. Chamber of Commerce also joined the fight against the FSA, arguing that rural rehabilitation programs subsidized inefficient farmers, thereby constricting the national labor supply and artificially boosting wages. FSA Administrator Baldwin answered such allegations by asking whether the country should allow the large commercial interests to take advantage of the war to "accumulate large land holdings and to make laborers out of farmers." Though agency officials continued to argue that small farms could contribute to the war effort, the FSA's funding was slashed and its employees scattered. Congress also ordered it to liquidate all the resettlement and cooperative farming projects. By 1946, only a weak Farmers' Home Administration remained.[44]

Unlike the AAA, Extension Service, Soil Conservation Service, or Rural Electrification Administration – USDA agencies that all survived the war – the BAE and the FSA never developed a strong political base. Contrary to the Farm Bureau's charges, these agencies never attempted to build interest-group support from the most indigent farmers and agricultural workers. Part of the problem stemmed from the disparate interests of the country's poor farmers: sharecroppers, tenants, and migrant workers had different problems and different needs. The New Dealers were able to unite the dominant and middling farmers of the South, the Midwest, and the West behind conservation assistance and high commodity prices, but they were unable to sustain a constituency composed of the poorest and the landless. Farmworker unionization would certainly have made a difference, but attempts at organization met violent resistance by California growers and southern planters. Nor did New Deal administrators risk the political ire of these southern and western interests in order to take up the question of union rights for agricultural wage laborers. Deeply divided by economic interest, and subject to myriad forms of repression, the country's poor farmers benefited occasionally from New Deal programs but found themselves without political clout when the war emboldened large growers, the Farm Bureau, and congressional conservatives.[45]

[44] Donald Holley, *Uncle Sam's Farmers: The New Deal Communities in the Lower Mississippi Valley* (1975), 245–74; Grant, *Down and Out*, 191; Baldwin, *Poverty and Politics*, 347–404.
[45] Holley, *Uncle Sam's Farmers*, 243; Jess Gilbert and Carolyn Howe, "Beyond 'State vs. Society': Theories of the State and New Deal Agricultural Policies," *American Sociological Review* 56 (1991); Badger, *The New Deal*, 182–4.

Neither, it must be said, did the FSA face the basic dilemma of its policy of helping farmers remain on the land in a time of rapid economic change. World War II transformed American agriculture dramatically. It solved the problem of low prices and eliminated crop surpluses. With government help, farmers used more fertilizer and adopted new machinery. They also expanded their holdings by buying or leasing more land. For the first time in years, farmers found themselves struggling with manpower shortages because so many people left to work in factories or to join the armed services. The war drained off many tenants and marginal farmers, who left in search of higher wages. Some of these farmers included many who willingly abandoned their homes in FSA-sponsored programs and resettlement communities. In fact, more farm people (an estimated 5 million) left the countryside between 1940 and 1945 than during any other five-year period of the twentieth century. Given these changes and the prospect of industrial recovery, could the FSA really have insured the small and marginal producer a standard of living commensurate with the other segments of society? This question was not the focus of congressional discussion, but it did weaken the agrarian liberals' internal defenses.[46]

The economic recovery catalyzed by World War II transformed the New Deal, revealing the long-term political incompatibility of efficiency, equity, and sustainability. The war required increased production above all else. It also opened up alternative employment opportunities for "marginal" farmers. Together these factors empowered efforts to undermine production restrictions, conservation controls, and rural rehabilitation programs. The agrarianism that fueled the New Conservationist policies of the 1930s and early 1940s lost influence with the demise of the BAE and the FSA, as did both the USDA's urban liberals and its agricultural pragmatists. However, the New Conservation underwent a transformation that revealed neither the death of the New Deal nor the end of federal intervention. Elated by wartime economic gains, many liberals now turned to an alternate prescription for rural poverty: full employment. New industry, they believed, could provide jobs and high wages; industrial expansion would underpin rural prosperity. During World War II Congress continued to pump

---

[46] Wilcox, *Farmer in the Second World War*; John L. Shover, *First Majority – Last Minority: The Transforming of Rural Life in America* (1976), 6; Holley, *Uncle Sam's Farmers*; Brian Q. Cannon, *Remaking the Agrarian Dream: New Deal Rural Resettlement in the Mountain West* (1996), 140; Baldwin, *Poverty and Politics*; McConnell, *Decline of Agrarian Democracy*.

money into resource development programs, especially in the South and the West, and the conservation agencies developed an altered worldview that guided and justified this industrial transition.

JOBS FOR ALL: INDUSTRIAL EXPANSION AND WARTIME RESOURCE POLICY

Writing in 1940 on the problem of rural poverty, the Extension Service's new director M. L. Wilson had worried that government policy would depopulate farm areas in the name of efficiency. The country, he pleaded, should retain a larger farm population than many economists – the "Rational Organizers of Agriculture and Industry" – advised. Of these economists, Wilson sadly remarked that "efficiency, low-cost production of goods, expansion of industrial production, and an era of abundance are their watchwords." As an example of such a rational organizer Wilson mentioned his former associate Mordecai Ezekiel, economic adviser to Secretary Henry Wallace. Wilson's choice proved both accurate and prescient, for no one figure worked harder during the 1930s and 1940s to replace agrarian with industrial liberalism.[47]

Wilson and Ezekiel had worked together in the early 1930s to bring the voluntary domestic allotment plan to FDR's attention and to design the AAA. The two men had agreed that farm assistance would hasten national recovery. Restoring rural purchasing power, they argued, would create demand for manufactured products and put industrial employees back to work. "To a very considerable degree the unemployment in cities is associated with the lack of buying power on farms and in rural communities," Ezekiel declared. "Emergency farm relief measures, directed at controlling production, will help initiate the readjustment." In 1933, Howard Tolley brought Ezekiel to work for the Agricultural-Industrial Relations Section of the AAA's Program Planning Division. Here Ezekiel explored the relationship between farmers and consumers and collected data on national income, farm income, and the income of industrial laborers. He soon came to the conclusion that agricultural welfare was closely bound to the welfare of other classes of people, especially those engaged in

---

[47] Wilson, "The Problem of Poverty in Agriculture," *Rural America*, 6; Kirkendall, *Social Scientists and Farm Politics*, 226; David E. Hamilton, "Mordecai Ezekiel, the Food and Agriculture Organization, and the Search for World Prosperity," paper presented at the annual conference of the Social Science History Association, November 2001.

manufacturing. In contrast to widespread assumptions within the USDA –
that rural underconsumption fueled the Depression – Ezekiel began to
argue that agricultural recovery required industrial expansion.[48]

During the 1930s Ezekiel proposed that the federal government spend
more money on public works and that it purchase large quantities of
industrial goods to "prime the pump." Though he did not campaign
against the FSA or the BAE's county planning program, Ezekiel harbored
grave doubts about the capacity of these efforts to help the rural poor.
He did not believe that land use planning or expanded systems of rural
credit could solve the nation's economic troubles. Only a movement of the
farm population out of agriculture, he claimed, could bring balance to an
economy in which too many people remained farmers and in which too
many small and unproductive farms yielded such low standards of living.
This transition, however, depended on government action to secure levels of industrial production and employment that exceeded those of the
1920s.[49]

Ezekiel was not the only one to move away from the agrarian interpretation of the Depression; indeed, he represented the ascendance of an
increasingly influential form of industrial liberalism. Central to the new
analysis, at least within the USDA, where agricultural fundamentalism
had formerly been taken as gospel, was the idea that farm recovery now
really depended on the expansion of urban consumption. "Farmers get
40 to 50 percent of the average dollar spent for food," as Ezekiel's BAE
colleague Louis Bean explained, "and urban workers probably receive
in wages about 60 percent of what farmers spend for industrial products
and services . . . Because of this interdependence, farmers have a vital interest in any program or policy that will help to bring about full employment of the working population in the cities."[50] Prodded by advisers
such as Ezekiel and Bean, Henry Wallace also expanded his conceptions of agricultural democracy to include government promotion of economic security for urban workers.[51] Most important, though, the growing

---

[48] David E. Hamilton, *From New Day to New Deal: American Farm Policy from Hoover to Roosevelt, 1928–1933* (1991); Ezekiel, "Agriculture: Illustrating Limitations of Free Enterprise as a Remedy for Present Unemployment," 1932, WP 00003, 16:21; Kirkendall, *Social Scientists and Farm Politics*, 79–80; Tolley oral history, CUOH.

[49] Ezekiel oral history, CUOH; Hamilton, "Mordecai Ezekiel"; Ezekiel, "Population and Unemployment," *Annals of the American Academy* 188 (1935).

[50] Louis H. Bean, "The Farmer's Stake in Greater Industrial Production," *Yearbook of Agriculture 1940*, 343.

[51] Badger, *The New Deal*, 151, 164; also see Kirkendall, *Social Scientists and Farm Politics*.

contingent of industrial liberals did not view industrial expansion simply as a way to expand the market for farm products; they also hoped an increasing supply of manufacturing jobs would solve the vexing question of low-income farmers. "It should be borne in mind," Bean wrote, "that increased [urban] purchasing power has greater significance for commercial than for subsistence farmers... For the latter an improvement in living standards depends ultimately on nonfarming sources of income."[52]

Ezekiel's 1939 book, *Jobs for All Through Industrial Expansion*, presented these ideas in a more popular format. Ezekiel called for a "full-bodied War on Poverty" and claimed that the country lacked no essential ingredients – its people were intelligent and its natural resources plentiful. What it did require, however, were "arrangements for keeping men at work to make the things they need, and for providing them the income to buy the things they make." He argued for better systems of industrial planning and for a more active approach to federal fiscal policy. Above all, Ezekiel insisted that the government must serve as an economic coordinator, because "private capitalism... seems unable to keep our men at work and our economy running at full production." As much as any agrarian liberal, Ezekiel felt sure that state intervention would benefit the ill-housed, the ill-clad, and the ill-nourished.[53]

Other analysts echoed these concerns. "In a broad view of a nation's welfare," wrote one economist who also challenged the agricultural fundamentalists, "it appears unwise to maintain an unnecessarily large farming population, with attendant problems of excessive output of farm products or low standards of living, in order that rural living may be enjoyed by a larger fraction of the population." Such worries, however, did relatively little to alter the agrarian tenor of conservation policy planning before the war. In 1940, the BAE launched the county planning program, and it recommended that Congress strengthen programs of rehabilitation lending and expand employment programs in soil, water, and forest conservation. More such projects, the BAE claimed, would permanently raise rural incomes. "Human erosion and soil erosion are but twin aspects of a single problem on the land," a BAE spokesman informed a Senate committee. "If these unemployed and under-employed men on farms and this great task of conserving natural resources can be brought together through such a program, both human and natural resources can be conserved by

[52] Bean, "Farmer's Stake," 346–7.
[53] Ezekiel, *Jobs for All Through Industrial Expansion* (1939), 7, 12, 282.

the same activity, one check would pay two bills, and a single stone would slay two Goliaths."[54]

The BAE's rural conservation works proposal was not about to be passed by a Congress that soon eviscerated the county planning program and the Farm Security Administration. And so, following the lines of thought developed by Ezekiel and Bean, some within the bureau began seriously to reassess the desirability of agrarian policy and to propose another option for farm unemployment – rural industrialization. Helped by government policy and by the wartime recovery of urban wages, farmers had stepped up production tremendously without employing more people. Many farmers left to join the military, and large numbers of other rural people, mostly marginal and landless farmers, moved to cities and factory jobs. Still, many poor farmers remained in rural areas during the war, and the BAE thought that out-migration must be accompanied by efforts to encourage industry in rural areas – not to sustain the rural way of life or to nurture small, craft-based factories, but to make it easier for low-income farmers to move immediately from agriculture to high-wage manufacturing or service jobs. Many munitions factories and other war industries had located in rural areas, but the concern was that demobilization would eliminate these new sources of employment. Permanent rural prosperity, one BAE report concluded, must include a sustained attempt to expand the rural industrial base and to shift postwar production from war materials to consumer goods. Because industry was highly concentrated in the northeastern part of the country (in 1935, the Northeast contained 82 percent of the country's manufacturing jobs), the report's author pinpointed the South and the Pacific West as areas ripe for further industrial development.[55]

Ezekiel heartily endorsed this ideological turnaround and returned to the BAE in 1944 to participate in its postwar planning efforts. He led the Agricultural-Industrial Relations Section, which sought to encourage industrial growth in rural areas after the war, and he helped Henry Wallace

[54] Joseph S. Davis, *On Agricultural Policy* (1939), quoted in R. R. Renne, "On Agricultural Policy," *Journal of Farm Economics* 20 (1940), 485; Raymond C. Smith, "A Statement on Two Suggested Solutions for the Problem of Farm Unemployment and Under-Employment," 24 May 1940, Records of the Division of Program Analysis and Development, NA RG 83, Entry 206, Box 1.

[55] Raymond B. Christensen, "Can Industry Be Developed in the Country?" 1943, General Correspondence, 1923–1946, NA RG 83, Entry 19C, Box 10; Wilcox, *Farmer in the Second World War*. On defense migration, see Collis Stocking, "Reallocation of Population and the Defense Program," *Social Forces* 20 (1941).

prepare *Sixty Million Jobs,* a book that championed industrial expansion and influenced the Full Employment Act of 1944. By the end of World War II, Ezekiel and his allies had concluded that farm poverty could be alleviated by the movement of poor farmers into better-paying jobs in the cities or into new factories closer to home. They also thought that industrialization would help the remaining farmers consolidate their holdings and mechanize their operations.[56]

The ascendance of industrial liberalism and of Ezekiel's role in that process accompanied the emergence of a revised conception of the liberal state. The inconsistent regulatory attempts of the early New Deal, as Alan Brinkley has demonstrated, produced few real economic gains and yielded little political agreement. But liberals, influenced by Keynesian theories of consumer demand, found they could adapt to the growing anti-statism of the war years by embracing a model of government intervention that steered clear of micromanaging the institutions of the economy and instead used macroeconomic fiscal tools (like public spending) to stimulate mass consumption.[57] Rural policy underwent a similar transition. Liberals moved away from the idea that farm security depended on equalizing and stabilizing the existing rural population and instead defended a less reformist but still aggressive government role in expanding the country's industrial base and increasing its aggregate purchasing power. Significantly, policymakers did not jettison the New Conservation, but altered and adapted it for new ends. Many now believed that resource policy, especially hydropower expansion, contained the potential to raise the incomes of farmers as well as those who took up other occupations. Electricity became the industrial genie waiting to be summoned from the agrarian lamp.

From his base in the BAE Mordecai Ezekiel both encouraged the emergence of the industrial approach and watched as the major resource

---

[56] Hamilton, "Mordecai Ezekiel"; Kirkendall, *Social Scientists and Farm Politics,* 226–7. Ezekiel's correspondence records are located in General Correspondence, 1929–1946, NA RG 83, Entry 19C, Box 11. I thank David Hamilton for directing me to these documents. Michael Flamm has argued that the "agrarian liberalism" of the National Farmers Union (NFU) contributed to the Full Employment Bill of 1944; the NFU, he claims, quickly understood the limitations of agricultural fundamentalism and saw that small- and family-farm welfare was linked to expanded consumer demand and Keynesian fiscal policy. That is, the NFU attempted to protect the small producer by embracing certain aspects of what I am labeling "industrial liberalism." See Michael W. Flamm, "The National Farmers Union and the Evolution of Agrarian Liberalism, 1937–1946," *Agricultural History* 68 (1994).

[57] Alan Brinkley, *The End of Reform: New Deal Liberalism in Recession and War* (1995).

agencies adapted on their own. He was especially intrigued by the wartime efforts of the Rural Electrification Administration, which quickly positioned itself to supply power and light to military installations and new rural industries. Already by the summer of 1940, 20 percent of the energy supplied by REA lines went to these new businesses and other large power users, and the figure only crept higher as the war continued. When hydro projects came on-line during the war, the REA boasted that they supplied power for expanded manufacturing as well as for area farmers. The new rural factories included more of the traditional processing concerns that had always cropped up in farm areas – those that added value to local food, forest, and mineral products before shipping them out – but the REA also encouraged a different kind of industrial decentralization by supplying cheap power to manufacturers that relocated from the city and that used no locally produced crop or raw material. These newcomers were attracted to rural areas solely because of the more flexible labor supply and the REA's inexpensive electricity.[58]

Ezekiel also communicated with the Tennessee Valley Authority, an agency that had recently launched a project in southern industrialization by designing a similar development strategy. During the early 1930s, the authority assumed that its conservation programs could address rural poverty by helping farmers make changes in land use and by providing them with inexpensive hydropower. Thick dairy pastures would replace eroded cotton fields, and small strawberry patches would provide as much income as entire fields of corn. These adjustments could be financed and sustained by the extra income provided by cooperative enterprises: small processing or craft concerns that "grew on the land," also powered by affordable electricity. This policy of decentralization reflected TVA's initial agrarian character and its administrators' belief that the agency could strengthen the southern economy while preserving its rural character and protecting the region from unsightly factories and crowded, unhealthy cities.

---

[58] "The Place of Rural Electrification Administration in Preparation for National Defense," "The Place of Rural Electrification Administration in Decentralization of Industry," "REA Mobile Power Reserve Units as a Factor in Total Defense," 1940, File on Defense Planning, NA RG 221, Entry 21, Box 4; "REA and the National Defense," "REA Systems Open Way for New Rural Industries," *REN* (July 1940); "More Power for National Defense," *REN* (November 1940); "Possum Kingdom Dam Dedicated – Will Serve 150,000 Texans," *REN* (September 1941); "Streamlined for War," *REN* (April 1942); "Industry Takes Root in the Land," *REN* (July 1942); "Grand River Dam Power Serves War Industry, Oklahoma Farms at Low Rates," *REN* (April 1943).

TVA's successes were limited in its first few years, however, and the South remained the nation's poorest region. In 1938, USDA researchers determined that it contained the highest proportion of disadvantaged farmers in the country, and an influential federal report issued the same year inspired the president to label the South "the Nation's No. 1 economic problem." Such thinking began to erode the appeal of TVA's philosophy of decentralization, which had failed to deliver significant economic gains. Its agrarian policies had also rested on an unstable administrative foundation. TVA chairman A. E. Morgan, the primary force behind the small rural cooperatives, intended to use electricity to create a new cooperative society. He often clashed with power director David Lilienthal, a fledgling industrial liberal who wanted TVA to provide an infrastructure for private investment and electricity for expanded manufacturing.[59] Chief agriculturalist H. A. Morgan agreed with A. E. on the merits of agrarian policy, but recoiled at his colleague's penchant for alienating the valley's established interests. The personality clashes broke out into the open when A. E. publicly accused his two colleagues of criminal misconduct. FDR removed A. E. in 1937, and his dismissal paved the way for a transition in the agency's development strategy.[60]

By 1938, TVA operated four dams with a total annual capacity of over 2 billion kilowatt-hours of primary or continuous power. These installations also produced significant amounts of secondary or dump power, which the agency had begun to sell to large industrial concerns such as Monsanto and the Aluminum Company of America (Alcoa). The TVA Act of 1933 had specified that local public agencies such as farm cooperatives and municipalities would be considered "preferential customers," but the legislation also authorized the agency to sell power to industry to permit domestic and rural use at the lowest possible rates. Claiming that municipalities and cooperatives could not use the secondary power, Lilienthal and his staff negotiated contracts with several large manufacturers and public utilities beginning in 1936. Though no public entity within feasible transmission distance was refused a wholesale power contract, A. E. Morgan had opposed the industrial policy on the grounds that Lilienthal

[59] David E. Nye, *Electrifying America: Social Meanings of a New Technology* (1990), 309.
[60] Carl C. Taylor, Helen W. Wheeler, and E. L. Kirkpatrick, *Disadvantaged Classes in American Agriculture* (GPO, 1938); Bruce J. Schulman, *From Cotton Belt to Sunbelt: Federal Policy, Economic Development, and the Transformation of the South, 1938–1980* (1991), 3, 35–7; Erwin C. Hargrove, *Prisoners of Myth: The Leadership of the Tennessee Valley Authority* (1994); Richard Lowitt, "The TVA, 1933–45," in Erwin C. Hargrove and Paul K. Conkin, eds., *TVA: Fifty Years of Grass-Roots Bureaucracy* (1983).

never sought approval for large industrial sales and that he never asked municipalities or cooperatives if they wanted to use the secondary power. "It is not necessarily a good policy in the public interest to favor large industries as opposed to smaller industries served by public agencies," A. E. explained. "It gives large industries preferential advantages over small industries; likewise preferential advantages over public agencies."[61]

Such anti-industrial sentiments no longer constrained Lilienthal's ambitions after Morgan's ouster in 1938. Bolstered by a Supreme Court case that finally sanctioned the agency's power program, and empowered by the final capitulation of the region's private utilities in 1939, Lilienthal steered the agency away from its earlier agrarian emphasis. Sensing an opportunity to catalyze southern industrial development, he positioned TVA's power program firmly within the Roosevelt administration's wartime mobilization plans, much as Lyndon Johnson had done for Central Texas. In 1940, Lilienthal worked out an agreement to build airplane and munitions factories and to supply electricity to Alcoa and military installations such as the secret atomic work soon undertaken at Oak Ridge. Helped by presidential support and congressional appropriations, TVA more than doubled its power capacity between 1940 and 1945 and used over 75 percent of this power for defense. It built several new dams, acquired five more, and supervised Alcoa's operation of another five. Symbolizing the final demise of agrarian concerns, one of these new projects – Douglas Dam – flooded over fifteen thousand acres of fertile bottomland and was built over the objections of area farmers, H. A. Morgan, the president of the University of Tennessee, and Tennessee Senator Kenneth McKellar. During the war TVA also constructed its first steam-generating plant, the most visible sign that the navigation and flood control programs no longer limited the amount of electricity the agency would produce.[62]

TVA emerged from the war as the largest integrated power system in the country, having contributed one-tenth of the total power for the nation's war effort. By facilitating the establishment of defense industries in the South, the agency also pointed the way toward a new approach to rural poverty. In search of better-paying jobs, rural southerners left the farms in

[61] J. A. Krug testimony, *TVAH*, 5227–309; A. E. Morgan testimony, *TVAH*, 11.

[62] Schulman, *From Cotton Belt to Sunbelt*, 91–2; Steven M. Neuse, *David E. Lilienthal: The Journey of an American Liberal* (1996), 150–66; Lowitt, "The TVA, 1933–45"; William H. Droze, "The TVA, 1945–80: The Power Company," in Hargrove and Conkin, *TVA*; Hargrove, *Prisoners of Myth*, 56–60; Ralph C. Hon, "The South in a War Economy," *Southern Economic Journal* 8 (1942).

droves; wartime work and military service drained off almost one-quarter of the region's farm population. Manufacturing employment increased threefold in Alabama, Florida, Georgia, Mississippi, South Carolina, and Tennessee, and weekly wages jumped up almost twofold. TVA, it seemed, had helped demonstrate that it was easier to help poor farmers by giving them incentives to migrate than by assisting them to regain their foothold on the land. As Lilienthal explained near the war's end, "The insistent demand of the people of the South for a higher level of income and the things that go with it cannot be met so long as we rely principally for the production of wealth upon agriculture, forestry, and mining... *Upon that as a base* we must develop, add, and build our industries."[63]

Industrial liberalism, that is, was not so much a rejection of agrarian policy as an expansion or addendum. The New Conservationists did not abandon the cause of agricultural modernization – on the contrary, they continued to believe that proper land use would create greater farm security and yield permanently high incomes. But efficiency was now in the driver's seat, and Lilienthal now found a larger audience for the argument that agrarian policy alone could not possibly raise the living standards of the country's entire farm population. As Lyndon Johnson had also discovered, a region's natural resources could be channeled into new industry while being developed simultaneously to serve a region's remaining farmers. These liberals envisioned a world where federal resource policy underpinned both rural and urban prosperity. The result would be bigger, more modern farms, an expanded industrial workforce, and larger towns and cities. "The region has made long strides toward a better balance between agriculture and industry," wrote Gordon Clapp, Lilienthal's successor. "With it have come arrangements for more efficient use of the region's resources, greater production, higher incomes, and a wider range of personal choice for farmers, businessmen, and wage-earners."[64]

---

[63] Hargrove, *Prisoners of Myth*, 60; Schulman, *From Cotton Belt to Sunbelt*, 102; Dillard B. Lasseter, "The Impact of the War on the South and Implications for Postwar Developments," *Social Forces* 23 (1944); David Lilienthal, "The Coming Industrialized South – Curse or Blessing?" 1944, LVF (italics in original). Lilienthal's thinking coincided with the general views of southern liberals: see Schulman, *From Cotton Belt to Sunbelt*; Clarence H. Danhof, "Four Decades of Thought on the South's Economic Problems," in Melvin L. Greenhut and W. Tate Whitman, eds., *Essays in Southern Economic Development* (1964); and George B. Tindall, "The 'Colonial Economy' and the Growth Psychology: The South in the 1930s," *South Atlantic Quarterly* 64 (1965).

[64] William H. Droze, "TVA and the Ordinary Farmer," *Agricultural History* 53 (1979); Gordon R. Clapp, *The TVA: An Approach to the Development of a Region* (1955), 55. Also see David Lilienthal, *TVA: Democracy on the March* (1944).

World War II also transformed resource policy in the West by accelerating existing trends. This was the domain of Interior Secretary Harold Ickes, whose influence over the region derived from the interlocked water and power programs of the Reclamation Bureau and the Public Works Administration. The reclamation program had begun in 1902 with the intent of building up more family farms with government-sponsored irrigation works, but until the 1930s the federal government watered only a small fraction of the irrigated acreage in the West. This changed during the 1930s, as the national public works budget soared and as almost half of that money (40 percent by 1939) paid for water and power projects like dams and irrigation canals. Following the example of Boulder Dam after its completion in 1935, power sales began to subsidize the cost of irrigation throughout the region.[65] Indeed, New Deal resource policy in the Great Basin, California, and the Pacific Northwest always bespoke a more optimistic sense of unlimited production and unlimited possibilities than elsewhere, for instance on the plains, where the drought and dust storms had provoked severe bouts of agricultural soul-searching. "If Henry A. Wallace, the Department of Agriculture, Franklin Roosevelt, and numerous others viewed the Great Plains in terms of lowering expectations to save the soil," as one western historian has remarked, "Harold Ickes and his allies viewed his domain largely in terms of expanding horizons, chiefly through the development of water facilities, especially hydroelectric power, and enhanced production."[66]

Still, despite these differences, Ickes and his allies shared with the agrarian New Dealers the initial expectation that conservation policy could shore up, perhaps even expand, the number of family farms. These hopes were stirred in large part by a vast movement of population westward. During the 1930s, many farm people had moved to the Pacific states from the Great Plains and parts of the Cotton Belt. Displaced by drought, dust, or the AAA, these migrants captured the attention of reformers, and their plight – caught on camera and in literature – served as a stinging reminder of the Depression's cruelty. The pathos, however, was due not simply to an unprecedented volume of migration but also to the restricted economic opportunities these already-disadvantaged migrants encountered upon their arrival. Particularly in California, they confronted a closed,

---

[65] Donald J. Pisani, *From Family Farm to Agribusiness: The Irrigation Crusade in California and the West, 1850–1931* (1984); Pisani, "Federal Water Policy and the Rural West," in R. Douglas Hurt, ed., *The Rural West Since World War II* (1998).
[66] Lowitt, *New Deal and the West*, 64.

industrial agricultural system sharply divided between landowners and seasonal, underpaid laborers. "The concentration of control in production is matched by concentration of control in employment," explained documentarians Dorothea Lange and Paul Taylor in *An American Exodus*; "opportunity turns out to be not land, but jobs on the land."[67]

While some federal officials managed workers' camps and attempted to enforce wage and housing standards, others hoped that an expanded reclamation program could provide irrigated homesteads for many of these migrants. The Reclamation Bureau had begun to work on community projects with the Resettlement Administration and the Farm Security Administration, and some New Dealers wanted to infuse the bureau's (and the Corps of Engineers') large dam plans with similar agrarian goals. Understanding that the displaced people would not find factory work in the midst of the Depression, they wanted them to find genuine opportunity on the land. "While it obviously would not be possible or desirable to resettle all families," conceded Agriculture Undersecretary M. L. Wilson, "it does appear that ... a large amount of resettlement on reclaimed lands could be carried out to advantage." The president agreed. Irrigation projects, Roosevelt argued, should be undertaken "not for the benefit of the man who happens to live there at the time, but rather with the idea that we will provide comparatively small irrigated tracts which we can offer for settlement." He claimed that the country should have initiated river development projects long before, for these would have prevented the plow-up of the Great Plains and halted the subsequent migration of thousands of destitute farmers. "In other words," he explained, "I want to give first chance to the 'Grapes of Wrath' families of the nation."[68]

Many factors worked against these hopes. Foremost among them was the conflict between the Reclamation Bureau's original raison d'être and the economic and political pressures of the 1930s. Intended to create more family farms and to encourage widespread landownership, the early Reclamation Acts prevented recipients from using irrigation water on more than 160 acres. But this rule was easily bypassed because of the

---

[67] Davis McEntire, "Migration and Resettlement in the Far Western States," *Journal of Farm Economics* (1941); Walter J. Stein, *California and the Dust Bowl Migration* (1973); Lowitt, *New Deal and the West*; James N. Gregory, *American Exodus: The Dust Bowl Migration and the Okie Culture in California* (1989); Dorothea Lange and Paul S. Taylor, *An American Exodus: A Record of Human Erosion* (1939), 145.

[68] Wilson to Hayden, 14 March 1938, Records of P. K. Hooker, NA RG 114, Entry 35, Box 5; Presidential Drought Conference, 1936, *FDRC*, 565; Speech at Bonneville Dam, 1937, *FDRC*, 132; Roosevelt to Ickes, 1939, *FDRC*, 405.

vociferous demands of large landholders and well-established communities. The 1930s witnessed a steady pattern of acreage exemptions in order to justify new water and power works in the West. For example, the Colorado–Big Thompson Project begun in 1938 provided irrigation water for eastern Colorado by sending water underneath the Continental Divide through a vast network of tunnels and reservoirs. Colorado–Big Thompson marked a significant departure for reclamation policy by providing supplemental water to existing farms and by exempting those farms from the 160-acre rule.[69]

Of course, nowhere was this pressure to aid existing farmlands more pronounced than in California, where a patchwork of large corporate landholdings – agribusinesses, really – already dominated the scene. There, efforts to enforce the 160-acre rule suffered the same fate as efforts to protect the Farm Security Administration. Additionally, while reclamation officials claimed that federal water projects would provide resettlement opportunities for fifty thousand Dust Bowl migrants, the focal point of administrative debate was never whether to build any new communities, but whether to enforce limits on water subsidies to existing or potential beneficiaries. Congress chose not to enforce the 160-acre rule when the Reclamation Bureau took over California's massive Central Valley Project (CVP) in 1935. Nor did it ever seriously attempt to prevent the bureau from continuing to aid larger landowners, or to stop the bureau's rival – the Corps of Engineers, never bound to the regulation – from doing so. Occasionally Harold Ickes raised a progressive objection to the arrangement, even announcing in 1940 that the bureau would indeed apply the 160-acre limit to the CVP. But Congress reacted to Ickes's proposal in 1944 by officially exempting the project from the restriction. Pressured by the valley's large growers and the California Farm Bureau, Congress yielded to the wartime political environment that stressed increased food production at any cost. Efficiency never really overwhelmed equity in California; equity never stood a chance.[70]

---

[69] Lowitt, *New Deal and the West*, 86.

[70] Lawrence B. Lee, "California Water Politics: Depression Genesis of the Central Valley Project, 1933–1944," *Journal of the West* 24 (1985); Clayton R. Koppes, "Public Water, Private Land: Origins of the Acreage Limitation Controversy, 1933–1953," *Pacific Historical Review* 47 (1978); Clayton Koppes, "Environmental Policy and American Liberalism: The Department of the Interior, 1933–1953," *Environmental Review* 7 (1983). On Western reclamation policy, also see Lowitt, *New Deal and the West*; Donald Worster, *Rivers of Empire: Water, Aridity, and the Growth of the American West* (1985); Norris Hundley, Jr., *The Great Thirst: Californians and Water* (1992); and especially Donald J. Pisani, *Water and American Government: The Reclamation Bureau, National Water Policy, and the West, 1902–1935* (2002).

The agrarian liberals' attention then turned to the Pacific Northwest, where federal officials intended to enforce the small-farm standard and to build a new rural community in the Columbia River Basin from scratch. Federal money had poured into Oregon and Washington during the 1930s, financing the construction of Bonneville and Grand Coulee Dams on the Columbia River. In 1937, Congress created the Bonneville Power Administration (BPA, placed in the Interior Department) to coordinate the distribution of electricity and to supervise a regional wholesale system. Though Congress, the Corps of Engineers, and the Interior Department fended off a "Columbia Valley Authority," lawmakers still modeled the Bonneville legislation after TVA's enabling act. Both TVA and the BPA were required to transmit power for the particular benefit of domestic and rural consumers, and to sell it at the lowest possible rates. BPA Administrators J. D. Ross and Paul Raver subsequently worked to expand rural markets and to help the REA establish rural cooperatives in the region.[71]

Many officials also viewed the BPA as TVA's western analogue: an anticolonial engine that would help the region escape from eastern financial domination. Though its officials always intended to encourage industrial growth, the BPA's initial vision also reflected TVA's early agrarianism. J. D. Ross, the administration's first director, painted a picture of small industries "diffused" throughout rural areas. Journalist Richard Neuberger also predicted that the industries established in the Columbia Basin would be decentralized and spread out. "What would be so unorthodox," he asked, "about every worker having his acre or so of peas and beans back of the house, as an anchor to windward if the work should give out?" Nothing stirred agrarian hopes more, though, than the prospect that thousands of poor, dusty migrants would find homes and water in the "Promised Land," America's new northwest empire and its last frontier. The focus of such dreams was the Columbia Basin Project, a large area in Central Washington to be irrigated by water pumped from the Grand Coulee. "Wandering men and women, looking for new opportunity, form a migratory population all over the West," Neuberger declared. "Their rehabilitation is a crucial problem. Grand Coulee will irrigate land for as many farms as there are in the entire state of New Jersey. All this will be

---

[71] The BPA was called the "Bonneville Power Project" until 1940, though I will use the abbreviation "BPA" when referring to its activities after 1937. J. D. Ross, "The Kilowatt Year: Your Money's Worth of Electricity," Misc. Records, 1925–1938, NA RG 221, Entry 12, Box 2; Harold Ickes, "Memorandum on Power Policy," 3 January 1946, Roscoe Bell Papers, Box 1, HSTL; "Bonneville Power Accelerates Rural Electrification in Northwest," *REN* (July 1940), 9–10. Also see Richard White, *The Organic Machine* (1995), 64–70.

controlled by the government, with speculation and profit subordinated to the general welfare."[72]

World War II delayed the basin's irrigation, and not until 1946 did the Interior Department begin construction of the Columbia Basin Project. The project never lived up to its promises; more residents of Washington and Utah took up farms than did migrants from Oklahoma or Arkansas. Very few of the settlers were poor, many were war veterans, and none remained content with the forty-acre plots approved by the original legislation. Postwar policy abandoned the family-farm ideal and soon subsidized large landholders. As had happened in the South, war mobilization also soaked up much of the West's farm population. The Reclamation Bureau and the Corps of Engineers expanded power capacities; federal planners located defense industries in Washington, Oregon, and California; and government dams provided electricity for war factories, military installations, and urban growth. Okies became steelworkers, aluminum processors, shipbuilders, and permanent residents of Los Angeles, Portland, and Seattle. Anticipating an influx of grateful Dust Bowl refugees, Columbia Basin planners had failed to consider how World War II would alter economic expectations. Agrarian options now struck many as rustic relics of a bygone age: wartime reports touted high-wage, industrial growth – not the maintenance of a stable farm population – as the only way to insure the West's continued prosperity.[73]

By the end of the war, industrial liberals had thus steered New Deal conservation policy away from its initial agrarian focus. Believing that rural incomes would remain stagnant if all farmers remained on the land, they crafted an altered intellectual landscape and a new policy regime. While a few agrarian stalwarts attempted to craft enhanced systems of agricultural planning and to expand the Farm Security Administration, other New Dealers channeled rural resources into manufacturing and defense concerns. The new commitment to sustained industrial growth entailed

---

[72] Ross, "The Kilowatt Year," 7, 8; Richard L. Neuberger, "The Columbia Flows to the Land," *SG* (July 1939), 439–41; Richard Neuberger, *Our Promised Land* (1938).

[73] Pisani, "Federal Water Policy and the Rural West"; Paul C. Pitzer, *Grand Coulee: Harnessing a Dream* (1994), 267–310; Gerald D. Nash, *World War II and the West: Reshaping the Economy* (1990); Philip J. Funigiello, "Kilowatts for Defense: The New Deal and the Coming of the Second World War," *Journal of American History* 56 (1969); Stein, *California and the Dust Bowl Migration*, 279; National Resources Planning Board, *Pacific Southwest Industrial Development* (GPO, 1942); National Resources Planning Board, *Pacific Northwest Region Industrial Development* (GPO, 1942).

a rapprochement with big business, with agribusiness, and with the military, but the shotgun wedding did little to disrupt the federal government's involvement in regional resource development.

While the prescription for rural poverty shifted dramatically, industrial liberalism grew out of agrarian policy. New Conservationists had always thought farmers should be able to find alternate employment. The agrarians, however, had hoped that small factories would employ farmers in the off-season, prevent out-migration, and sustain rather than undermine the rural way of life. Initially, federal money financed dam projects with agrarian aims in mind: the power would be distributed widely and cheaply, serving rural and urban areas with comparable rates. The war then prompted the expansion of these electric systems, and administrators channeled the additional power into large industries. The industrial transition was built upon the agrarian base. A similar pattern characterized the agricultural programs, in which conservation policy helped build a new farm constituency. Agricultural regions lost the poor and the unorganized, but the remaining farmers continued to expect federal assistance.

What emerged from the war was a model of rural resource development that put more emphasis on encouraging agricultural out-migration than on sustaining smaller farms, maintaining rural populations, or requiring soil conservation districts to implement measures that might limit farm incomes. A triumphant industrial paradigm held that only the expansion of factory and urban employment could provide a standard of living commensurate with postwar expectations, while government assistance could nurture an ever-decreasing number of farmers who nonetheless produced more and more with the aid of consolidated landholdings, mechanized operations, and the new chemical inputs that became widely available after the war. To be sure, government policy alone did not create the forces that ultimately rationalized and industrialized the farm sector. By the 1940s, however, policymakers no longer offered alternatives to those forces or presented social or environmental reasons for resisting them.

Conclusion

The New Conservation was a movement for social and environmental justice. Building upon the arguments of the Progressive era, these land planning specialists and rural electrification advocates asserted that rural resources should be developed for the use and benefit of an area's most immediate inhabitants. Their arguments gained political power and state-building capacity after the onset of the Depression. With the economic crisis came the widespread belief that the collapse had somehow begun in the rural sector, and that the nation as a whole would remain mired in depression as long as farmers continued to lag behind. Many New Dealers assumed that rural assistance would function as an engine for national recovery, and they launched genuine efforts to provide inexpensive electricity to underserved rural areas and to help farmers remain in place with commodity-support programs and better soil management practices.

There is no doubt these efforts constituted a real redistribution of wealth and opportunity. Rural electrification was so effective – and so profitable – that after the war private utilities adopted the models developed by the New Deal's public agencies. Areawide coverage at reasonable rates is no longer the hotly contested issue it once was. Wartime industrialization, made possible in large part because of this government-sponsored infrastructure, decentralized economic power and launched the postwar development of the South and West.

The New Deal also introduced lasting and positive environmental change. While serious environmental problems continue to beset farm practices, rarely does one encounter the violently gullied, scarred, and denuded landscapes that were so prevalent before the 1930s. In fact, the problems created by the postwar introduction of synthetic and petrochemical compounds so quickly changed the focus of environmental debate that it becomes far too easy to overlook just how much the New Deal was able to accomplish – how many landscapes contoured, regrassed, and reforested despite the reliance on short-term financial incentives and noncoercive means. Indeed, these imperfect yet undoubtedly ameliorative policies helped to launch the modern environmental movement.[1]

Yet the New Conservation rested on a set of conflicting commitments that would have weakened its reform potential even without the development of a conservative coalition in Congress or the ideological transition brought about by World War II. These New Dealers honestly believed that rural modernization and rational resource use would save the family farm, perhaps even expand its reach and influence. For a while, in rhetoric and in practice, they labored to balance the ideals of efficiency, equity, and sustainability. Of course, there were those who probably cared more about poor soils than poor people, and those who wanted to bring the countryside into the industrial era no matter the number of displaced farmers or the environmental consequences. To deny the sincere attempts to assist both poor people and poor land, however, is to ignore the initial range of New Deal policy and the complex intentions of New Deal policymakers. Efficiency triumphed over equity and sustainability not because it was the only goal, but because liberals were sometimes unwilling, and more often unable, to challenge two persistent forces: a political system in which representatives from the class-stratified South and West checked even modest efforts to assist the rural poor, and farmers' own understandable desires to increase their incomes both before and after the economic emergency had passed.

These conditions established the rural contours of New Deal state building. The federal government financed policies that were voluntary rather than coercive; it offered continuous assistance to landowners rather than to tenants, sharecroppers, and migrants; and it instituted programs that yielded immediate short-term returns rather than comprehensive plans for the long term. The enlarged state left in place after World War II is best described as neither especially strong nor weak, but as a vigorous developmental state committed to making markets less volatile and to increasing the value of private property. Herein, then, lie the promises and limits of midcentury liberalism. Correcting market failures and increasing the value of private property can indeed produce a wider and fairer

---

[1] See Neil Maher, *Nature's New Deal: Franklin Roosevelt's Civilian Conservation Corps and the Roots of the American Environmental Movement* (forthcoming).

distribution of wealth; such actions can even address the most heinous examples of natural resource exploitation. However, a developmental state could not challenge the institutions and political arrangements that perpetuated and sustained inequality, nor could it ask for sacrifice in the short term to institute social and environmental reform over the long run.

In the end, the New Deal formed a critical juncture in which intellectuals and policymakers attempted to embrace both progress and restraint, perhaps for the last time. No one more embodied this effort than Henry Wallace, who with one hand established a multinational corporation to sell hybrid seed while with the other he labored to revive the lost arts of soil maintenance and self-sacrificing economic cooperation. Wallace personally resolved the ideological contradictions of his professional life by surmising that once farmers appreciated the possibilities of high-yielding hybrids, they would gladly set aside the remaining acres for conservation purposes and return them to grass.[2] However incorrect his prediction turned out to be, Wallace's hopeful assessment of his fellow citizens reveals a great deal about the general obstacles facing any reform effort attempting to promote both modernity and stability. He sincerely believed that when American farmers achieved a certain level of output they would then be capable of saying: "Now we have enough." He also believed American consumers capable of exercising the same restraint. While Wallace could embrace both increased productivity and profit-limiting sacrifice, neither American producers nor the consumers whose demands they met followed suit. They never chose that moment to say "enough."

Writing over fifty years ago, historian Richard Hofstadter commented of the American farmer that he "had innocently sought progress from the very beginning, and thus hastened the decline of many of his own values."[3] Hofstadter was referring to the values of rural fundamentalism and farm moralism, qualities he disliked because of their backward-looking nature and irrational political potential. But Hofstadter put his finger on the paradox nonetheless: if one seeks both stability and modernity, progress can easily outrun traditional habits, in this case the traditions of conservation, social cooperation, and entrepreneurial restraint that Wallace learned from his grandfather and that he hoped to nurture nationwide. New Deal policy attempted to hew simultaneously to the values of upward mobility and to those of land stewardship, but the kind of state building it put in place relied on voluntary measures and short-term financial

---

[2] Russell Lord, *The Wallaces of Iowa* (1947), 143.
[3] Richard Hofstadter, *The Age of Reform* (1955), 35.

benefits. These methods do not restrain economic expansion, but encourage it; they do not put a brake on consumers' needs and wants, but accelerate their accumulation. Ultimately, modern Americans must look in the mirror to understand the inadequacies of New Deal resource policy and the unanticipated consequences of liberal reform.

Epilogue

Exporting the New Deal

Rarely have I presented parts of this study that someone hasn't asked about the connection between New Deal domestic policy and the post-war export and influence of these attitudes and techniques. "Now I understand why Lyndon Johnson would have proposed a TVA for the Mekong Delta," many say, often shaking their heads sadly to acknowledge Johnson's naiveté. In this epilogue I'd like to trace a few aspects of this international story, not by analyzing the route to Vietnam, of course, but by exploring how New Deal personnel traveled abroad to assist developing countries and how they helped create a new institutional network for assisted modernization. My intent here is not to make decisive claims about U.S. foreign policy but to suggest the existence of overlap and continuity between domestic and foreign affairs. What shaped many of these overseas rural development efforts was the favorable assessment of the recent American experience and the belief that war-ravaged and developing countries alike would benefit from similar agrarian and industrial resource policies.

An anecdote sets the stage. In the autumn of 1942, as war raged in Europe and the Far East, Vice President Henry Wallace stood before a group of conservation advocates. He called attention to the poor incomes and desperate living conditions of most of the world's inhabitants, and drew connections between rural poverty and misguided land use. Wallace believed the United States had something special to offer the depressed regions. In the previous nine years, he maintained, American farmers had left behind the soil-ruining ways of their forebears, increased crop yields, and embraced the help of the federal government to ensure continued progress. "The work that has been done on the land here has made a difference between success and failure," he concluded. "We should share everything we can with our good neighbors to the South and the West. In time to come I am sure that conservation will make a vital difference in determining whether we have another war or an abiding peace."[1]

Wallace's remarks encapsulated the ideology that propelled hundreds of American resource technicians abroad to strengthen allies in the war effort, reconstruct war-torn economies, and check the spread of communism. These "shirt-sleeve diplomats" emanated from the Department of Agriculture, the Extension Service, the agricultural colleges, the Interior Department, the Corps of Engineers, and the Tennessee Valley Authority. County agents, crop breeders, pasture specialists, soil conservation experts, foresters, fishery managers, irrigation engineers, and hydropower designers fanned out across the globe in the 1940s and 1950s. In return, American institutions welcomed overseas personnel: the land-grant colleges, the Soil Conservation Service, the Rural Electrification Administration, and the Fish and Wildlife Service provided in-house instruction for foreign students, and the Bureau of Reclamation operated an engineering center and laboratory in Denver, Colorado, where it offered training for hundreds of visiting engineers.[2]

Of course, Americans had been dispensing advice for years.[3] During the 1940s, however, Americans transformed the intensity and character of their overseas technical missions as the State Department began coordinating rural development projects as a well-defined objective. U.S. political and military strategy during World War II and the Cold War

---

[1] Wallace, "A Billion People," *The Land* 2 (1942–43), 241–5.
[2] On the Bureau of Reclamation's international activities, see U.S. Interior Department, *Point Four in Action: Department of Interior's Role* (GPO, 1951).
[3] Jonathan Bingham, *Shirt-Sleeve Diplomacy: Point 4 in Action* (1953); Merle Curti and Kendall Birr, *Prelude to Point Four: American Technical Missions Overseas, 1838–1938* (1954); Lewis S. Feuer, "American Travelers to the Soviet Union, 1917–32: The Formation of a Component of New Deal Ideology," *American Quarterly* 14 (1962); Deborah K. Fitzgerald, "Blinded by Technology: American Agriculture in the Soviet Union, 1928–1932," *Agricultural History* 70 (1996); Philip M. Glick, *The Administration of Technical Assistance: Growth in the Americas* (1957); Gove Hambidge, *The Story of FAO* (1955); Sarah T. Phillips, "Lessons from the Dust Bowl: Dryland Agriculture and Soil Erosion in the United States and South Africa, 1900–1950," *Environmental History* 4 (1999); Randall E. Stross, *The Stubborn Earth: American Agriculturalists in Chinese Soil, 1898–1937* (1986); Frank Pinder, "Point Four: A New Name for an Old Job," *Extension Service Review* (January 1952); USDA Extension Service and Office of Foreign Agricultural Relations, *Conference Report on Extension Experiences Around the World* (GPO, 1951); Russell Lord, "Governor Rex: A Tough Poet," *The Land* 2 (1942). Rexford Tugwell recounted his experiences in Puerto Rico in *The Stricken Land: The Story of Puerto Rico* (1946).

provided the specific context for this turn in foreign policy. First dispatched in the early 1940s, technical experts worked with the State Department and private organizations such as the Rockefeller Foundation to increase wartime production of food and raw materials in Latin America. After the war, resource specialists traveled on behalf of international relief organizations and the new Food and Agriculture Organization of the United Nations (FAO). These multilateral surveys of relief and rehabilitation functioned as pilot demonstrations for more extensive American bilateral aid to Greece and Turkey in 1947, and then throughout Europe in 1948. Then, in 1949, President Harry Truman's inaugural address challenged the country to extend the benefits of scientific knowledge to the entire underdeveloped world, to improve its natural and human resources. Inspired by this address, the resource agencies worked with lawmakers to formulate a "bold new" program of international assistance, a program that became Point Four (named after the idea's numeric position within Truman's speech).

Animating many of these wartime and postwar assistance efforts were distinct ideas about what had caused the Great Depression, and what had fixed it. In fact, many of the overseas food and resource specialists had worked in New Deal agencies, and they believed that the federal conservation programs of the 1930s and 1940s – land planning, soil conservation, flood control, irrigation, hydroelectric power, rural electrification, and industrialization – uplifted farm areas, raised farm incomes, and set the nation on the road to recovery. Experience derived from the rural resource programs of the New Deal at home often served as the starting point for technical assistance abroad. "We have a golden opportunity to help the people of the so-called 'underdeveloped' areas do things right," said Henry Bennett, the first director of Point Four, "to put roads and dams and ditches in the right places; to divide up units of land so they're neither too large nor too small for the average family; and to determine what land should be cultivated and how it should be cultivated so that they won't have the erosion, soil depletion and dust storms that we have brought upon ourselves here in the United States."[4]

This conservationist influence in postwar foreign policy represented the culmination of a project in domestic American state building. Mature federal resource agencies, born of Depression constituencies and war production schedules, now faced the world with the personnel, the experience,

---

[4] Henry G. Bennett, 1951, SA-HB. It was no accident that Bennett mentioned the Dust Bowl – it served as a particularly potent symbol both domestically and abroad.

and the attitude to change it. Americans were neither special nor superior, these universalists insisted; they were simply first to discover the appropriate technology and forms of government organization. Why should the United States sit still and watch painfully while others "drift to it the slow and hard way?"[5] After all, the reasoning continued, soils, forests, rivers, even people were much the same the world over. "Our foreign visitors see that the Tennessee Valley Authority speaks in a tongue that is universal," wrote TVA Chairman David Lilienthal in 1944:

No English interpreter is needed when a Chinese or a Peruvian sees this series of working dams, or electricity flowing into a single farmhouse, or acres that phosphate has brought back to life. For it is not really Norris Dam on a Tennessee stream or a farm in Georgia that he sees, but a river, a valley, a farm in China or Peru. The changes that are taking place here are much the same as those that men all over the world are seeking. The technical problems, too, at bottom are essentially similar, whether one is dealing with soil erosion along the Yangtze or the Hiawassee, the malaria mosquito in Burma or Mississippi's Tishomingo County, power production in Sweden or Swain County, North Carolina.[6]

By 1950, when the United States set out to assist the so-called underdeveloped nations, this resource universalism melded with an international political and economic agenda. Because most of the Third World remained agricultural in character, the experts insisted that the Cold War battle would be waged for the "hearts and minds" of *rural* people in particular and that American practice should serve as a model. American conservation programs, they believed, had integrated poor, rural regions into the national economy, and U.S. foreign policy could do the same for other areas of the globe. By fostering overseas what Interior Secretary Julius Krug called "coordinated area development," the United States could help put each nation's resources to work for the benefit of its people, and in turn each nation could participate in the world economic system on an equal, rather than colonial, basis. "Conservation and development is the very opposite of exploitation," wrote Henry Bennett. "This work produces opposite results by helping other peoples become self-sustaining and economically independent."[7]

[5] Morris Cooke, *Brazil on the March* (1944), 248.
[6] David Lilienthal, *TVA: Democracy on the March* (1944), 198–9.
[7] Julius Krug testimony, Congress, House, Committee on Foreign Affairs, *Hearings on the International Cooperation Act of 1949*, 81st Cong., 1st sess., September–October 1949, 300; Bennett, "The Point Four Program: To Conserve and Develop," in U.S. Interior Department, *Point Four in Action*, 2–3; Bennett, "The Problem and the Solution," 1951, SA-HB.

Of course, such optimistic and relentlessly universalistic language reflected the characteristic habit of mind of most postwar Americans. They assumed that people were basically the same worldwide – surely everyone desired material prosperity, increased living standards, and the political liberty required to exercise one's freedom of choice in a privatized marketplace. Linked to a social worldview that overlooked cultural and political differences was a scientific cast of mind that similarly eliminated ecological specificity and downplayed environmental distinctions. These naive assumptions, however, arose from the belief that the United States had discovered the recipe for sustained economic prosperity, and this buoyant outlook seems to have provided many Americans with the ideological ammunition to build a new institutional network for development assistance.

Certainly, the export of American expertise entailed no monolithic program, and it certainly produced no homogeneous result. Current opinion is widely divided on how to assess the effects of American influence in any given country, let alone the entire world. Still, an examination of the rural resource specialists' part in forming policy reveals some underappreciated links between the domestic arena (especially the tensions between agrarian and industrial liberalism) and how the United States shaped its posture in the postwar era. At the time, almost everyone agreed that programs of economic assistance should not be linked with demands for military alignment (though this eventually came to pass), but the agreement usually stopped there. Deeper divisions arose over whether change should come from the bottom up, from incremental improvements in agricultural practice and land use, or whether developing countries needed massive infusions of capital to catalyze the industrial sector and pull workers from the farms. "Point Four agrarians" such as Henry Bennett envisioned a set of long-term commitments to small but tangible projects in agriculture, health, and education, and fought an ideological battle for "modernization, not mechanization." On the other side, officials like Morris Cooke and David Lilienthal, whose loyalty lay with the engineers of large multipurpose water and power projects, believed that agencies such as the Rural Electrification Administration and the Tennessee Valley Authority had aptly demonstrated that cheap and abundant hydroelectric power could transform rural regions. The evidence suggests that the agrarian influence faded and that devotees of assisted industrialization saw their recommendations implemented as the State Department began to promote large-scale multipurpose river projects as part of its strategy to pump more money into nations deemed most critical in the effort to contain the Soviet Union.

In other words, the recent domestic experience seems to have influenced the initial evolution of Cold War foreign policy. The favored methods for rural rehabilitation at home had shifted from an agrarian to an industrial model, and it appears that many policymakers working abroad also jettisoned the idea that conservation policy should help farmers remain on the land. It seemed that only new industries could jumpstart regional economies, provide factory jobs, and quickly modernize backward agricultural sectors. Efforts to address rural poverty would henceforth entail a commitment to state-sponsored industrialization.

This methodological transition, however, revealed a pattern of continuity rather than one of change. Despite their differences in policy preferences, both the agrarians and the industrial planners had absorbed the collective vision of the New Conservationists: government responsibility for rural welfare. Both camps viewed the U.S. experience in universal terms and argued that conservation assistance could strengthen rural areas and national economies everywhere. This unified assessment of their home country and of the developing world's possibilities, honed during the New Deal and World War II, might help to explain the resilience, influence, and eventual combination of the American resource development models.

WARTIME ASSISTANCE, POSTWAR INSTITUTION BUILDING, AND THE COLD WAR

Technical assistance as a form of organized diplomacy arose from the unique relationship between the United States and the Latin American republics during the 1930s and World War II. Influenced by the Good Neighbor Policy and a growing spirit of pan-American solidarity, Congress in 1939 set up a systematic framework for cooperative technical exchange. It authorized the president, upon request by a host nation, to temporarily assign any U.S. government employee qualified to offer expert advice. Congress soon broadened the legislation, empowering the president to use the services of any government department "to render closer and more effective the relationship between the American republics." By the end of the year Roosevelt had established the Interdepartmental Committee on Scientific and Cultural Cooperation to organize requests for assistance. Members from more than twenty-five separate government bureaus assumed responsibility for each project, although the State Department handled overall coordination.[8]

---

[8] Glick, *Administration of Technical Assistance*, 6–8; Office of Inter-American Affairs, *History of the Office of the Coordinator of Inter-American Affairs* (GPO, 1947), 3.

The program in its early stages was conceived not as an economic development program for Latin America but as a manifestation of diplomatic goodwill and a way of codifying numerous requests for consultation with U.S. experts. The committee first began operations in 1940 with a small allocation of $370,500 (though its yearly allowance grew to $4 million by 1949). The missions remained small, consisting mostly of only one or two technicians, and advisory in character. The Latin American governments received assistance in a wide range of fields, from civil aviation to geologic mapping, but most of the missions addressed some aspect of food production. From 1940 to 1948, the committee assigned U.S. agricultural experts overseas, brought agricultural trainees to the United States, and set up agricultural research and experiment stations in fifteen countries.[9]

During this period the United States also conducted a second, parallel operation in Latin America. As the war in Europe and Asia choked off sources of raw materials, the Roosevelt administration moved more urgently to solidify commercial relations between the United States and the southern republics. In 1940 the president established the Office of the Coordinator of Inter-American Affairs as a body subordinate to the Council of National Defense, and appointed Nelson A. Rockefeller to the coordinator's post. Though the effective procurement of strategic war materials (and the dissemination of anti-Axis propaganda) was always central to Rockefeller's mission, he broadened this initial objective on the theory that friendly relations would best be secured by cooperating with Latin America on a wide array of cultural and scientific activities. In 1942 Rockefeller secured a charter for a government corporation, the Institute of Inter-American Affairs (IIAA), and initiated a broad program in agriculture, health, and education. From 1942 to 1950, the IIAA spent about $65 million on its cooperative programs in Latin America (almost three times the amount spent by the Interdepartmental Committee). Unlike the committee, which contributed very little to actual program costs, the IIAA paid for supplies, equipment, materials, and technicians.[10]

9 Glick, *Administration of Technical Assistance*, 8–12; Charles Brannan, "Agricultural Research and Point Four," 1950, WP 2100, 2:27; Department of State, *Point Four* (GPO, 1950), 130; Oscar L. Chapman, "Cooperation in the Development and Conservation of Fishery and Wildlife Resources," *The Record* 4 (September–October 1948).

10 Stanley Andrews oral history, HSTL; Office of Inter-American Affairs, *History of the Office of the Coordinator*, 3–10; Glick, *Administration of Technical Assistance*, 14–26. A second corporation, the Inter-American Educational Foundation, was organized in 1944 specifically for the educational efforts, but insofar as Congress consolidated both corporations in 1947 as the Institute of Inter-American Affairs I will use the abbreviation "IIAA" for all of these activities.

The Department of Agriculture participated more than any other resource agency in the Latin American activities. The USDA's Office of Foreign Agricultural Relations (OFAR), along with the Federal Extension Office, coordinated independent projects in the region as well as the agricultural missions and foreign fellowship programs for both the Interdepartmental Committee and the Food Supply Division of the IIAA. Henry Wallace took particular interest in Latin American issues in the 1930s and continued to do so after leaving the USDA to become vice president in 1941.[11]

One of the most dynamic and visible of the USDA's agricultural ambassadors was Hugh H. Bennett, chief of the U.S. Soil Conservation Service (SCS). Bennett had built his agency in the early 1930s after Congress appropriated funds for soil conservation experiment stations in 1929. During the 1930s, the SCS grew in size and prestige as it set CCC men to work on terraces and pastures, battled the Dust Bowl, and sustained hundreds of regional soil conservation districts. By the mid-1930s, SCS publications reached audiences around the world, and foreign officials often sought Bennett's presence as an expert observer. After the Interdepartmental Committee and IIAA set up official frameworks for exchange, the SCS helped develop soil conservation programs in Mexico, Venezuela, Colombia, and Ecuador.[12]

Bennett relished the international spotlight and articulated well the universalist assumptions underlying technical aid in general, and U.S. conservation assistance in particular. "Today we have on our hands the greatest war of all history," he observed after a trip to Venezuela in 1941, "and we have got to settle that with guns. But it seems to me when you get out on the land and work with people and talk with them about the productivity

---

[11] Brannan, "Agricultural Research and Point Four"; M. L. Wilson, "Report on Agriculture's Third Inter-American Conference," *Better Farming Methods* (September–October 1945); "Office of Foreign Agricultural Relations: History and Functions," n.d., ca. 1949–1950, Stanley Andrews Papers, Box 2, HSTL; Wilson, "The Latin-American Fellowship Program of the Extension Service," 1943, WP 00003, 12:35; Office of Inter-American Affairs, *History of the Office of the Coordinator*, 127–36; Wallace, "Sustained Yield: From a Talk to Latin-American Soil and Water Technicians Visiting Washington," *The Land* 2 (1943). OFAR was created in 1939 when the Foreign Agricultural Service was transferred to the secretary's office from the Bureau of Agricultural Economics.

[12] Atherton Lee, "Soil and Good Neighbors," *The Land* 1 (1941), 239; Bennett, "The Increasing Interest Abroad in Soil Conservation," *The Record* 4 (September–October 1948). For an example of SCS influence abroad, see Sarah T. Phillips, "Drylands, Dustbowl, and Agro-Technical Internationalism in Southern Africa," in James C. Scott and Thomas Summerhill, eds., *TransAtlantic Rebels: Agrarian Radicalism in Comparative Context* (2004).

of the soil, there is a common denominator. You always come to some sort of understanding . . . and our statesmen, our educators, and all of our great men have missed that." In Venezuela he found poverty, malnutrition, slopes denuded of trees, uncontrolled runoff, and "good land in the hands of other people." He left Caracas with a few other Americans and conducted an exhibition tour in the countryside, helping farmers build terraces, contour land, and plant thousands of trees. Bennett could have told this story about Baca County, Colorado, or Fayette County, Georgia. But that was precisely his point: "Wherever and whenever you begin to talk about the fertility of the soil and how it relates to the welfare of humanity," he declared, "you are talking a common language that will bring nations closer together."[13]

M. L. Wilson, director of USDA Extension, shared Bennett's steadfast internationalism. This New Conservationist began his career as Montana's first county agent in 1912 and worked with the Bureau of Agricultural Economics in the 1920s. During the New Deal, he helped craft and implement the Agricultural Adjustment Act, directed the Subsistence Homesteads program, and served as undersecretary of agriculture. In 1940, Wilson took the position as extension director in order to build support for the USDA's county planning program. He also helped position the Extension Service as one of the major sources of personnel for the overseas technical assistance programs. Equal parts scientist, philosopher, and social engineer, Wilson championed comprehensive rural rehabilitation programs and democratic forms of education and administration. Believing that conservation assistance could help all farmers remain on the land, Wilson represented the agrarian impulse in domestic as well as foreign assistance philosophy.

By the time World War II provided the opportunity, Wilson and his colleagues were ideologically prepared for enlarged activities in Latin America, for what he called the "humanitarian application of the Good Neighbor Policy." During the 1940s, Americans aided agricultural research and extension programs in fifteen Central and South American countries. In Costa Rica, for example, they helped set up programs in crop development, pasture and soil conservation, and insect control. In El Salvador, U.S. personnel assisted with erosion control methods such as check dams, terracing, and grass barriers. With aid from the IIAA, the Haitian government established an agricultural experiment station, an agricultural

---

[13] Bennett, "Soil, a Common Denominator: The Opening Talk at St. Louis," *The Land* 2 (1942): 146–8.

college, an extension service, a school for rural teachers, and a forestry service. The USDA's Rural Electrification Administration also participated in IIAA activities, sponsoring year-long courses on U.S. distribution systems and rural cooperatives for visiting engineers.[14]

Most of the wartime programs in Latin America, however, focused on supplying the armed forces and Allies quickly and efficiently. For example, the expansion of rubber production in Brazil required extensive health and sanitation projects, and U.S.-sponsored hospitals served migrant labor camps along the Amazon. Procurement of foodstuffs also received top priority, and in most instances the programs for food storage facilities, transportation improvements, crop and livestock demonstrations, and agricultural extension functioned with this objective in mind. As a result of these arrangements an uneasy relationship existed between the IIAA and the Department of Agriculture. The IIAA maintained that the USDA's dogged determination to guard its turf hampered long-term planning and development in Latin America, and the USDA argued in return that its long-term projects should not become subordinate to temporary wartime needs.[15]

Not only were the IIAA's agricultural activities undertaken for the purpose of defense, its plans for industrial expansion in Latin America also reflected the exigencies of war. As submarine attacks obstructed shipping in the Atlantic, the Board of Economic Warfare and the IIAA organized a U.S. Technical Mission to Brazil to "soften the economic impact of the loss of imports." A White House memo set out four basic objectives for the mission – to increase local production of essential products in order to save shipping space, to convert local industries to the use of substitute raw materials, to maintain and improve transportation facilities, and "to lay the foundation for a long-range strengthening of Brazil's whole industrial economy." According to Morris Cooke, the Brazil mission chief, the war hurt Brazil's nascent industries more dramatically than its far larger agricultural sector. He believed delivery failures in coal, gasoline, and fuel

---

[14] Wilson, "Latin-American Fellowship Program"; "Summary Statement of Foreign Student Program as of January 1, 1945," WP 2100, 1:26; USDA Extension Service and OFAR, *Conference Report on Extension Experiences*; "What Latin Americans See in REA," *REN* (December 1941); "Electrification in Latin America," *REN* (March 1944); "Latin American Engineer-Trainees, 1946–1947," *REN* (October 1946); "New Power for Chile," *REN* (December 1947/ January 1948).

[15] Claude C. Erb, "Prelude to Point Four: The Institute of Inter-American Affairs," *Diplomatic History* 9 (1985). Office of Inter-American Affairs, *History of the Office of the Coordinator*, 128–36, 213–17, details the food procurement operations and the rivalry between OFAR and the IIAA. Also see Andrews oral history, HSTL.

oil "became the basis of an interrelated shortage in supplies and in land transportation that threatened the stability of the whole economy."[16]

Though not affiliated with a single agency or government department like Hugh Bennett or M. L. Wilson, Morris Cooke nonetheless spent the years prior to the Brazil mission promoting New Deal conservation measures. He worked with Governor Gifford Pinchot on Pennsylvania's Giant Power Survey during the 1920s, and served as chairman of the Mississippi Valley Committee under Franklin Roosevelt. After directing the Water Resources Section of the National Resources Board, Cooke served as the first administrator of the Rural Electrification Administration and chairman of the Great Plains Committee. He worked closely with the Tennessee Valley Authority and electrification projects across the United States. Cooke fervently believed that the wise stewardship of land and water would yield improvements in rural welfare, and saw hydroelectric power as the foundation for a multipurpose system of agricultural modernization and industrialization designed to develop regional economies.

Cooke well understood that while U.S. federal policy promoted cheap hydropower, rural electrification, land rehabilitation, and flood control just about everywhere in the country, the Tennessee Valley Authority had become the unrivaled model of American regional development. A felicitous wartime combination of modernized farms and mechanized industries appeared to have ameliorated the rural exodus of the Depression almost overnight. Hydroelectric dams sent kilowatts to new factories, rural cooperatives distributed power to the homes and barns of valley residents, and phosphate fertilizers revived sagging fields. Foreign visitors, including heads of state, flocked to view the gleaming steel and concrete and to speak with TVA technicians about turbines, public health, contour plowing, and electric milking machines.[17]

TVA's international reputation stemmed from the authority's unique administrative structure and the skill of its propagandists. While other agencies such as the Reclamation Bureau, the Corps of Engineers, the Rural Electrification Administration, the Soil Conservation Service, the USDA Extension Service, and the Forest Service could claim credit for similar (or even more dramatic) results across the nation, only TVA

---

[16] Cooke, *Brazil on the March*, vii, 51.
[17] David Lilienthal described international interest in *TVA: Democracy on the March*. Also see "TVA as a Symbol of Resource Development in Many Countries: A Digest and Selected Bibliography of Information" (Knoxville: TVA Technical Library, January 1952).

held exclusive jurisdiction over a single geographic region. As a result, authority spokesmen like Chairman David Lilienthal could create the "TVA Idea" and imbue the agency with an aura of comprehensive expertise, an expertise suited for the present global emergency. The TVA experience, its chairman believed, constituted the "brass tacks of world reconstruction," and that explained why the agency had so quickly become a center of international attention. "It is obvious," Lilienthal wrote in 1944, "that the development of one people's land and forests and minerals for the sole benefit of another people has started many a fire of hatred that later exploded into war. It has not been quite so apparent that methods of unified development to create sustained productivity rather than quick exhaustion relieve war-creating tensions of impoverishment."[18] Herman Finer, writing in the same year for the International Labour Organization, echoed Lilienthal's thesis and brandished it as a lesson in world responsibility:

The cardinal feature of the TVA is that it was deliberately established and given responsibility for the welfare of an undeveloped area. It was the answer to a complex of economic and social problems, which involved the relationship between a nation and one of its regions, poverty-stricken but with resources capable of development. National authorities felt that the welfare of any region of the United States was an important contribution to the whole nation... With this evolution of the TVA in mind, it may be asked whether the richer nations of the world recognize the value to the world economy of international assistance to the underdeveloped areas within it.[19]

Therefore, when Morris Cooke traveled to Brazil and looked out the airplane window, he surveyed the vast country as others had looked at Appalachia in the early 1930s – seeing a colonial economy rich in natural and human resources but economically and institutionally underdeveloped. The North American "technological inheritance," Cooke declared, could put Brazil's rich resources to work for the betterment of its people. The waterfalls and rapids dotting Brazil's rivers would become "a future source of wealth to the country that neither gold nor diamonds, nor coffee, nor rubber, nor cotton can be, for [the rivers] represent such amounts of potential electricity as cannot even be estimated." Citing Lilienthal's *TVA: Democracy on the March*, Cooke affirmed that Brazilians should

[18] Lilienthal, *TVA: Democracy on the March*, 199–200. David Ekbladh also looks at the international establishment of the TVA Idea in "'Mr. TVA': Grass-Roots Development, David Lilienthal, and the Rise and Fall of the Tennessee Valley Authority as a Symbol for United States Overseas Development, 1933–1973," *Diplomatic History* 26 (2002).

[19] Herman Finer, *The TVA: Lessons for International Application* (1944), 217.

emulate the example of TVA, an agency that had successfully transformed a poverty-stricken, flood-prone region plagued by eroded soils and deforested slopes into the showpiece of the nation. "We in the United States have been the first to explore the possibilities of multiple-purpose river development," he boasted as he mulled over Brazilian plans to develop the Sao Francisco River along American lines and with American assistance. Cooke also warned that harnessing the hydropower would not be enough – it "must be sent to the people who need it."[20] Such faith in the American model of hydropower development – which required aggressive rural electrification to fulfill a complementary program of social justice – illustrated well the buoyant universalism of these former New Dealers, few of whom paused to consider whether developing countries possessed the means or the will to distribute resources such as power and water equitably among much denser rural populations.

On the tenth anniversary of the IIAA, Secretary of State Dean Acheson applauded the institute's ten years of technical cooperation. "Its pioneer experience," he affirmed, "is being utilized in technical assistance projects in many other areas of the free world."[21] Acheson spoke correctly. Although the IIAA was not particularly popular in Congress, many Latin American programs continued after the war, and they do seem to have provided the initial models for postwar projects of rehabilitation and technical aid in the underdeveloped world. But technical assistance to Latin America was not the only forerunner of later development programs. U.S. agricultural and natural resource experts also traveled to North Africa, Europe, and Asia to feed allies during World War II and to rebuild liberated regions. These specialists worked with national agencies such as the Lend Lease Administration, the Board of Economic Warfare, and the Foreign Economic Administration, as well as multinational organizations such as the United Nations Relief and Rehabilitation Administration (UNRRA) and the United Nations Food and Agriculture Organization (FAO). They gained similar international experience and voiced similar rationales for U.S. involvement in underdeveloped nations.

---

[20] Cooke, *Brazil on the March*, 10–11, 65, 30, 184, 187, 195. Also see Cooke, "Cinderella the Great," *SG* 33 (November 1944); Cooke, "World Industrialization: The Challenge of Social Engineering," *The Land* 6 (1947); and Cooke, "Down to Earth with Point Four," *New Republic*, 11 July 1949.

[21] "Statement by Secretary of State Dean Acheson on the Occasion of the Tenth Anniversary of the Institute of Inter-American Affairs," State Department Press Release no. 243, 1952, Kenneth Hechler Files, Box 3, HSTL.

The career of Stanley Andrews exemplifies this wartime export of former New Dealers and American technical personnel. Andrews edited the *Arkansas Farmer* and the *American Cotton Grower* during the 1930s and moved to New Orleans in 1941 to take a job with the Farm Credit Administration. After joining the army, Andrews became an agricultural officer with the Allied Military Governments in North Africa, Italy, and Germany, and he served as a U.S. delegate to the FAO. He traveled to Greece in 1947 as a member of the Greek-Turkish aid committee, spent more time in Europe as the civilian director of the Food, Agriculture, and Forestry Group for the U.S. and British zones of Western Germany, and returned to the United States in 1949 to head the USDA's OFAR. While still with OFAR, Andrews joined two food survey missions to East Asia relating to the recovery of Japan. In 1951, President Truman appointed Andrews director of the Technical Cooperation Administration (Point Four) after the death of Henry Bennett, its first director.[22]

As Andrews's professional path suggests, the theaters of battle created an avenue for the internationalization of U.S. technical personnel that paralleled the wartime activities in Latin America. Andrews and other agricultural officers followed in the wake of the Allied military forces as they moved through North Africa and Italy and finally into Germany. In Algiers, Andrews fed civilians under the Civilian Supply Program and shipped food to the army. As he pulled out of North Africa, he also noted that Russians were carrying out road-building and construction projects, and that a few Americans were coordinating reforestation and reclamation efforts.[23]

Andrews moved on to Italy to work with the Allied Military Government. With a mixed American and British staff, he began "helping Italy set up Democratic institutions" by addressing its agricultural outreach methods. "We were deeply imbued with the American system of research, education, and extension established in the U.S. under the Land Grant College system," Andrews later remembered. He criticized the Italian rural advisory system in which the bureaucrats "took a superior

---

[22] Stanley Andrews, "Journal of a Retread," unpublished manuscript, Andrews Papers, Box 30, HSTL; "Truman Names Arkansas Ex-Editor Administrator of Point 4 Program," *New York Times*, 22 April 1952; "A Missourian Feeding a Hungry World," *St. Louis Post Dispatch*, 7 May 1952.

[23] Andrews, "Journal," 93–9. The Civilian Supply Program in North Africa is also discussed in William A. Brown, Jr., and Redvers Opie, *American Foreign Assistance* (1953), 71–2.

tack and required the peasant to come to them with hat in hand for advice and supplies." In contrast, Andrews's office worked with sympathetic Italian officials to schedule peasant meetings and to require the "desk-bound" gentlemen to give talks and answer questions.[24]

In 1945 Andrews proceeded to Germany, where the occupation forces faced the urgent task of feeding civilians. Food shipments from the United States often made the difference between survival and mass starvation. Andrews worried constantly about shortages and nutritional deficiency in Germany, and his agency supervised rationing and the processing of agricultural products. From his post Andrews also observed the onset of the Cold War and subsequent adjustments in American strategy. "U.S. policy," he noted, "was gradually shifting from tearing down Germany under a plan which was to make it a cow pasture to a more constructive approach in the hope that this country would survive as an important member of the New Europe . . . it was plain that the Russians were going to take over Eastern Germany and as much of Eastern Europe as possible." His division received orders from the Military Government to "democratize" German agriculture, which had been centrally planned under Hitler. In his view, U.S. personnel from OFAR, the Extension Service, and the land-grant colleges helped return "the planning and development of production down to local levels."[25]

In North Africa, Italy, and Germany, Andrews witnessed countless scenes of devastation, and he discovered how violently war interrupted the daily routines of economic existence. Farmers and shepherds died while tending mine-laden fields, and families huddled in mountain caves to protect small remnants of grain. American troops, cold and hungry after a long campaign, cut down even the seed stock for a national reforestation program in the Italian highlands. But what affected Andrews more than the wreckage was the "medieval state" of agriculture in those regions, the great divisions between rich landlords and poor peasants, and the primitive hoe-and-sickle technology. Andrews's experiences in Algiers, Rome, and Berlin resembled those of Americans stationed in Latin America. They all perceived agricultural backwardness and compared

---

[24] Andrews, "Journal," 114–202, quotations 264, 265, 266.
[25] Andrews, "Journal," 788–9, 913, 931; Andrews, "Food and World Tensions," 1951, Andrews Papers, Box 5, HSTL. For a discussion of the postwar politics of European food relief efforts, see Allen Matusow, *Farm Policies and Politics in the Truman Years* (1967). The reconstruction of the German extension system is also discussed in USDA Extension Service and OFAR, *Conference Report on Extension Experiences*, 102–9; and Wilson, "Abundance and Our World Responsibilities," 1949, WP 00003, 12:14.

those conditions unfavorably with American progress. "To the casual observer the first impression of farming methods in most countries of Europe is its primitiveness," Andrews noted in the *Arkansas Farmer*. "It appears in the ox cart stage rather than the tractor stage."[26]

American technical advisers also accompanied U.S. occupation forces in Japan and South Korea, where they increased agricultural yields (often with new rice varieties developed by the Rockefeller philanthropies) and instituted adjustments in land tenure. For example, Laurence Hewes, who worked during the 1930s in the Resettlement Administration and Farm Security Administration as special assistant to Rexford Tugwell, helped implement General MacArthur's land reform program in the Japanese countryside. In Okinawa, the army contracted with the Agricultural Research Service of the USDA and Michigan State University to devise a research and extension system.[27]

U.S. military forces were not the only parties working to feed civilians and to reconstruct economies during and immediately following the war. The UNRRA, established in 1943, pooled the resources of UN member governments to provide assistance in liberated areas not under the control of military authorities. China, for example, received more UNRRA aid than any other nation, and the United States contributed well over half the funding and almost a third of the program's foreign staff. The China UNRRA not only distributed immediate relief assistance but also resumed long-term agricultural development and river engineering work sponsored in the 1920s and 1930s by nongovernmental organizations such as the YMCA, the Rockefeller Foundation, and U.S. universities.[28]

By the end of 1947, UNRRA programs in Europe and the Far East came to a close. American policymakers initially stipulated that wartime aid efforts not become long-range reconstruction programs, but Congress did

[26] Andrews, "Journal," 986–7. Henry Bennett, president of Oklahoma A&M and the first director of Point Four, also looked aghast at the state of the peasantry in Bavaria when the Military Government asked him to observe the agricultural situation in Europe in 1949. He was particularly distressed to see farmers harvesting by hand. See "We Must Win the Peace," n.d., Bennett Papers, Box 1, HSTL.

[27] Michael Schaller, *The American Occupation of Japan* (1985); Congress, House, Committee on Foreign Affairs, *Hearings on Aid to Korea*, 81st Cong., 1st sess., 1949; Laurence Hewes, *Boxcar in the Sand* (1947); Andrews, "Journal."

[28] David Ekbladh, "To Reconstruct the Medieval: U.S. Non-Governmental Organizations and the Modernization of Inter-War China, 1914–1937," paper in possession of author. Also see George Woodbridge, *UNRRA: The History of the United Nations Relief and Rehabilitation Administration* (1950); and J. Franklin Ray, Jr., "UNRRA in China," Secretariat Paper No. 6, Tenth Conference of the Institute of Pacific Relations, September 1947.

allocate funds for some post-UNRRA aid. It authorized an extension of
the Civilian Supply Program of the War Department (for which Andrews
worked in North Africa and Europe), and extended limited amounts of
aid with the Relief Act of 1947. Still, few Americans believed that this
foreshadowed the advent of an extensive new program of U.S. assistance.
Instead, they regarded post-UNRRA relief as the final phase in the transition from war to peace.[29]

Indeed, a new international agency stood poised to take over UNRRA
work and to sponsor worldwide rural development and food security
activities: the UN Food and Agriculture Organization. The FAO was conceived in the spring of 1943, when the United States hosted a Conference
on Food and Agriculture in Hot Springs, Virginia, at the urging of Franklin
Roosevelt. "Eventually," one inspired delegate remarked, "*freedom from
want* will be adopted as a world policy because the driving force of modern
science and technology is in the direction of unrestricted, expanding production and universal, adequate distribution." Conference-goers agreed
that scientific discoveries in nutrition, agriculture, and conservation made
it possible to raise world production levels, and that a permanent international organization to carry out this mission should be established as
quickly as possible. But the delegates at Hot Springs did not envision agricultural development as their single aim. They also proposed that nations
cooperate to raise consumer purchasing power and create new demand
for agricultural products; to this end they recommended increased industrial production, expanded world trade, improved employment and educational opportunities, and better transportation facilities.[30]

After the Hot Springs conference an Interim Commission on Food and
Agriculture, composed of representatives from forty-five nations, drafted
a constitution and planned the technical duties of the new organization. The commission, along with subcommittees in agriculture, nutrition,

[29] Charles Wolf, *Foreign Aid: Theory and Practice in Southern Asia* (1960), 14–15; Brown
and Opie, *American Foreign Assistance*, 76–9, 108–13.
[30] Gove Hambidge, "Freedom from Want: A Report on the Hot Springs Conference," *The
Land* 3 (1943), 40; Henry Jarrett, "FAO: A Matter of Mechanics," *The Land* 5 (1945–6),
91; Hambidge, *Story of FAO*, 51. Two other studies of the FAO include P. Lamartine Yates,
So Bold an Aim: Ten Years of International Cooperation Toward Freedom from Want
(1955); and Sergio Marchisio and Antonietta di Blase, *The Food and Agriculture Organization (FAO)* (1991). The FAO, of course, did not spring forth from a single conference;
an assortment of ideas and organizational precedents influenced its conception. It took
over the work of the International Institute of Agriculture in Rome, which distributed
statistical and technical data: the League of Nations publicized influential scientific work
in nutrition (and malnourishment) that also shaped the organization's mission.

forestry, fisheries, and economics, submitted a general report (*The Work of FAO*), which reiterated many of the proposals from the Virginia conference – that producer welfare was inseparable from consumer welfare, that nations should work toward full employment and high purchasing power, and that agricultural development in the less advanced countries would become the focus of attention in the decade following the war. The report also put forward specific project ideas, from small improvements in agricultural technology (such as steel hoes and village incubators) to reforestation, soil conservation, and multiple-purpose river schemes. Thus the commission explicitly endorsed local agricultural work modeled after the U.S. Extension Service as well as large-scale development projects to promote irrigation, hydroelectric power, and industrialization. From the start the FAO endorsed an approach that combined the agrarian and industrial points of view.[31]

Contemporary accounts of the organization's formation repeatedly describe the persuasive influence of U.S. universalism. For example, one early FAO chronicler observed how U.S. achievements during the 1930s and 1940s convinced Americans "that the application of science and technology could obtain results as startling as those obtained in industry . . . Not for them the 'slow continuous epic of the soil' but rather the commando approach, namely that shock tactics and fine equipment could overcome any obstacle." Indeed, what this author found most astounding was that U.S. rural improvement projects materialized so swiftly and so decisively. "Once, shortly after the war, a farm was remodeled in one day as a conservation demonstration – fields shaped and contoured, drains laid, windbreaks planted, crops drilled, farm buildings and home redesigned . . . The passionate conviction that science has now made it possible to transform the oldest and slowest of human occupations is something wholly new in the world."[32]

Forty-four governments officially established the FAO at the Quebec Conference in October 1945. In its first year, the FAO conducted

---

[31] Hambidge, *Story of FAO*, 51–9. Notable New Dealers worked with the Interim Commission – Paul Appleby was a member, Howard Tolley chaired the economics panel, and M. L. Wilson served on the science panel. See Paul Appleby, "Some Implications of the Hot Springs Conference in Relation to Extension Work," in *Conference Report on the Contribution of Extension Methods and Techniques Toward the Rehabilitation of War-Torn Countries* (GPO, 1945); Howard Tolley, "The United Nations Interim Commission on Food and Agriculture," *Journal of the American Dietetic Association* 21 (1945); and Wilson, "Nutrition and Agriculture," *Journal of the American Dietetic Association* 21 (1945).

[32] Yates, *So Bold an Aim*, 47.

a world food survey covering seventy nations and assumed UNRRA responsibilities, including reclamation and flood prevention projects in China, rinderpest control in Ethiopia, soil conservation and pasture improvement in Italy, and a hybrid corn program in Europe. At the request of the Greek government in January 1946, the FAO sent its first technical mission to make a reconnaissance study of Greek agricultural problems and to recommend a general program for the rehabilitation and development of Greek land, water, and industrial resources.[33]

Though several European specialists served on the FAO Mission to Greece, more than 60 percent of its personnel hailed from the United States – from the Bureau of Agricultural Economics, OFAR, the agricultural colleges, and the Bureau of Reclamation. The mission traveled throughout Greece during the summer of 1946, consulting with the UNRRA and conferring with Greek officials, bankers, merchants, farmers, and the directors of construction, irrigation, and power companies. The mission concluded that the country could double or triple its national income within a few decades. "This can be done," it proclaimed, "by effective development and use of irrigation and hydroelectricity, by the development and use of improved agricultural technologies, and by the expansion of industry to use unemployed labor effectively." The mission recommended that the United Nations, World Bank, and International Monetary Fund offer financial support. In the end, however, the international agencies did not supervise postwar development in Greece because the United States embarked on an extensive bilateral program of military, economic, and technical assistance soon after the FAO mission sent its report to the press.[34]

By 1946 and 1947, Greece had emerged as the site of a Cold War showdown. The Soviet Union, after consolidating its hold over Eastern Europe, appeared ready to push southward into areas historically dominated by the British. Western leaders viewed Soviet actions in Iran and Turkey as a systematic attempt to expand Moscow's control beyond the sphere of influence allotted to it by the Allied wartime conferences. So when a communist insurrection in northern Greece threatened the country's stability, American and British leaders interpreted the situation as part of this larger Soviet scheme. Though the United States and Britain supplied small amounts of assistance to Greece throughout 1946, by early

---

[33] Jarrett, "FAO," 94; Hambidge, *Story of FAO*, 30, 64, 71–5; "Report of the FAO Mission for Greece" (1947), filed in WP 2100, 30:5; Andrews, "Journal," 743–5.

[34] "Report of the FAO Mission for Greece"; Sumner P. Wing, "Global 'Hydro-Economics' Advanced by Reclamation Visitors," *The Record* 4 (September–October 1948).

1947 a communist victory appeared imminent. Britain, unable to shoulder the burden owing to the precarious position of its own economy, informed the U.S. State Department that it planned to terminate financial and military assistance to Greece.[35]

At a joint session of Congress on 12 March 1947, Truman declared that the United States would assume responsibility for the economic and financial stability of Greece and Turkey. The president, however, had more than the Mediterranean crisis in mind. "I believe," he declared, "that it must be the policy of the United States to support free peoples who are resisting subjugation by armed minorities or by outside pressures." Soon known as the "Truman Doctrine," this pledge significantly altered American geopolitical strategy. Henceforth, Truman implied, the Unted States would contain Soviet expansion by supporting friendly nations along the Russian periphery as well as those susceptible to internal communist insurgency. Interestingly, the FAO report on Greece played a critical role in the administration's new initiative. Secretary of State Dean Acheson often quoted from the report and distributed copies to the House Foreign Affairs Committee. Perhaps convinced in part by the concrete measures suggested by the FAO mission, Congress authorized several hundred million dollars in military and economic aid for Greece and Turkey, and sent American advisers to assist in reorganization and reconstruction. The assumption that relief programs alone would guarantee stability in wartorn regions was brushed aside; the United States now committed itself to far more comprehensive schemes of assistance. "Our missions in Greece and Turkey," wrote Stanley Andrews, "were actually reconstruction and development missions which took over the work of the UNRRA and, in effect, took up where the UNRRA left off after World War II in many countries."[36]

The American advisers drew extensively from the FAO report. As recommended by the FAO mission, the reconstruction projects combined both agrarian and industrial goals. The U.S. Army Corps of Engineers sent technicians to help restore land and water transportation; rebuild homes, factories, and utilities; and reconstruct irrigation and reclamation works. The USDA also sent personnel to restore farm output and to increase agricultural exports. These rehabilitation projects were gradually supplemented with long-term projects, especially after the Greek and

[35] William Keylor, *The Twentieth-Century World: An International History* (1996), 251–60; Bruce Kuniholm, *The Origins of the Cold War in the Near East: Great Power Conflict and Diplomacy in Iran, Turkey, and Greece* (1980).

[36] Keylor, *Twentieth-Century World*, 261; George Britt, "The Greeks," *SG* (May 1947), 279–80; Andrews, "Journal," 848.

Turkish aid programs were folded into the Marshall Plan in 1948. First among these goals was the construction of electric power projects to support the development of light industries such as textiles and processed foods. An American firm prepared engineering plans for the construction of a national power grid and the development of hydroelectric facilities, and a Public Power Corporation, designed in part after the TVA, administered the industrial power program as well as some rural electrification efforts. U.S. agricultural experts also helped their Greek counterparts design and outfit a new extension service. The Division of Agricultural Extension, created by the Greek Parliament in 1951 and modeled after the U.S. Extension Service, employed trained agents to conduct demonstrations, meet with farmers, distribute technical bulletins, and work with homemakers and young people. The extension agents introduced improved varieties of wheat, maize, fruits, and livestock. They encouraged extensive use of farm machinery such as tractors and seed drills, helped construct small irrigation and drainage systems, and promoted soil conservation measures such as contour plowing, terracing, and range rehabilitation. Similar programs began in Turkey, and Marshall Plan funds brought Turkish civil engineers to the United States to study with the Bureau of Reclamation.[37]

Indeed, the Marshall Plan followed closely on the heels of the Greek-Turkish crisis, and by the end of 1948 U.S. commitment abroad had changed dramatically. Military support, economic aid, and technical assistance now constituted essential instruments in halting communist expansion and integrating the world economy. Strategic infusions of bilateral aid underpinned recovery in Europe, and American administrators like Stanley Andrews remained there well into the 1950s. While aid to Europe far exceeded aid to other areas from 1948 to 1950, planning for European (and Japanese) recovery did focus attention on other parts of the world,

---

[37] *Fourth Report to Congress on Assistance to Greece and Turkey* (GPO, 1948); William H. McNeill, *Greece: American Aid in Action, 1947–1956* (1957), 71–3; "Electric Power Program in Greece," Congress, Senate, Committee on Foreign Relations and Committee on Armed Services, *Hearings on the Mutual Security Act of 1951*, 82nd Cong., 1st sess., July–August 1951, 122–3; "M. L. Wilson on Assignment to Greece as Extension Consultant," 1948, WP 2100, 57:35; Wilson, "Final Report," 1948, WP 2100, 15:26; Division of Agricultural Extension and Education Ministry of Agriculture, Greece, and the Advisory Group on Agricultural Extension, Food and Agriculture Division, Mutual Security Agency, "More Production Through Agricultural Extension in Greece," 1953, WP 2100, 30:4; Turkish General Secretary's Office of the Organization for International Economic Cooperation, "Quarterly Report on the Marshall Plan in Turkey," 1953, WP 2100, 30:4.

especially Asia. The legislation establishing the European Recovery Program in 1948 authorized a China Aid Program under the same administrative agency – the Economic Cooperation Administration (ECA). And after the Chinese communist victory in 1949, the ECA supplanted military-directed relief programs in Korea, deeming the country critical to checking communist expansion in the Far East.[38]

In China, American strategists faced a country not only struggling to rebuild but also entangled in civil war. ECA administrators believed that attention to rural areas would speed economic recovery and secure peasant support, both vital to strengthening the Nationalist government's ability to fend off a communist victory. Drawing personnel and program ideas from the UNRRA and earlier efforts, the ECA and the Nationalist government established the Joint Commission on Rural Reconstruction (JCRR) to modernize Chinese rural life. The JCRR recruited both American and Chinese technical advisers and provided assistance for the repair of water control facilities, cooperative associations, the introduction of improved varieties of seed, irrigation expansion, and land reform in Taiwan and three mainland provinces.[39]

After the 1949 communist victory in China, the JCRR moved operations to Taiwan and expanded its range of activities. OFAR staff worked with the JCRR on land reform and helped set up rural cooperatives. The ECA financed large shipments of fertilizer, which the JCRR distributed to the cooperatives along with improved seed and advice on green manuring. In addition to broad programs in education and public health, the commission also directed irrigation, fisheries, and forestry projects. And though the ECA hired an American firm to restore and expand hydroelectric power facilities with industrial recovery in mind, Stanley Andrews (who traveled to Taiwan while director of OFAR) reported that "rural electricity was developed and even the smallest bamboo hut had at least one electric light bulb." The JCRR, inspired by its own success, gradually set up international research and educational institutions to train foreign technicians.[40]

---

[38] Wolf, *Foreign Aid*, 28–52; Congress, House, *Hearings on Aid to Korea*.

[39] David Ekbladh, "To Reconstruct the Medieval"; Sergei Shenin, *The United States and the Third World: The Origins of Postwar Relations and the Point Four Program* (2000), 5; Economic Cooperation Administration, "The Program of the Joint Commission on Rural Reconstruction in China," 1951.

[40] Economic Cooperation Administration, "U.S. Economic Assistance to Formosa, 1 January to 31 December 1950"; Andrews, "Journal," 1053; Joseph A. Yager, *Transforming Agriculture in Taiwan: The Experience of the Joint Commission on Rural Reconstruction* (1988).

Like the IIAA activities in Latin America, the battle theaters and occupation zones of World War II served as pilot projects for U.S. development assistance. American specialists such as Stanley Andrews followed behind military operations, fed civilians and allies, and remained in occupied Italy, Germany, and Japan to rebuild and refashion the rural infrastructure. Americans also worked with international organizations like the UNRRA and FAO, and with private interests such as the Rockefeller Foundation, to provide relief as well as long-term agricultural and industrial assistance. When the Cold War upped the ante in 1947 and provided a revised context for technical assistance, the U.S. government sent technical advisers along with military and economic aid to Greece and Turkey, and then created a new agency – the ECA – to coordinate resource development efforts in Europe, Asia, and parts of colonial Africa. Still, in 1950, such programs remained tied to areas of strategic concern; there existed no commitment to the underdeveloped world as a whole.

THE POINT FOUR PROGRAM

In April 1946, State Department press officer Benjamin Hardy waited with his family aboard a freighter in the harbor of Santos, Brazil. Hardy and his wife grew tense as news of Soviet activities trickled in through the ship's wireless. Then, while observing Brazilian communists staging strikes on the docks, they grew alarmed that communist activity was not contained within Europe and Asia. During his wartime years with the IIAA, Hardy had observed how agricultural, medical, and educational facilities had helped Brazilians, and now he decided that the same measures would work in all underdeveloped countries. "He believed," remembered his wife, "that they would have to be taught to have a mind for themselves ... and he said that by teaching these people to do for themselves they wouldn't be such easy prey to the Communist ideas."[41]

Not much came of the idea until August 1948 when Hardy, now a speechwriter in the State Department, pitched the proposal to his boss. Arguing that a third of the world's people lived in hunger and poverty, he maintained that the United States should extend its know-how to the less fortunate countries of the world. They would soon be demanding a greater portion of the world's products; if thwarted, they would shortly prove "ripe for revolution." In the long run, he believed, such a program of technical assistance would prove more important than the Marshall

---

[41] Christine Hardy Little oral history, HSTL.

Plan. When later that year Truman and his aides began casting about for themes to include in the inaugural address, Hardy expanded his proposal. The new initiative would have four significant advantages: the cost was low in comparison with the Marshall Plan, it would pick up where the European Recovery Program left off, the United States could coordinate its efforts with those of international and private organizations, and charges of imperialism could be deflected if technical aid was extended only to those countries requesting it. Truman had indicated that he desired a "democratic manifesto" directed to the world rather than the American people, and he approved the plan in January 1949.[42]

Hardy's proposal dovetailed with the administration's emerging emphasis on the less developed countries. Until 1948, a Europe-centered position prevailed among U.S. planners; they believed the recovery of Europe would restore the world market, thus aiding underdeveloped regions. Europe, however, still lacked dollars to pay for raw materials and industrial equipment from the United States, despite infusions of Marshall Plan assistance. American strategists then focused on the less developed countries, especially in Southeast Asia, where development might create raw-materials sources for Europe and Japan, as well as markets for export goods. So by 1949, as Cold War concerns merged with flagging world recovery, the United States stood ready to initiate new policies in the underdeveloped world as a whole.[43]

Truman announced the new initiative in the fourth point of his inaugural address on 20 January 1949. After pledging support for the United Nations, the European Recovery Program, and the formation of a North Atlantic security alliance, the president proposed a "bold new program" for "making the benefits of our scientific advances and industrial progress available for the improvement and growth of underdeveloped areas." Declaring that misery, hunger, and disease constituted threats to underdeveloped and prosperous nations alike, Truman maintained that the United States in cooperation with other countries and organizations should make available technical knowledge and foster capital investment in areas requesting assistance. Yet the president made it clear that he did not conceive the program as another Marshall Plan. Material resources, he admitted, were limited. But American technical expertise, the key to greater

---

[42] Shenin, *United States and the Third World*, 8–12.
[43] Harold H. Hutcheson, "Government and Capital in Point Four," *Foreign Policy Reports* 25 (June 1949): 66–75; Brown and Opie, *American Foreign Assistance*, 383–84; Shenin, *United States and the Third World*, 15–21.

production, was inexhaustible. In the end, Truman argued that Americans would benefit as much as the world from the expanded commerce that development would foster. Although the president never mentioned communism specifically, he did conclude by implying that economic development would yield democratic societies.[44]

Truman insisted that the Point Four idea had been with him since he approved the Greek-Turkish aid program in 1947. Ever since then, the president told reporters, he had "spent most of his time looking over his globe, trying to find how to make peace in the world." Point Four embodied the president's (admittedly naive) belief that peace could be obtained by integrating the lesser-developed nations into the world economic system without encouraging "the old imperialism – exploitation for foreign profit." Secretary of State Dean Acheson repeatedly explained that Point Four was not a "big money" program; the United States intended to export skills, not capital. The natural and human resources of each country could be developed for the benefit of its residents, thus countering Russian accusations of exploitation while speeding European and Japanese recovery and expanding U.S. markets.[45]

Also in the president's mind were the American conservation and agricultural programs of the 1930s and 1940s. Special assistant Ken Hechler remembered that Truman drew from "his knowledge of the success of the Tennessee Valley Authority in bringing prosperity to the southeastern states, and his awareness of the way that scientific and educational programs of the Department of Agriculture had increased farm production." River valleys all over the world, the president had predicted, could be "made to bloom" with American help. Such references suggest that the New Deal programs exerted a powerful influence on the formation of U.S. assistance policy. Just as the natural resources of rural and poverty-stricken areas in the United States were "put to work" for the benefit of residents, the natural resources of underdeveloped nations could be developed for their people. Just as poor U.S. farmers were integrated into

---

[44] "Inaugural Address," in Congress, House, Committee on Foreign Affairs, *Point Four: Background and Program* (GPO, 1949), 21.

[45] "President Orders New Plan Speeded," *New York Times*, 28 January 1949; "Inaugural Address," 21; "The World from Capitol Hill," *New York Times*, 23 January 1949; "Truman's Four Points Have Wide Implications," *New York Times*, 23 January 1949; "President's New, Bold Program Unveils Real Truman Doctrine," *Washington Star*, 25 January 1949; "Truman Aid Plan Lauded by Acheson," *New York Times*, 27 January 1949.

the national economy, poor nations might be integrated into the world economy.[46]

Because the Point Four announcement took the country by surprise, Congress did not pass legislation establishing the program until almost two years later. Many interests competed to influence the legislation, and administration goals often shifted during the many months between Truman's inaugural address and the Act for International Development, which authorized Point Four. The most heated arguments erupted over how best to foster the appropriate "atmosphere" for capital development and foreign investment abroad. Many maintained that corporations should receive special concessions protected by bilateral treaties, while others insisted that only the U.S. government could create the conditions for development by funding basic technical programs in agriculture, health, and education. Still another faction, influenced in large part by the Marshall Plan, believed that development would depend on large transfers of government capital. A State Department compromise split up the technical assistance and investment provisions into separate bills, and opened the way for final debate during the spring and summer of 1950.[47]

"The bill now before you," explained Dean Acheson to the Senate Foreign Relations Committee, "establishes economic development of underdeveloped areas for the first time as a national policy. Its purpose is to encourage the exchange of technical skills and promote the flow of private investment capital where these skills and capital can help raise standards of living, create new wealth, increase productivity and expand purchasing power." This aim constituted an essential component of U.S. military security, Acheson maintained, because "increasing numbers of these people no longer accept poverty as an inescapable fact of life... so when Communists offer quick and easy remedies for all their ills, they make a strong appeal to these people."[48]

At this point the State Department espoused a "pure technical assistance" approach. That is, it believed the U.S. government should export the skills and techniques – not the capital – to create conditions conducive to development. Acheson conceded that philanthropies such as the Rockefeller Foundation had demonstrated the success of giving money,

---

[46] Ken Hechler, *Working with Truman* (1982), 118; Congress, House, *Point Four: Background and Program*, 1–7.

[47] Shenin, *United States and the Third World*, 24–57.

[48] Congress, Senate, Committee on Foreign Relations, *Hearings on the Act for International Development*, 81st Cong., 2nd sess., March–April 1950, 4–5.

but he pointed out that private resources were limited. Business, he continued, could not be expected to invest in basic skills such as training county agricultural agents or undertaking irrigation surveys because such activities were not designed to maximize profits. "What this bill deals with," Acheson concluded, "is the skills and techniques. It hopes that, having created that knowledge, then the private investors, the entrepreneurs, the managerial skill and all of that, will follow." Acheson also believed the international lending agencies, the Export-Import Bank and the Bank for Reconstruction and Development (World Bank), would step in to finance worthy projects.[49]

The Departments of Agriculture and Interior also testified on behalf of Point Four. Secretary of Agriculture Charles Brannan portrayed Point Four as "a natural outgrowth of our internal program for farmers." Brannan was eager to share with Congress the successful experiences of the USDA's Latin American activities, and to demonstrate international interest in the department with statistics on the fellowship program and foreign visitors. Secretary of Interior Julius Krug also pointed to past experience to show that "enormous results can be achieved with technical assistance for remarkably small outlay." He argued that small American teams from the Bureau of Reclamation, the Fish and Wildlife Service, the Bureau of Mines, and TVA had already made a difference in several countries, and that Point Four funds would help the department better serve all the foreigners requesting technical advice on irrigation, power, and flood control projects. Both secretaries agreed with the State Department's contention that U.S. prosperity ultimately depended on the prosperity of its neighbors.[50]

Krug explicitly linked foreign development assistance to the American resource conservation model. What made the Point Four idea new, Krug believed, was the recognition of U.S. responsibility for extending coordinated area development abroad. Drawing on his experience as chief power engineer for TVA, Krug argued that the natural resources of poor areas should be developed "for the benefit of the peoples of an area, not merely for production for its own sake." Such resource development would integrate those areas into the world economic system on a permanent basis, rather than for extractive or monopolistic purposes. "Our American history of resource development has taught us that nature cannot sensibly

---

[49] Congress, Senate, *Hearings on the Act for International Development*, 5, 19–20.
[50] Congress, House, *Hearings on the International Cooperation Act of 1949*, 43–5, 295–7.

be brought to serve mankind by a series of blind stabs," Krug passionately declared.

We would be sorry friends to the world if we exported our skill in lumbering without giving with it our skill in flood control; if we aided in the conversion of new areas for agriculture but kept the secrets of soil conservation . . . In short, we would have little claim on the affection of mankind if we led it not only into the successes of twentieth-century technology but also into the mistakes of nineteenth-century resource exploitation.[51]

The Act for International Development, finally approved in June 1950, made it the policy of the United States to promote long-term economic development in underdeveloped nations by encouraging the exchange of technical knowledge. Excluded were those areas covered by existing legislation – nations still under military occupation, the Philippines, and country programs administered by the Economic Cooperation Administration. Congress authorized the president to plan and execute bilateral technical cooperation programs, to allocate funds to the U.S. agencies of his choice, and to cooperate with international organizations such as the United Nations and the Organization of American States. Yet the act stipulated that assisted countries contribute a "fair share" of the costs, and that participation of private organizations and persons be sought to the greatest extent possible. The September Appropriation Act made available to Point Four a little over $32 million, a small fraction of the billions allotted to other military and economic assistance programs. In fact, Congress took steps to protect Point Four from becoming a "big money" program like the ECA by decreeing that the funds be used only to construct demonstration or instruction projects, and that surveys or project preparations not constitute loan or grant obligations.[52]

Despite attempts by the USDA and the IIAA to acquire the administration of Point Four, the president assigned it to the State Department. The Technical Cooperation Administration (TCA, the Point Four agency) absorbed the activities of the Interdepartmental Committee and

---

[51] Congress, House, *Hearings on the International Cooperation Act of 1949*, 298–300. Krug had also developed these ideas in *National Resources and Foreign Aid*, Report of the Secretary of the Interior, October 1947, in which he concluded that the United States was "physically capable of providing the resource requirements of a considerable program of foreign aid" (iii).

[52] "Act for International Development," Public Law 535, Chapter 220, Title IV, 81st Cong., 2nd sess., 5 June 1950; Vernon W. Ruttan, *United States Development Assistance Policy: The Domestic Politics of Foreign Economic Aid* (1996), 51; Brown and Opie, *Foreign Economic Assistance*, 394–6; Shenin, *United States and the Third World*, 67.

the IIAA, although the IIAA persisted as the program's Latin American arm. Because the Economic Cooperation Administration had already commenced programs in Europe, colonial Africa, and parts of Asia, TCA operations were confined to the Middle East, Latin America, five sites in Africa (Liberia, Libya, Egypt, Ethiopia, and Eritrea), and five countries in Asia (Afghanistan, Pakistan, India, Nepal, and Ceylon). The development of Point Four also inspired a host of similar initiatives – in 1950 the United Nations launched an expanded technical assistance program, Great Britain instituted the "Colombo Plan" for underdeveloped areas of the Commonwealth, the Organization of American States began technical assistance projects on a hemispheric basis, and other countries such as France and Norway established smaller but similar bilateral programs.[53]

Unlike the FAO or the ECA, however, Point Four initially had an entirely agrarian emphasis, very much influenced by the USDA/land-grant college complex. Indeed, Truman's choice for TCA director – Henry G. Bennett – cemented the influence of this extension model. Bennett had served as president of Oklahoma A&M from 1928 to 1950, spent time in Germany in 1949 to advise the U.S. Military Government on agricultural extension, and traveled to Ethiopia in 1950 to make suggestions for organizing agricultural training centers. As head of the TCA, Bennett doggedly defended the extension and demonstration method against ever more urgent calls for large grants-in-aid to finance the export of advanced American technology and machinery.[54]

Bennett's devotion to the extension approach stemmed from his agricultural fundamentalism and his universalistic assessment of the American experience. "We will do well to take note," he reminded the sympathetic Land Grant College Association, "that while industrialization made us powerful, agriculture is the rock bed of our existence." Furthermore, he noted that progress in farming took place gradually, incrementally assisted and judiciously adjusted by the USDA, the experiment stations, the Extension Service, and the New Deal improvements in land use, credit, and

---

[53] Andrews oral history, HSTL; Douglas Ensminger oral history, HSTL; Brown and Opie, *American Foreign Assistance*, 397; Glick, *Administration of Technical Assistance*, 217; Hambidge, *Story of FAO*, 82–6; Amy L. S. Staples, "Norris Dodd and the Connections Between Domestic and International Agricultural Policy," *Agricultural History* 74 (2000).

[54] SA-HB; Andrews oral history, HSTL. Much "international extension philosophy" was also set down during two conferences organized jointly by OFAR and the Extension Office, and chaired by Dougles Ensminger – see *Conference Report on the Contribution of Extension Methods*; and USDA Extension Service and OFAR, *Conference Report on Extension Experiences*.

tenancy conditions. Therefore, what the United States should contribute to the "underdeveloped" world was not the advanced American farming systems of 1950 but a particular method of solving problems – the state-sponsored educational approach. Because three-fourths or more of the people in the affected nations farmed for a living, Bennett understood Point Four as a program to produce more food and to fight communism by improving the social and economic conditions of rural life. "Even if factories were to spring up in the underdeveloped areas like mushrooms," he warned, "we would not see an end to mass misery because there would still be mass hunger." More specifically, what Bennett advocated was "modernization" as opposed to "mechanization." By espousing "modernization," Bennett meant that technical cooperation should aim to increase yields per acre, rather than increasing acreage under cultivation. The introduction of simple and inexpensive methods – better seed, better tools, and better practices – would immediately increase food production without commercial fertilizer, without expensive machinery, without "the necessity for handouts."[55]

Bennett's favorite illustration of these principles in action was the Etawah pilot project on the Ganges Plain in India, begun in 1948 with the aid of Horace Holmes, a former Tennessee county agent and UNRRA agricultural adviser in China. Holmes, who soon directed the Point Four Agricultural Group in India, became for Henry Bennett the very symbol of small-scale "shirt-sleeve diplomacy" at work. With a few changes in methods and technology, the Etawah project increased wheat and potato yields several times over. Critical to this success was the introduction of an improved variety of wheat (Punjab 591, a forerunner of Green Revolution strains), green manuring of native legumes, the use of dung and compost, and a new tool – a small steel turning plow. The results even required a fair bit of cultural literacy – religious law appeared to prohibit the "killing" of a growing crop of legumes, but Holmes and his Indian colleagues convinced the farmers to interpret the Vedic Laws in a manner more favorable to this practice. "Holmes began with the good old American demonstration method, adapted to the problems of Indian farmers," Bennett testified before the Senate. "There's a mistaken idea that Point Four is pouring out billions of dollars, but compared to what we are spending on military defense, Point Four is peanuts... One of the

[55] Bennett, "Land and Independence – America's Experience," 1951, SA-HB; Bennett, "Point IV: Philosophy of Plenty," 1951, SA-HB; Bennett testimony, Congress, Senate, *Hearings on the Mutual Security Act of 1951*, 409–57.

remarkable things about Point Four is that you can see results in a relatively short space of time – two or three years."[56]

Bennett persistently defended the small-scale extension approach, not only to win the support of economy-minded congressmen but also because he sincerely believed that grass-roots improvements in agriculture, health, and education constituted prerequisites for development. After such needs were met, he maintained, private capital and international loans would flow freely to the countries so badly in need of investment. Bennett's vision for the new program also provided him with ammunition in the bureaucratic and ideological struggle over the direction of Point Four. Though the State Department initially presented Point Four to Congress as a low-cost program to transfer skills, it eventually amended its stance to advocate more capital transfers along the lines of the European Recovery Program and the ECA's programs in Southeast Asia. Only government capital, the State Department insisted, could fill the gap quickly enough to ensure steady economic development and to quell communist sympathies in strategic areas. The rivalry came to a head in March 1951, when Truman presided over a special conference to determine the direction of the TCA. Though State Department officials argued persuasively for the capital-assistance point of view, Bennett carried the day with his insistence and firm demeanor. At least for a while, the issue was settled and Bennett could turn his attention to Point Four activities.[57]

During its first year, the TCA received 690 requests for assistance from 43 nations. It approved 500 of these requests, signed bilateral agreements with 36 countries, and put 1,200 technicians in the field. It allocated over one-third of its budget to the United Nations and the specialized agencies, and signed contracts with 56 private organizations such as the land-grant colleges, the Near East Foundation, the Ford Foundation, and

---

[56] *Point Four Pioneers: Reports from a New Frontier* (GPO, 1951); Bingham, *Shirt-Sleeve Diplomacy*, 44–8, 170–88; Albert Mayer, *Pilot Project, India: The Story of Rural Development at Etawah, Uttar Pradesh* (1959); J. C. Kavoori and Baij Nath Singh, *History of Rural Development in Modern India* (1967). Also see Carl C. Taylor et al., *India's Roots of Democracy: A Sociological Analysis of Rural India's Experience in Planned Development Since Independence* (1965); SA-HB; Testimony of Bennett and Horace Holmes, Congress, Senate, *Hearings on the Mutual Security Act of 1951*, 409–77.

[57] SA-HB; Andrews oral history, HSTL; Andrews, "Journal," 1073–6; Shenin, *United States and the Third World*. At the start of fiscal year 1951 the ECA launched a large program of economic assistance and technical aid in the "STEM" countries – Burma, Thailand, Indochina, Indonesia, and the Philippines. The ECA intended to raise output in these countries by increasing the supply of capital, in contrast to Point IV, which in 1950–1 set out to raise output in recipient countries by changing methods of production. See Wolf, *Foreign Aid*, 58–72.

the American University at Beirut. Of the American agencies, the Department of Agriculture received the most money from Point Four, followed closely by the Interior and Commerce Departments. In the individual countries, TCA administrators worked with U.S. State Department officials and representatives of the host governments to put programs in place. While increased food production, natural resource development, improved health and sanitation, and education remained the primary goals of the program, Point Four also aided projects in communications, roads and highways, and civil aeronautics.[58]

The initial agrarian emphasis of the program, however, seems to have begun to give way to a mixed approach that combined the agrarian and the industrial models. In Iran, for example, small-scale projects initially characterized what soon became one of the most extensive country programs in the Near East. The transition occurred after 1951, when a new prime minister came to power on a platform of oil nationalization. In response to this perceived socialist threat, the TCA authorized a twentyfold expansion of Point Four activities in Iran. William Warne, the new country director, resigned from his upper-level post in the Interior Department and launched extensive work in Iranian water supply, river surveys, agriculture, livestock improvement, insect control, rural education, health, and industrial development.[59]

Interior Department participation in Point Four provided a counterpoint to the agrarian extension model. While TCA leaders like Henry Bennett and Stanley Andrews upheld the Etawah experiment and other small-scale projects as the genuine basis for the program, other forces worked to expand and redefine that mission. It appears that one of the most powerful influences came from ideological and institutional allies of Interior and TVA, the U.S. resource agencies engaged in large-scale river engineering and hydroelectric projects. Morris Cooke, for example, continued to publicize the benefits of river development after his trip to Brazil. He argued in 1947 that hydroelectric power would prove to be the "prime factor" in the advancement of the underdeveloped world. The energy provided by hydropower, he predicted, would help "build up local purchasing power so that locally grown agricultural products can be consumed locally while manufactures and excess agricultural products

---

[58] Congress, Senate, *Hearings on the Mutual Security Act of 1951*, 410–11; William Warne oral history, HSTL; Shenin, *United States and the Third World*, 90.
[59] "Dr. Harris Says Iran 'Most Critical Area,'" *Salt Lake City Tribune*, 4 August 1952; Warne oral history; William Warne, *Mission for Peace: Point 4 in Iran* (1956), 22.

are exported." Cooke described the vision as one of a "better balanced but socially-minded industrialization." And when Truman's inaugural address introduced the Point Four idea, Cooke reiterated his message, this time highlighting the international fame of TVA : "The TVA is almost custom-made for Point Four use, because its techniques can be employed on streams of varying size, because it affords the electric power needed to infiltrate agriculture with industry, and because the development provides an adequate foundation on which to base all phases of an enriched and growing economy." Rather than anticipating Henry Bennett's agrarian vision for Point Four, such thinking echoed the stated aims of the recently created FAO, and accurately reflected the character of U.S. Marshall Plan/ECA assistance in Greece, Turkey, and Asia.[60]

Personnel linked to TVA also joined Cooke in publicizing the idea of hydropower-based industrial expansion and widespread electrification as supplements to the agrarians' emphasis on agricultural modernization. Gordon Clapp, who served as TVA chairman after David Lilienthal, shared Lilienthal's interest in the authority's international application. Clapp especially enjoyed working with the United Nations, and led the UN Economic Survey Mission to the Middle East in 1949. Like Julius Krug and William Warne of the Interior Department, Clapp endorsed and recommended the cooperative and multipurpose development of rivers to stimulate industrial growth. Such a "balanced" strategy of regional development, Clapp believed, would integrate poor regions into an expanding world economy just as TVA had done for the Tennessee Valley. At one point in U.S. history, he claimed, the underdeveloped regions of the United States were a source of weakness for the nation. "It has taken depressions and threats of war," Clapp continued, "to make us realize that we have to share our internal strength to make all regions strong... Much of the foreign policy of the United States is an extension of that idea."[61]

After leaving the Atomic Energy Commission in 1950, Lilienthal also renewed his work in international affairs and resource issues. He took

---

[60] Cooke, "World Industrialization," 51, 55; Cooke, "Down to Earth with Point Four," 21.
[61] Lilienthal to Clapp, 2 September 1949, Clapp Papers, Box 2, HSTL; Clapp, "The Experience of the Tennessee Valley Authority in the Comprehensive Development of a River Basin," in *Proceedings of the United Nations Scientific Conference on the Conservation and Utilization of Resources*, 1949 (1950); "Integrated Development of River Basins – UNSCCUR Plenary Hears Gordon Clapp on Experience of the TVA," 1949, Kenneth Hechler Files, Box 3, HSTL; Clapp, "Aid to Underdeveloped Areas," 1951, Clapp Papers, Box 2, HSTL; U.S. Interior Department, *Point Four in Action*.

a particular interest in the situation on the Asian subcontinent, where he believed that the TVA experience might serve a useful purpose in diffusing tensions between India and Pakistan and in thwarting any alliance between India and communist China. Bankrolled by *Collier's* (and encouraged by the U.S. State Department), Lilienthal and his wife spent three weeks in India and Pakistan visiting with officials from both countries. Lilienthal especially enjoyed long talks with Nehru, and he delighted in examining Indian development projects such as the Damodar Valley Corporation, which had been modeled in large part on TVA and built with help from Indian engineers trained in Tennessee. In the summer of 1951, he published two articles in *Collier's*, the first urging U.S. support for Nehru's efforts to modernize his country and the second recommending the comprehensive development of the Indus River to benefit both India and Pakistan.[62]

Not only did certain Americans tout the benefits of assisted industrialization, the host countries themselves seem to have exerted similar pressures for Point Four assistance in multipurpose river development. Although TVA continued to serve as the reigning symbol of U.S. resource expertise, foreign leaders and engineers often viewed the works of TVA, the Interior Department, and the Corps of Engineers as the mass multiplication of a certain political and technological model, not as the products of competing agencies. As a result, Point Four representatives often found that officials first requested general technical help in the related fields of hydroelectric infrastructure, flood control, navigation, irrigation improvements, and industrial expansion. In its first year, the TCA arranged for personnel from the Reclamation Bureau and TVA to undertake surveys and help design water development plans for Libya, Egypt, Lebanon, Israel, Ceylon, India, Pakistan, Costa Rica, Nicaragua, and Honduras. The bureau also hosted hundreds of foreign students and technicians at its engineering center in Denver, Colorado. Still, the TCA (unlike the Economic Cooperation Administration) did not yet commit large amounts of capital overseas for construction. "The Point Four theory," Stanley Andrews recalled, "was that we could pay for training, [but] that training had to precede industry."[63]

[62] Steven M. Neuse, *David E. Lilienthal: The Journey of an American Liberal* (1996), 256–61; "New Receives Post in India: TVA Man to Advise in Dams Planning," *Chattanooga News-Free Press*, 28 July 1952; Lilienthal, "Are We Losing India?" *Collier's*, 23 June 1951; Lilienthal, "Another 'Korea' in the Making?" *Collier's*, 4 August 1951.

[63] Andrews oral history, HSTL; Warne, *Mission for Peace;* Bingham, *Shirt-Sleeve Diplomacy;* U.S. Interior Department, *Point Four in Action.*

Despite Andrews's emphatic assessment of the "Point Four theory," a growing murmur of dissent could be heard from the TVA enthusiasts. Lilienthal and Clapp, for example, cast their votes in favor of more direct capital assistance. For Clapp, an American program of economic aid, technical assistance, and collective security constituted a "single free world policy... financial aid and technical assistance to help the peoples of the under-developed areas produce more food, control floods and pests and diseases, [and] to help them increase and improve their supply of water and electrical energy are the surest material means to helping them become self-supporting." Lilienthal, deeply concerned with India's strategic importance in the Cold War, similarly pressed Americans to sympathize with Nehru's ambitious plans to "produce a revolution in the manner of life" with increased food production, irrigation, flood control, and hydroelectric power. Such projects, Lilienthal maintained, reflected America's belief in the advancement of the individual rather than a Soviet-style collectivist agenda. Most important, he argued that Nehru's trust in science, technology, and industry would help India protect its newly acquired independence against foreign domination. But the former TVA chairman warned that "how far and how fast Nehru's program actually can go will be determined not so much by engineering limitations as by India's future relations with America and upon India's ability to raise capital."[64]

Soon after Point Four's inception, these methodological differences appear to have played into the hands of those in the larger foreign policy establishment who desired more uniformity in U.S. assistance administration. Influenced by the growing severity of the Korean conflict, many State Department and ECA officials argued that the underdeveloped countries were failing to attract private investment, and that government capital transfers (like those overseen by the ECA) would bring much-needed coordination to foreign aid programs. Yet throughout 1951, Henry Bennett steadfastly defended the grass-roots approach of the TCA, even preserving its mission intact when Congress combined technical, economic, and military assistance under a single agency (the Mutual Security Agency) in the fall of 1951.[65]

---

[64] Clapp, "Aid to Underdeveloped Areas"; Lilienthal, "Are We Losing India?" 44.
[65] Public Affairs Institute, "Conflicting Views on American Foreign Policy: A Summary of Several Important Foreign Policy Proposals Including an Analysis of the Rockefeller Board's Report to the President" (1951); Bingham, *Shirt-Sleeve Diplomacy*, 187; Andrews oral history, HSTL; Ensminger oral history, HSTL; Shenin, *United States and the Third World*, 78–92.

Defenders of Point Four's small-scale emphasis did not just argue that basic improvements in agriculture, health, and education must precede industry. They also voiced concerns that large capital investments would exacerbate inequalities of wealth. Senator J. W. Fulbright, for example, responded negatively to the State Department's requests for special economic aid. "One of the curses of Iran and Iraq," he asserted, "is the fact that but few people own the land...the benefits would accrue to those who already have all the wealth in the country." Fulbright maintained that production for production's sake would not serve U.S. interests if economic aid subsidized the wealthiest landowners. Stanley Andrews, who became director of the TCA after the death of Henry Bennett in late 1951, voiced similar misgivings about the direction of foreign assistance policy. "There are a lot of 'Big Money Boys' out here," he wrote from Iran in 1952. "Most of it swings around the elite few in control and the masses will rarely get in on the benefits. We would be making a terrible mistake if we got away from the basic concept of Point Four – technical aid plus some modest funds to support the TCA program rather than a big money show."[66]

Yet the State Department continued to press for economic aid, viewing Point Four as a vehicle for delivering direct capital assistance. Douglas Ensminger, M. L. Wilson's assistant, remembered that many of the diplomats involved in the European Recovery Program drifted home and assumed tasks related to Point Four. "They just couldn't quite see how we could make a contribution to these developing countries unless we really talked in terms of economic aid," he recalled. Henry Bennett's tragic death also made it easier for the State Department to advance its position. "The TCA lost thirteen of its top seventeen advisers and policy men in that one plane crash," Ensminger continued,

and from that point forward you begin to get the infiltration of the other point of view...we got into the period of what you call 'big economic aid,' where the theory was that you don't work at where poverty is, but at building big enterprises [with the belief that] this will increase your GNP, and you will have a trickle-down benefit to the poor.

Intense debate persisted throughout 1952 and 1953. Eventually the State Department succeeded in acquiring congressional appropriations for special economic aid to three regions deemed particularly strategic: the Near

[66] Congress, Senate, *Hearings on the Mutual Security Act of 1951*, 447; Andrews to Charles Brannan, 14 February 1952, Charles Brannan Papers, Box 5, HSTL.

East (Israel, the Arab States, and Iran), India, and Pakistan. Despite Stanley Andrews's hesitance, the TCA began to supervise capital transfers to these politically critical areas.[67]

Evidence drawn from the congressional hearings suggests that closely connected with this new emphasis on direct financial aid was the belief that multipurpose river projects would quicken the pace of economic and industrial development, and thus check communist influence abroad. State Department officials argued that the less developed countries along the Soviet periphery looked to the combined agricultural and industrial successes of Greece and Turkey, and that they should receive similar assistance. The Nile, the Jordan, the Euphrates, the Indus, and the Ganges Rivers all presented great potential for large-scale development projects. In this way, State Department presentations of reclamation, navigation, and hydroelectric power possibilities became entwined with justifications and subsequent appropriations for special economic assistance.[68]

Perhaps India can provide an example of how Point Four seems to have expanded with this new category of special economic assistance. Planning for India began entirely in step with the agrarian extension model. In consultation with Prime Minister Nehru and Chester Bowles, U.S. ambassador to India, the TCA and the Ford Foundation began to assist India in its plans to replicate the Etawah project as part of the country's larger rural development aims. The U.S. and Indian governments signed an agreement in June 1952 providing for fifty-five community development projects to be started the first year, with at least one in each of the country's twenty-eight states. The project plans drew primarily from Nehru's goals for village improvement, but the program was also informed by the JCRR's approach in China and Taiwan, where extension workers focused on specific villages with a multipurpose program. Specific projects in the Indian community development "blocks"

---

[67] Ensminger oral history, HSTL; Shenin, *United States and the Third World*, 92–103; Ruttan, *United States Development Assistance Policy*, 63–8; Congress, Senate, Committee on Foreign Relations, *Hearings on the Mutual Security Act of 1952*, 82nd Cong., 2nd sess., March–April 1952; Congress, Senate, Committee on Foreign Relations, *Hearings on the Mutual Security Act of 1953*, 83rd Cong., 1st sess., May 1953; Congress, House, Committee on Foreign Affairs, *Hearings on Foreign Economic Policy*, 83rd Cong., 1st sess., March–May 1953; Congress, House, Committee on Foreign Affairs, *Hearings on Mutual Security Act Extension*, 83rd Cong., 1st sess., March–June 1953.

[68] Congress, Senate, *Hearings on the Mutual Security Act of 1952*; Congress, Senate, *Hearings on the Mutual Security Act of 1953*; Congress, House, *Hearings on Foreign Economic Policy*; Congress, House, *Hearings on Mutual Security Act Extension*.

centered on training programs in agriculture, health, basic education, and developing small village industries. In addition, the program included general work in agricultural extension, forestry, groundwater development, soil conservation, pest control, and the distribution of fertilizer and steel farm implements. Douglas Ensminger, who served as the Ford Foundation representative in India, remembered that this idea of U.S. aid tied to community development "got a *very* great response, because it was not a U.S. imposed program."[69]

Ensminger, however, grew increasingly disenchanted with U.S. government assistance in India. "The leaders in Congress," he said, "began to get restless, saying that India needed massive economic aid and that community development was too slow, that India needed to put its foreign aid into big economic development projects." Indeed, Congress earmarked $25 million of special economic aid in 1953 for such river valley development, including construction equipment and supplies for irrigation dams and canals, flood control dams and reservoirs, and hydroelectric power installations.[70] The responsibility for this shift lay not only with Congress, as Ensminger claimed. Nehru also desired and promoted such large-scale enterprises, as Lilienthal and the State Department well understood.

Expansive foreign aid outlays did not fare well politically. Concerned by the ballooning budget, the Eisenhower administration trimmed expenses and succeeded in merging technical, economic, and military aid into a single agency, the Foreign Operations Administration. The Cold War became the rationale for the change; more attention was given to short-term geopolitical and military strategy, and less to long-term programs. The TCA ceased to exist as a separate entity – technical assistance activities were folded into specific country "packages" and linked directly to military and economic goals. Eisenhower and his Republican allies in Congress, more sympathetic to private capital, also set up new incentive structures for private investment overseas. These actions eased the way for large corporate involvement, especially the raw-materials giants.[71]

[69] Congress, Senate, *Hearings on the Mutual Security Act of 1952*, 697–9; Congress, Senate, *Hearings on the Mutual Security Act of 1953*, 399–405; "Program for Special Study in the United States of the Extension Principles, Organizations and Methods by Extension Service Directors From India," 21 July 1952, WP 2100, 15:30; Ensminger oral history, HSTL.

[70] Ensminger oral history, HSTL; Congress, Senate, *Hearings on the Mutual Security Act of 1953*, 405.

[71] Shenin, *United States and the Third World*, 116–22.

Some Point Four devotees expressed dismay at how the technical assistance programs had been folded in with military and short-term economic aid. "What we essentially did," concluded Ensminger, "was make it possible for the small elites to further entrench themselves, to further exploit their poor people." Stanley Andrews resigned and went to work for the Kellogg Foundation. Many others also drifted to work in private foundations, finding programs like the Ford Foundation's community development activities in India and Pakistan more congenial to their own outlook. However, the United States never abandoned the technical assistance programs completely, and the goals of agricultural modernization and industrialization remained intertwined. Government aid agencies continued to support programs in food production, resource conservation, health, and education, along with large-scale river engineering works. They also maintained and expanded contracts with universities and other nongovernmental organizations. Furthermore, international agencies and multilateral lending institutions stepped in with increased financing as it became clear that neither private nor state capital alone could support worldwide initiatives.[72]

By the 1950s, the United States and the international organizations supported a mixed model of agricultural and industrial development. For the most part, the resource specialists closed ranks and supported what they perceived to be the swiftest path to economic independence. In later years, the division between the agrarian and the industrial positions appeared far less salient than their methodological similarity: the idea that publicly sponsored resource development projects should pull poor and lagging regions into the economic mainstream. This reflected the New Dealers' success in building domestic support for enlarged government responsibilities, an exercise in state development that Americans then exported during the Cold War. "The emerging nations need to be integrated into the structure of the developed world's economy," wrote

[72] Stanley Andrews to Harold Stassen, 8 January 1953, Stanley Andrews to Harry Truman, 13 January 1953, Andrews Papers, Box 9, HSTL; Ensminger oral history, HSTL; Wilson, "Comments on Community Development Projects and National Extension Service Blocks in India," May 1956, WP 2100, 14:27; Carl C. Taylor, "Content and Scope of Community Development in India," April 1957, WP 2100, 51:27; "Sixth Meeting of USDA Retired Overseas Group," 22 August 1957, WP 2100, 14:1; "Summary Statement of FOA-Financed University Contracts in Operation," 2 April 1955, WP 2100, 51:40; "International Cooperation Administration Fact Sheet" (1955), and "Recommended Policy Statement on Community Development for ICA Consideration," 24 March 1956, WP 2100, 9:6; Patrick McCully, *Silenced Rivers: The Ecology and Politics of Large Dams* (1996), 19–20.

one commentator and former Interior Department planner. "No amount of bootstrap-pulling can do the job: outside assistance is essential."[73]

THE NEW CONSERVATION ABROAD

American natural resource specialists traveled abroad to feed allies during the war, to reconstruct damaged economies, and to contain communist expansion. Bolstered by universalist assumptions, they drew from their experience with the U.S. agricultural and conservation programs of the 1930s and believed that the resource development methods developed during the New Deal and World War II could be applied successfully elsewhere. Current interpretations of the Marshall Plan and European reconstruction emphasize the continuity between American domestic and international economic goals, and the evidence presented here, while far from conclusive, supports a corresponding thesis – that rural reconstruction ideology and practice evolved along similar lines, from the domestic policies of the interwar years to the new bilateral and multilateral aid efforts of the 1940s and 1950s.[74]

Indeed, a composite definition of "exploitation" forged in the domestic policy context formed a central concept in U.S. assistance philosophy. Beginning in the 1920s, the new rural conservationists had imbued the word with two related meanings: first, the unsustainable abuse of land, woods, and water; and second, the monopolistic or neocolonial extraction of resources. They thought monopolies and entrenched interests kept resource-rich regions in a colonial state by exploiting their natural assets for some far-off business or metropole, rather than developing them for the permanent use of the region's inhabitants. This dual meaning of exploitation appears to have provided a natural path from domestic to international concerns. Those "resource ambassadors" who took this path believed that underdeveloped regions of the United States – whether

---

[73] Arthur Goldschmidt, "The Development of the U.S. South," *Scientific American* (September 1963), 228. Goldschmidt claimed that the New Deal's rural and industrial development projects had integrated the South into the national economy, and argued that outside capital must do the same for the underdeveloped world. Goldschmidt sent a copy of this article to his friend and former New Deal colleague Lyndon Johnson with the annotation: "A nostalgic look into our earlier days." Johnson replied: "We are in a better position to handle some of the problems of the developing countries because of the problems we faced so recently in developing our own." I thank David Ekbladh for sending me copies of these documents.

[74] See Michael J. Hogan, *The Marshall Plan: America, Britain, and the Reconstruction of Western Europe, 1947–1952* (1987).

the Tennessee Valley, or the South, or rural America in general – had been successfully integrated into the national economy because they had conserved and developed their land and water for their own people. Therefore, they argued that similar social and technical solutions would enable poor and newly independent nations to join the world economy as equal (and democratically inclined) partners.

To examine the connections between U.S. resource practice and postwar foreign assistance is not to argue that the Americans held a monopoly on these development concepts (certainly that was not the case), nor is it to justify the ecological and social devastation that resulted in part from U.S. involvement and from the flaws of this resource universalism. Rather, the story illuminates underappreciated threads connecting domestic and foreign policy. In particular, the tensions highlighted here between hydroelectric industrialism and Henry Bennett's agrarianism clarify a critical transformation in domestic policy as well as a similar change in foreign assistance philosophy. Certainly, it was not inevitable that the agrarian vision of Point Four should fade – Henry Bennett drew from a long tradition of agricultural fundamentalism when he declared that farming and farmers constituted the foundation of a nation's health. Opponents of large-scale aid projects voiced a similar populist credo when they feared that direct economic assistance would bypass the neediest and further entrench the wealthy. Finally, Bennett promised results on the cheap, without large amounts of money or another Marshall Plan. So one must ask why the "Big Money Boys" prevailed.

One answer, of course, is that the Point Four concept was an aberration from the start. Other aid programs – the ECA, the FAO – combined the goals of agricultural modernization and industrialization from the beginning, viewing both as necessary for balanced development and full employment. National leaders also desired industries and factories in addition to increased food production and, like many Americans, viewed their untapped rivers as a source of endless power. Indeed, Point Four's initial emphasis on agriculture and raw materials could have certainly appeared colonial in intent, despite an underlying philosophy that stressed regional control of resources. "The political leaders in these developing countries," remarked one observer, "quickly began to find their position was attached to the things that had a prestige symbol, a big dam, a fertilizer plant, a steel plant ... I used to have the very distinct feeling that if we [had stayed] by the bullets to provide the small farmers a better hoe, they would have thought we wanted to keep them a peasant society."[75]

[75] Ensminger oral history, HSTL.

   Still, the agrarians lost abroad mainly because they represented the last expression of an already-discarded domestic strategy. During the 1930s, federal agencies had attempted to help farmers remain on the land – providing credit, technical assistance, and electricity, and often building entirely new rural communities. Congressional conservatives, of course, always deemed such approaches to rural poverty socialistic. During World War II, industrial decentralization proceeded apace as war factories moved to take advantage of cheap hydropower. In turn, defense employment provided an answer to the question that had dogged rural planners from the very beginning – how to rehabilitate marginal farmers after increases in efficiency and government purchase of submarginal lands made their existence unnecessary. Consequently, a revised model for rural development emerged after the war: not to build up more family farms but to attract industry, encourage farm out-migration, and subsidize the larger remaining farm operations.

   Henry Bennett was out of step not only with other foreign assistance programs but also with the recent American experience. By the 1940s and 1950s, politicians and planners saw little need for conservation programs designed to help the poorest rural inhabitants remain farmers; industrial production, they believed, would create prosperity. The industrial transition did not mean, however, that New Deal liberalism died or that state-sponsored rural resource development diminished. Most Americans continued to support an enlarged federal government, especially a federal government that built and managed a new hydroelectric, flood control, and irrigation infrastructure, and one that subsidized commercial farm production directly. This experience informed the course of U.S. assistance abroad. While the foreign aid programs began initially as a contest between the agrarian and the industrial points of view, Americans' universal assessment of their own experience and of the world's possibilities appears to have yielded a somewhat unified ideological approach to rural poverty. We inherit a world both richer and poorer.